DELIVERING FAMILY JUSTICE IN THE 21ST CENTURY

Family justice requires not only a legal framework within which personal obligations are regulated over the life course, but also a justice system which can deliver legal information, advice and support at times of change of status or family stress, together with mechanisms for negotiation, dispute management and resolution, with adjudication as the last resort.

The past few years have seen unparalleled turbulence in the way family justice systems function. These changes are associated with economic constraints in many countries, including England and Wales, where legal aid for private family matters has largely disappeared. But there is also a change in ideology in a number of jurisdictions, including Canada, towards what is sometimes called neoliberalism, whereby the state seeks to reduce its area of activity while at the same time maintaining strong views on family values. Legal services may become fragmented and marketised, and the role of law and lawyers reduced, while self-help web-based services expand.

The contributors to this volume share their anxieties about the impact on the ability of individuals to achieve fair and informed resolution in family matters.

Oñati International Series in Law and Society

A SERIES PUBLISHED FOR THE OÑATI INSTITUTE FOR THE SOCIOLOGY OF LAW

Recent titles in this series

Shooting to Kill: Socio-Legal Perspectives on the Use of Lethal Force
Edited by Simon Bronitt, Miriam Gani and Saskia Hufnagel

Managing Family Justice in Diverse Societies
edited by Mavis Maclean and John Eekelaar

Making Human Rights Intelligible
Towards a Sociology of Human Rights
edited by Mikael Rask Madsen and Gert Verschraegen

European Penology?
edited by Tom Daems, Dirk van Zyl Smit and Sonja Snacken

Rights and Courts in Pursuit of Social Change
Legal Mobilisation in the Multi-Level European System
edited by Dia Anagnostou

Women's Rights to Social Security and Social Protection
edited by Beth Goldblatt and Lucie Lamarch

For the complete list of titles in this series, see 'Oñati International Series in Law and Society' link at www.hartpub.co.uk/books/series.asp

Delivering Family Justice in the 21st Century

Edited by
Mavis Maclean
John Eekelaar
and
Benoit Bastard

Oñati International Series in Law and Society

A SERIES PUBLISHED FOR THE OÑATI INSTITUTE FOR THE SOCIOLOGY OF LAW

•HART•
PUBLISHING
OXFORD AND PORTLAND, OREGON
2017

Hart Publishing
An imprint of Bloomsbury Publishing Plc

Hart Publishing Ltd
Kemp House
Chawley Park
Cumnor Hill
Oxford OX2 9PH
UK

Bloomsbury Publishing Plc
50 Bedford Square
London
WC1B 3DP
UK

www.hartpub.co.uk
www.bloomsbury.com

Published in North America (US and Canada) by
Hart Publishing
c/o International Specialized Book Services
920 NE 58th Avenue, Suite 300
Portland, OR 97213-3786
USA

www.isbs.com

HART PUBLISHING, the Hart/Stag logo, BLOOMSBURY and the Diana logo are trademarks of Bloomsbury Publishing Plc

First published in hardback, 2015
Paperback edition, 2017

British Library Cataloguing-in-Publication Data
A catalogue record for this book is available from the British Library.

ISBN: PB: 978-1-50991-775-4
HB: 978-1-84946-912-8

Typeset by Compuscript Ltd, Shannon
Printed and bound in Great Britain by
Lightning Source UK Ltd

Acknowledgements

We would, as always, like to thank the Oñati Institute for hosting this workshop. For the participants it was a stimulating and productive exchange of facts, views and argument of the kind which can only take place in such a supportive environment.

Mavis Maclean, John Eekelaar and Benoit Bastard, 12 January 2015

Table of Contents

List of Contributors

Bill Atkin is Professor of Law, Victoria University of Wellington, New Zealand

Anne Barlow is Professor of Family Law at the University of Exeter, UK

Benoit Bastard, sociologist, is Directeur de Recherche, CNRS, Institut des Sciences Sociales du Politique, École normale supérieure de Cachan, France

Becky Batagol is Senior Lecturer in the Faculty of Law, Monash University, Victoria, Australia

Emilie Biland is Associate Professor of Political Science at the University of Rennes 2 (CRAPE), France

David Delvaux, sociologist, is Maître de Conférences, Centre de recherche et d'intervention sociologique, University of Liège, France

John Eekelaar is Emeritus Fellow, Pembroke College, Oxford, UK

Jan Ewing is research Associate at the University of Kent, UK

Małgorzata Fuszara is Professor at the University of Warsaw, Institute of Applied Social Sciences and also Secretary of State – Plenipotentiary for Equal Treatment in the Polish government

Peter G Harris is a barrister who, as a senior civil servant, spent nearly 30 years advising governments on policies and legislation concerned with the reform of various aspects of the justice system. He is now a Research Member of Exeter College in the University of Oxford where he teaches and continues to research and write about the law and its social, economic and political underpinnings

Rosemary Hunter is Professor of Law in the School of Law, Queen Mary University of London, UK

Jacek Kurczewski is Professor in Sociology and Anthropology of Custom and Law at the University of Warsaw, Institute of Applied Social Sciences, Poland

Karen Laing is Research Associate at the School of Education, Communication and Language Sciences, Newcastle University, UK

Kirsteen Mackay is Research Fellow, Child Protection Research Centre, University of Edinburgh, UK

Mavis Maclean CBE is Co-Director of the Oxford Centre for Family Law and Policy in the Department of Social Policy and Intervention, and Senior Research Fellow in the Faculty of Law, University of Oxford, UK. She is a former President of the RCSL, a Fellow of the IISL and academic adviser to the UK Ministry of Justice.

Jane Mair is Professor of Private Law, School of Law, University of Glasgow, UK

Angela Melville is Senior Lecturer, Flinders Law School, Flinders University, Adelaide, Australia

Muriel Mille is Postdoctoral Fellow in Sociology, CNRS, Centre Maurice Halbwachs, France

Christian Mouhanna, sociologist, is Chargé de Recherche, CNRS, Director of CESDIP, University of Versailles Saint-Quentin, France

Teresa Picontó-Novales is Lecturer of Legal Philosophy and Sociology of Law at the University of Zaragoza, Spain

Encarna Roca Trías is a Judge of the Constitutional Court, Spain

Carol Rogerson is Professor in the Faculty of Law at the University of Toronto, Canada and co-author of the Canadian Spousal Support Advisory Guidelines

Frédéric Schoenaers, sociologist, is President of the Centre de recherche et d'intervention sociologique, University of Liège, France

Janet Smithson is Senior Lecturer in Psychology in the School of Psychology, University of Exeter, UK

Hilary Sommerlad is Professor of Law and Research Director of the Centre for Professional Legal Education and Research, Birmingham Law School, University of Birmingham, UK.

Hélène Steinmetz is Associate Professor of Sociology, Normandie Université (IDEES) Le Havre, France

Frank Stephen is Emeritus Professor of Regulation, School of Law, University of Manchester, UK

Velina Todorova has been Associate Professor at the Faculty of Law, Plovdiv University, Bulgaria, since 2000. She has worked for 20 years as a Researcher and Senior Research Fellow at the Institute for Legal Studies, Bulgarian Academy of Sciences. She was Deputy Minister of Justice in two governments (December 2011–May 2013).

Rachel Treloar is Professor in the Sociology Department, Simon Fraser University, Burnaby, British Columbia, Canada

Liz Trinder is Professor of Socio-Legal Studies at the University of Exeter, UK

Fran Wasoff is Emeritus Professor, University of Edinburgh, UK

Lisa Webley is Professor of Empirical Legal Studies, Faculty Research Director, Faculty of Social Sciences and Humanities, School of Law, University of Westminster, London, UK

Introduction

THE SCOPE AND PURPOSE OF THE BOOK: DEFINITIONS AND BOUNDARIES

BY FAMILY JUSTICE we mean not only Family Law, the legal framework within which personal obligations over the life course are managed and regulated, but also the justice system which delivers legal knowledge, advice and support at times of change of status or family stress, together with the mechanisms for dispute resolution, and adjudication where agreement cannot be reached.

The past few years have seen unparalleled turbulence in the way family justice systems function across a number of jurisdictions. These changes are stimulated by economic constraints in many countries, for example England and Wales and Spain have seen a drastic reduction in public funding for private family law cases, and in France judges are under pressure to accelerate their activity rate to control costs. In other settings change seems to have been driven by political pressures, for example British Columbia's new Family Law Act 2013 and the procedural changes in New Zealand sit firmly within a neoliberal political landscape, while the Bulgarian justice system is under pressure to conform to the requirements for accession to the EU, and in Poland increased public questioning of all institutions in the period after transition has been associated with a decrease in confidence in the courts and judiciary. The climate is calmer in Scotland, where court use is traditionally low and clear legislation seems to make private contracting in the shadow of the law work well. And in Australia a great deal of thought, accompanied by resources, has resulted in a considered though not always unquestioned shift towards Alternative Dispute Resolution. But whether the policy context is turbulent or calm, well-resourced or struggling, we are seeing an increase in private ordering and the marketisation and fragmentation of legal services, together with an overarching reduction in the role of law and the delivery of traditional legal services.

We therefore came together as a multidisciplinary group including judges, lawyers, mediators, researchers and policy-makers, from civil and common law countries in Europe and beyond, including England and Wales, Scotland, France, Poland, Spain, Bulgaria, Canada, and Australia and New Zealand to share our experiences and knowledge of the changing delivery of family justice, and to discuss possible outcomes and concerns. We shared anxiety about the impact of these changes on access to justice, and on the achievement of a fair and informed resolution of family difficulties for those without the resources to enable them to turn to the newly developing family legal services market, or the computer literacy to choose and use the newly developing web-based services. At the same time, we were aware of the economic and political pressures for change, and of the inventiveness of the response to these pressures being displayed by the legal professions and others in developing new ways of working: cutting costs by working from home with sophisticated IT, making effective use of the internet, and developing new professional relationships with ADR practitioners, including mediators, arbitrators and others. We found ourselves both starting and ending with comments on the part played by the law within the justice system, and reached the inescapable conclusion that justice without law is hard to find. For example, in England and Wales we noted with sympathy the principles which guided the Review of Family Justice in England and Wales which reported in 2011, chaired by David Norgrove,[1] which included paramountcy for the interests of the child in any decision affecting them; protection for the vulnerable and the avoidance of intervention by the state except where it is of clear benefit; and the right of adults to information and support to enable them to take responsibility for the consequences of separation and to make their own decisions, wherever possible outside the courts. Conflict should be minimised, process should be clear and simple, and administrative or non-adversarial in nature, and mediation should be preferred to legal process.

But while applauding the focus on the interests of children and the vulnerable, we also noted an apparent more widespread change in views of the role of law, including the idea that law is not important to all, but only to a subgroup of 'the vulnerable', although perhaps, as John Eekelaar suggests in our final chapter, anyone who needs to have recourse to the law with respect to his personal affairs might be properly regarded as vulnerable.

Systems and terminology vary across the countries discussed here, but we have aimed to include within our discussion of the family justice delivery system all those institutions whose primary purpose is to define, protect and enforce the legal rights family members have as family members, and to resolve conflicts family members have concerning those rights. These are the court system (judiciary, court-based staff and court-based agencies), lawyers and mediators, and experts. But we have excluded the counselling, medical and psychotherapeutic services which support the justice system.

STRUCTURE AND ANALYTICAL FRAMEWORK

Structure

The volume is presented in four parts: the first is concerned with the role of substantive law in the delivery of family justice. We look at the way in

[1] *Family Justice Review, Final Report* (London, Ministry of Justice, 2011).

which the role of law in the justice system has been changing, and been reformed either as a result of traditional governmental 'top-down' decree, or more gradually by osmosis or the absorption of developing social norms, or even by direct consumer action where those using the law take matters into their own hands. The second part looks at change in the heart of the justice system, the work of courts and judges, and the way in which political and economic pressures are affecting both the role of the judiciary and the way in which they are regarded in society. The third part looks at the impact of austerity on access to family justice, and at the changing pathways for users through the system, often involving less recourse to courts and lawyers and increased use of private ordering processes including mediation. The fourth and final part discusses newly developing aspects of the family justice system, including new ways of using courts, redefining the role of lawyers, and finding web-based alternatives to traditional legal services. The final chapter takes us back to the central but no longer unquestioned role of law in the delivery of justice.

Analytical Framework

This group of researchers has interests which differ; some are more concerned with the content of the law; others with how cases are treated in different situations; others with how courts function. But we share a common starting point: the state has withdrawn from the private sphere when dealing with couples, but control has been maintained or even reinforced when dealing with children and parenting. This evolution is not happening in the same way with the same rhythm everywhere, but is influenced by many background factors including the economic situation, social organisation, gender roles, culture and religion. And the change is not completely homogeneous, even in some instances moving in different directions. Our aim has been to try and ask a range of questions to show where each country is situated on the pathway of change, to investigate, first, how society tries to ensure people do what is expected from them, and do it properly when they have responsibility for action, and secondly, how society manages such cases efficiently when the responsibility is a private matter, always keeping in mind how gender or economic inequalities are managed, given that they are key determinants of access to the justice system. We know that the same problems are dealt with in different ways in our different countries. In particular, we start from the following questions, 'What is public, what is private? What is subject to judicial action, what is not? Where do we need a judge and where do we not'? For the French, the idea that 'private ordering' could be the norm, without any need for state intervention in family matters, is difficult to understand. There has been resistance recently to proposals for administrative divorce as the judges are currently always active in the process in France, whereas in England the procedure for undefended divorce has been essentially administrative with minimal judicial involvement since 1976. We are also aware that the scope of court activities varies widely across the jurisdictions represented here. As a consequence, we need to consider the question of the professions and professionalism in a comparative way. 'Who is doing what? Who is in charge of solving conflicts: lawyers, mediators or computers'? There is competition between the professions, each trying to demonstrate its own competence and the superiority of its techniques, while governments focus on cost-effectiveness.

The issue of scope leads directly to questions about the management of family cases. In France, for example, where family judges see all cases, sometimes without any preview of the case by a lawyer or other professional, the management of cases is a serious problem, with judges deciding up to a hundred cases each month. In countries where court use is lower and more decision-making takes place outside them, the courts may see only the more contentious cases, which will be fewer in number but take longer. Management issues then tend to centre around deciding which cases should be in court and which dealt with by Alternative Dispute Resolution.

The common unifying factor however remains, that justice systems are poor and this lack of resources impacts on access to justice, contributes to delay, and in the current economic crisis gives an air of precariousness to each system. But whether cases are dealt with in or out-of-court, the same questions arise about the treatment of family problems: how do we find a way to fit private ordering within some degree of control? How do we provide solutions for families that fit with both their values and with general societal norms? Do we keep matters within the private domain but with some issues reserved for public control, and if so which? We know that there is a gap between how people live and how they are expected to behave in court. They cannot expect recognition of who they are and what they feel when they enter the family justice system, and many aspects of their stories have to be abandoned.[2] The conflict between individuals develops long before the conflict becomes a judicial one, and rarely ends with the judicial decision.[3]

At the same time, our view of law is predominantly proactive. We expect law to mould behaviour. Through the justice system we seek settlement, and the making of arrangements for the future. But there is a paradox here with respect to collaborative law and mediation in that we seem to be asking people to make agreements and to reach a shared view about the future for their children when they are at their most conflicted. This leads to questions about whether people are able to respond to these expectations, and what

[2] Renchon, J-L, 'Droit et pauvreté affective' (1983) 10 *Revue interdisciplinaire d'études juridiques* 17.

[3] Noreau, P, 'La superposition des conflits: limites de l'institution judiciaire comme espace de résolution' (1998) 40 *Droit et société* 585.

should happen if they cannot. Do we help them? Educate them? Or punish them? At the present time we do not seem to have a clear answer.

Finally there is the question of inequality among those coming to the justice system. In family justice, the private conflict reflects and expresses the broader tensions in society. Divorce or separation is the moment when the specialisation of parenting roles or the difference in resources available to the parties is made visible. The gap between aspiration and reality is revealed. The impact of any justice system is limited. In fact when justice is privatised and relies on private ordering, little can be expected except the reproduction of societal inequalities by the justice system and indeed by the parties themselves.[4]

These questions arise from our combined researches into the changing delivery of family justice. The individual chapters which will be described in more detail below arise from, though they cannot answer, the questions just raised. Hopefully, in the best tradition of the Oñati Workshops which offer such a rich environment for reflection and debate, they may add to and develop that list of questions, and thus develop the next generation of empirical studies.

ORGANISATION OF CHAPTERS

Part I: Law and Delivering Family Justice

Part I examines the role of law in the changing delivery of family justice. Taking substantive law as the starting point for the family justice system, we begin the volume by looking at where changes to the law may come from, and whether the origins of change affect the delivery of justice.[5] Rachel Treloar looks at top-down reform with a political agenda in her description of the introduction of the Family Law Act in British Columbia, Canada, which came into effect in 2013. The background of the economic, political and social context, with increasing economic disparity within the population and precarious employment, reveals a neoliberal approach to politically inspired governmental lawmaking, seeking to emphasise parental responsibility and choice while de-emphasising any active role for the state, including adjudication through the courts. And while asking families in conflict to take more responsibility, the Act also included significant cutbacks to public funding for legal aid and the broad range of services that support families. Treloar quotes research on the impact of leaving family disputes unresolved

[4] Le Collectif Onze, *Au tribunal des couples: enquêtes sur des affaires familiales* (Paris, Odile Jacob, 2013).

[5] For further discussion, see Maclean, M, with Kurczewski, J, *Making Family Law* (Oxford, Hart Publishing, 2011).

which argues that perpetuating social problems in this way ultimately adds to overall social costs.[6] The Act gives interesting new and precise rules on relocation, defines domestic violence and replaces the terms custody and access with an expanded definition of guardianship, paving the way for independent decision-making. While these rules may work well for many families, for those with a serious dispute the restriction of legal aid means that parties without resources will either self-represent at great personal cost, or concede. Confidence in the family law system is at risk. So at the beginning of the volume we are alerted, however highly we value the law, to the problems associated with the content of the law in this case as a result of top-down law reform. The second chapter in Part I from Bill Atkin in New Zealand, looks at how court process can reflect the role of the state to achieve the same kind of outcome, moving towards 'user pays', 'privatisation' and 'secret justice'. The third chapter also comes from Canada, but has a more positive account of legal reform as taking on board the common practice of people undergoing in this case divorce or separation and making financial arrangements. Carol Rogerson was one of the team of lawyers involved in deciding whether the system for deciding property and maintenance at the end of a relationship should remain largely discretionary or whether there should be a move towards a rule-based system. As in other jurisdictions, including England and Wales, there had been interest in developing rules, but lack of agreement about which rules to adopt. Professor Rogerson and colleagues carried out research to discover social norms, by looking at what arrangements separating couples in a variety of circumstances had adopted and been able to live with. They analysed actual arrangements made according to age, length of marriage, number and age of children, wealth and income. They created tables showing the range of outcomes chosen for each set of circumstances. These were made available on the internet, so that couples could see where they stand, and choose an option within the range adopted by others in similar circumstances. No law was 'made' but the guidelines were popular with separating couples and with the judiciary and are now so widely used that there is some concern that this information has become used prescriptively as if it were a formal legal requirement. But the gradual progress from actual behaviour, to information, to acceptance of de facto rules worked well. Becky Batagol describes an earlier stage in the move towards change in Australia, where the government is attempting to support traditional forms of marriage through a required text of the civil marriage service, which refers to marriage as the union between one man and one woman. But Australians who support same-sex marriage are taking

[6] Currie, A, *The Legal Problems of Everyday Life: The Nature, Extent and Consequences if Justiciable Problems Experienced by Canadians* (Department of Justice, 2009) www.justice.gc.ca/eng/rp-pr/csj-sjc/jsp-sjp/rr07_la1-rr07_aj1/rr07_la1.pdf.

matters into their own hands by following their formal vows with an immediate statement of their disagreement with the formulation. It remains to be seen whether law reform will follow in response to this form of direct action. Part 1 therefore asks us to think carefully about what we mean by law, and where it may be coming from.

Part II: Judges and Courts Delivering Family Justice

The next part turns to the traditional heart of any family justice system, the judges and their courts. The first chapter in this part from Biland and colleagues presents empirical data on the working of family courts in France and in Québec, both with high divorce rates, but with very different kinds of hearings, partly as a result of the difference between civil and common law traditions, but also of the expectations about levels of state control. In France, the government has responded to austerity by concentrating on internal reforms to the courts, where lawyers are heavily involved and the career judges, often young women, who deal with every case, are under pressure to meet targets for cases dealt with each month. All family matters remain in court, including the calculation of child maintenance, and mediation is used by only a minority. In Québec, the encouragement of private ordering and no-fault divorce has led to less investigation by the court, resulting in more privacy for the parties and more agreements being made out-of-court. Mediation is used in less than half of the cases, but other services by various kinds of 'sub judge' are also offered to the parties to reduce the need for time in court. Judges now concentrate on the most highly conflicted cases. Legal aid helps the poor, the rich can buy what they need, and it is the middle income cases which are most likely to avoid court hearings because of the cost. The authors refer to the different ways of managing cases in the two jurisdictions, but interestingly point to the possibility for parties in private ordering, in both areas, of maintaining increased privacy by doing so. The remaining chapters in this part reveal an interesting set of political influences operating in the heart of the justice system. In Bulgaria, the judges in family courts are being pressured into taking more and more cases to comply with the requirements for the way courts work set by the EU on agreeing to accession. While in Poland, drawing on national survey data over time, it appears that, while under communism the courts and judges were held in high regard as places of independent thought and judgment, following transition this regard has lessened along with the increased questioning of all institutions now that this is possible. The emphasis on inquisitorial judicial activity is under discussion. So again, as in Part I, we are encouraged to question our assumptions, in this case about the role of the state through the mechanism of judges and their courts, as well as the substantive law.

Part III: Current Context of Practice and Policy—(I) Bypassing Courts and (II) Reducing Public Funding

Part III considers directly the impact of economic pressures, often in a neo-liberal policy landscape, on the delivery of family justice. A common factor across a number of the jurisdictions represented in this volume has been the attempt to reduce the role of law and the courts in the family justice system by cutting public funding for legal help and encouraging other forms of dispute management which increase individual responsibility and reduce public expenditure. This part begins with a description of the existing pathways to justice, including private ordering, taken by parties seeking divorce or separation, and then of how these are being affected by resource issues; it concludes with comment on governmental decision-making, the aims, the process and the possible outcomes.

The first chapter reports on the major study *Paths to Justice* carried out in England and Wales 2011–14, led by Rosemary Hunter and colleagues, which presents survey results on awareness of and use and satisfaction with three main paths to divorce settlement, all of which seek to avoid contest in court: lawyer-led negotiation, collaborative law and mediation. It is combined with interview data from professionals and clients, and recordings of examples of each process. The authors conclude that some cases need to go to court, and that private ordering or Alternative Dispute Resolution in the form of mediation as currently offered as a stand-alone service is unlikely to meet the current needs of the divorcing population as a whole, despite government's preference for this route. Angela Melville and colleagues then describe an earlier experiment in moving from lawyer-based intervention to multi-agency support in England, which has not been continued partly because the lawyers were better at receiving referrals than making them. Another form of private ordering through the use of contracts is described by Jane Mair and Fran Wasoff and their colleague in Scotland, Kirsteen Mackay, where the legal framework for property division on divorce or separation is relatively clear, court use is traditionally low and parties are accustomed to seeing a lawyer together to prepare a legally binding contract known as a Minute of Agreement which is then registered in the Books of Council and Session. The cost is low (a few hundred pounds sterling), and satisfaction and use are high (most divorces with property use this method and the agreements are rarely challenged). The contract is legally binding, but courts are bypassed. The system is widely thought to work well, with the caveat that the bargaining takes place in the shadow of the law, and requires a fresh supply of court decisions to keep the bargaining process up to date.

Part III(II) then focuses more directly on the impact of austerity on the delivery of family justice. Teresa Picontó-Novales describes the recent changes to Spanish law which have increased court fees, require payment in advance and have cut the provision of other non-lawyer services within the courts such as social workers. This has given rise to serious concern about access to justice for women and children. We are fortunate to have further comment on this issue from the judicial perspective by Encarna Roca Trías of the Constitutional Court of Spain. The range of court fees in other jurisdictions, and whether they are set for economic or political reasons, requires further research, for example the constitutional challenges to rising court fees in British Columbia compared with the absence of court fees in family courts in Ontario. Liz Trinder provides an account of how litigants in person affect and are affected by the court process in Canada, Australia and England and Wales. Numbers may increase in other jurisdictions experiencing reduction in public funding for legal help. Data from the study by Trinder and colleagues for the Ministry of Justice study in England and Wales published as we go to press throws new light on their need for support, and indicates how judges might be given specific training for dealing with cases where one or both parties are without legal representation.

Detailed concerns expressed in an ongoing study of a small qualitative sample of those directly involved in the delivery of family legal aid (lawyers, mediators, judges and court staff) about the impact of the Legal Aid Sentencing and Punishment of Offenders Act 2012 on access to justice in family matters are then set out by Hilary Sommerlad in chapter fourteen. A barrister suggested that absence of legal representatives could increase the length of a hearing from half an hour to all day; a solicitor referred to 'a whole industry of unregulated paralegals who charge for services with no insurance, no liability: DIY divorce and other IT platforms'; a judge raised the problem 'about provisions for disadvantaged parties ... usually battered women'. Another barrister was concerned about the wider impact on society, saying: 'It's making access to justice unavailable for the ordinary man in the street ... we're becoming a nation of two halves'. The final chapter in this part by Peter Harris draws on his experience as a British civil servant in observing opposition to various government policy moves, and advocates taking care not to undermine the position of those in government charged with responsibility for the justice system, and to be aware of the possibilities of exploiting changes in the machinery of government for delivering publicly funded legal services in order to maintain or expand them. This pragmatic approach may be of some interest in the context of Sommerlad's contention that the disintegration of the family justice system may, in effect, be the aim of governments who wish to withdraw from intervention in the private family affairs of citizens.

Part IV: Innovation in Delivering Family Justice

The final part of the volume looks to the future, identifying new forms of delivery developing to reduce state costs and the issues arising from this, before closing with a return to our initial concern with the place of law in delivering family justice. It begins with Benoit Bastard and colleagues' account of the French response to economic pressure which does not try to remove family matters from the oversight of the judiciary, nor limit the involvement of lawyers, but instead aims to reduce the time spent on each matter by accelerating the court process, seeking quick answers not lengthy consideration. Rather than privatising family responsibilities, the state aims to keep control over the family's situation, but limits costs by using the techniques of public management, pushing parties to compromise, pressing lawyers not to speak, not to postpone. Bastard contrasts this with the Belgian approach where family matters are divided into their different components, to be dealt with in different courts, for example post-divorce parenting comes to the juvenile court, division of patrimony to the notary and so on. The delays which may arise from this segmentation are best avoided by private negotiation, leading back to the promotion of mediation. In England and Wales, Lisa Webley alerts us to the question of what exactly is meant by the term 'lawyer' in a jurisdiction where most legal activities are not reserved to lawyers who have been admitted to the profession of barrister or solicitor. Family arbitration, negotiation or advising a client on family law, assisting in drafting a consent order which a court may be asked to ratify, even when a fee is charged, may be done by anyone. A market is developing in unregulated legal services, which in some ways could be beneficial in increasing access to justice and encouraging working partnerships between lawyers, social workers or mediators. But the potential problems of lack of professional indemnity and quality control are worrying. Mavis Maclean looks at new sources of legal information and advice, describing the development of web-based services offering advice which may or may not be free and may or may not be advice and sit outside any recognised regulatory framework, and at the possibility of finding legal help within family mediation, especially where the mediators are qualified as lawyers also. Some of these services are high quality, and both web-based and mediation services have established relationships with firms of lawyers. The web can work well for divorcing couples without property, children or dispute, and mediation for those who are able to cope with it. But where there is conflict, vulnerable parties may be at risk of failing to reach a fair and informed settlement without legal backup.

To conclude this informative and provocative series of debates, our final chapter from John Eekelaar takes us full circle to the fundamental question 'Can there be family justice without law?' Governmental hostility to legal process in family courts and lawyers in a number of jurisdictions seems to sit with reluctance to intervene in private life, combined with a clear view of the way people should be required to behave: an uncomfortable combination, especially when exacerbated by economic constraints. Substantive law is more popular with government when it is seen as a way of delivering a message, for example about the desirability of opposite sex marriage or cooperative parenting after separation. Interestingly, there are some signs of the emergence of a more positive approach to law and legal process exemplified by the Law Commission of Ontario Report 2013,[7] which argues for treating family problems in a holistic manner, drawing on law and lawyers, and also in the introduction of lawyers into the Australian Family Relationship Centres and the New Zealand government's recent drawing back from excluding family lawyers from certain courts.

Are family disputes best dealt with by law? Should individuals reach their own solutions, if necessary with the help of dispute resolution services? Are legal services just another service which the market will provide in varying ways in varying circumstances according to demand?

Eekelaar argues for the place of law, the rule of law and the need for law in providing a framework within which to organise the complexities of family life and to provide a safe place in which if all other attempts fail to secure guidance when conflict arises. Law is far more than dispute resolution. Private ordering outside law is an invitation to perpetuate in individual cases the inequalities of the wider society. The outcome of a dispute needs to be not only acceptable to the parties, but to be perceived as such by what Adam Smith (and later Amartya Sen) called 'an impartial spectator', in this context, the family justice system which includes legal norms, courts and lawyers advising and representing parties, and mediators resolving disputes. Eekelaar closes the volume with the following words: 'Family justice is concerned with more than simply bargaining, fairly or otherwise. It is concerned with upholding some elemental features of personal relationship. It cannot do this without the law, and effective means of upholding it'.

[7] Law Commission of Ontario, *Increasing Access to Family Justice through Comprehensive Entry Points and Inclusivity*, available at: www.lco-cdo.org/en/family-law-reform-final-report.

Part I

Law and Delivering Family Justice

1

The Neoliberal Context of Family Law Reform in British Columbia, Canada

Implications for Access to (Family) Justice

RACHEL TRELOAR

INTRODUCTION

THIS CHAPTER BEGINS with a brief overview of the economic, social and political context[1] that formed the backdrop for British Columbia's new Family Law Act[2] (FLA) which came into full effect in March 2013. This context is best described as neoliberal. After a brief overview of the FLA as it pertains to post-separation parenting, the extent to which it is fulfilling its potential in such an environment will be assessed, with particular attention to high-conflict, complex disputes. The chapter concludes with the question of whether family justice is indeed possible in this neoliberal context and an examination of what would be required to make family law more accessible and just.

Neoliberalism is defined here as a social, economic and political framework, underpinned by a philosophy of liberal individualism that centres on the free market and state withdrawal from responsibility for social well-being or welfare. In practical terms, neoliberalism involves privatisation, deregulation and individualisation, with substantial cuts to public spending alongside the promotion of individual and family responsibility and 'responsible choices'.

Although significant reductions were made to public spending in Canada, beginning in the late-1970s, with social programs most affected,[3]

[1] This context is described at greater length in Treloar, R and Boyd, SB, 'Family Law Reform in (Neoliberal) Context: British Columbia's New Family Law Act' (2014) 28(1) *International Journal of Law, Policy and the Family* 77.

[2] British Columbia Family Law Act, SBC 2011, c 25.

[3] Christie, N, *Engendering the State: Family, Work, and Welfare in Canada* (Toronto, University of Toronto Press, 2000).

in British Columbia (BC) 'fiscal austerity' began with a renewed vengeance in 2002, following the 2001 election of a new provincial Liberal government. Spending cuts affected a broad range of programs and services that support families in need. Broad welfare reforms were instituted, including strict changes to eligibility requirements and a focus on paid employment for mothers with children over the age of three. At the same time, funding for childcare resource and referral agencies was terminated. Cuts to agencies serving women and community-based organisations were particularly severe. Substantial cuts to legal aid also began during this period, with family and poverty law services particularly affected. Against this backdrop, the FLA also came into force during a period of increasing income inequality and precarious employment.

BC, like most of Canada,[4] has seen increased income disparity in recent years. This 'growing gap', with increasing wealth at the top of the income distribution and low incomes and casualisation of employment for those at the bottom,[5] is characteristic of societies that are governed by neoliberal economic policies. Indeed, in Canada, the median after tax income has not changed for the past four years,[6] with the exception of a slight increase for two-parent households with children. BC also has both the highest overall poverty rate[7] (15.6 per cent) and the highest child poverty rate at 18.6 per cent[8] of all Canadian provinces or territories. While BC is not unique either in its circumstances or in its response to factors such as the global economic crisis,[9] such a context is likely to have a significant bearing on the challenges faced by, and experiences of, individuals and families in the midst of separation and divorce (and beyond).

Although the 'success' and 'impact' of the new FLA are likely to be officially measured by reduced court costs and backlogs, as well as fewer families accessing the courts, the effect of this social and political context on families is likely to be far more complex and variable than would be painted by such a statistical picture. Indeed, some parents with family law related disputes do not access the courts at all, while others are able to pay for legal services yet later find themselves with ongoing difficulties but without the

[4] See Statistics Canada, 'High-income Trends among Canadian Tax-filers, 1982 to 2010' *The Daily* 28 January 2013. Available at: www.statcan.gc.ca/daily-quotidien/130128/dq130128a-eng.htm.

[5] Women (many of whom are mothers with care responsibilities), recent immigrants and young people are most affected.

[6] See Statistics Canada, 'Income of Canadians, 2011' *The Daily* 27 June 2013. Available at: www.statcan.gc.ca/daily-quotidien/130627/dq130627c-eng.htm.

[7] Based on Low Income Cut Offs (LICO) before tax data; ibid *Table 202-0802. Persons in low income families, annual.*

[8] ibid.

[9] In the context of family law reform see the chapters by Picontó-Novales, Atkin, Sommerlad, Eekelaar and Maclean (this volume).

means (let alone the time and energy) to return. Still others attempt to represent themselves in court but very quickly find themselves overwhelmed, frustrated and isolated.[10] This raises concern not only about meaningful access to justice but also the long-term personal and social consequences of unresolved justiciable disputes.[11] In this context, Currie points out that it is erroneous to equate demand for legal assistance with need.[12] A review of provincial needs assessments and other studies, conducted by McEown for the Law Foundation of British Columbia, found family law problems to be the area with the greatest unmet need.[13] Thus, given the stringent eligibility criteria for family law legal aid and limited services provided, it is likely that many family law disputes, especially those that are complex, go unresolved—or at least unaddressed—in the formal legal system. This potentially leaves some families in perpetual strife, thereby undermining the principle that the best interests of the child be protected.[14]

Considerable research highlights the long-term health consequences of divorce,[15] particularly for individuals embroiled in post-separation conflicts.[16] A UK study[17] also indicates that legal conflicts disproportionately affect those who are vulnerable, therefore *reinforcing*, rather than alleviating their vulnerability. Thus, unresolved legal problems, in further perpetuating

[10] Macfarlane, J, *The National Self-represented Litigants Project: Identifying and Meeting the Needs of Self-represented Litigants. Final Report* (May 2013) http://representingyourselfcanada.files.wordpress.com/2014/02/reportm15-2.pdf.

[11] See eg Currie, A, *The Legal Problems of Everyday Life: The Nature, Extent and Consequences of Justiciable Problems Experienced by Canadians* (Department of Justice, 2009) www.justice.gc.ca/eng/rp-pr/csj-sjc/jsp-sjp/rr07_la1-rr07_aj1/rr07_la1.pdf; and Genn, H, *Paths to Justice: What People Do and Think about Going to Law* (Oxford, Hart Publishing, 1999).

[12] Currie, ibid.

[13] McEown, C, *Civil Legal Needs Research Project*, 2nd edn (March 2009) www.lawfoundationbc.org/wp-content/uploads/Civil-Legal-Needs-Research-FINAL.pdf.

[14] Notably, this puts more vulnerable family members at risk. Many thanks to Jane Pulkingham for this point.

[15] See eg Avison, W, 'Single Motherhood and Mental Health: Implications for Primary Prevention' (1997) 156(5) *Canadian Medical Association Journal* 661; Hughes, ME and Waite, LJ, 'Marital Biography and Health at Mid-life' (2009) 50(3) *Journal of Health and Social Behavior* 344; Lorenz, F, Wickrama, K, Conger, R and Elder, G, 'The Short-term and Decade-long Effects of Divorce on Women's Midlife Health' (2006) 47(2) *Journal of Health and Social Behavior* 111; Wickrama, K, Lorenz, F, Conger, R, Elder, G, Abraham, W and Fang, S, 'Changes in Family Financial Circumstances and the Physical Health of Married and Recently Divorced Mothers' (2006) 63(1) *Social Science & Medicine* 123.

[16] Treloar, R and Funk, L, 'Mothers' Health, Responsibilization, and Choice in Family Care Work after Separation/Divorce' (2008) *Canadian Journal of Public Health* (Suppl Nov–Dec) 33; Treloar, R and Funk, L, 'Mothers' Health, Responsibilization, and Choice in Family Care Work after Separation/Divorce' in C Benoit and H Hallgrimsdottir (eds), *Valuing Care Work: Comparative Perspectives on Canada, Finland and Iceland* (Toronto, University of Toronto Press, 2011) 153.

[17] Buck, A, Balmer, N and Pleasence, P, 'Social Exclusion and Civil Law: Experience of Civil Justice Problems among Vulnerable Groups' (2005) 39(3) *Social Policy and Administration* 302.

social problems, ultimately add to overall social costs.[18] It is also worth noting that 27.7 per cent of those in Buck et al's study[19] who had an unresolved civil legal problem reported a stress-related illness and 14.2 per cent reported a physical illness with most illnesses involving a medical visit. Given the extent of these findings, it is hard to find justification either for legal aid cuts or cuts to programmes and services that families depend on. Instead, the evidence overwhelmingly points to the need for robust service improvements rather than moving these costs downstream (ie to communities, families and individuals) or into the future (ie beyond the political business cycle).

From the outset of the family law reform process leading up to the FLA, a neoliberal orientation was clearly apparent. Terms such as 'responsibility' and 'choice' were frequently deployed and the role of the state (including adjudication through the courts) was de-emphasised.[20] Instead, separating parents were frequently incited to 'self-manage' their disputes for the sake of their children, and fiscal responsibility for their resolution was held to belong to the parties rather than to the state. The inculcation of self-management and the individualisation of responsibility alongside cuts to services are hallmarks of neoliberal forms of governance, and such strategies are associated with the broader decollectivisation of welfare.[21] Rose and Miller[22] refer to this as 'governing at a distance', wherein individuals come to regulate themselves in accordance with government aims and policies. In other words, they are 'responsibilised'. Thus individualisation, alongside an emphasis on out-of-court dispute resolution, means that those who 'divorce responsibly' are those who self-manage their disputes in accordance with contemporary social and legal norms,[23] whereas those who do not, or cannot, are regarded as morally suspect and undeserving of support or services.[24]

Such a view was implied by the former Attorney General of British Columbia during legislative debates on the FLA, when questions were raised

[18] ibid; see also Currie, *The Legal Problems of Everyday Life* (n 11).

[19] Buck, Balmer and Pleasence, 'Social Exclusion and Civil Law' (n 17).

[20] In the UK context, see Eekelaar (this volume) and '"Not of the Highest Importance": Family Justice under Threat' (2011) 33(4) *Journal of Social Welfare and Family Law* 311, regarding the downgrading of family legal issues allegedly arising from personal choice.

[21] Rose, N, 'The Politics of Life Itself' (2001) 18(6) *Theory, Culture and Society* 1.

[22] Rose, N and Miller, P, 'Political Power beyond the State: Problematic of Government (1992) 43(2) *British Journal of Sociology* 173.

[23] Reece, H, *Divorcing Responsibly* (Oxford, Hart Publishing, 2003); see also Diduck, A, *Law's Families* (London, LexisNexis, 2003) 2.

[24] Day Sclater, S, *Divorce: A Psychosocial Study* (Aldershot, UK, Ashcroft, 1999); Elizabeth, V, Gavey, N and Tolmie, J, 'Between a Rock and a Hard Place: Resident Mothers and the Moral Dilemmas they Face during Custody Disputes' (2010) 18(3) *Feminist Legal Studies* 253; Kaganas, F and Day Sclater, S, 'Contact Disputes: Narrative Constructions of "Good" Parents' (2004) 12(1) *Feminist Legal Studies* 1.

about who would pay for the cost of a parenting coordinator[25] if it became necessary. The Minister responded that 'those families already pay, and pay a fair bit, to go back through the court legal process'.[26] When pressed further, as to whether women who are trying to leave abusive relationships and already face prohibitive legal costs would receive assistance in order to access a parenting coordinator, the Minister was adamant that 'those families' would see an overall reduction of their costs by paying for out-of-court dispute resolution. Furthermore, resources would be deployed to assist the majority of divorcing couples who do not need parenting coordinators or occupy court time, whereas the 10 per cent who do require these services and 'take up 90 per cent of court time related to family issues'[27] would find that their overall costs would be reduced.[28] Essentially, these 'high-conflict parents'[29] will now be responsible to find, and pay for, their own resources for the resolution of their disputes (if, indeed, that is possible). Such a monolithic view of parents who are in dispute regarding children's arrangements post-separation is highly problematic, not only because of the range of issues and child welfare concerns involved in post-separation disputes, but also because it represents—at least potentially—state abandonment of families without the means or who are otherwise vulnerable, and constructs them as undeserving of support (including care and social inclusion) or justice.

Unfortunately, a kind of paradox results. Parents appear to have greater autonomy and choice but, in fact, there is a narrowing of choices such that only decisions or behaviours that fit these norms (eg ability to self-manage their disputes) are endorsed. Those outside such narrow boundaries are 'othered' and abandoned, without access to justice and the support and services necessary, either to resolve their disputes or to move on in spite of them. Although some exception is made for those who are deemed to be vulnerable (eg where family violence has occurred), drawing boundaries around those who are vulnerable, or 'deserving' of support portrays those outside the boundaries as able to resolve their disputes on their own if they so 'choose'. That is, those who are 'reasonable' and willing to put

[25] A parenting coordinator is a dispute resolution professional who: (1) meets the requirements set out in the regulations; and (2) may assist the parties in implementing an agreement or order where there is an agreement or court order that they do so (FLA, Div 3). Typically this involves consensus-building. However, if that is unsuccessful the parenting coordinator may make a binding decision.

[26] British Columbia, Legislative Assembly, *Official Report of the Debates of the Legislative Assembly* 21 November 2011, vol 28 at 8937 (Hon S Bond) Debates of the Legislative Assembly (Hansard) www.leg.bc.ca/hansard/39th4th/index.htm.

[27] ibid.

[28] ibid.

[29] ibid. The categorisation 'high-conflict parents' raises a number of concerns but it is beyond the scope of this chapter to expand on them.

their children first are potentially excluded from access to justice and to support.[30]

Legal aid for some family law matters was first introduced in Canada in 1973.[31] At one time, BC had a noteworthy legal aid system with stable funding, largely through a provincial grant. Following the election of a provincial Liberal government in 2001, however, the funding situation has involved significant cuts to provincial funding, brief periods of redevelopment, followed by another funding crisis with service and/or staff cuts and coverage restrictions. This cycle repeated itself several times. Since Canada's Charter of Rights and Freedoms and case law protect those who require representation for criminal or immigration matters, most of these cuts occurred in civil law legal aid (primarily involving family and poverty law). In 2010, a fifth round of cuts ensued, resulting in reductions for criminal law coverage and further reductions to family law coverage.[32] Plans to expand Justice Access Centres[33] (JAC) in the province were shelved and the LawLine telephone information service was discontinued. A further legal aid funding crisis occurred in 2012–13; however, this was resolved with additional provincial funds. Since the new FLA came into effect, some of these cuts to legal services have been partially restored and a new provincial domestic violence plan has been implemented.[34] These changes will be evaluated in more depth later in this chapter. However, it is worth noting that in the 2014 World Justice Report,[35] Canada ranked only 13th out of 30 high-income countries on civil justice and ranked poorly on accessibility and affordability of legal counsel.[36]

[30] Such boundaries may also obscure the gendered dimensions of family life and family responsibilities and recognition of how these factors, and consequently unequal access to material resources, can result in particular vulnerabilities for women in post-separation disputes concerning children; see Boyd, SB, *Child Custody, Law, and Women's Work* (Toronto, Oxford University Press, 2003); and Pulkingham, J, 'Private Troubles, Private Solutions: Poverty among Divorced Women and the Politics of Support Enforcement and Child Custody Determination' in N Larsen and B Burtch (eds), *Law in Society: Canadian Readings* (Toronto, Harcourt Brace Canada, 2006) 296.

[31] Beveridge, A, *History of Social Justice (Poverty) Law Services Pre-2002. Report to Coalition for Public Legal Services* (December 2009). www.cba.org/dev/BC/Public_Media/PDF/beveridge_memo_12_30_09.pdf.

[32] ibid.

[33] Justice Access Centres are sites designed to assist people with family and civil law issues. They provide information and limited services. The Victoria Centre is also affiliated with the University of Victoria's Student Law Centre Clinic. See: www.ag.gov.bc.ca/justice-access-centre/index.htm.

[34] *British Columbia's Domestic Violence Plan* (2014) www.mcf.gov.bc.ca/podv/pdf/dv_pp_booklet.pdf; *Government Launches Three Year Domestic Violence Plan [Press release]* www.newsroom.gov.bc.ca/2014/02/government-launches-three-year-domestic-violence-plan.html

[35] See The World Justice Project (2014): http://worldjusticeproject.org/sites/default/files/files/country_profiles.pdf.

[36] Canada received a score of .54 on accessibility and affordability, ranking behind a number of countries with a lower Gross Domestic Product (GDP).

Leading up to the introduction of the FLA, BC's Ministry of the Attorney General increased its focus on the provision of basic family law information via the internet, as did the Legal Services Society (LSS). In 2013, six months after the introduction of the FLA, the province opened a third JAC in Victoria. The current focus appears to be on providing basic legal 'information' (widely available to literate individuals with internet access and arguably most useful to those with straightforward family law issues), and limited legal 'advice' (eg through JAC's and pro bono duty counsel). Only those with the most dire family circumstances (eg those who require protection orders) are eligible for legal aid, providing they meet the strict eligibility criteria.[37] The LSS has also replaced the former LawLine with a FamilyLawLINE, although in order to be eligible to obtain advice (rather than information) the financial eligibility criteria are the same as for legal aid. In its 2014–15 budget[38] the BC Ministry of Justice restored two million dollars of legal aid funding for both criminal and civil legal aid, with a commitment to an additional four million dollars to be distributed over the next two years. However, this amount falls far short of the overall cutbacks and does not restore funding to the Court Services Branch. This means that many of the pressures on the justice system that result in backlogs and delays will go unaddressed, potentially offsetting any funding increases. Notably, these delays are likely to add to the financial and emotional stresses of those who must resort to the court system.

In addition to overall cutbacks to legal aid funding, BC has also instituted severe funding reductions to a broad range of services and programmes that support families, with a particular impact on the most vulnerable (ie those with low incomes and families in crisis). As with family law legal aid, it is predominantly poor and marginalised women that utilise social welfare services and provisions; thus those most in need of assistance bear the greatest impact of cuts. In sum, these changes—scaling back fiscal responsibility for the services and supports that families need and may depend on to successfully navigate the divorce process and privatisation of the costs alongside the individualisation of responsibility—reflect a neoliberal orientation.[39] As Maclean notes in this volume, this is in stark contrast with a welfare state ethic of justice which was formerly understood to be a central aspect of citizenship.[40]

[37] See http://legalaid.bc.ca/legal_aid/doIQualifyAdvice.php.

[38] See www.bcbudget.gov.bc.ca/2014/sp/pdf/ministry/jag.pdf.

[39] See Treloar and Boyd, 'Family Law Reform in (Neoliberal) Context' (n 1) for a full discussion of these changes in the context of neoliberalism. See also Treloar and Funk (n 16) for a discussion of neoliberalism in the context of the law reform process and the post-separation consequences for mothers.

[40] See also Sommerlad (this volume) and Sommerlad, H, 'Some Reflections on the Relationship between Citizenship, Access to Justice and the Reform of Legal Aid' (2004) 31 (3) *Journal of Law & Society* 345.

OVERVIEW OF THE FLA

This section addresses important statutory changes pertaining to parenting after separation,[41] with particular emphasis on the new provisions regarding guardianship, family violence and relocation. These changes are framed in an approach to family dispute resolution that promotes 'out-of-court' dispute resolution processes and parental agreements. Such changes are also intended to reflect the fact that the majority of family law disputes now settle out-of-court.[42] Space does not permit a provision by provision analysis of the Act; however, in an earlier co-authored article,[43] a number of these provisions were examined in detail. Boyd has also investigated whether the Family Law Act manages to avoid the pitfalls of formal equality and its effects on women's autonomy, given the extant gendered division of care.[44] These are the only published analyses of the Act to date.

Although the Act contains a number of important changes, three of these are central to the discussion that follows: (1) replacing the terms 'custody' and 'access' with expanded definitions of guardianship; (2) an explicit definition of domestic violence; and (3) rules to guide relocation. Other innovative provisions include a list of specific factors that both parents and the courts must consider in determining a child's 'best interests' and explicit definitions of legal parenthood and the ability of the court to make conduct and compliance orders. It is also important to note that the Act does not make presumptions regarding the preferred form of parenting arrangements. To date, Canada has not introduced legislated joint custody or 'equal' parenting presumptions per se.[45] Quote marks are used for the term 'equal' since it is a contested term and, furthermore, the merits of such a presumption in the context of marital separation are not borne out by empirical research.[46]

[41] For a comprehensive discussion of these changes, see Treloar and Boyd (n 1).

[42] See Department of Justice Canada, *Resolving Disputes-Think about your Options* www.justice.gc.ca/eng/rp-pr/csj-sjc/dprs-sprd/dr-rd/index.html.

However, this may not be as big of a change as it is claimed to be since most family disputes always did settle outside a judicial decision. In fact, the biggest change in this regard is the considerable emphasis on trying to make everyone settle outside court. The author is grateful to Susan Boyd for this point.

[43] Treloar and Boyd (n 1).

[44] Boyd, SB, 'Equality: An Uncomfortable Fit in Parenting Law' in R Leckey (ed), *After Legal Equality: Family, Sex, Kinship* (New York, Routledge, 2014) 42.

[45] In 2014, a private member's bill was introduced that would amend the federal Divorce Act to include a presumption of 'equal' parenting; however, the bill was defeated at second reading.

[46] For reviews of this literature, see Fehlberg, B, Smyth, B, Maclean, M and Roberts, C, 'Legislating for Shared Time Parenting after Separation: A Research Review' (2011) 25(3) *International Journal of Law, Policy and the Family* 318; Trinder, L, 'Shared Residence: A Review of Recent Research Evidence' (2010) 22(4) *Child and Family Law Quarterly* 475.

In fact, as Rhoades has noted in the Australian context, such a presumption can be problematic.[47]

One of the key changes in the FLA is the elimination of the terms 'custody' and 'access'. Instead, the Act sets out a model of 'parenting arrangements' in which each parent who is also a guardian has a significant role with their responsibilities and parenting time specified (FLA pt 4, Div 2). 'Parental responsibilities' of guardians include the day-to-day care and control of a child and an explicit list of responsibilities (eg deciding where the child will live, go to school, and how they will be raised) (FLA, s 41). In place of the term 'access', each guardian's 'parenting time' allows them to exercise day-to-day decision-making, care and control (FLA, s 42). The allocation of these responsibilities can be varied by order or contract, but like the Children and Families Act 2014, England and Wales, the default is ongoing parental responsibilities.

The Act also makes a number of improvements where family violence is involved. First, the list of factors that both courts and parents must consider in determining a child's best interests (FLA, s 37) explicitly emphasises 'the child's physical, psychological and emotional safety, security and well-being' (FLA, s 37(3)) and pays careful attention to the presence and impacts of family violence on a child. A second key change is the explicit definition of domestic violence that recognises the multiple forms that domestic violence may take (FLA, s 1), including:

(a) physical abuse of a family member, including forced confinement or deprivation of the necessities of life, but not including the use of reasonable force to protect oneself or others from harm;
(b) sexual abuse of a family member;
(c) attempts to physically or sexually abuse a family member;
(d) psychological or emotional abuse of a family member, including
    (i) intimidation, harassment, coercion or threats, including threats respecting other persons, pets or property;
    (ii) unreasonable restrictions on, or prevention of, a family member's financial or personal autonomy;
    (iii) stalking or following of the family member; and
    (iv) intentional damage to property; and
(e) in the case of a child, direct or indirect exposure to family violence (FLA, s 1).

Thirdly, the FLA provides tools to address family violence, including a new protection order to assist police and the courts in addressing family violence

[47] Rhoades, H, 'The Dangers of Shared Care Legislation: why Australia Needs (yet more) Family Law Reform' (2008) 36(3) *Federal Law Review* 279; Rhoades, H, 'Legislating to Promote Children's Welfare, and the Quest for Certainty' (2012) 24(2) *Child and Family Law Quarterly* 158.

situations (pt 9). Breaching a protection order is now a Criminal Code offence. Family dispute resolution professionals are also required to screen for the presence of family violence and the extent to which it may adversely affect safety of a party or family member and the ability of a party to negotiate a fair agreement (FLA, s 8).

Finally, the Act includes new provisions to assist parents and the courts when a parent wishes to relocate. Related to the general 'best interests' considerations, these provisions vary according to the existing parenting arrangements. Generally, if a guardian wishes to move they must provide 60 days' notice to other guardians or persons with contact with that child (FLA, s 66). If they object, they must go to court within 30 days (FLA, s 68). If the guardians do *not* have substantially equal parenting time, then the relocating guardian must satisfy a court that the proposed relocation is in good faith and that he or she has proposed reasonable and workable arrangements to preserve the relationship between the child and other guardians or significant persons in the child's life (FLA, s 69). If the court is satisfied in this regard, then the relocation must be considered as in the best interests of the child unless another guardian is able to satisfy the court otherwise. However, if the guardians have 'substantially equal parenting time' with the child, then the relocating guardian must satisfy the court of both the factors described above and that the relocation is in the best interests of the child (FLA, s 69(5)). Thus, the burden is heavier on the relocating guardian when an arrangement along the lines of shared parenting exists. Otherwise, the Act largely seems to acknowledge the interrelationship of child and caregiver well-being. However, while each of these provisions is positive on its face, when viewed in the context of how neoliberalism affects access to justice, and in particular taking into account the cutbacks and assumptions described above, there is also some cause for concern.

Although the intent of the FLA is to divert most parties away from court processes, consideration of legal decisions is still important. Court decisions can have a significant effect on people's lives; thus, it is in the public interest to know how the law is interpreted and why certain results are reached in particular cases. Legal decisions can also provide some indication of how well the justice system is functioning.[48] Several court decisions have been made in relation to guardianship and relocation under the FLA (although it is early days yet and there are no or few appellate decisions to date). These decisions will be briefly evaluated, followed by a more extensive discussion of decisions where findings of family violence were made under the

[48] There are also a number of limitations involved in using legal decisions when attempting to understand the impact of the FLA, one of the most obvious being that only a small minority of separating parents resolve their disputes in court. Consequently, it is not possible to use legal decisions to assess the effect of 'new' social and legal norms (as promoted in the FLA) on parents.

new statute. The discussion will focus on a key decision regarding family violence and engage a broader examination of a new provincial Domestic Violence Plan (DVP) which includes specific provisions for vulnerable groups. This plan, particularly in the context of BC's FLA, has important implications for access to justice.

KEY LEGAL DECISIONS

A particular concern expressed by Treloar and Boyd[49] was the default of ongoing guardianship in the context of intra-household gendered power relations and patterns of care. We were concerned that such a provision would place a parent who resisted shared guardianship for good reason in a difficult situation and also that it might actually become a site for *increased* conflict and litigation (as was seen in the UK and Australia when those countries moved to a similar model). However, in that the Act avoided presumptions about shared parenting or contact rights and included a clear focus on children's safety, we were cautiously optimistic that similar problems could be avoided. In the Act's first year no published decisions suggest that these concerns have been borne out; however, it is very difficult to assess the effect of such a default after such a short period. Moreover, it is impossible to assess people's reasons for resisting shared guardianship through legal decisions alone. Many of the published guardianship cases to date involve transitional provisions (eg interim orders that were made under the former Family Relations Act (RSBC 1996, c 128)) or situations where children were/had been in care. Therefore, further research is necessary in order to determine what, if any, effect these provisions (and the new norms inherent in the FLA) have on an individual's decision to engage in family law litigation and their expectations regarding the likely outcomes. Research that assesses the extent of unmet legal (and extralegal) needs would also be invaluable. A preliminary discussion with contacts in the field suggests that these unmet needs are considerable. Indeed, unless one can pay or qualify for legal aid, short of self-representation, there are only two alternatives: concede or remain in an untenable situation.

As noted by Treloar and Boyd,[50] how 'substantially equal parenting time' and other provisions were interpreted would be of crucial importance when assessing decisions regarding relocation. To date, most reported relocation decisions explicitly lay out the factors considered by the court in their analysis, making them unremarkable. However, in less clear cut situations, the court still appears to exercise some discretion based on their impressions of each parent as a *parent* and their assessment of the 'good faith' (s 69(4)(a)(i))

[49] Treloar and Boyd (n 1).
[50] ibid.

of a relocating parent. Thus those who appear to self-manage their disputes in accordance with contemporary social and legal norms[51] are now understood as 'deserving' (at least to some degree) the right to make autonomous decisions regarding where they will live and how they will parent their child. This is because they are seen as acting in the best interests of their children. Yet it is extremely difficult for any parent to (self-re)present themselves in such a way in court, making access to justice crucial to ensuring 'just' outcomes when arguing against the 'default position'. In relocation cases the default position is often viewed as the status quo. That is to say, in current thinking, a move away from the other parent is not generally in the child's best interests.

An assessment of court decisions regarding family violence, particularly in light of a new provincial Domestic Violence Plan,[52] highlights both the transformative potential of the Act and positive steps to date. However, as argued below, a number of issues remain, particularly where disputes are multifaceted or where considerable conflict is involved. To date, under the new Act, the court has decided cases where the expanded definition of family violence was applied. These include emotional or psychological abuse of a child[53] or parent and child,[54] potential risk of sexual abuse by a parent,[55] indirect exposure to family violence,[56] a party's conduct of a court proceeding[57] and financial abuse.[58]

Next, this chapter turns to a court decision (*J.C.P. v J.B.*),[59] involving financial (and other) abuse in the context of divorce litigation. This case has a number of important implications, not the least because of its basis in the expanded definition of family violence and the considerable impact on the mother and child involved, but also in light of the concerns raised by Boyd[60] and others regarding the generally diminished material circumstances that mothers experience (compared to fathers) following marital separation. Mothers tend to earn lower wages owing to a gender wage gap,[61] the concentration

[51] Reece, *Divorcing Responsibly* (n 23); Diduck, *Law's Families* (n 23).
[52] See n 34.
[53] *D.N.L. v C.N.S.*, 2013 BCSC 809.
[54] *J.C.P. v J.B.*, 2013 BCPC 297.
[55] *L.J.S.M. v L.T.S.*, 2013 BCSC 796.
[56] ibid.
[57] *M.W.B. v A.R.B.*, 2013 BCSC 885.
[58] *J.C.P. v J.B.*, 2013 BCPC 297.
[59] ibid.
[60] Boyd, SB, *Child Custody, Law, and Women's Work* (Toronto, Oxford University Press, 2003).
[61] Fortin, N and Huberman, M, 'Occupational Gender Segregation and Women's Wages in Canada: An Historical Perspective' (2002) 28 *Canadian Public Policy* S11; Statistics Canada, *Women in Canada: A Gender-based Statistical Report* (2011). 89-503-X. Available at: www.statcan.gc.ca/pub/89-503-x/89-503-x2010001-eng.htm.

of women in low-paid fields and a 'motherhood wage penalty'.[62] Mothers also assume greater overall responsibility for care work,[63] which is typically non- or under-compensated. As such, this case has important ramifications for the material basis of access to justice and mother and child well-being.

J.C.P. v J.B.[64] involved a four-year-old girl who lived with her mother and extended family. There were mutual allegations by the parents of physical assault. In addition, the mother contended that the child was conceived as a result of sexual assault by the father and that on occasion he had touched their daughter inappropriately. Although there was conflicting evidence, the Court found the father's behaviour to be abusive on a number of grounds: he had used a hidden surveillance camera to record a parenting time exchange which was then presented as evidence in court, he had tried to intimidate and manipulate the mother in the presence of the child, and he had failed to pay child support in full and on time. This combination of factors was the basis upon which the Court found that 'family violence' under section 1 of the FLA had occurred.

In giving reasons, the Court said that the father's

> failure to pay child support on time and in the full amount … combined with his other actions and words constitutes family violence. I am satisfied that his failure to pay was a calculated and deliberate act designed to inflict psychological and emotional harm and control [the mother's] behaviour. I am satisfied that [the father's] goal was to destabilise the mother's parenting (para 15).

The Court further noted that the father could well afford to pay, and that although

> the failure to pay child support will not often constitute an act of family violence, when the failure is the result of a determined decision not to pay, knowing the impact it would have on [the mother], who had limited income, and my rejection of [the father's] explanation for failing to pay, I have concluded that this was designed to inflict psychological and emotional trauma to [the mother] and is therefore an act of family violence (para 18).

Finally, the Court said, 'I am also of the view that this has impacted [the child's] well-being and that [the father's] ability to care for [the child] is impaired' (para 19).

[62] Budig, MJ and England, P, 'The Wage Penalty for Motherhood' (2001) 66(2) *American Sociological Review* 204; Budig, MJ and Hodges, MJ, 'Differences in Disadvantage: Variation in the Motherhood Penalty across White Women's Earnings Distribution' (2010) 75(5) *American Sociological Review* 705; Caranci, B and Gauthier, P, *Career Interrupted: The Economic Impact of Motherhood. Toronto Dominion Bank, Special Report* (October 2010) www.td.com/document/PDF/economics/special/td-economics-special-bc1010-career-interrupted.pdf.

[63] Statistics Canada, *Women in Canada* (n 61).

[64] ibid.

Overall, the Court clearly doubted the father's commitment to the child, his willingness to cooperate with the mother regarding the best interests of their child, and found that he had demonstrated a clear pattern of putting his own interests ahead of the child. In the final disposition of the case, the mother received sole decision-making authority regarding all matters except for health, education, culture, religion and spiritual upbringing, which were to be shared. However, both parties would continue to be responsible for day-to-day care during their parenting time. The Court also issued a conduct order under section 199(1)(b) of the FLA, providing that '[the father] shall attend, participate in, and successfully complete counselling, including psychological counselling and parenting courses, and provide proof of his attendance at counselling' (para 51).

Thus the Court in *J.C.P. v J.B.* sent a strong message that it would not tolerate efforts by one party to manipulate, undermine or intimidate another. As such, controlling behaviour when intended to inflict harm—whether through psychological, financial or a combination of means—falls under the definition of family violence. Importantly, this harm inevitably affects children and is part of a 'best interests' determination. Hopefully the Court's message will reduce the frequency with which such behaviour occurs and increase recognition of the impact on both the intended recipient and on children. However, in that the abusing parent received unsupervised and generous parenting time before there was evidence of behavioural change, this strong message loses some of its meaning. If indeed the father's goal was to destabilise the mother's parenting, a better option would have been to reduce his parenting time (or have it supervised) at least in the short term. This would restore stable parenting for the child as well as provide a more consistent message on family violence. Although the mother had proposed the division of responsibilities and parenting time[65] that was ultimately adopted by the Court, it seems that the Court favoured her proposal over an arrangement that was in the child's best interests (s 37). Indeed, the Court had determined that the father's ability to care for the child was impaired as a result of the family violence (para 24) and family violence is a factor that must now be considered in determining a child's best interests (s 37(2)). Thus we are left wondering whether the mother made this proposal largely to counter the father's claim that she was trying to limit his role (and so satisfy the court that his allegations were untrue),[66] rather than because she genuinely believed it was in their child's best interests. If so, then the mother was caught in a paradoxical situation—the only proposal she could make (ie one that seemed to be in 'good faith' and would, therefore, counter the father's allegations of her intent to exclude him from their child's life)—was

[65] Full details of the mother's proposal were not included in the Court's decision.

[66] Which she did: the Court found that the evidence did not support the father's assertions (para 26) and that the mother will make decisions that are in the child's interests (para 27).

one that was likely not in her child's best interests. However, the FLA explicitly states that the best interests of a child must be the parents and the court's *only* consideration in making agreements or orders involving children (FLA, s 37(1)). Given the mother's very limited means and the father's proclivity to controlling and litigious behaviour, as well as his greater financial power, this example highlights the important interrelationship between access to justice and family justice.

ASSESSMENT OF THE FLA: ONE YEAR ON

Shortly after the Act came into force, Treloar and Boyd offered a preliminary assessment of the strengths and weaknesses of the Act, critically reflecting on how the Act might ultimately fulfil its transformative promise given the contemporary neoliberal context.[67] Specifically, the article concluded that the Act has both strengths and weaknesses as well as several areas that would benefit from further attention. Positive changes identified were: the redefinition of parentage; revisions to the 'best interests criteria'; the comprehensive definition of domestic violence and explicit attention to its effects; new protection orders; new relocation provisions; and the statement against presumptions of preferred parenting arrangements. However, concerns were raised about the default of ongoing guardianship and, given the neoliberal impetus to reduce public spending and individualise responsibility for social problems, there was particular concern about the adequacy of investment in support resources. Shifting responsibility to individuals and/or households and cutting funding for social programmes including legal aid, has significant implications for access to justice. For the FLA to attain its full potential, changes must also occur outside the family legal system. Without labour force policy initiatives and a strong system of public childcare to support parents who attempt to balance paid work and care responsibilities, the FLA could instead contribute to broader social tensions regarding work and family life and make the interpretation of legal norms more challenging.

This section revisits that very preliminary assessment and considers the extent to which the concerns expressed have played out in the first year following implementation of the Act. With few exceptions, legal decisions regarding guardianship, family violence and relocation have been unremarkable; some funding issues have been addressed, albeit rather minimally, but the broader implications of cuts to social services and programmes have not. Thus access to justice and access to services remains a significant concern. In combination, they severely constrain the possibilities of access to justice

[67] Treloar and Boyd (n 1).

for all families. Currie,[68] Pleasence, et al[69] and others have documented the huge personal and social costs when justice (and its many interrelated dimensions) is out of reach for those who need it. In fact, researchers have found that when justiciable problems go unresolved they tend to intersect with social problems in a mutually reinforcing manner and often worsen over time (Currie). In some cases, particularly for members of vulnerable groups, this can result in social exclusion (Pleasence et al). What is sometimes lost in the broader access to justice literature, however, is that lack of access to family law legal aid and other family support services disproportionately affects women[70] and indirectly affects children. In part, that is because most legal aid referrals are for criminal law,[71] an area of law in which men make up the majority of those receiving services. Gender differences in access to financial resources can also have a significant impact on access to justice in family law disputes and, therefore, on outcomes. Thus there is also a risk of what Sommerlad, in this volume, describes as an 'intensification of gender injustice'. If one party has access to funds through employment or investments but the other does not (eg is a stay home parent), it is possible that the former, with ready access to cash or capital, could retain a top lawyer, while the latter is unlikely to qualify for legal aid and could struggle to meet their essential expenses. In this way, access to justice loses its purchase as a democratic right and instead becomes something that is purchased on the market.

The section next explores the new BC Domestic Violence Plan, reflecting on its strengths as well as raising some concerns. First, the background and details of the plan are described. Secondly, concerns are raised about the identification of individuals and groups as 'more' and 'less' vulnerable in this context, particularly as it has implications for access to justice and to resources. Finally, in thinking about how this plan might play out in practice, given both the complex circumstances often faced by survivors of domestic violence and the knotty intersections of social and legal policies, concerns are raised both in regard to access to justice and in access to needed services.

In February 2014, almost a year after the FLA came into full effect, the BC government launched a three-year domestic violence plan (DVP) which

[68] Currie (n 11).

[69] Pleasence, P, Balmer, NJ, Buck, A, O'Grady, A and Genn, H, 'Civil Law Problems and Morbidity' (2004) 58(7) *Journal of Epidemiology and Community Health* 552.

[70] Treloar and Boyd (n 1); Brewin, A, *Legal Aid Denied: Women and the Cuts to Legal Services in BC* (Vancouver, BC, Canadian Centre for Policy Alternatives, 2004); Mossman, MJ, 'Gender Equality, Family Law and Access to Justice' (1994) 8(3) *International Journal of Law and the Family* 357; Track, L, *Putting Justice Back on the Map: The Route to Equal and Accessible Family Justice* (February 2014) www.westcoastleaf.org/userfiles/file/FINAL%20 REPORT%20PDF.pdf.

[71] In the most recent Legal Services Society Annual Service Plan reports this figure was 72%. Only 16% of referrals were for family law: see www.lss.bc.ca/assets/aboutUs/reports/annualReports/annualServicePlanReport_2012.pdf.

is to be coordinated through the Provincial Office of Domestic Violence. This Office was established in 2012, with the mandate to coordinate government programmes and come up with a comprehensive plan to tackle domestic violence, following the 2008 murder of three children by their mentally ill father. In her report,[72] BC's independent Representative for Children and Youth found that a coordinated and effective provincial domestic violence programme could have prevented these deaths. The same year, while out on bail following charges of domestic violence, a man killed his estranged wife, their son and her parents. The Representative for Children and Youth[73] similarly detailed the gaps in service provision and missed opportunities for intervention, and made numerous recommendations for improvements to services, policy and practice that could prevent similar deaths in the future. According to the press release,[74] this plan is the result of extensive consultation with domestic and anti-violence groups and members of the public. It provides start-up funding for two new specialised domestic violence units (for a total of six);[75] includes programmes designed for Aboriginal families, new immigrant and refugee women and women with disabilities; direct services for perpetrators; and improved access to services and social housing for women who live in rural and remote communities.

In many respects the DVP is a positive step forward and responds to frequently raised concerns about the impact of domestic violence on vulnerable groups. However, all women exiting violent relationships are vulnerable, as are their children. Categorising women who have experienced domestic violence into 'more' and 'less' vulnerable based on their social or geographic location, could obscure the needs and experiences of women who do not fit the category of 'most vulnerable'. Moreover, notions of vulnerability often accompany perceptions of blameworthiness; thus, there is a risk that those who are not seen as vulnerable could, in some way, be regarded as culpable for their abuse.[76] As a result, such divisions could serve to exclude those who are deemed 'not vulnerable' from needed services as well as (potentially) portraying them as culpable owing to their agency. As Brown points out, a structural view of vulnerability suggests an absence of agency, whereas an individualistic conceptualisation of vulnerability obscures the structural factors that play a role in people's vulnerability.[77] Furthermore, she argues

[72] See http://www.rcybc.ca/sites/default/files/documents/pdf/reports_publications/honouring_christian_lee.pdf.

[73] See https://www.rcybc.ca/sites/default/files/documents/pdf/reports_publications/honouring_kaitlynne.pdf.

[74] *Government Launches Three Year Domestic Violence Plan* (n 34).

[75] The four units that currently exist are found in the 'Lower Mainland' area surrounding and including Vancouver (3), and the provincial capital (1). It is currently unknown where the two new units will be located.

[76] Indeed, under the new DVP they may be less able to access free or low-cost services, and may face greater difficulty accessing legal aid during the separation process.

[77] Brown, K, '"Vulnerability": Handle with Care' (2011) 5(3) *Journal of Ethics and Social Welfare* 313.

that the tension between these two accounts raises critical ethical issues. Although the term 'vulnerability' serves as justification for resources and moderates concerns about blameworthiness, it also conflicts with notions of rights and can play a role in the 'patronising and negative treatment of some groups in society'.[78] It is precisely such treatment that discourages Aboriginal women, for example, from seeking assistance in the first place. Thus the DVP's focus on known vulnerable groups has implications not only for individuals or groups that are deemed to be vulnerable, but also for those who are regarded as not, since it is assumed that they make their own choices and can do so without need to seek remedy through legal mechanisms. Those that are not deemed vulnerable in this view are likely to be expected to self-manage their post-separation family disputes and any difficulties they face are obscured. The identification of vulnerable groups also conveys an implicit message about who the presumed perpetrators are.[79] Typically, they are assumed to be Aboriginal men, immigrant and refugee men, and deviant men who prey on identifiably vulnerable women.[80] Therefore this strategy may make sense in terms of targeting scarce resources, but it undermines efforts at effectively dealing with the true magnitude and extent of the problem at a societal level because it misrepresents the nature and extent of the problem in terms of who is on the receiving end of abuse, as well as who metes out such abuse. Finally, it is also unclear whether the needs of individuals whose experiences fit the expanded legal definition of family violence (eg financial or emotional abuse) would be recognised in the new domestic violence plan.

Despite these concerns, the DVP does, for the most part, seem to be a positive step forward, particularly in that it identifies gaps in service provision and aims to provide services that are more useful or appropriate for their recipients. For example, given that persons with disabilities who have justiciable problems are at greater risk of social exclusion,[81] in situations where domestic violence is also an issue, such a plan should go some distance to alleviating the complex challenges these women face. However, how this plan plays out in practice and the extent to which it will assist survivors of domestic violence with their often complex and interconnected needs remains to be seen. Importantly, a significant factor in meeting these interconnected needs is whether services exist in the communities where they are required. As such, it is rather ironic that at the same time as the

[78] ibid 318.

[79] Thanks to Jane Pulkingham for this point.

[80] Ironically, some Aboriginal women and immigrant women may not disclose domestic violence because of concern about reinforcing these racial stereotypes. Aboriginal women may also lack faith in the police and justice system (and in the government more generally).

[81] O'Grady, A, Pleasence, P, Balmer, NJ, Buck, A and Genn, H, 'Disability, Social Exclusion and the Consequential Experience of Justiciable Problems' (2004) 19(3) *Disability & Society* 259.

provincial government developed their DVP with the intent of providing improved services to Aboriginal women and their communities, the federal government cut core funding for long established Native Friendship Centres. These centres are the social welfare hub of many Aboriginal communities, providing a wide range of programmes and services. Instead, funding was reassigned to an 'improved Urban Aboriginal Strategy aimed at increasing the economic participation of urban Aboriginal people'.[82] Prioritising the economic participation of urban Aboriginal people over their broader social welfare needs as they exist and are required across the province is short-sighted, to put it bluntly. Again, the prioritising of economic concerns by government speaks clearly to who is seen as deserving (ie those who participate in the labour force and are visible in urban areas) and has important implications for social exclusion.

In assessing the extent to which the FLA can fulfil its potential in a neoliberal environment, given the interconnected nature of family law problems and other social issues, along with a lack of accessibility to the courts and cutbacks to services, it is unlikely that many individuals who are engaged in high-conflict and complex disputes will fare well. In addition to the situations described above, families where one or more members have complex health issues (eg mental health or addictions, severe or chronic pain or illness, brain injury) often fell between the cracks under the previous statute. Given ongoing austerity measures they are likely to face even greater challenges under the new statute. Even *with* money and support these situations are challenging and are often exhausting for families.

A further concern is that of uneven access to justice when there is a significant disparity in financial resources (or ability to access these resources) *between* parties in family law disputes. Whether or not people turn to law often depends on a number of factors, money being an important one. Public confidence in the justice system has been diminished,[83] in part because of perceptions that justice is the provenance of the wealthy, ie those with the financial autonomy to be able to access it. A recent Canadian Bar Association summary report on access to justice concluded that 'the reality today is that not everyone has meaningful access to justice regardless of income. The justice system is aggregating, rather than mitigating inequality'.[84]

[82] See the government news release at: www.newswire.ca/en/story/1301619/harper-government-invests-in-aboriginal-people-living-in-urban-centres.

[83] According to the 2008 Statistics Canada General Social Survey on Social Engagement (survey conducted every five years), only 53% of British Columbians have confidence in the justice system.

[84] Canadian Bar Association, *Reaching Equal Justice: An Invitation to Envision and Act. A summary Report by the CBA Access to Justice Committee* (August 2013) 12: available at:www.cba.org/CBA/equaljustice/secure_pdf/Equal-Justice-Summary-Report-eng.pdf. See also Canadian Bar Association, *Reaching Equal Justice: An Invitation to Envision and Act. Final Report of the CBA Access to Justice Committee* (November 2013) www.cba.org/CBA/equaljustice/secure_pdf/EqualJusticeFinalReport-eng.pdf.

This conclusion has profound moral and ethical implications for family justice central to which is the question of whether access to justice is a fundamental democratic right. If so, how does that right sit next to the increasing privatisation and marketisation of justice? Furthermore, is family justice possible in this neoliberal context where both access to the courts (when necessary) and to needed services has become more and more difficult? The next section takes a brief look at this question and reflects on what would be required to make family law more accessible and just.

FAMILY JUSTICE IN NEOLIBERAL CONTEXT: WHAT DOES (FAMILY) JUSTICE REQUIRE?

In asking whether family justice is indeed possible in this neoliberal context, we might first consider whether family justice is possible without concomitant social justice. Of course, to insist that it is not possible is an idealistic (and some may argue, naive) view. Indeed, the project of social justice cannot be evaluated in binary terms (ie as achieved or not achieved) as change tends to be incremental and uneven.[85] Regardless, transformative change requires a vision.

Although liberal political theorists might agree, at least in principle, that justice is possible in capitalist societies; principle and practice are not the same things. Such an economic system generates inequality more than it alleviates. As neither a political theorist, nor a moral philosopher, this author cannot adequately review the extensive literature and debate concerning what is just, fair or right. Instead, from a social justice perspective, it is argued that there must be a fair distribution of benefits and burdens across society and that it is the responsibility of the state to ensure their just distribution. Where this distribution impacts on rights that are central to democracy, such as the right to assert or protect one's rights (as well as those of one's dependants), dignity or well-being, then the state has a responsibility to ensure that those with heavier burdens can do so. This means ensuring that law and policy processes are fair and inclusive (ie just and accessible) as well as responsive to structural inequalities. However, on a more practical level, justice requires resources as well as a vision.

Real access to justice for families requires meaningful access to legal services and, more broadly, services that assist them to move on and flourish. As Atkin notes in chapter two, even in fairly ordinary separations people are frequently vulnerable and many cases that reach court involve complex issues. Therefore, given the significant personal and social costs when broader issues are not adequately addressed, he says it must be asked

[85] Sen, A, *The Idea of Justice* (Cambridge, MA, Harvard University Press, 2009).

whether family justice reforms involving privatisation and a reduced state role are, in the end, in the common good.[86]

Given the neoliberal context described above, most notably a governmental emphasis on fiscal constraint that is rooted in an understanding of 'the common good' in primarily economic terms, the restoration of funding to programmes and services that have been cut is unlikely. Similarly, there is little purpose in suggesting the creation of new programmes or services. Despite these limitations, this chapter now turns to explore a few specific and practical changes that would go some distance towards making family law more accessible and just. Drawing from the author's ongoing examination of social policy reforms in British Columbia as well a number of recent law reform reports,[87] many of which draw similar conclusions—that the justice system is broken and action is needed *now*, the focus is on better integration of services and systems along with a few practical suggestions.

First, and most importantly, government ministries and departments must think beyond their own borders when shifting 'strategic priorities' and cutting programme funding. Before doing so, it would be helpful to consider the intersection of policies and programmes across branches and levels of government, asking: who would be affected by these cuts and what else is in place to ensure that needs are met? For example, if the federal government cuts core funding to Native Friendship Centres—the most likely site for programmes and services through the provincial government's new DVP in remote communities, how is that going to work and who will be affected? Similarly, why is it that the federal Department of Justice is ending its 'Supporting Families Initiative' funding, just as the BC FLA has come into effect? If families are going to seek help outside the courts, surely this would be a time to maintain or even improve extra-legal programmes. Finally, if a lone parent on social assistance is categorised as 'expected to work' and has an ongoing complex family law dispute to deal with, *without* continuing access to legal advice and representation and *with* the requirement to seek or engage in paid employment, how exactly is he or she to do so? Although many other examples spring to mind, it is clear that greater foresight, integration and collaboration are necessary. Indeed, Cromwell argues that change must come from the ground up.[88] His report on behalf of the Action Committee on Access to Justice in Civil and Family Matters proposes a substantial shift in legal culture. Although Cromwell's argument is compelling, a concomitant shift in political culture is also necessary.

[86] We might also ask whether some of these changes are penny wise and pound foolish.

[87] With the exception of Track, *Putting Justice Back on the Map* (n 70), these reports address access to justice or law reform broadly, rather than focusing on family law exclusively.

[88] Cromwell, TA, *Meaningful Change for Family Justice: Beyond Wise Words. Final Report of the Family Justice Working Group of the Action Committee on Access to Justice in Civil and Family Matters* (Ottawa, Canada, April 2013).

Fortunately, the legal profession is also advocating for improved accessibility to the courts and access to justice and is prepared to play a part. In a November 2013 report, the Canadian Bar Association (CBA) laid out its vision for 'equal justice'.[89] This vision involves 31 measurable goals to be achieved by 2030. Of the strategies it proposes, three seem most immediately viable and practical: more people-centred law practices where services are provided by integrated teams; more focus on 'access to justice' in law schools; and clearly setting out the expectation that all lawyers will do pro bono work at some point in their careers, with a particular focus on 'lawyers who do not regularly provide people law services, such as lawyers in large law firms, corporate counsel and government lawyers'.[90] Another excellent suggestion, to include lawyers working directly in community agencies servicing women, comes from Track.[91] Many other ideas can be found in these and other reports; however, it is not possible to address them all within the scope of this chapter.

As well as practical and incremental steps that can be implemented right away, 'big thinking' ideas can significantly alter the way we think about the place of justice in Canada's social welfare system, and must be seriously considered in the long term. For example, in his 2011 Report of the Public Commission on Legal Aid,[92] Doust proposed that legal aid be regarded as an essential public service, similar to health and education. As well, noting the tremendous impact on families and the 'downstream economic and social consequences' (p 7) of the current system, he recommended expanded eligibility, increased public engagement, stable funding and greater collaboration among stakeholders as crucial to change. In regard to public engagement, although public sentiment towards the legal profession is not always positive, if all bar members did participate in pro bono work public perceptions of the legal profession would likely improve. Furthermore, such evidence of strengthened commitment to improving access to justice would set the stage for renewed dialogue about how access to justice is everyone's problem, thus putting it on the political agenda.

CONCLUSION

Although the FLA makes some innovative changes and goes some distance in recognising and responding to family violence, it largely ignores inequities

[89] *Reaching Equal Justice Report: An Invitation to Envision and Act. Final Report* (November, 2013) www.cba.org/CBA/equaljustice/secure_pdf/EqualJusticeFinalReport-eng.pdf.

[90] (n 89) 117.

[91] Track (n 70).

[92] See Doust, L, *Foundation for Change: Report of the Public Commission on Legal Aid in British Columbia* (March 2011).

in material and emotional resources among divorcing parents. Family law and policy reform that either assumes parents have equal and sufficient resources, or gives with one hand while taking away with the other, is likely to fall short of its potential. In order to fully achieve this potential *and* ensure family justice, it is essential that all relevant government ministries, along with other stakeholders (eg community organisations and professional groups), work in an integrated manner. If a party does not have the means to access the legal system (which citizens are entitled to access to enforce their legal rights), then their democratic rights are meaningless. In family law, the need to access this system does not necessarily happen once, or in a tidy way. An example of this is where a parent has a legal decision that is not being complied with, but cannot access the system to pursue additional measures to address the non-compliance. A further issue, that of inequity of resources *between* disputing parties, occurs when one party has the means to initiate (or alternately, drag out) proceedings[93] and the other does not, or one party has an income that enables them to hire an expensive lawyer.[94] In that case, there is unequal access to justice between parties. Even if the party with fewer resources can access legal aid, they may lack reasonably equal odds of a just outcome. Such uneven outcomes are more likely where divorcing spouses have significantly unequal incomes and ignores the (gendered) 'internal justice' of the family.[95] Together, such inequities result in a two tiered system and further reinforce public perceptions of the justice system as market based and unfair.

For those who cannot afford legal representation (in the context of marital disputes this could be one or both parties), difficult decisions must be made. If parties cannot come to agreement, those without access to funds or adequate assistance must self-represent or concede. As a recent study by Macfarlane clearly demonstrates, self-representation often results in significant personal costs, which may ultimately also result in greater health and social service costs in the long run.[96] This failure to support litigants with legal assistance is short-sighted, particularly in light of the voluminous literature that shows the high health and social costs of family law disputes, as discussed above. Although justice cannot serve as the single guiding principle in deciding on the 'correct' course of action or policy, making courts more accessible for those who do need them goes some distance to ensuring greater fairness of

[93] Those with means may also engage in the strategic use of self-representation in order to drag out proceedings (and bearing considerably lower financial costs than would otherwise be the case) until the other party is financially or emotionally depleted. Such tactics are well known as part of a pattern of abuse or control, often consistent with family violence. If the other party is eligible for legal aid, such tactics also waste precious legal aid resources.

[94] To clarify, a more expensive lawyer is not necessarily a better one, but such inequity does affect public perceptions and questions regarding the fairness of outcomes.

[95] Okin, SM, *Justice, Gender, and the Family* (New York, Basic Books, 1989).

[96] Macfarlane, *The National Self-represented Litigants Project* (n 10).

outcomes. In addition to the immediate impacts on families, the reduced risk of potential negative social and economic consequences would be considerable. Finally, greater access to justice is likely to go some way to restoring public confidence in the legal system. However, in the case of family law, access to necessary services and support is also required. To slightly rephrase the words of Canada's Chief Justice Beverley Mclachlin, who famously said, 'There is no justice without access to justice',[97] there is no family justice without access to justice, including meaningful access to the broader services families need when they are in crisis.

[97] Ciccocioppo, L, 'There is no Justice without Access to Justice: Chief Justice Beverley McLachlin' (University of Toronto Faculty of Law, 14 February 2014) www.law.utoronto.ca/news/there-no-justice-without-access-justice-chief-justice-beverley-mclachlin.

2

The Revised Family Court System in New Zealand: Secret Justice and Privatisation

BILL ATKIN*

THE ROLE OF THE STATE—A UNIVERSAL QUESTION?

WHAT LESSONS OF universal significance can be asked about changes at the local level to the family law of one particular country? This chapter focuses on changes to the New Zealand system of 'family justice' that came into effect at the end of March 2014. Most of the changes relate not to the substantive law but to the procedures used to deal with family breakdown. They affect the Family Court, the role of lawyers and the place of other professionals in the system, not to mention the parties themselves and their children.

While other countries have made similar changes, the New Zealand version may be seen as extreme. Changes in the direction of 'user pays', privatisation and 'secret justice' raise some significant questions about the jurisprudential basis of the new model. In part, the changes have been made because of financial pressures caused by the global financial crisis but New Zealand has actually weathered that crisis comparatively well. The real reasons for the changes in fact appear to be ideological. This is more fundamental because a country's finances can improve; ideology remains. The ideology in question relates to the fundamental question of the role of the state: the position taken is that, while the state may provide a framework within which people can determine the best outcomes for their own circumstances, beyond this the state should take a back-seat role. To put it another way, the state should not interfere in our private lives.

The issues raised here have synergies with several other contributions to this volume. One such topic is affordability. Irrespective of the global

* This chapter is based on a presentation at the World Conference of the International Society of Family Law, Recife, Brazil, 6–9 August 2014. A version appears on the conference website. Special thanks to my fine research assistant, Sean Brennan.

financial crisis, governments have been asking how much of their budgets should be devoted to family justice. Another theme is de-legalisation. How much detail does the law need to provide in spelling out the rights and responsibilities of parties in family breakdown situations? Has the tendency been to over-prescribe? This is linked to 'contractualisation' under which family law should be seen as much more a matter of contract between the parties than as an imposed regime. Yet a contractual regime may fail to address all the questions and may provide answers that exploit one or other of the parties. Self-determination is not always the best approach.

The New Zealand law has moved in the direction of greater self-determination, and a lesser role for the state. However, in so doing it has given rise to a number of question marks that relate to universal issues that can be explored at different levels.

MORE ON THE STATE: UNDERLYING TENSIONS

The role of the state in the resolution of family disputes, as already touched on, is a basic issue that affects the way that specific policies are developed. Underlying this issue are some important tensions that need to be explored.

First, the opposite of state involvement is what we might call a privatisation approach. Put in a positive way, this allows former partners to work out for themselves the best way forward. If they reach an agreement that they are both happy with, then they are likely to stick with the arrangement and make sure that it works.[1] While the arrangement may include matters to do with property and finances, the crucial issues are often those relating to the children. Most separating couples will realise that they have to cooperate for the benefit of the children. Thus, an amicable scheme that the parents are committed to is likely to be beneficial for the children. So, private arrangements can be very positive. However, these are not the ones that family law tends to get involved with, unless it is to get a formal court order to reflect the parties' agreement. Family law's involvement arises where the parents fail to reach an agreement and where they may have taken up intractable positions. To what extent should the state take an active role in resolving the problems and to what extent should it take a back-seat and regard the issues as essentially ones for the parties to sort out privately?

This question is sometimes framed in another way. The classic distinction between public law and private law is invoked. In short, cases involving child abuse and vulnerable adults are regarded as part of public law and the state, historically as *parens patriae*, has a responsibility to protect those at risk. This responsibility arguably carries over into partner abuse, although

[1] See eg Barlow, A, 'Out-of-court Family Dispute Resolution: the Lessons of Experience' [2014] *Family Law* 620, commenting inter alia on lawyer-led negotiation.

in the not too distant past this was seen as part of the private sphere. In contrast, ordinary family breakdown, where a married or unmarried couple decides to separate, is seen as part of private law. The role of the law is to provide a vehicle for the resolution of a 'private' dispute, not unlike a dispute over a contract. The state's interest is in providing an appropriate judicial framework so that business can function smoothly but beyond this the state has no particular interest in the outcome.

The chapter returns later to the public/private divide and suggests that it is no longer a very helpful distinction to make in the family law context. It in effect sidesteps the crucial questions about the shape of family law and the proper role of the state.

Questions about the role of the state, and the private sphere, raise further sub-issues. Who should pay for what? To what extent should the state pay and to what extent should the individuals pay? Traditionally, the state pays for the court system while the parties will pay for their own negotiated settlements. Inevitably sharing of costs occurs. However, what if the state puts in place rules that force parties to undertake certain activities, such as mandatory mediation? What if the family law system also provides for lawyers for the child and reports from experts such as child psychologists? In New Zealand, these have largely been paid for by the state but since the changes in March 2014 a significant share of the costs has been shifted to the individuals concerned. New Zealand has thus added to the financial burdens of separating couples. As a matter of principle, is this appropriate? Does it turn on ideological positions about the role of the state?

Another issue is the place of legislation. If the role of the state is minimal and family breakdown is in essence seen as a private matter, then legislation should be as least prescriptive as possible. However, if the public/private divide is seen as unhelpful and the state's protective role is wider than conceived by that divide, then legislative policy should be more detailed in setting out key ground rules. The latest New Zealand system is somewhat equivocal in its approach to this issue. In some respects it is so excessively detailed that it is very hard to understand aspects of the system—even for lawyers. In other important respects, including rules about the rights of children, it is silent. It forfeits policy-making to the contractual relationships between the parties and mediators, a form of 'contractualisation', but going well beyond the 'contracts' between the parties themselves. The legislative vacuum, explored further in the rest of this chapter, could be aptly described as a version of 'secret justice'.

MORE UNIVERSAL QUESTIONS?

The universal question of the role of the state gives rise to several tensions, as we have seen. Some other universal questions of a more specific nature are raised by the New Zealand scheme. Three are mentioned here.

Access to Justice

It is usually axiomatic that people should not be denied access to the courts except in extreme cases, such as abuse of process and where a litigant is vexatious. Yet, access to the courts can be made difficult in other ways. Where, for example, mediation is made a mandatory step before an application can be made to the court, is the principle of access to justice breached? Is this question rather more acute where mandatory mediation is not paid for by the state that mandates it? Or should parties pay for it just as they pay for lawyers whom they hire?

One immediate response to this question is to ask what 'justice' means. Can 'justice' not include various dispute mechanisms other than conventional adjudication? If so, access to mandatory mediation is sufficient. However, if mediation is mandatory, then by necessary implication people's choices are restricted. Mandatory mediation is putting most of the eggs into one basket rather than offering a range of options. The New Zealand scheme arguably does not deny access to justice but does impose restrictions that did not exist before, both in terms of the pre-conditions before an application can be made to the court and in terms of monetary barriers put in place by having to pay for the mandatory alternative.

Right to Legal Representation

As with access to justice, the New Zealand scheme imposes new restrictions on legal representation. Such representation is also usually regarded as axiomatic when a case goes to court. Whether that extends to alternative forms of dispute resolution is debatable but arguably, if an alternative form such as mediation is mandatory, then the case for representation is stronger, and even more so if the parties must pay for mediation.

Representation for children is a further issue. As discussed later, appointment of a lawyer for the child was mandatory in New Zealand in the past but this is no longer the law. New hurdles have been created. Does this breach the right to legal representation?

The Place of Children

The last point about legal representation for children is part of a wider issue about the place of children in a family justice system. If the dispute is seen as essentially one between two private citizens who happen to be parents, then children may have little claim to a place in the proceedings. However, this sounds contrary to contemporary jurisprudence given that the children are usually at the centre of the dispute. Should the children not have clearly defined rights in such situations? We return to this when we explore where children fit into the New Zealand system.

THE LATEST NEW ZEALAND SYSTEM

The Old and the New

New Zealand has had a Family Court since 1981.[2] This followed recommendations by a Royal Commission on the court system.[3] A key element in the system was the free use of counsellors, to whom people were referred by the court. Key hallmarks of the system included:

— an integrated approach whereby counselling and other services were seen as clearly linked to the court, even if carried out by independent professionals;
— ready access to justice and the court;
— an endeavour to avoid a full adversarial hearing; and
— legal representation, in particular for children.

The latest system places overriding emphasis on the third of these and backtracks on the other three. The changes were originally incorporated in the Family Court Proceedings Reform Bill. The Bill was enacted in 2013, at which point it was split into various separate Acts, the main ones being amendments to the Care of Children Act 2004 and the Family Courts Act 1980, and a new Act entitled the Family Dispute Resolution Act 2013. Important aspects of the new system are also found in other places, most notably the Family Courts Rules 2002 (as amended) but, for present purposes these will be ignored. Cutbacks to legal aid are found in the Legal Services Act 2011 and are also not covered in any detail here. Enough has already been said to indicate that the changed system is complex. The discussion here is inevitably a simplified version.

The two novel features of the new system are:

1. parenting information programmes (PIPs); and
2. private 'family dispute resolution' (FDR).

These two steps are in most instances mandatory before the court can be approached in relation to a disagreement about children. They are also separate from the court, unlike the previous connections between the court and counselling.

[2] Family Courts Act 1980, in force on 1 October 1981.
[3] *Report of the Royal Commission on the Courts* (Wellington, Government Printer, 1978) paras 463–602.

Parenting Information Programmes

The mandatory nature of PIPs is somewhat obscurely provided for in section 47B of the Care of Children Act 2004. An application for a parenting order or a variation of an order must contain a statement that the applicant has undertaken a PIP within the previous two years. Alternatively, the application can state that 'the applicant is unable to participate effectively in a parenting information programme'[4] and, thus, undertaking a PIP is not necessary. Just exactly what this means is unclear. However, the applicant must produce evidence of attendance or inability to participate, and, in the absence of adequate evidence, the Court Registrar can refuse to accept the application. Attendance at a PIP is not necessary where the application has been made without notice to the other party, typically in urgent circumstances.

Participation in a PIP is hardly demanding and the information received may be useful as parties endeavour to negotiate a settlement or else go on to FDR. Nevertheless it does constitute a formal legal barrier to accessing the courts. It is not a matter of choice but a pre-condition.

Mandatory Mediation

Family dispute resolution, echoing the terminology used in Australia and elsewhere, is a long-winded way of referring to mediation. The principal rule that mandates mediation is found in section 46E of the Care of Children Act 2004, as amended in 2013: a person cannot apply for a parenting order or go to court over a guardianship dispute unless 'a family dispute resolution form' accompanies the application. The form must have been obtained within the previous year: thus, for example, a form following mediation that occurred two years earlier will not suffice.

Although mediation is mandatory, several significant exceptions to the need for a 'form' are provided for:

- where the other party has already applied for an order;
- where the application is 'without notice', that is, it has some urgency;
- where it is for a 'consent order', that is, one that both parties agree should be made;
- where it seeks to enforce an existing order;
- where separate proceedings about alleged abuse of the child are under way;
- where a party 'is unable to participate effectively in family dispute resolution', an echo of the exception that applies to PIPs; or
- where one party has subjected the other, or a child, to domestic violence.

[4] Care of Children Act 2004, s 47B(2)(i).

Most of these are self-explanatory but the second is worth highlighting. Some anecdotal speculation has suggested that people can get around compulsory mediation quite easily by designating their claim as without notice.

The situation is further complicated by rules relating to the FDR forms themselves. Usually a form will be obtained either where FDR has been successful or where FDR has been tried but failed. However, mediators must undertake an initial process of filtering out certain cases that can go straight to court without FDR. This relies heavily on the mediator's good judgement. So, mediation may be considered inappropriate because one or both of the parties cannot participate effectively in the process (duplicating the same point as mentioned above), one of the parties has been subjected to abuse, or the mediator decides on 'reasonable grounds' that FDR 'is inappropriate for the parties to the family dispute'.[5] In these cases, a form is still provided but it will state that FDR is 'inappropriate'.

Some aspects of the FDR system are governed by legislation. The rules on FDR forms are quite detailed. The appointment of mediators ('FDR providers') is also dealt with by statute: mediators are approved by the Secretary for Justice or by an organisation that the Secretary has approved.[6]

However, other important aspects of the system are not legislated for. In short, they are determined by the contract between the parties and the mediator, ie by means of a form of secret justice. One of these is the cost. Unlike the previous system of counselling which was free and unlike the free PIP sessions, FDR must be paid for. The amount is not laid down but the common understanding is that FDR will cost the parties NZ$897 (US$780). The state will cover a person's costs if they meet the strict legal aid tests—although this is not expressly provided for in legislation.

The number of sessions is not stipulated, which is odd given that the cost would depend, one would think, on the amount of time that the process takes. Likewise, who can attend is not provided for—it depends on the secret contract. What if the parties both have lawyers who have been privy to prior negotiations? Should these lawyers be excluded? What if one of the parties has a lawyer? Again outside the legislative framework, the government is providing four hours' legal advice to people who meet the legal aid threshold.[7]

[5] Family Dispute Resolution Act 2013, s 12. In regard to the third reason, s 12(1)(c) is distinctly circular in saying that FDR is 'inappropriate' because it is 'inappropriate'!

[6] Family Dispute Resolution Act 2013, s 9. See also the Family Dispute Resolution Regulations 2013.

[7] It is considered to be a 'specified legal service' under s 68(2)(b) of the Legal Services Act 2011, which gives the Secretary for Justice wide powers in relation to legal aid. The 'Operational Policy' is found in *Family Legal Advice Service*, available at: www.justice.govt.nz/services/information-for-legal-professionals/information-for-legal-aid-providers/legal-aid-provider-manuals/family-legal-advice-service-operational-policy/view?searchterm=Family+Legal+advice. See more generally O'Dwyer, M and Doyle, C, 'Family Court Reforms—The Nuts and Bolts' in *Family Law Conference—Reclaiming the Ground* (Auckland, NZ Law Society CLE Ltd, 2013) 16–17.

Those hours will not equate to much work on behalf of the client but is that lawyer included in the process or excluded?

What if one of the parties is inarticulate but has an articulate support person? What if the parties are Māori, for whom a communal approach rather than an individualistic one is preferred? Can family members (members of the 'whānau') participate?

Some flexibility in the way in which mediation is carried out is understandable. Perhaps the timing and number of sessions fall into this category. On the other hand, FDR is a legal barrier to proceedings in the Family Court. Although it is a privatised system, it is part of the official framework for dealing with family breakdown. Some matters such as who has a right to attend are matters of principle of sufficient importance that, arguably, should be determined by Parliament, not by secret contracts.

Counselling

The previous system that provided for pre-hearing counselling, which was often successful in resolving issues, has gone. Counsellors nevertheless have residual roles. During a child-related hearing the Family Court can refer parties to counsellors.[8] This will be rare.

Counsellors may also be used to help people prepare for mediation,[9] a somewhat obscure role for counsellors. This is not actually legislated for and is provided for 'operationally', a further example of 'secret justice'. If this sort of counselling is considered necessary for the success of FDR, why did Parliament not address it and lay down the ground rules?

Lawyers

It has already been noted that the place of lawyers in FDR is not covered by legislation. Legislation does provide for the role of lawyers in the Family Court but, rather counter-intuitively, on a restrictive basis. Section 7A of the Care of Children Act 2004, as amended, aims to keep lawyers out-of-court until a case goes to a full hearing. While some exceptions have been built in, the thrust of the new law is that the parties will have to represent themselves in many of the preliminary matters that arise in this kind of litigation.

The result of this is that 'litigants in person' or 'self-litigants' will increase in number not because they cannot afford lawyers but because of a conscious choice made by Parliament. Judges already despair of self-litigants

[8] Care of Children Act 2004, ss 46G–46N.

[9] *Family Court Proceedings Reform Bill Departmental Report* (Wellington, Ministry of Justice, 2013) para 160.

because of the extra time they take and their frequent inability to address the relevant issues.

A further aspect of this policy is that it may exacerbate the inequalities that are already inherent in self-litigation. Some people will be able to represent their case better than others simply because of their innate talents. Further, under the new system, nothing stops a self-litigant who can afford it from getting advice from a lawyer. Such people will be at an advantage over the other party if that other party has not been schooled by a lawyer. The new rules raise many questions about the rationale for their existence. Is mandatory self-representation not taking the private/public distinction rather too far?

WHERE DO CHILDREN FIT IN?

One of the most worrying features of the New Zealand scheme is uncertainty over where children fit in. This relates especially to mediation but the changes to the rules on lawyers for children are a signal that their status is now downgraded.

With respect to mediation, a range of options for child involvement can be considered:

1. a right to attend mediation, depending upon age and maturity;
2. a right to attend part of a mediation in order to be heard and questioned;
3. a right to have views presented, either by a legal or other representative, through discussion with the mediator, through a child-version of an affidavit, or by other means;
4. a right to be consulted after the conclusion of the mediation sessions but before an agreement is signed off;
5. a right to have the child's best interests independently presented to those at the mediation; and
6. a right to have the parties reminded of the need to keep the child's best interests paramount.

Variations on these themes are also possible, but they capture the key ideas.

The weakest option is the last one and it is the one that New Zealand has chosen. One of the two purposes of FDR is 'ensuring that the parties' first and paramount consideration in reaching a resolution is the welfare and best interests of the children'.[10] Framed rather strangely in slightly different language, a mediator 'must make every endeavour to … assist the parties to reach an agreement on the resolution of those matters that best serves the welfare and best interests of all children involved in the dispute'.[11]

[10] Family Dispute Resolution Act 2013, s 4.
[11] ibid, s 11.

What exactly do these provisions mean? No one questions the need to focus on the child's welfare and best interests: this almost goes without saying. However, what role is the statute demanding of the mediator? Is the mediator to become an advocate for the child instead of being neutral, the usual function of a mediator? What does the mediator do, from the statutory point of view, if the parties appear to be heading for an agreement that is not in the child's interests? To do nothing appears to breach the legislative rubric. To do something positive appears to be taking sides.

Where do the views of the children fit in? When it comes to court hearings, the New Zealand law takes a very strong position. Children must be given reasonable opportunities to express their views, irrespective of their age and maturity, and these views must be taken into account. In contrast, with regard to mediation and FDR, the New Zealand law is silent. The role that the children's views might play is left to the contract between the parties and the mediator. In other words, it is covered by secret justice. If legislation spells out obligations in relation to the views of the child in one context—in court cases—why is this not sufficiently important to be spelt out in the mandatory FDR context? Should such an important issue be left to private arrangements instead of being a matter of legislative policy? This is an important matter of universal significance that is highlighted by the inadequacies of New Zealand's scheme.

The position on representation for children has been weakened. In the past it was in effect mandatory for a lawyer to be appointed to represent the children once a case was heading to a court hearing.[12] Since the recent amendments came into force, two hurdles have been inserted into the law before an appointment can be made:[13]

1. the court must have 'concerns for the safety or well-being of the child'; and
2. the court must consider 'an appointment necessary'.

These hurdles enshrine a movement away from mandatory child representation but what do they mean and how will they work out in practice? A judge may have concerns for a child's well-being whenever a dispute reaches the adjudication stage, but this is reading down the legislative language. What is meant by 'necessary'? Many would argue that child representation is a child's right and is always necessary for a satisfactory hearing to occur. However, this is also reading down the language of the section. 'Necessary' is surely something more than useful or desirable but less than absolutely essential. Parliament must surely have expected judges to deliberate with some care over the appointment and not treat it almost as automatic.

[12] Previous version of Care of Children Act 2004, s 7.

[13] New version of Care of Children Act 2004, s 7. The role of the lawyer for the child is spelt out in s 9B of the Family Courts Act 1980 (as amended in 2013).

A further new twist to this process is that, again in contrast to the past, the court must now make a supplementary order requiring the parties to pay for part of the costs of the lawyer for the child.[14] Thus, what was regarded as a community cost in the past is now, in part, the private responsibility of the parties to the dispute.

In summary, while the law makes reference to the welfare and best interests of the child in the mandatory mediation process, it otherwise ignores the place of children including the obtaining of their views. In disputes that reach the Family Court, legal representation for children has been watered down. Are all these changes good for the children involved?

RETURNING TO THE PUBLIC v PRIVATE DIVISION

As indicated above, one of the driving notions behind the New Zealand changes is the distinction drawn between public law and private law. The categorisation of family disputes not involving violence as 'private' enables arguments to be made that the parties should participate in procedures that assist them reach their own solutions before they can go to court. It also appears to justify expectations that the parties pay for both mediation and for lawyers appointed to represent the children. In court, the parties are now required to represent themselves rather than using lawyers, although the removal of lawyers from the courtroom is not so obviously a logical outcome of treating disputes as 'private'. The indifferent provision of rules affecting children, most notably in the mediation process, is consistent with seeing the dispute as essentially between the parents.

The underlying ideology of the private law classification is that the role played by the state is wheeled back. The state still provides a legal structure for the resolution of disputes but leaves crucial questions to be determined in secret by way of contract with dispute resolution professionals. It minimises its involvement and its funding, in contrast to situations of child abuse and domestic violence, which are seen as part of public law and criminal law.

The use of the public/private division no longer has any real value in the family law context. Instead, we should simply ask what the proper role of family law or the state is in the context of family breakdown. I suggest that society has a significant interest in family breakdown, whether violence is present or not. This is because social cohesion and solidarity depend in part on the strength of our personal relationships. Where such relationships run into trouble, society has a real interest, for the common good, in easing the path to sorting out differences, in reducing the emotional and physical upset

[14] Care of Children Act 2004, ss 131(4) and 135A: there is an exception for serious hardship. Similar orders are to be made where, eg, the court orders a report from a psychologist.

that may ensue, and in clearing the way for new beginnings. Many people will settle their own differences and the wider community can step back. In other situations, the community may have to be more active.

The community interest becomes even more obvious when the welfare and best interests of children are factored in. No contrary argument is raised when children are abused or neglected. Nor should there be when children are caught up in the separation of their parents. The protective role of the community is surely not restricted to situations of defined peril: it is much more extensive than this. An emphasis on 'private law' risks leaving children in a state of vulnerability.

Yet, this same point can be made of the adults caught up in relationship breakdown. Some will survive the situation largely unscathed, but others will face real uncertainties—financial, emotional, physical etc. In ordinary cases of separation, we find vulnerable people. The New Zealand Ministry of Justice's own discussion paper that preceded the latest changes made the point tellingly enough. A survey by the Ministry revealed that most cases that reached the Family Court had factors at work other than the relationship breakdown itself: mental health, alcohol, abuse and other matters of considerable public concern.[15] To treat these cases as essentially 'private' is to miss the point.

CONCLUSION

The recent changes to the family justice system in New Zealand are controversial. They greatly affect the Family Court, judges, lawyers, mediators, counsellors and the parties, including children. They place much more emphasis on mediation. This in itself is not objectionable but when it is made mandatory and when it is combined with a range of other changes, then some fundamental or universal questions are raised. Does the cutting back of the role of the state jeopardise our children? How much family policy should be left to alternative systems and how much should be determined by legislation? Do greater 'privatisation' and 'user pays' fulfil the wider common good? Ultimately, what is the interest of society in family breakdown and how should it be implemented in practice? In these days of cutbacks, are there fresh issues that people interested in family policy should be alert to?

[15] Ministry of Justice, *Reviewing the Family Court A public consultation paper* (Wellington, Ministry of Justice, 2011) paras 69–70.

3

Shaping Substantive Law to Promote Access to Justice: Canada's Use of Child and Spousal Support Guidelines

CAROL ROGERSON

ACCESS TO FAMILY JUSTICE: PROCEDURAL OR SUBSTANTIVE?

DISCUSSIONS OF THE crisis in access to family justice tend to be dominated by a focus on procedural and institutional issues. The list of issues is a familiar one—clogged courtrooms, complex procedures, high costs, limited public and private resources, lack of access to legal advice and representation, and the turn to alternative methods of dispute resolution and private settlement. Without in any way detracting from the importance of those issues, this chapter focuses on substantive law, asking us both to think about substantive law reform as one way of responding to some of the problems of accessibility to family justice and to recognise the inter-connectedness of process and substance in the family justice system.[1] More specifically the focus will be on the turn away from discretionary standards toward more rule-like provisions as a response to the increasing emphasis in family law systems on efficient dispute resolution and settlement outside of court. The evolution of the Canadian law governing financial relief, in particular the development of formulaic, income-sharing guidelines for the determination of child and spousal support, will be drawn on as a primary example to illustrate both the possibilities and limitations of substantive law reform in increasing access to family justice.[2]

[1] See Parkinson, P, 'The Challenge of Affordable Family Law' Sydney Law School Legal Studies Research Paper No 14/78, August 2014, available at: http://papers.ssrn.com/sol3/papers.cfm?abstract_id=2484274.

[2] Parts of this chapter draw on earlier reviews of these developments; see Rogerson, C, 'Child Support, Spousal Support and the Turn to Guidelines' in J Eekelaar and R George (eds), *Routledge Handbook of Family Law and Policy* (Abingdon, Routledge, 2014) 153; and Rogerson, C, 'Child and Spousal Support in Canada: The Guidelines Approach Part 1' (2011) 14 *Irish Journal of Family Law* 72 and 'Part 2' in (2012) 15 *Irish Journal of Family Law* 18.

In 1997, following the path taken by the United States, England, Australia and New Zealand, Canada legislated the federal Child Support Guidelines (CSG) under which child support is assessed as a specified percentage of parental income rather than on the basis of an individualised, budget-based determination of a specific child's needs.[3] While many Western jurisdictions have adopted child support guidelines, Canada has gone further in extending that methodology of income-sharing guidelines to the much more contentious and complex area of spousal support. The final version of a set of Spousal Support Advisory Guidelines (SSAG) was released in July of 2008, the culmination of a seven-year project directed by two law professors and supported by the federal Department of Justice.[4] Unlike the child support guidelines, the Canadian spousal support guidelines are not legislated and their application is not mandatory. They are informal, advisory guidelines, developed through consultation with family lawyers and judges and intended to reflect current practice under the existing legislation. Although only advisory, they have received the endorsement of several appellate courts as a useful tool and are now widely used across the country by lawyers and judges both in negotiation and litigation.

Both the CSG and the SSAG are regarded as fairly successful policy developments that have improved the fairness and consistency of outcomes and made these issues easier to resolve. To the extent that they have not eliminated discretion entirely and that contentious and complex issues remain, this illustrates difficult trade-offs between fairness of outcomes and efficient dispute resolution. The need for legal advice and representation has not been eliminated, and reform of substantive law is clearly only one component of improved access to family justice. While Canada has made significant progress on this front, at least with respect to the law governing financial remedies, a recent barrage of studies has nonetheless made clear the growing crisis in access to family justice—marked in part by growing numbers of self-represented litigants[5]—and the need for significant procedural and institutional reforms.[6]

[3] Federal Child Support Guidelines, SOR/97–175 as amended. The CSG were enacted as regulations pursuant to the federal Divorce Act, RSC 1985, c 3 (2nd Supp).

[4] Rogerson, C and Thompson, R, *Spousal Support Advisory Guidelines* (Department of Justice Canada, July 2008) www.justice.gc.ca/eng/rp-pr/fl-lf/spousal-epoux/spag/index.html.

[5] See Macfarlane, J, *The National Self-Represented Litigants Project: Identifying and Meeting the Needs of Self-Represented Litigants: Final Report*' (May 2013) http://representingyourselfcanada.files.wordpress.com/2014/02/reportm15-2.pdf; and Birnbaum, R et al, 'The Rise of Self-Representation in Canada's Family Courts: The Complex Picture Revealed in Surveys of Judges, Lawyers and Litigants' (2013) 91 *Canadian Bar Review* 67.

[6] See Bala, N, 'Reforming Family Dispute Resolution in Ontario: Systemic Changes and Cultural Shifts' in MI Trebilcock et al (eds), *Middle Income Access to Justice* (Toronto, University of Toronto Press, 2012) 271; Semple, N and Rogerson, C, 'Middle Income Access to Justice: Policy Options with Respect to Family Law' in MI Trebilcock et al (eds), *Middle Income Access to Justice* (Toronto, University of Toronto Press, 2012) 413; Law Commission of Ontario, *Increasing Access to Family Justice Through Comprehensive Entry Points and Inclusivity: Final Report* (February 2013) www.lco-cdo.org/en/family-law-reform-final-report;

RULES vs DISCRETION IN FAMILY LAW

Family law is frequently analysed in terms of the tension between rules and discretion.[7] Dewar has identified as one of the characteristics of modern family law systems a retreat from discretionary standards and an increasing reliance on more rule-like provisions. He ties this development to an increasing emphasis on efficient dispute resolution and on reducing both the financial and emotional costs of resolving the issues that arise as a result of marriage breakdown and divorce.[8] The certainty and predictability provided by more rule-like provisions not only facilitate efficient judicial (or administrative) decision-making, but even more importantly can reduce conflict and promote settlement.[9]

Substantive family law now operates in systems that emphasise reduction of conflict and settlement. As Dewar has recognised, in many cases the substantive rules will not be applied by judges in the context of a hearing in a courtroom, rather they will be the backdrop to settlement outside of court. In some cases the interpretation and application of the legal norms will be mediated by lawyers, but in other cases they will be applied by non-legal personnel or the parties themselves. Dewar has thus described current family law systems as 'high reach, low intensity' systems of mass dispute resolution. By this he means that many people see their problems as legal ones but are unlikely to engage in any formal process of adjudication or even of seeking legal advice.[10] Instead legal norms will be interpreted and applied in a range of settings and by a range of actors. This requires that family laws be drafted with a greater emphasis on the need for clear norms that can be understood not only by lawyers and judges but also by a wide range of non-legal actors, including parties themselves.

Action Committee on Access to Justice in Civil and Family Matters, *Access to Civil & Family Justice: A Roadmap for Change* (Ottawa, Canada, October 2013), which in turn drew on the Final Report of the Committee's Family Justice Working Group: *Meaningful Change for Family Justice: Beyond Wise Words* (April 2013) www.cfcj-fcjc.org/sites/default/files/docs/Report%20of%20the%20Family%20Law%20WG%20Meaningful%20Change%20April%202013.pdf.

[7] See Schneider, CE, 'The Tension Between Rules and Discretion in Family Law: A Report and Reflection' (1993–94) 27 *Family Law Quarterly* 229. For a nice review of the literature on this tension both in family law and in law more generally, see Leckey, R, 'Particular Justice: Michel Bastarache and Family Law' in N Lambert (ed), *À l'avant-garde de la dualité: Mélanges en l'honneur de Michel Bastarache* (Cowansville, Éditions Yvon Blais, 2011).

[8] Dewar, J, 'Family Law and Its Discontents' (2000) 14 *International Journal of Law, Policy and the Family* 59.

[9] Dewar also sees this shift as a way of creating normative order. Here, it is the consistency and clarity provided by rules that are significant, generating a sense of legitimacy and fairness.

[10] Dewar, J, 'Can the Centre Hold? Reflections on Two Decades of Family Law Reform in Australia' (2010) 24 *Australian Journal of Family Law* 139; Dewar, J, 'Regulating Families' in C Parker et al (eds), *Regulating Law* (Oxford, Oxford University Press, 2004) 82; and Dewar, J, 'Families' in M Tushnet and P Cane (eds), *The Oxford Handbook of Legal Studies* (Oxford, Oxford University Press, 2003) 413. Dewar suggests that we should speak about negotiating in the 'light' of the law rather than in its 'shadow'.

Along similar lines, Parkinson contrasts 'centripetal' laws, laws which assume that courts will make the decisions and regulate the conduct and adjudication of cases within the court setting, with 'centrifugal' laws, laws which send clear messages to people about their rights, obligations and entitlements so that judicial resolution of disputes is made necessary only where the facts of the case or the scope of the rule are in question. In order to provide a framework within which alternative dispute resolution may operate successfully, centrifugal laws

> will usually require general rules or principles which may not be sensitively attuned to all the different circumstances that might arise, but they simplify the messages the law gives, thereby reducing the numbers of disputes, and assisting in the resolution of disputes by conferring bargaining chips.[11]

In Parkinson's view, an emphasis on private ordering, combined with the conferral of broad discretion on judges in the few cases that come to courts, is 'the worst of all worlds'.

The advantages of rules must, of course, be balanced against their disadvantages—the sacrifice of finely-tuned individual justice, undue rigidity and arbitrary and unfair results. Ironically, it is at the very time that family law has come to recognise the diversity of family forms that the need for rules and standardisation has increased.[12] However, as a practical matter, there are many points on the spectrum between rules and discretion from which policy-makers can choose, with presumptions and guidelines falling somewhere in the middle. Default rules can be crafted for typical cases, with more discretion allowed for complicated cases. Rule-based schemes often provide for exceptions and rules can be made more complex to deal with a greater variation of circumstances although at the cost of clarity and transparency. Dewar himself has been careful

> not to suggest that family law has become a seamless code of rules, but rather that new techniques are steadily being superimposed on old.… [T]he question of which technique is best, and of the costs and benefits of each, is yet to be settled.

Indeed, it has been suggested that 'the continuing search for the third way between discretion and rules is a key feature of modern family law'.[13] As the two different examples of support guidelines in Canada show, there are many ways of structuring such guidelines to allow scope for flexibility and discretion while providing much needed structure and guidance.

[11] Parkinson, 'The Challenge of Affordable Family Law' (n 1) 32.

[12] Baker, K, 'Homogenous Rules for Heterogeneous Families: The Standardization of Family Law When There is No Standard Family' [2012] *University of Illinois Law Review* 319.

[13] Dewar, 'Families' (n 10) 418.

When considering substantive law reform from the perspective of access to justice and promoting settlement, a range of issues arise. Policy-makers in this area must search for the appropriate balance between standardisation and efficient dispute resolution, on the one hand, and discretion and responsiveness to diverse family circumstances on the other. Rules may be determined to be more appropriate in some areas than others. The shift towards more rule-like provisions has been most obvious in the area of financial relief.[14] Child custody law is often seen as the area where it is most difficult to generate a sensible, non-discretionary rule,[15] and the move in some jurisdictions, such as Australia, to shared parenting presumptions, has generated intense controversy and raised concerns about harmful outcomes for children.[16] Canadian law, while embracing a more rule-based approach for financial relief, has thus far retained the discretionary approach guided by the best interests of the child principle for determining parenting arrangements, although following the successful experience with the SSAG there is now some interest in developing guidelines for relocation disputes.[17]

As the following discussion of the development of support guidelines will show, the process of reforming substantive law in a more rule-like direction is a complex and fascinating mixture of the theoretical and the practical, of substance and process. Debates over normative principles and what constitutes fair outcomes merge into the search for somewhat crude proxy measures that can be effectively administered in a system of mass dispute resolution and these proxy measures in turn shape the understanding of the obligation. Discretionary rules may mask normative disagreement which must first be resolved. The implementation of more rule-based provisions may be part of a bold process of law reform intended to depart dramatically from the past and set new norms or it may simply involve clarifying norms that have evolved from practice under an existing discretionary regime.

[14] See Ellman, I, 'The Maturing Law of Divorce Finances: Towards Rules and Guidelines' (1999) 33 *Family Law Quarterly* 801. The American Law Institute, in its ambitious project on the *Principles of the Law of Family Dissolution: Analysis and Recommendations* (St Paul, MN, ALI, 2002), for which Ellman was the chief reporter, defended the development of rebuttable presumptions to govern financial issues at 33: 'In many divorces the parties' assets and incomes are not great, and it will not be sensible or even possible to devote significant legal resources to divorce proceedings. Expeditious settlement with a minimum of legal process is the preferred result'.

[15] Ellman, I, 'Inventing Family Law' (1999) 32 *UC Davis Law Review* 855. The ALI, ibid, did propose an 'approximation' presumption based on the pre-separation allocation of parenting time, although this alternative has had little legislative take-up. The options more frequently considered are presumptions of joint custody or shared parenting time.

[16] See Fehlberg, B et al, 'Parenting Issues after Separation: Developments in Common Law Countries' in Eekelaar and George, *Routledge Handbook of Family Law and Policy* (n 2) 215.

[17] See Bala, N and Wheeler, A, 'Canadian Relocation Cases: Heading Towards Guidelines' (2012) 30 *Canadian Family Law Quarterly* 271; Thompson, R, 'Where is BC Law Going? The New Mobility' (2012) 30 *Canadian Family Law Quarterly* 235 and the new Family Law Act, SBC 2011, c 2, ss 65–71, in force 18 March 2013.

Given the fragmentation of the modern family law system, it is not surprising to see that rules, presumptions or guidelines can be generated by various legal actors, not only by legislatures but by courts and lawyers. There are many ways in which support guidelines can be developed and structured. They can be formal or informal; mandatory or advisory; and more or less complex both with respect to the structure of the basic formulas and the openings for discretion and deviation. In Canada, the child support guidelines are legislated, mandatory and fairly rigid, whereas the spousal support guidelines, dealing as they do with a much more complex and normatively contested area of law, as they do are informal, advisory guidelines based on norms that have evolved through practice that allow greater scope for discretion and deviation.

THE CANADIAN CHILD SUPPORT GUIDELINES

The current package of laws governing the financial aspects of separation and divorce in Canada is the result of an ongoing process of law reform that began in 1968 with the enactment Canada's first national divorce act[18] and the introduction of no-fault divorce. Three distinct financial remedies are provided for: division of matrimonial property, spousal support and child support.[19] The cornerstone of the initial wave of family law reform in the 1970s was the enactment of matrimonial property legislation. While each province enacted its own scheme, they all incorporate the basic concept of marriage as an equal partnership which in turn justifies a prima facie equal division of a defined pool of marital assets when the partnership ends—a choice reflecting both the symbolic value of equality and the desire to minimise litigation and encourage settlement. Unlike England and other common law jurisdictions, Canada thus adopted an approach closer to that of civilian jurisdictions in clearly separating issues of property from those of maintenance and in adopting a clear rule of equal division. Over time, as problems were identified in the highly discretionary areas of child and spousal support, the adoption of more rule-based solutions was facilitated by these earlier choices in the area of matrimonial property.

During the 1980s, in Canada, as in other Western jurisdictions, inadequate levels of child support became the focus of public policy in response to growing concern over the disadvantage experienced by children in single-parent families and the growing costs of state support to such families. Increasing levels of child support and developing effective and efficient mechanisms for its assessment and enforcement became a policy priority. The discretionary

[18] Replaced by a new Act in 1985: see n 3.

[19] The federal Divorce Act governs support issues in the context of divorce proceedings; provincial legislation applies in contexts not involving divorce.

determination of child support by courts through application of the vague concept of 'need' was identified as contributing to the problem of historically low and inadequate levels of child support and formulas and guidelines emerged as one possible solution.[20] In the common law world, the American states were the pioneers in developing child support guidelines as a result of federal requirements imposed in 1988,[21] with Australia,[22] England[23] and New Zealand[24] quickly following suit. Thus when Canada decided to develop guidelines to deal with the problem of child support, culminating in the enactment of the CSG in 1997,[25] it was not treading into uncharted territory. The stated objectives of the CSG were fairness, predictability, consistency and the reduction of conflict.[26] Although Canada, like the American states, decided that child support determinations using the guidelines would continue to be made by courts, rather than an administrative agency,[27] one of the clear objectives of the CSG was to encourage out-of-court settlement. The terminology of 'guidelines' is somewhat misleading. The CSG, like the schemes in the other common law jurisdictions, are formally legislated, mandatory rules that generate precise amounts of child support.[28]

The guideline models developed in the American context have to a large extent provided the framework and starting point for the development of child support guidelines in other common law jurisdictions, including Canada.[29] Although there are different models, they share a basic shift in approach by abandoning an individualised, budget-based assessment of a child's needs and instead determining child support on the basis of *average* expenditures on children. The construction of child support guidelines requires clarification of the substantive, normative principles that structure

[20] For a comparative overview, see Parkinson, P, *Family Law and the Indissolubility of Parenthood* (Cambridge, Cambridge University Press, 2011).

[21] The Family Support Act 1988 (now found in scattered sections of 42 U.S.C.) required states to implement mandatory child support guidelines as a condition for receipt of federal funding of their welfare programs.

[22] The Child Support Assessment Act 1989 significantly amended in 2008 by the Child Support Legislation Amendment Act 2006.

[23] The Child Support Act 1991, which has undergone successive major reforms; see Fehlberg, B and MacLean, M 'Child Support Policy in Australia and the United Kingdom: Changing Priorities But a Similar Tough Deal for Children?' (2009) 23 *International Journal of Law Policy and the Family* 1.

[24] The Child Support Act 1991, significantly amended by the Child Support Amendment Bill 2011.

[25] See n 3. The federal CSG apply to determinations of child support under the federal Divorce Act. All of the provinces subsequently enacted guidelines applicable to child support determinations in other contexts, with all but one scheme identical to the federal guidelines.

[26] s 1.

[27] The other common law jurisdictions moved child support determinations to an administrative agency that both assesses and enforces child support.

[28] Although prior to the CSG some courts did create their own informal guidelines.

[29] See Harris, L, 'The New ALI Child Support Proposal' (1999) 35 *Williamette Law Review* 717.

the child support obligation. What do parents owe their children financially? What are the costs of raising children? Because children require caregivers and share a household standard of living with them, challenges arise in delineating the boundary between child support and spousal remedies. Most child support guidelines have addressed this challenge through adoption of what has been called a 'marginal cost' approach, whereby child support is based on the costs of adding a child to an already existing household.

For the purposes of developing formulaic guidelines, aggregate economic data has been used to determine average measures of these costs. Typically the evidence used to construct child support guidelines has been household expenditure surveys from which it is possible to determine the additional costs to households at different income levels when children are added. From this aggregate data economists calculate what percentages of parental income are spent as additional children are added to the household and these percentages are used in turn to construct the formulas on which the child support guidelines are based.[30] Child support amounts under the guidelines are thus determined as a percentage of parental incomes: a shift from *cost*-sharing to *income*-sharing. The percentages of income used in the child support formula vary between jurisdictions, reflecting not only different data sources and methods of analysis but also different political and legal contexts, including the availability of other financial remedies within the family law system and government benefits. The percentages in Canada, for example, are roughly 11 per cent of gross income for one child; 18 per cent for two children, and 23 per cent for three children.[31] From a comparative perspective, these percentages are in the middle of the range that exists in common law jurisdictions.[32]

The methodology used to create child support guidelines is not without its problems. Critics point to the flawed assumptions that underlie the guidelines—the marginal cost approach, the use of economic data from intact families to determine costs where parents live apart, the failure to take into account base income disparities between the parents—as well as to contentious interpretations of the economic data.[33] Despite the aura

[30] See Ellman, I, 'Fudging Failure: The Economic Analysis Used to Construct Child Support Guidelines' [2004] *University of Chicago Legal Forum* 162. In Canada, attempts to use household expenditure data proved unsuccessful and instead Statistics Canada 40/30 household equivalency scales were used to construct the formula; see Federal/Provincial/Territorial Family Law Committee, *Summary Report and Recommendations on Child Support* (Ottawa, Department of Justice, Communications and Consultation Branch, January 1995).

[31] Because the Canadian formula is based upon the 40/30 household equivalency scales and works on net incomes there are no explicit percentages of gross income set out; these percentages are extrapolated and will vary somewhat with income level.

[32] In Wisconsin in the United States the comparable percentages are 17, 25 and 29; in Australia and New Zealand, following the recent reforms, the basic percentages for one, two and three or more children respectively are 17, 24 and 27; and in England 12, 16 and 19.

[33] See Ellman, 'Fudging Failure' (n 30); and Allen, D and Brinig, M, 'Child Support Guidelines: The Good, the Bad, the Ugly' (2011) 45 *Family Law Quarterly* 135.

of mathematical precision that attaches to child support guidelines, they are based on very crude economic data and their adoption is governed as much by politics as technical expertise. To the extent they are accepted, it is because they generate numbers that appear overall to be reasonable while offering the advantages of certainty and predictability, and they acquire legitimacy through their consistent application.[34]

Within the framework of this general methodology for constructing child support guidelines, there is much room for variation and significant differences exist between the particular schemes adopted in different jurisdictions. The specific formulas chosen can vary in their degree of complexity, involving trade-offs between simplicity and efficiency, on the one hand, and more finely-tuned justice on the other. As will be seen, the Canadian guidelines clearly fall on the less complex end of the spectrum. The CSG take into account only the income of the payor, whereas many second-generation guidelines look to the incomes of both parents. As well, in more complex schemes, the income percentages vary with the income level of the parents[35] and with the ages of the children. The degree to which the formula is calibrated to take into account variations in the amount of time each parent spends with the child also varies. Although many first generation formulas, like the Canadian formula, provide for no adjustment until arrangements come close to equal time-sharing,[36] increasing politicisation around the issue of shared custody has resulted in new guideline models in Australia, New Zealand and England that incorporate more complex sliding scale approaches in which child support amounts are proportionately reduced as time spent with the child increases.

The basic (formula) amount of child support under the CSG is determined by support tables based on two factors: the payor's income and the number of children.[37] The amount of support can be increased above the table amount, on a discretionary, individual basis to take account of certain special or extraordinary expenses and can be reduced in cases of undue hardship. Additional provisions create exceptions for shared care, children over the age of majority, high incomes and step-parent support, where a more discretionary approach is allowed. Some degree of discretion would seem to be required for successful operation of any scheme of child support guidelines,[38] an element more easily included in jurisdictions where child support remains within the purview of the courts.

[34] See Baker, 'Homogenous Rules for Heterogeneous Families' (n 12).

[35] Under the CSG a discretionary approach is allowed for incomes over $150,000, but Canadian courts have largely ignored that 'ceiling' and have continued to apply the formula to extraordinarily high income levels.

[36] Section 9 of the CSG establishes a 40% time threshold for any adjustment for shared care.

[37] Available at: www.justice.gc.ca/eng/fl-df/child-enfant/ft-tf.html.

[38] See Oldham, JT, 'Lessons from the New English and Australian Child Support Systems' (1996) 29 *Vanderbilt Journal of Transnational Law* 29.

The experience with child support guidelines has been more positive in some jurisdictions than in others. In England, the scheme originally introduced in 1991 was plagued by monumental administrative shortcomings combined with a complicated formula, the potential for unreasonably high awards and no discretion to depart from the formula. The scheme has been the subject of successive reforms, the most recent of which have focused on simplifying the formula and the administration of the scheme, with an emphasis on encouraging private settlement. In Australia, ongoing debates about the design and reform of the Australian child support guidelines have been shaped by the heated politics in that jurisdiction around post-divorce parenting arrangements.[39] Recent reforms have introduced many refinements and exceptions to what was originally a very simple formula to better reflect the diversity of family situations. However, these reforms, intended to generate 'fairer' outcomes, have resulted in a scheme of guidelines so complicated that parties are unable to understand the scheme or calculate child support on their own.

In Canada, on the other hand, the experience with child support guidelines has been very positive. They are widely supported by family lawyers, judges, mediators and parents.[40] Despite the somewhat crude nature of the Canadian formula, the table amounts have, on the whole, come to be seen as an objectively fair measure of child support and they have facilitated settlement and reduced parental conflict over child support.[41] One of the main virtues of the Canadian scheme is its relative simplicity. In a standard case the calculation of child support is relatively easy. In the vast majority of cases parents are able to work out the appropriate levels of child support on their own, using the easily accessible and straightforward child support tables,[42] and will at most request of a court that their agreement be embodied in a consent order.[43] The main issue in dispute in most child support cases is the income of the payor; cases dealing with complex or uncertain incomes account for the bulk of litigated child support cases. In most cases,

[39] Fehlberg, 'Parenting Issues after Separation' (n 16).

[40] In its review of the CSG five years after they were introduced the federal government concluded that they were working well in meeting their goals of fair, predictable and consistent awards: see *Children Come First: A Report to Parliament Reviewing the Provisions and Operation of the Federal Child Support Guidelines* (Minister of Justice and Attorney General for Canada, April 2002) www.justice.gc.ca/eng/pi/fcy-fea/lib-bib/rep-rap/2002/rp/index.html.

[41] The percentages of income transferred under the Canadian guidelines may not be as high as in some other jurisdictions, but spousal support is more widely available to top up child support where there is additional capacity to pay.

[42] Two-thirds of child support orders are based on the table amount alone.

[43] While settlement is encouraged, there are strict limits on parties' ability to contract out of the CSG, reflecting a clear policy choice to prevent child support from being bargained away by women in the context of negotiations over parenting arrangements; contrast with the unlimited ability to contract out recently introduced in England.

once the payor's income is determined, the appropriate amount of child support is easily calculated.

For the most part judges have preferred to constrain rather than expand their discretion under the Guidelines. Courts routinely apply the formulas in high-income cases even though the Guidelines allow for deviation when incomes are over $150,000 and have largely been unwilling to allow claims for a reduction of child support on the grounds of undue hardship.[44] The Guidelines have created a strong desire for structure and guidance amongst Canadian family law lawyers. The provisions of the Guidelines that continue to generate uncertainty and conflicting interpretations—those dealing with step-parents and shared custody—are increasingly seen as problems which require the development of some formulaic presumptions or clearer starting points.

THE CANADIAN SPOUSAL SUPPORT GUIDELINES

While child support guidelines have become a familiar feature of the family law landscape in the common law world since the late-1980s and early-1990s, spousal support guidelines are rarer. In jurisdictions where spousal support has become an extremely limited remedy and where financial relief is accomplished almost exclusively through property division there is no pressing need for spousal support guidelines. They are only of interest in jurisdictions where spousal support, as a distinct obligation that attaches to post-divorce incomes, remains as a significant but disputed remedy. That is the case in Canada.

In Canada, as is typical in other jurisdictions, spousal support is governed by highly discretionary legislation that lists a multiplicity of objectives and factors, reflecting the lack of a clear theoretical or political consensus with respect to this contentious obligation and leaving much scope for judicial interpretation.[45] In the 1980s, Canadian spousal support law had begun to move in the direction of other jurisdictions, with support legislation being interpreted and applied so as to favour time-limited support obligations and to promote the interests of clean breaks and finality.[46] However, in a series of major decisions interpreting the spousal support provisions of the Divorce Act, the Supreme Court of Canada rejected the approach that prioritised spousal self-sufficiency after divorce. In the 1992 *Moge*[47] case,

[44] Both of these tendencies have been the subject of some criticism.

[45] As with child support, spousal support in the divorce context is governed by the federal Divorce Act (n 3) s 15.2, with provincial legislation applying in non-divorce contexts. In all provinces except Québec the spousal support obligation has been extended to de facto couples.

[46] For a review of the Canadian law of spousal support, see Rogerson, C, 'The Canadian Law of Spousal Support' (2004) 38 *Family Law Quarterly* 69.

[47] [1992] 3 SCR 813.

the Court emphasised the important compensatory role of spousal support and subsequently, in the 1999 *Bracklow*[48] decision, spousal support's continuing role in meeting post-divorce need (what Canadians call non-compensatory support). Thus Canadian law recognises a broad basis for entitlement to spousal support in compensating for economic disadvantage, meeting post-divorce needs and more generally recognising the reliance and expectations generated by the merger of lives over time. Although not all will agree with this expansive role for spousal support, it reflects the priority Canadian law places on ameliorating the economic disadvantage of marriage breakdown and divorce, with particular sensitivity to gender-based disadvantage.

However, as the basis for spousal support in Canada expanded, the law became more discretionary and uncertain as judges and lawyers struggled with implementing the broad and vague concepts of compensation and need and with balancing the range of factors and objectives to be taken into account. The clean break approach, although rejected as unfair, had had the advantage of more certainty. Lawyers increasingly expressed their frustration with this area of family law practice. Similar fact situations could generate a wide variation in results. Individual judges were provided with little concrete guidance in determining spousal support outcomes and their subjective perceptions of fair outcomes seemed to play a large role in determining the spousal support ultimately ordered. Lawyers in turn had difficulty predicting outcomes, thus impeding their ability to advise clients and to engage in cost-effective settlement negotiations. And for those without legal representation or in weak bargaining positions, support claims were often simply not pursued.

In the past, the multiplicity of competing objectives in this area had tended to lead to the conclusion that it was inherently fact-based and not amenable to guidelines. However, circumstances had changed and pragmatic concerns with the lack of certainty, predictability and consistency in this area of law prompted a new interest in exploring the possibility of spousal support guidelines. Canada's family law culture had already become fairly rule-oriented as a result of reforms to matrimonial property law and child support. The successful introduction of the child support guidelines in 1997 had accustomed judges and lawyers to the use of income-sharing formulas to determine support. Indeed, some lawyers and judges had begun to develop their own income-sharing formulas for spousal support, attempting to carry this new methodology over to spousal support. As well, some concrete models for developing spousal support guidelines had emerged in the US.[49] In particular, the influential American Law Institute had developed a very sophisticated formulaic approach under which the percentages of

[48] [1999] 1 SCR 420.
[49] Many of the early American guidelines dealt only with interim or temporary support.

income used to determine spousal support varied depending upon the length and type of marriage.[50]

In 2001, the federal Department of Justice in Canada decided to support a project, headed by two law professors, to development spousal support guidelines. The culmination of the project was the release in 2008 of the final version of the Spousal Support Advisory Guidelines,[51] a set of informal, advisory guidelines with national scope intended to assist in the determination of the amount and duration of spousal support under the federal Divorce Act.[52] Here we see a different, more flexible form of guidelines, a 'halfway house between rules and discretion',[53] reflecting the more complex nature of this area of law. Unlike the child support guidelines, the SSAG are not legislated and their application is not mandatory. They are informal, advisory guidelines developed through consultation with family lawyers and judges and intended to reflect current practice under the existing legislation rather than to change the law. Their development was a practical rather than a theoretical exercise.

The SSAG were developed through an intensive consultative process with judges and lawyers. The academic directors of the project worked with an advisory group of lawyers and judges. Much of the work in developing the guidelines involved identifying the dominant patterns of outcomes across a range of *typical* cases, relying both on reported case law and on the practical experience of the advisory working group. The premise underlying the guidelines project was that despite the uncertainty and unpredictability in this area of law, there were some dominant patterns emerging in typical cases that required clearer identification. Mathematical formulas were then developed to capture these patterns in the law, both with respect to amount and duration. The results obtained suggested two basic formulas, reflecting strong distinctions between cases with and without dependent children. Because results clustered rather than converged on precise outcomes, the formulas were constructed to generate ranges rather than precise numbers for both amount and duration. The guidelines went on to identify a list of circumstances or 'exceptions' that would justify departure from the formula

[50] ALI, *Principles of the Law of Family Dissolution* (n 14) ch 5 (draft version published in 1997). In the US the ALI proposals have had little direct take-up, in part because they contemplated active legislative reform, thereby unleashing an unresolvable theoretical debate about the normative basis for the spousal support obligation. A modified version of the ALI formulas was the basis for informal guidelines introduced in Maricopa County, Arizona.

[51] Rogerson and Thompson, *Spousal Support Advisory Guidelines* (n 4). For a more extensive discussion of the SSAG, see Rogerson, C and Thompson, R, 'The Canadian Experiment with Spousal Support Guidelines' (2011) 45 *Family Law Quarterly* 241; and Thompson, R, 'Canada's Spousal Support Advisory Guidelines: A Half-way House between Rules and Discretion' [2010] *International Family Law* 106. All of the documents relating to the SSAG project may be found at: http://library.law.utoronto.ca/spousal-support-advisory-guidelines.

[52] Although expressly developed for use under the federal Divorce Act, the SSAG are also as a matter of practice used in support determinations under provincial law.

[53] Thompson, 'Canada's Spousal Support Advisory Guidelines' (n 51).

outcomes. A draft version of guidelines was produced and released in January 2005. Then, after an extensive process of consultation with the Family Law Bar and judiciary across the country, a final version was released in July of 2008.

At the heart of the SSAG are a set of formulas to be applied after entitlement has been established. These formulas generate ranges for both amount and duration of support based upon factors such as the parties' incomes, the length of their relationship, their ages, the presence of dependent children, the ages of the children and the allocation of custodial responsibility. There are two basic formulas, distinguished by the presence or absence of minor children and hence a concurrent child support obligation. The 'without child support' formula relies upon two main factors—the length of the marriage and the income difference between the parties, with both amount and duration increasing incrementally with the length of the marriage. The formula is described as reflecting the concept of 'merger over time' which encompasses elements of both compensatory and non-compensatory support. In simplified form, the amount generated under this formula is 1.5 to 2 per cent of the income difference for each year of marriage (capping at 50 per cent) and duration is one half to one year of support for each year of marriage, with no specified time limit after a martial duration of 20 years or more. In the case of a 15-year marriage without children the guidelines would suggest an amount in the range of 22.5 to 30 per cent of the income difference between the spouses for a period of between seven and 15 years. In the case of a 27-year marriage where the children are now adults the amount would be 37.5 to 50 per cent of the income difference and there would be no time limit set.

The 'with child support' formula is more complex as it must take into account both the priority given to child support as the first claim on income under Canadian law and also adjust for differences in tax treatments of child and spousal support (spousal support is deducted from the payor's income for tax purposes and included in the recipient's income, but child support is not), requiring computer-based calculations. The formula works with net parental incomes after removal of amounts dedicated to child support and allocates this remaining income so that the lower-income spouse with primary care of the children is left with between 40 to 46 per cent of this income. Thus under this formula amount does not vary with length of the marriage. As well, the ranges for duration are sensitive not only to the length of the marriage but also, in shorter marriages, to the ages of the children and thus the length of the post-divorce child-rearing period. This formula represents distinctive patterns found in Canadian law in cases involving minor children captured by the concept of 'parental partnership'. It provides a formulaic measure for what Canadian law recognises as strong compensatory spousal claims based on past and ongoing responsibility for childcare.

The formulas are only one part of what is a complex and flexible scheme that still has many openings for exercises of judgement and discretion.

These elements reflect both the complexity of this area of law and the informal nature of the guidelines. The guidelines do not determine entitlement to support; the formulas only operate to determine amount and duration after entitlement has been established. The formulas generate ranges for amount and duration—often quite significant ranges—that require fact-based determinations of where within the range awards should be made. The formula outcomes are based on outcomes in typical cases and the guidelines identify a non-exhaustive range of circumstances in which deviation might be appropriate.[54] Initial determinations under the SSAG will often require ongoing variation in response to changing circumstances over time, including changes in incomes, re-partnering and second families; in many cases the SSAG do not provide formulaic solutions to these changes.

While there continue to be some concerns surrounding the use of the SSAG, on the whole they have been viewed as a successful policy initiative. Initial reactions to the SSAG were admittedly mixed. Concerns were voiced both about their illegitimacy and about applying 'cookie cutter' justice to complex, fact-specific issues. Often these initial reactions were based on mistaken assumptions about the actual nature of scheme and assumed a more rigid scheme than the one that was actually developed. It took some time to convey the idea that the income-sharing formulas were not a new scheme of spousal support but rather proxy measures for the well-established factors of compensation and need. Some of the criticisms also reflected disagreement with the broad basis for spousal support recognised in the Canadian law. The guidelines made the dominant patterns more explicit and exposed substantive disagreement and outliers. Over time the response has become largely positive.

Evidence drawn from ongoing consultations with lawyers and judges and reviews of judicial decisions, confirmed by a 2012 formal evaluation,[55] shows that although only advisory, the guidelines are now widely accepted and used both by lawyers and judges across the country, resulting in greater consistency and predictability of outcomes and reduced conflict. Their use has been facilitated by the development of computer software to perform the calculations under the formulas. Lawyers find the guidelines very useful in shaping client expectations and providing a structure for negotiation. Typical cases are resolved much more easily. The SSAG have received strong endorsement from several appellate courts across the country, which have identified them as a useful tool and have treated their legal status as

[54] Including compelling financial circumstances in interim period; debt payments; prior support obligations; illness and disability; disproportionate losses or gains in short marriages; high and low incomes.

[55] Prairie Research Associates, *Assessing the Impact of the Spousal Support Advisory Guidelines (SSAG)* (30 January 2012, prepared for the Department of Justice Canada) [on file with author].

analogous to a compilation of precedent.[56] While emphasising that the SSAG do not eliminate the need for an individualised analysis, appellate courts have recognised that they provide a useful starting point or litmus test. Within the judicial arena, the SSAG have provided a clearer structure for analysing spousal support cases, making the basis for discretionary decisions more transparent, constraining outlier decisions and enhancing the substantive legitimacy of the spousal support obligation. The SSAG have also provided clearer standards for judicial intervention in unfair spousal support agreements and lawyers, in turn, are beginning to absorb the message that extremely one-sided agreements will not stand.[57]

On the less positive side, the SSAG are undoubtedly complex. They have not eliminated uncertainty, inconsistency and conflict. The document is long and complex; computer software is required for calculations in cases involving child support; and the ranges and exceptions leave many openings for exercises of discretion. All of this reflects the fact that spousal support remains a complex area of law. From the perspective of other jurisdictions, an easier solution might be to eliminate or significantly reduce the obligation, thereby avoiding potentially long-term obligations that entail continuing entanglement with the legal system. However, Canadian law has made different normative choices and the SSAG represent the current limits of what is possible in terms of standardisation and clarification.[58] One of the main problems that has been identified is that of unsophisticated use—a tendency among lawyers and judges to turn the SSAG into default rules, to ignore the exceptions and choose the midpoint of the ranges by default. In part this reflects lack of knowledge of or misunderstandings of the guidelines and is a problem that should ease over time with increased use and education. However it also reflects the strong attraction of rules and easy solutions in an over-burdened family justice system.

Given their complexity the SSAG fall somewhat short of the standards of clarity and simplicity articulated by Dewar and Parkinson for the 'centrifugal' laws demanded by modern family law systems. Ideally the SSAG envision parties who have access to legal advice and to expensive computer software[59] and have thus been criticised from an access to justice perspective.

[56] For two examples, see *Yemchuk v Yemchuk*, 2005 BCCA 406 and *Fisher v Fisher* 2008 ONCA 11.

[57] While Canadian law allows parties a fair amount of scope to contract out of the spousal support obligation in prenuptial and cohabitation agreements as well as separation agreements, spousal support agreements may be overridden on grounds of procedural and substantive unfairness; see Rogerson, C, 'Spousal Support Agreements and the Legacy of *Miglin*' (2012) 31 *Canadian Family Law Quarterly* 13.

[58] Their primary objective is to facilitate well-drafted agreements that will govern both initial determinations and the subsequent issues of variation and termination, thus avoiding resort to courts and secondarily, to provide a clearer starting point for those cases that do go to court.

[59] Lawyers can purchase the software. In addition, the software providers will provide calculations to anyone for a fee.

However, although not ideal, the guidelines, which are accessible online, do provide some assistance to spouses attempting to settle spousal support on their own without lawyers, particularly in cases without children where the formula can be applied without computer calculations. Recently one of the software providers has decided to make a free simplified version of software available online—an extremely positive development.[60] In addition, in some courts family law information centers will produce the SSAG calculations for unrepresented parties, but this is not true across the country and more needs to be done.

The Canadian experience with the Spousal Support Advisory Guidelines offers some useful lessons to other jurisdictions; it shows that spousal support can be amenable to a guidelines regime provided the guidelines are sufficiently flexible and sophisticated; that guidelines can accommodate multiple support objectives in a practical way; that they can resolve large numbers of typical cases and offer a structure that can inform resolution of more difficult cases; and that legislative reform is not the only way that guidelines may be introduced. Since the Canadian initiative, interest in spousal support guidelines has continued to grow. In the United States, the American Association of Matrimonial Lawyers, putting to the side the grand theoretical project of reconceptualising spousal support envisioned by ALI guidelines, released a set of guidelines in 2008 based on outcomes in practice.[61] The English Law Commission has also floated the idea of guidelines, making specific reference to the Canadian SSAG.[62]

CONCLUSION

Canada has gone very far along the path of reforming its substantive family law in a more rule-based direction with the explicit objective of encouraging out-of-court settlement. We have come to accept some degree of 'average' rather than individualised justice in the interests of efficient dispute resolution. Post-divorce parenting arrangements is the one area that remains highly discretionary, and the ideological push for a presumption of shared parenting time has thus far been resisted as inconsistent with the interests of children.[63]

[60] 'My Support Calculator', available at: www.mysupportcalculator.ca/Welcome.aspx, discussed at: http://bcfamilylawresource.blogspot.ca/2011/05/divorcemate-posts-free-advisory.html. The service is funded by lawyers advertising on the site.

[61] See Kisthardt, M, 'Re-thinking Alimony: The AAML's Considerations for Calculating Alimony, Spousal Support or Maintenance' (2008) 21 *Journal of the American Academy of Matrimonial Lawyers* 61. These guidelines have been the basis for recent legislative reforms in New York and Massachusetts and for proposed reforms in Connecticut and Ohio.

[62] Law Commission, *Matrimonial Property, Needs and Agreements: A Supplementary Consultation Paper* (Law Com No 208, 2012).

[63] Relocation guidelines are, however, being considered: see n 17.

It is important to keep in mind, however, that the project of reforming substantive law to promote access to justice rests on the assumption that a role remains for law in the family justice system. It assumes a system in which substantive legal norms continue to structure processes of settlement and dispute resolution. This in turn requires that parties have information about these norms, access to legal advice and representation to deal with the more complex cases that will fall outside any easily-applied default rules or presumptions, and a realistic possibility of enforcement of those norms, including oversight by legal institutions of significant departures from those norms. The substantive and institutional/procedural components of access to justice are closely linked and Canada, despite its positive achievements on the substantive law front, still has many problems to solve.[64]

[64] See n 6.

4

Performing the Marriage Act Straight: The Legal Regulation of Marriage in the Australian Civil Wedding Ceremony

BECKY BATAGOL

INTRODUCTION

THIS CHAPTER EXAMINES how Australian marriage law is used to regulate family formation and considers how the conflict between conservative family views and personal autonomy in law may play out in civil wedding ceremonies across Australia. Much attention has been paid to the role of the state in family life following separation, including other chapters in this volume. Other contributors to this volume, in particular Bill Atkin, Hilary Sommerlad and Rachel Treloar, have observed a trend in family justice policy across multiple jurisdictions towards neoliberalism, whereby the state seeks to reduce its area of activity, while at the same time imposing conservative family values on separating families.[1] This chapter examines the tension between neoliberal choice and conservative family values in the context of the Australian law of marriage.

Marriage of same-sex couples is not permitted in Australia, a situation which must be announced at every civil marriage ceremony by law. This hetero-normative requirement has been in place since the Marriage Act 1961 (Cth) (the 'Marriage Act') was enacted as Australia's first national marriage law. The provision reflects both the common law and religious views which were dominant at the time. Since the 1960s however, civil marriage has moved from a minority event to become the most popular way of getting married in Australia. The introduction of Australia's world-first civil celebrancy program in the 1970s transformed civil wedding ceremonies from

[1] See also Batagol, B and Brown, T, *Bargaining in the Shadow of the Law: The Case of Family Mediation* (Sydney, Themis Press, 2011) 63–66.

dry, brief affairs in registry offices to events where couples choose a highly personalised non-religious wedding ceremony that reflects their own values.

Multiple opinion polls have shown that an overwhelming majority of Australians now support marriage equality, enabling any couple, gay or straight, to marry. For heterosexual Australian brides and grooms who believe in marriage equality and the civil celebrants who marry them, there is enormous potential for conflict between the conservative and neoliberal policies around civil wedding ceremonies. It appears that some couples and celebrants may be resolving this conflict by obeying the legal requirements but including statements of protest in their ceremonies to campaign for law reform. Ultimately the attempt by the Australian state to impose conservative family values on marrying couples may fail because progressive brides and grooms subvert the law and question the homophobic nature of that law. These actions show that rather than protecting the institution of marriage in enforcing these laws, the Australian government is acting in a discriminatory manner on this issue and is out of touch with widespread Australian understandings of the nature of marriage.

CIVIL MARRIAGE IN AUSTRALIA

Marriage law in Australia is pluralistic in that both religious and civil ceremonies are recognised. Civil marriage is overwhelmingly the most popular way of getting married in Australia. In 2012, 71.9 per cent of marriages were performed by a civil celebrant rather than a minister of religion.[2] These numbers represent a major shift towards civil weddings over the last half of the twentieth century. In 1959, just prior to the enactment of the Marriage Act, just 11.4 per cent of marriages were civil marriages.[3] Civil marriages have outnumbered religious marriages in Australia since 1999.[4]

Religious marriages may be solemnised under law according to the practices of a broad range of registered religious denominations.[5] There are currently 128 religions and religious denominations recognised under the Marriage Act, each of which is permitted to nominate officials as marriage celebrants.[6] Religious marriage ceremonies are comparatively unregulated by the state compared with civil ceremonies under the Marriage Act. Where a marriage is officiated by a minister of religion, the ceremony may be conducted according

[2] Australian Bureau of Statistics, *Marriages and Divorces in Australia 2012* (Cat no 3310.0, 2013).

[3] Parliament of Australia, *Parliamentary Debates, House of Representatives* (Garfield Barwick, Attorney General, 19 May 1960).

[4] Australian Bureau of Statistics, *Marriages and Divorces in Australia 2012* (n 2).

[5] Marriage Act 1961 (Cth), s 32.

[6] Marriage (Recognised Denominations) Proclamation 2007 (Cth) and the Marriage (Recognised Denominations) Amendment Proclamation 2013 (Cth).

to whatever form and ceremony is recognised by the religion to which the minister belongs.[7] No other requirements are imposed by law upon religious marriage ceremonies.

Civil marriage has been possible in Australia since the various Australian colonies permitted it between the 1830s and 1870s. The Australian colonies inherited many of their laws from England, sometimes automatically and sometimes when the colonial parliaments enacted legislation that replicated English law.[8] In 1901, with the birth of the independent nation of Australia, Australia's Constitution gave the newly created federal Parliament the power to enact laws for marriage.[9] That power was not exercised until 1961, when Australia's first national marriage law, the Marriage Act, was enacted. Previously, marriage law had been regulated separately and somewhat inconsistently by each Australian State and Territory. A key aim behind the federal Marriage Act in 1961 was to create a single national marriage scheme in Australia so that the rules of private international law would not have to be employed to recognise marriages across state borders.[10] The Marriage Act complemented the Matrimonial Causes Act 1959 (Cth) which introduced Australia's first national divorce laws. The Family Law Act 1975 (Cth) followed not much more than a decade later, which introduced divorce on a single no-fault ground and created the specialist Family Court of Australia to deal exclusively with family law cases.

There are two basic types of civil marriage possible in Australia. Registry marriages are conducted by State or Territory officials at Registry offices or official registry venues in each Australian State and Territory.[11] Registry marriage ceremonies, comprising around 10 per cent of all marriages in Australia,[12] are generally cheaper and quicker to organise than other marriage ceremonies (or 'elegant and affordable' as described by the government in the Australian State of Victoria). Marriage by a federally registered marriage celebrant is the other form of civil marriage in Australia.[13] Marriage celebrants offer couples the chance to create a unique and personalised wedding ceremony that reflects the values and tastes of the bride and groom. For both types of civil ceremonies, two adult witnesses must be present[14] and at least one month's notice of the marriage must usually be given.[15]

[7] Marriage Act 1961 (Cth), s 45(1).
[8] Parliament of Australia, *Parliamentary Debates, House of Representatives* (n 3).
[9] Constitution of Australia, s 51 (xxi).
[10] Parliament of Australia (n 3).
[11] Marriage Act 1961 (Cth), s 39.
[12] Messenger, D, *Murphy's Law and the Pursuit of Happiness: A History of the Civil Celebrant Movement* (Melbourne, Spectrum Publications and the International College of Celebrancy, 2012) 119.
[13] Marriage Act 1961 (Cth), s 41.
[14] ibid, s 44.
[15] ibid, s 42.

The notice period was extended from seven days in 1976 and the longer time provides space for couples to develop their ceremony with their celebrant.[16] Civil ceremonies may take place at any time of day and any place in Australia.[17] Couples, celebrants and witnesses must sign the marriage certificate immediately after the ceremony.[18]

THE AUSTRALIAN CIVIL CELEBRANCY PROGRAM

The establishment of the civil celebrancy program in Australia in the early-1970s brought with it social change just as profound as the contemporaneous introduction of no-fault divorce in Australia. A key feature of the program is choice of ceremony for marrying couples, matching the neoliberal philosophy of personal autonomy. The civil celebrancy program made civil marriage ceremonies attractive and accessible to brides and grooms because weddings could be personalised and celebrated as the couples chose in the presence of friends and family. These reforms, alongside the secularisation of Australian society, have meant that marriage ceremonies performed by civil celebrants have become the way that the vast majority of Australians now get married today. There are around 9000 civil marriage celebrants currently registered in Australia. Secular civil celebrants officiated at around 65 per cent of all Australian weddings in 2012.[19] The federal government has stated that 'Commonwealth-registered marriage celebrants play a critical role in Australian society'.[20]

After the Marriage Act was passed in 1961 and until 1973, civil weddings could only take place in State and Territory Registry offices. Most couples at this time chose a religious wedding. Registry ceremonies were usually dry, brief legal affairs used by a small minority of brides and grooms. One of Australia's first civil celebrants, Dally Messenger, described Registry office weddings in the 1960s and early-1970s:

> [T]hey were stark, austere, offensive, brief and completely legal. Couples, with their witnesses, sat on a long bench and were called up, four by four (ie the bride and groom with two witnesses), by a poker-faced official behind a desk, in the manner of a soup queue. A brief, legal marriage then ensued.[21]

In 1973, the Australian civil celebrancy program was created. It has been claimed that this program was a world first.[22] Unlike the no-fault divorce

16 Messenger, *Murphy's Law and the Pursuit of Happiness* (n 12) 67.
17 Marriage Act 1961 (Cth), s 43.
18 ibid, s 50(2).
19 Messenger (n 12) 118.
20 Attorney General's Department, *Marriage Celebrant Program Reforms: Frequently Asked Questions* (Canberra, Australian Government, 2012) 4.
21 Messenger (n 12) 18.
22 ibid 49.

reforms debated and passed by the federal Parliament at the same time in the Family Law Act 1975 (Cth), the celebrancy program was created without legislation and went under the publicity radar.[23] The civil celebrancy program appears initially to have been established by the Attorney General, Senator Lionel Murphy alone, who was also architect of the Family Law Act.[24] In an interview, Senator Murphy explained his reasons for initiating the celebrancy program:

> There was dissatisfaction, during the period before I became Attorney General, with the way in which civil marriages were performed. Registries in the various states weren't open for marriages throughout the weekends or at nights, and often the marriages were performed in an undignified way.[25]

The aims of the program for the Attorney General were, according to Messenger, first, to provide a choice of ceremony which was consistent with the marrying couple's beliefs in terms of place, symbols, dress and celebrant chosen; second, to allow for a civil alternative to religious marriage ceremonies that were also dignified and non-humiliating; and finally to enhance respect for the institution of marriage by developing the culture of marriage and to strengthen couples' relationships and commitment to marriage.[26] The Attorney General appointed a small group of civil marriage celebrants in 1973 and 1974.[27] Sections 39(2) and 41 of the Marriage Act permitted 'authorised celebrants' to conduct civil marriage ceremonies and provided scope for the Attorney General to appoint 'suitable persons' to solemnise marriages. The Attorney General used this section to create the program without the need for further legislation. In 1973, Senator Murphy selected a number of 'disciplined, dignified professionals' under these existing provisions who were efficient in record keeping and legal procedures as the first civil marriage celebrants. The celebrants were asked to be conscious of people's needs and to dress as those who were getting married would want.[28]

Since 1973, the civil celebrancy program in Australia has become increasingly professionalised and more intensely regulated by the federal government. The neoliberal principle of choice of ceremony still prevails. However, the more intensive monitoring of celebrants' work has ensured that particular family forms are promoted through civil celebrants. Additional provisions have been inserted into the Marriage Act, delegated legislation passed and a Code of Practice has been developed to regulate civil celebrants. The program is administered by the Registrar of Marriage Celebrants from the federal Attorney General's Department. A register of marriage celebrants

[23] ibid 29.
[24] ibid 48.
[25] ibid 49.
[26] ibid 53.
[27] ibid 55.
[28] ibid 52.

is maintained and celebrants can only be included on the register if they have the qualifications and skills necessary to be a celebrant and they are deemed to be a 'fit and proper person'.[29] Section 39C(2) of the Act sets out criteria for determining what is 'fit and proper', which include knowledge of the law of marriage, good standing in the community, a clear criminal record, that there be no conflict of interest with another occupation the celebrant holds and that the celebrant does not stand to benefit from their role. Celebrants must comply with a Code of Practice and must undertake five hours of professional development annually.[30] They are subject to disciplinary measures if they fail to do this.[31] Celebrants must undergo regular performance reviews by the Registrar of Marriage Celebrants.[32] Disciplinary measures may be taken against individual celebrants by the Registrar for unsatisfactory performance in their review or if a complaint against them has been sustained.[33] These measures can include a caution, mandatory professional development, a periodic suspension of registration or complete deregistration.[34] In 2014, a significant annual registration fee for most civil marriage celebrants was introduced to fund the government's increased regulation of the celebrancy program.[35]

The civil celebrancy program has dramatically changed the celebration of weddings in Australia. One of the longest-serving civil celebrants, Messenger, describes the evolution of Australian civil ceremonies since 1973 towards an 'an equality-based wedding compact' born of the ability of brides and grooms to choose their own ceremonies:

> Those celebrants who allowed complete freedom of choice began to notice that chosen vows for grooms and brides had this same new wording. In the churches, many still had (and have today) the 'obey' phrase. The personally chosen or composed introduction to the ceremony, as well as the asking and especially the vows, began to articulate a 'compact' of equality.[36]

There is now a wide variety of wedding ceremonies conducted at a diverse range of venues in Australia. The lack of restriction on the time and venue of civil weddings in Australia (unlike in England and Wales) has encouraged this multiplicity. Messenger describes officiating at many 'gimmick' weddings, although he notes these weddings are less popular today:

> In these early years, I have to admit to officiating at the break of dawn at the beach on the spot at the time of day, where a couple first made love. I performed

[29] Marriage Act 1961 (Cth), s 39B, 39C.
[30] ibid, ss 39G(a) and (b).
[31] ibid, s 39I(1)(b)).
[32] ibid, s 39H.
[33] ibid, s 39I.
[34] ibid, s 39I(2).
[35] ibid, s 39FA.
[36] Messenger (n 12) 74–75.

> weddings on tops of mountains and at the winning post of a racecourse ... At another wedding I was on a houseboat on Eildon Weir in mid-Victoria. When I pronounced the couple husband and wife, they dived overboard for joy. We were all wearing swimming costumes so I and all the guests, followed.[37]

It is easy to find celebrants across Australia advertising services for garden weddings, weddings at family homes, beach weddings, skydiving weddings ('The idea is to do the formal exchange in the plane in front of your two witnesses, then all jump out just after the "I do" part'),[38] underwater weddings ('Imagine a dozen sharks being your wedding ceremony guests??'),[39] helicopter weddings and almost nude weddings ('The celebrant said their nudity showed, "there was nothing you wouldn't do to be together"').[40]

The changes to the civil marriage ceremony made in the 1970s reflected neoliberal ideals of minimal state involvement in family life and so encouraged choice of ceremony for brides and grooms. These changes were as profound as the no-fault divorce laws that took place at the same time. Civil marriage became accessible and attractive—weddings could be personalised and celebrated as the couples wanted. Many Australians, whether as brides and grooms or as family and friends of marrying couples, have participated in meaningful wedding ceremonies because of the legacy of these reforms.

LEGAL REQUIREMENTS FOR CIVIL WEDDING CEREMONIES

One of the attractions of civil weddings is that couples are able to choose the content of their own wedding ceremonies. However, there is a statement and a particular form of vows to be used by the couple which must be made at all civil (but not religious) marriage ceremonies, whether conducted by registered marriage celebrants or State and Territory registry officers. These statements, alongside the increased policing of their use, reveal that the Australian government still has a hand in determining the content of civil wedding ceremonies, imposing conservative, heteronormative values upon all couples married in secular ceremonies.

The statement required to be made at civil ceremonies, known commonly as the monitum, must be made by the celebrant to the parties before the couple exchange vows.[41] This part of the ceremony provides a warning to the bride and groom about the solemn nature of marriage and reiterates the

[37] ibid 118–19.
[38] www.adventureweddings.com.au/skydiving-weddings.html.
[39] www.adventureweddings.com.au/underwater-weddings.html.
[40] http://blogs.theage.com.au/entertainment/archives/2008/02/nude_wedding_fo.html.
[41] Marriage Act 1961 (Cth), s 46(1); Attorney General's Department, *Guidelines on the Marriage Act 1961 for Marriage Celebrants* (Canberra, Australian Government, July 2014) 74.

heterosexual exclusivity of marriage in Australian law. This statement from section 46(1) of the Marriage Act is:

> I am duly authorised by law to solemnise marriages according to law.
>
> Before you are joined in marriage in my presence and in the presence of these witnesses, I am to remind you of the solemn and binding nature of the relationship into which you are now about to enter.
>
> Marriage, according to law in Australia, is the union of a man and a woman to the exclusion of all others, voluntarily entered into for life.

Section 46(1) is one of the original sections of the Marriage Act. In the second reading speech for an early version of the Bill in 1960, then chief law officer of the federal government at that time, Attorney General Garfield Barwick, set out the reasons for enacting the provision. Key amongst them were protection of the institution of marriage and reminding young couples of the importance of marriage:

> The Government feels that the bill … is a contribution towards the stability of marriage which … will make for the well-being of this country throughout its great future. The bill goes a long way in this direction and endeavours to ensure that our people—particularly our young people—enter into marriage, in the familiar and eloquent words, not lightly but advisedly.[42]

Prior to 2004, section 46 represented the closest thing there was to a definition of marriage in the Marriage Act. This description of marriage as a monogamous, lifelong and heterosexual institution is a secular version of the common law definition of marriage applicable in Australia, inherited from England, that 'marriage, as understood in Christendom, may for this purpose be defined as the voluntary union for life of one man and one woman to the exclusion of all others'.[43] In 2004, the federal Parliament passed a law which introduced a definition of marriage into the Marriage Act with the intention of making clear that marriage of same-sex couples was not permitted in Australia.[44] Section 5 of the Marriage Act now contains a definition of marriage as 'the union of a man and a woman to the exclusion of all others, voluntarily entered into for life'. This definition matches the description of marriage in section 46.

If the celebrant fails to make this statement, the marriage is still valid under law.[45] The second reading speech for the Bill in 1960 made clear that this no-invalidity provision was enacted to ensure the certainty of

[42] Parliament of Australia (n 3).
[43] *Hyde v Hyde & Woodmansee* (1866) LR 1 P&D 130, per Lord Penzance.
[44] Marriage Amendment Act 2004 (Cth).
[45] Marriage Act 1961 (Cth), s 48(2).

marriage.[46] It is possible for individual celebrants to be excused from compliance with section 46 by the Attorney General.[47] For some time early in the civil celebrancy program, all celebrants were excused in their instruments of appointment made by the Attorney General from needing to recite the monitum in section 46.[48]

Since around 2004, compliance with section 46 has been increasingly enforced, ensuring this discriminatory statement is now made at all civil wedding ceremonies. The enforcement of section 46 coincided with the passing of Marriage Amendment Act 2004 (Cth) and broadcasts successive Australian governments' views that same-sex couples should be excluded from participation in marriage in Australia. The provision is enforced through soft pressure upon civil celebrants to comply, backed up by the threat of removing a civil celebrant's livelihood through disciplinary action by the Registrar of Marriage Celebrants. Disciplinary action can be taken when a ceremony performed by a celebrant is deemed not to have complied with section 46 as part of their performance review, or because the Registrar of Marriage Celebrants determines that they have not complied with the Code of Practice for marriage celebrants which requires celebrants to 'solemnize marriages according to the legal requirements in the Marriage Act'.[49] Disciplinary action can include a caution, mandatory professional development, a periodic suspension of registration or complete deregistration.[50]

In 2010, a review of 336 sample wedding ceremonies provided by marriage celebrants as part of their performance reviews found that 261, or around 80 per cent, failed to comply with section 45 or 46 of the Marriage Act.[51] The review found that in the seven years prior, 339 celebrants had been deregistered or chosen to resign as a result of their performance review. This suggests that the Department is actively pursuing celebrants who fail to state the heterosexual nature of marriage at wedding ceremonies. Civil celebrant Messenger suggested that there is a culture of fear created by the Department and that celebrants are fearful of losing their livelihoods if they do not comply:

> The problem the bureaucrats complain about is of their own making. Celebrants have become terrified of the Marriage Act bureaucrats, and have ceased even politely speaking truth to power. The verbose legalese that emanates from the Attorney General's Department is so overwhelming as to be ineffective.[52]

[46] Parliament of Australia (n 3).
[47] Marriage Act 1961 (Cth), s 46(2).
[48] Messenger (n 12) 127.
[49] Marriage Act 1961 (Cth), s 39I; Attorney General's Department, *Code of Practice for Marriage Celebrants* (Canberra, Australian Government, nd) cl.4.
[50] Marriage Act 1961 (Cth), s 39I(2).
[51] Horin, D, 'Invalid Wedding Vows Put Weddings in Doubt' *The Age Newspaper* 21 August 2010.
[52] Messenger, D, 'Celebrants want a divorce as bureaucrats go over the top' *The Age Newspaper* 27 August 2010.

There is a great deal of soft pressure to comply with the monitum in section 46. As a long-serving celebrant, Messenger is the author of a book used by civil celebrants setting out readings and sample ceremonies for civil weddings. He recalls being threatened with being reported to the Attorney General by a group of celebrants who were concerned that the book did not reproduce the words of section 46 precisely.[53] The Attorney General's Department has created a set of Guidelines on the Marriage Act 1961 for Marriage Celebrants.[54] These guidelines have no legal status (unlike the Code of Practice which celebrant must comply with under the Act). However, the Guidelines direct celebrants in how they should perform section 46 of the Marriage Act. The possibility of suspension or deregistration by the Department means that the Guidelines effectively become mandatory as they set out how the Registrar of Marriage Celebrants will interpret the Act in the event of disciplinary action. This ensures compliance with the Guidelines, despite their lack of legal status.

Section 46(1) of the Marriage Act states that 'words to that effect' may be used instead of the statement prescribed, suggesting that the words in the Act may be changed if the meaning remains the same. However, the Guidelines recommend that celebrants use the exact form of words as set out in the legislation:

> Commonwealth-registered marriage celebrants and State and Territory Officers have a legal obligation to say the words in subsection 46(1). It is the statement of their authority to solemnise the marriage. It also explains marriage under Australian law. The safest course for Commonwealth-registered marriage celebrants or State Officers in solemnising marriages is to always use the wording in the Marriage Act. Doing so will leave no room for doubt that the celebrant has complied with their obligations under the Marriage Act, and will ensure that parties are aware of the legal implications of marriage.[55]

These Guidelines reinforce the heteronormative, homophobic definition of marriage as set out in the Marriage Act. The Guidelines are clear that marriage celebrants and State and Territory Registry officers must not alter the words read out so that the definition of marriage is altered to include same-sex couples:

> Given that the third sentence is the legal definition of marriage in Australia the words cannot be changed. Reversing the order of the words 'man' and 'woman' would be acceptable, but that is all.

[53] Messenger (n 12) 127.

[54] Attorney General's Department, *Guidelines on the Marriage Act 1961 for Marriage Celebrants* (n 41).

[55] ibid 74–75.

> Commonwealth-registered marriage celebrants and State and Territory Officers must not make the following changes to the words in the third sentence because 'marriage' is specifically defined by law:
>
> — do not replace 'man' and 'woman' with 'people' or 'persons'. This could signify the marriage of two people of the same sex which is specifically excluded by the definition.
> — do not change the first part of the sentence to read: 'Marriage as most of us understand it is…', and
> — do not change 'for life' to 'with the intention/hope/desire that it will last for life.'[56]

The Attorney General's Department in the Guidelines anticipates a situation where couples request that the celebrant change this aspect of the ceremony so as to remove the homophobic nature of the statement. The Guidelines are clear that the celebrant must refuse the couple's request:

> The definition of marriage in the Marriage Act is the law in Australia. While everyone is entitled to their individual view about such matters, Commonwealth-registered marriage celebrants and State and Territory Officers are authorised to solemnise marriages in accordance with the law. Such celebrants will need to explain carefully to the couple that, despite their view, they are not authorised to change the definition and have a legal obligation to state it during the ceremony. This means the authorised celebrant is not able to agree to such a request.[57]

There is also a particular exchange of vows which must also be made at all civil weddings by both the bride and groom to each other in the presence of the celebrant and the two witnesses. It is: 'I call upon the persons here present to witness that I, A.B. (*or* C.D.), take thee, C.D. (*or* A.B.), to be my lawful wedded wife (*or* husband)'.[58] This section has also been narrowly interpreted by the Attorney General's Department who no longer provides leeway when interpreting this section as it did prior to 2006–07 so that the vows must be declared as written in the Act, rather than asked as a question by the celebrant and answered with 'I do' by the bride and groom.[59] The consequences of failing to comply with this section are potentially more extreme for the bride and groom than a failure to recite the monitum, as non-compliance with section 45(2) during the ceremony means the marriage is not valid (s 48(1)). An invalid marriage is considered void under section 23B(1)(c) of the Marriage Act and can be the basis of an application to the Family Court of Australia for a decree of nullity.

[56] ibid 75.
[57] ibid.
[58] Marriage Act 1961 (Cth), s 45(2).
[59] Horin, 'Invalid Wedding Vows Put Weddings in Doubt' (n 51); Attorney General's Department (n 41) 79.

While civil marriages have become a popular vehicle for Australians to wed in a way that reflects their own family values, the discriminatory and unpopular stance of the Australian government on marriage equality is imposed upon marrying couples and announced at all weddings. Together, the legislation and the Code of Practice and the Guidelines, alongside more intensive regulation of civil celebrants by the Australian government contribute to this picture. The rigid requirements of the monitum sit uneasily with the neoliberal choice of ceremony ethos that has become part of the culture of civil wedding ceremonies in Australia since 1973, when the civil celebrancy program was established. Because the conservative social values contained in the legislation do not match the views on marriage equality of the majority of Australians, there is great potential for conflict between celebrants and marrying couples around these aspects of the wedding ceremony.

MARRIAGE OF SAME-SEX COUPLES IN AUSTRALIA

Marriage of same-sex couples is prohibited in Australia. 'Marriage' was not defined in the relevant Australian legislation until 2004, although common law, inherited from England, defined marriage as the voluntary, exclusive union for life of one man and one woman. Amendments to the Marriage Act were passed in 2004 which expressly excluded marriage of gay and lesbian couples from the federal marriage scheme. As well as adding the discriminatory definition of marriage to the Marriage Act, amendments were also made at this time to the Marriage Act so that marriages of same-sex couples formalised in other countries would not be recognised in Australia.[60] The Explanatory Memorandum that accompanied the Act stated that the amendments were made to show 'the Government's commitment to protect the institution of marriage by ensuring that marriage means a union of a man and a woman and that same-sex relationships cannot be equated with marriage'.[61]

While there is some recognition of same-sex relationships at State and Territory level in Australia, a decision of Australia's highest court, the High Court in December 2013 established that only the federal Parliament has the power to make laws for the marriage of couples of the same sex under the Constitution and that as such, the Australian States and Territories cannot legislate to allow marriage equality.[62] This leaves marriage equality in the exclusive domain of the federal Parliament in Australia. There have been several attempts in the past decade to legislate federally for same-sex marriage but these bills have not gained a majority in either house of

[60] Marriage Act 1961 (Cth), s 88EA.

[61] Parliament of Australia, *Explanatory Memorandum, Marriage Amendment Bill 2004, House of Representatives* (Canberra, 2004).

[62] *Commonwealth v Australian Capital Territory* [2013] HCA 55.

Parliament. In 2013, Prime Minister Tony Abbott explained his opposition to permitting lesbian and gay couples to marry: 'My position on this is fairly well known. I'm fairly traditional. I support the standard definition of marriage as between a man and a woman'.[63]

Multiple recent opinion polls suggest that the majority of Australians back the ability of lesbian women and gay men to marry. A recent poll from July 2014 showed that 72 per cent of Australians supported the legalisation of marriage of couples of the same sex.[64] Support for marriage equality has been steadily increasing amongst Australians, rising from just 38 per cent agreeing with it in 2004, as shown by regular telephone polls.[65] A clear majority of heterosexual couples already in a marriage favoured marriage equality. One of those responsible for conducting the poll, Mark Textor, stated

> This poll definitively puts pay to some of the myths that married couples or those with religious beliefs are against same-sex marriage. It doesn't devalue their marriages or faith, and instead gives everyone equal access to the rights they are accorded.[66]

The high number of heterosexual Australians supporting marriage equality suggests that there will be a cohort of progressive heterosexual marrying couples who are attracted to civil marriage for choice of ceremony but who object to the recitation of the monitum because of its homophobic nature. The increasing number of Australians who support marriage equality and the refusal of Australia's politicians to legislate for the marriage of same-sex couples makes more conflict between celebrants and marrying couples around the content of their wedding ceremony inevitable.

STATEMENTS OF PROTEST IN CIVIL WEDDING CEREMONIES

There is evidence that some heterosexual Australian couples are requesting changes to their wedding ceremony that reflect values of marriage equality. These brides and grooms are including 'statements of protest' in their ceremonies, speeches made to guests before or after the required monitum is recited, acknowledging the couple's disagreement with the exclusively heterosexual nature of marriage under Australian law. In so doing, the intention behind the law, the protection of the institution of marriage through the denial of the human rights of same-sex attracted people, is subverted.

[63] Australian Associated Press, 'Abbott quizzed on gay marriage stance' *Sydney Morning Herald Newspaper* 15 April 2013.

[64] Cox, L, 'Poll Shows Growing Support for Same Sex Marriage' *Sydney Morning Herald Newspaper* 15 July 2014.

[65] Textor, M, 'Record Support for Same-Sex Marriage' (15 July 2014) www.crosbytextor.com/news/record-support-for-same-sex-marriage/.

[66] ibid.

Online discussion boards, wedding and bride forums as well as comment sections under articles about weddings all provide publicly available evidence of this phenomenon. These online sources were identified for this chapter through a Google search for the terms 'wedding ceremony same sex' and 'wedding ceremony marriage equality' with a filter limiting results to Australia. Although the quotes reprinted below are not necessarily representative of all marrying couples, they do provide evidence of a cohort of Australian marrying couples who are including the monitum in their ceremony but using it as an opportunity to agitate for law reform on marriage equality.

On the Vogue Australia bride forum, user 'Tabs' posted on 17 February 2010 that

> We have a lot of wonderful friends who are gay. They are invited to our wedding and, upon reading the legal parts of the ceremony given to us by our celebrant, I'm feeling like I need to address how homophobic the wording is. I'm hoping to ask our celebrant to include something about how unjust it is that adults who love each other cannot have their unions legally acknowledged. To borrow the phrasing from cupcake brides' blog 'in a just world, all adults will be free to celebrate their love in a lawful commitment'.[67]

In response to Tabs's post, 'Lindsay' wrote on the Vogue Australia bride forum on 17 February 2010:

> [O]ur celebrant said 'I am required to say that under Australian law, marriage is between a man and a woman to the exclusion of all others. However, X and Y have asked me to express their heartfelt desire that one day same-sex couples will be permitted the same privilege that is afforded to X and Y today.' A few people rolled their eyes, but we also got applause. I wouldn't have said anything about same-sex marriage if it weren't for the compulsory wording. If they're going to make us say something exclusionary like that, I'm going to speak up![68]

In the comments under an article on online magazine Offbeat Bride, user 'Hopium' wrote on 27 January 2010:

> I was an Aussie bride. My Maid of Honour was/is lesbian with a gorgeous girlfriend. We had the definition—had to as we wanted a legal ceremony. Then we had the celebrant say that marriage should be between two loving people regardless of race, creed, colour or gender … I am rather politically active I make it an issue. You should hear the screaming matches with my local pollies.[69]

Advocacy organisation Australian Marriage Equality has a webpage with suggested wording for five different statements of protest that wedding

[67] http://forums.vogue.com.au/showthread.php?t=355361.
[68] http://forums.vogue.com.au/showthread.php?t=355361&page=2.
[69] http://offbeatbride.com/2010/01/australia-wedding-recitation.

celebrants could make after reciting the monitum. Most of these statements advocate for law reform. For example, the celebrant could say after the monitum:

> So what are we waiting for? Well PARTNER 1 and PARTNER 2 have asked to me to pause for a moment, so we can all keep in mind those who ARE waiting to be married—but cannot do so under current marriage law. Special days like this belong to two people who love each other—irrespective of religion, race, gender or sexuality.[70]

These statements of protest fulfil legal requirements regarding wedding ceremonies in the Marriage Act but subvert the intention of the lawmakers. In asking their celebrants to make a protest statement after the monitum these brides and grooms are pushing back against the intrusion of conservative values in their family lives. These couples, empowered by the neoliberal rhetoric of choice of ceremony, have chosen to reject the imposition of conservative government values on their wedded lives and upon their guests.

One feature of the statements of protest reproduced here is that they all support the institution of marriage but disassociate the marrying couple from discriminatory Australian marriage law. It is the law which these brides publicly identify as diminishing the institution. Both the Marriage Act (including the 2004 amendments which explicitly excluded the marriage of same-sex couples) and the civil celebrancy program were created with the intention of enhancing respect for the institution of marriage. However, the incorporation of statements of protest into wedding ceremonies shows that enforcing the recitation of the monitum through increased policing of civil celebrants, appears to do little to enhance respect for the institution of marriage, and may well undermine the intention behind the law as it creates a platform for a public declaration of the unfairness of the law. These cases suggest that a more effective way of enhancing respect for the institution of marriage is through providing marrying couples with the unrestricted freedom to choose a ceremony that matches their values.

NEW DIRECTIONS FOR RESEARCH

This chapter has focused on the conflict between conservative family views and personal autonomy in Australian marriage law governing civil wedding ceremonies. The laws around civil marriage ceremonies purport to protect the institution of marriage. Australian law and simultaneously provides couples with choice, respect and dignity in their wedding ceremonies and promotes conservative, religiously-informed family values.

[70] www.australianmarriageequality.org/werewaiting/cant-wait/.

Since the development of the civil celebrancy program more than 40 years ago, civil marriage has grown significantly in popularity, providing Australian couples with a secular, dignified alterative to a religious wedding that reflects their own personal values. Choice of ceremony has been central to the success of civil marriage. It has enhanced respect for the institution of marriage by attracting couples who without choice, might not marry at all. However one of the key compulsory aspects of the civil ceremony, the monitum, explicitly excludes lesbian women and gay men from marriage, a sentiment which does not match the beliefs of the vast majority of Australians, gay or straight. The enforcement of section 46 of the Marriage Act has coincided with a sustained refusal by successive federal governments to legislate for marriage equality in a purported attempt to protect the institution of marriage. This imposition of conservative views regarding family structures sits uneasily with a ceremony based around choice. For the couples and their celebrants who resolve this conflict by obeying the legal requirements but include statements of protest in their ceremonies, the inclusion of conservative family values in the wedding ceremony generates agitation for law reform. Rather than protecting the institution of marriage, in enforcing these laws the Australian government may be diminishing the institution by rendering it discriminatory and out of touch with widespread Australian understandings of the nature of marriage.

A key area for further research is systematic documentation of how heterosexual Australian brides and grooms who believe in marriage equality negotiate the hetero-normative requirements of the Marriage Act with their civil celebrants and how the celebrants perform this aspect of the wedding ceremony. Such a project will uncover the nature of negotiations between marrying couples and their celebrants over these issues and the extent to which statements of protest are being included in civil wedding ceremonies. Such research will assist us to better understand how the conflict between conservative family views and personal autonomy in law may play out in civil wedding ceremonies across Australia.

Part II

Judges and Courts Delivering Family Justice

5

National Paths Towards Private Ordering

Professionals' Jurisdictions and Separating Couples' Privacy in the French and Canadian Family Justice Systems

EMILIE BILAND, MURIEL MILLE AND HÉLÈNE STEINMETZ

INTRODUCTION

SINCE THE MID-1970s, socio-legal scholars have extensively analysed changes in family law and family justice systems. The recognition of 'no-fault' divorce and the rise of undisputed proceedings have changed the nature of judicial intervention in family regulation. The concept of 'private ordering', as Mnookin and Kornhauser[1] called it, emphasises the institutionalisation of private decisions in family law. This trend accompanies the decline of adjudication through the courts and the redefinition of the role of legal professionals in family cases. Based on their recent study of the English family justice system, Eekelaar and Maclean[2] conclude that 'an important goal of late modern society is the empowerment of individuals to choose their own solutions, albeit that the state seeks to use various devices to control what those solutions should be. These devices have limited effects'. In this chapter, we aim to discuss this proposition through a double lens. First, we argue that the result of these policies of 'private ordering' varies according to whether the outcome or the process is taken into account. Settled decisions may not be as private as they seem to be if we observe the process that has led to them, as that has often involved professionals. To obtain a comprehensive approach to 'private ordering', we suggest distinguishing between two dimensions: decisions as the outcome of divorce ordering, but also the interactions between ex-partners and professionals

[1] Mnookin, RH and Kornhauser, L, 'Bargaining in the Shadow of the Law: The Case of Divorce' (1979) 88(5) *The Yale Law Journal* 950.

[2] Eekelaar, J and Maclean, M, *Family Justice. The Work of Family Judges in Uncertain Times* (Oxford, Hart Publishing, 2013).

as the process towards decision. Even if a decision is reached through an agreement between individuals, the ex-partners' private life is likely to be discussed in front of a variety of professionals during the process, and these professionals contribute to defining how the cases may be settled.

This hypothesis leads us to a second starting point. Although the trend towards 'private ordering' is shared by every Western jurisdiction, it has not reached the same level, and does not take the same form in all countries. Different paths have been experienced, depending on national patterns regarding the judicial system and the legal profession as well as public policy and family relations. The circumstances in which separating couples are led to expose private issues in court and in front of professionals may also vary between national judicial systems. To study these national paths, this study focuses on two family justice systems: France and Québec, the French-speaking province of Canada.

With respect to divorce rates, whose rise encourages the evolution of divorce adjudication, France and Québec are similar, since unmarried couples and divorced people are more numerous than in most Western jurisdictions: there is about one divorce for two marriages.[3] They are also comparable with respect to their shared legal tradition. Because of the legacy of French colonisation, Québec partly belongs to the civil law legal system. As in France, family law is codified in its Civil Code. Neither of these jurisdictions has allowed administrative divorce; and family litigation accounts for about half of the cases in each court system (French *Tribunaux de Grande Instance* and the Superior Court of Québec).

However, when it comes to the actual functioning of family justice, other national patterns differ between the two jurisdictions and account for variations in the treatment of family cases. In Québec, judicial proceedings are based on the common law tradition, whereas France is a 'pure' civil law country. As a result, the role of judges and lawyers during hearings and, more broadly, the social status[4] and the political influence of the legal profession, vary between the jurisdictions. Moreover, public policies regarding divorce adjudication differ. On a tight budget, the French Department of Justice has given preference to internal reforms, at the court level, inspired by new public management norms. In contrast, the Québec Department has implemented new services outside the courts, without changing the core of

[3] Prioux, F and Barbieri, M, 'L'évolution démographique récente en France: une mortalité relativement faible aux grands âges' (2012) 67(4) *Population* 597; Milan, A, 'Marital Status: Overview, 2011' Component of Statistics Canada Catalogue no 91-209-X, Report on the Demographic Situation in Canada (2013) www.statcan.gc.ca/pub/91-209-x/2013001/article/11788-eng.pdf.

[4] In France, most judges enter the *École Nationale de la Magistrature* immediately after graduate school, before the age of 30; they have civil servant-like careers, organised along a vertical scale. Trial judges working on family cases have a low or intermediate position within the judiciary and do not belong to the élite of their professional group. Québec trial judges form a more homogeneous and élitist group, whose salaries and social prestige are far higher. They are appointed by the federal Minister of Justice, usually in their late 40s or their early 50s, after a first career as successful lawyers.

judicial proceedings (ie adversarial trials), which is beyond its control. Finally, France and Québec have developed two contrasting ways for dealing with high rates of marital breakdown: the former still involves the judiciary in any and every case, while streamlining the proceedings to make them quicker and less intrusive; the latter focuses the judges' intervention on a smaller number of more complex, and more contentious, cases, while involving both legal and non-legal professionals to bargain out-of-court agreements.

To compare how each jurisdiction organises professional responsibilities over family dissolutions, from processes to decisions, this research combines macro data, based on legal provisions and institutional features, and the ethnographic study of judges' and attorneys' work (Table 1). The three authors, along with several students and colleagues[5] in both jurisdictions, have collected a great deal of data: we have observed hundreds of hearings and meetings with lawyers and clients, interviewed about 90 professionals, and analysed numerous judicial records (connected with the hearings observations). These data were gathered in different courthouses and offices (law firms and legal aid offices), in rural as well as in urban settings, in order to vary both the social characteristics of litigants and the type of court operations.

Table 1: Research Materials

		France (2009–10; 2014)	Québec (2011–14)
Courthouses		5 *tribunaux de grande instance* (2 in the Paris area, 3 outside)	3 districts of the Superior Court (Montreal, Québec City and a rural area, Albanel)[6]
Interviews		20 judges	18 judges
		4 court clerks	3 court clerks
		22 attorneys	23 attorneys
Observations	Court hearings	330 cases	130 cases
	Meetings with lawyers and clients	24 cases	61 cases
	Judicial records	100	36

[5] This work was supported by Mission de Recherche Droit et Justice (2008–10); Commission Permanente de Coopération Franco-Québécoise (2011–13); Fonds Québécois de la Recherche sur la Société et la Culture ('Nouveaux Professeurs-Chercheurs' Program, 2011–14); Social Sciences and Humanities Research Council (Insight Program, 2012–15); and Agence Nationale de la Recherche (ANR-12-JSH1-003-01 & ANR-10-IDEX-0001-02-PSL*).

[6] The name of this place has been changed, along with those of the French jurisdictions, in order to protect the confidentiality of the participants, whose names are pseudonyms.

These data highlight two types of change that the trend towards private ordering leads to, regarding both professionals and clients.

1. Changes in family law and in judicial organisation have transformed the exposure of individuals' private issues in court. In both countries, intimacy, especially the causes of the marital breakdown, is less likely to be exposed in front of the judge than it used to be. But this general trend corresponds to very different transformations of legal processes in Québec and in France, especially when it comes to the potential withdrawal of judges from family cases. Lastly, such changes are not neutral: middle-class parents are less exposed to in-depth investigation of private issues in court than working-class and upper-class ones. Such class differences are greater in Québec than in France, owing to the greater variety of legal processes.
2. Changes in divorce adjudication have transformed professionals' jurisdictions[7] and roles. Although there is a trend towards discouraging people from litigating about intimate issues, they are not left to themselves when they do so. In Québec, lawyers strongly contribute to shaping how individuals' lives are discussed outside and inside the courts. In France, judges have a more visible part in this process, although this work also relies on the lawyers' cooperation.

COMMON AND DISPARATE TRENDS IN LEGAL PROCESSES

In Québec: Inside and Outside Courts

In Québec, the trend towards private ordering reflects two complementary changes: first, the rise of 'undisputed' divorce, meaning divorces in which spouses agree not to dispute over marital offences and reach an agreement about the consequences of their divorce; secondly, the decline of adjudication through the courts and the partial withdrawal of judges in family law cases.

The first trend is connected to the evolution of the federal regulations on divorce. The 1985 Divorce Act[8] allowed 'no-fault' divorce where spouses have been separated for one year. In 2008, no more than 6 per cent of divorces involved either adultery or physical or mental cruelty in Canada.[9] Such a decline in fault-based divorces implies that the causes of separation are seldom explained in judicial proceedings. The intimacy of marital relations is far less scrutinised than in the past. As well as this evolution in

[7] Abbott, A, *The System of Professions. An Essay on the Division of Expert Labor* (Chicago, University of Chicago Press, 1988).
[8] Divorce Act (R.S.C., 1985, c 3).
[9] Milan, 'Marital Status' (n 3).

family law, changes in family structures explain how family privacy—in particular the reasons why couples separate—is less likely to be discussed in the courtroom. Québec has the highest incidence of unmarried cohabitation in relation to married cohabitation in Western jurisdictions and as a result about half the judgments rendered by the Superior Court of Québec concern unmarried couples.[10] In such cases, provincial provisions—ie the Québec's Civil Code—determine that the reasons for separation are irrelevant, since judicial proceedings regard exclusively children—not former partners.

Those two legal and family trends are not peculiar to Québec province nor to Canada: several Western countries have experienced similar changes. However, concerning the concrete organisation of legal processes, Québec has devised its own way of dealing with the large family caseload, choosing to reduce adjudication through the court. This is quite different from the French way of regulating marital breakdowns. To understand this process, one should remember that, owing to the influence of the common law system, family hearings in Québec in disputed cases are adversarial. Because of litigants' and witnesses' testimonies and cross-examinations, they are quite long—from half a day to five days, according to our observations. Such substantive hearings lead to a deep exposure of family life in court. Besides, they are rather impractical in this era of widespread marital breakdown. The encouragement of Alternative Dispute Resolution can be considered a way to handle these issues in Québec.

A strong shift in practice has indeed been implemented over the last two decades. Contested hearings have become less frequent, and judges nowadays only hear a few selected cases according to the common law trial norms. Most proceedings end with a written agreement, which does not always imply direct intervention by the judiciary. To sum up, the Québec legal processes are designed so that judges hear few people. A number of policies have favoured the decline of adjudication through the courts. Québec province is well known for financing Alternative Dispute Resolution in family law, especially family mediation. Since 1997, its Code of Civil Procedure makes it compulsory for parents who file an application to attend an information session on mediation (renamed 'parenting after separation' in 2012), which is followed, on a voluntary basis, by meetings free of charge for up to five hours.[11] Mediation services are also accessible to people who have not yet filed a judicial motion, and these are now the main users of the mediation service. As a whole, half as many separating couples used mediation services as ex-partners who resorted to court in 2011.[12] The success rate of mediation is high (82 per cent of mediation reports that were sent to court

[10] *Système d'information et de gestion, Direction générale des services de justice et des registres* (Québec, Department of Justice, 2011).

[11] Statutes of Québec, 1997, c 42.

[12] About 12,000 couples attended mediation meetings, compared to about 28,000 family law motions filed at the Superior Court: *Système d'information et de gestion* (n 10).

in 2008).[13] This policy has played a major part in the decline of adjudicated solutions without threatening the lawyers' leadership in family cases. During the 1980s and the 1990s, mediation was mainly promoted by social workers and psychologists,[14] while the Bar was strongly opposed to compulsory mediation, fearful of losing part of its clientele. However, legal professionals have since then taken hold of this new activity: in 2012, 75 per cent of mediators were jurists (58 per cent lawyers, 17 per cent notaries).[15] Finally, since 2013, people who agree to revise a judgment on family matters can access legal services to write and send their agreement to court at a reduced fee, which is fixed by government.[16]

As a consequence of these various incentives to seek agreement, the overall number of judges' decisions in Québec started to fall from the middle of the 1990s (from 60,000 to 40,000 in 2010) and the number of divorce trials on merits scheduled in the Superior Court of Québec has declined by 72 per cent over the last 30 years (from 6800 in 1981 to 1880 in 2011).[17] As a result, the judges' role in family law has changed. They hear fewer litigants and specialise in contested cases. As Gérard Boyer, a 55-year-old male judge in the small community of Albanel, puts it:[18] 'It didn't work with the mediator; it didn't work with the lawyer, the conciliation process. And then they come to us—we are the last resort. We only get the files that couldn't be settled. Most cases get settled'.

When couples who aim to divorce file a joint motion including an agreement, the judge will mostly approve it without hearing them in court. Unmarried parents' agreements as well as consensual reviews of judgments do not require hearings either. Since 1997, even the approval of these agreements is delegated to other professionals, namely proto-notaries, who are employed by the Department of Justice.[19] This corresponds to the tendency towards a 'proliferation of subjudges'—ie workers with an intermediate position between clerks and judges—, already noted by Fiss in American Federal Courts.[20] Québec judges may rely on several other professionals to

[13] *Étude sur la qualité de la prestation de services et la satisfaction des personnes ayant obtenu un jugement en matière familiale à l'égard du service de médiation familiale* (Québec, Department of Justice, 2008) www.justice.gouv.qc.ca/francais/publications/rapports/pdf/etude-med-f.pdf.

[14] Another shift in family law, the implementation of provincial guidelines on child support, in 1997, has also helped those non-legal mediators to get involved in family law cases. Statutes of Québec, 1996, c 68.

[15] Ministère de la justice du Québec, *Note d'information concernant le programme de médiation familiale* (Québec, 2012).

[16] $529 shared among ex-partners for counsel and legal fees: Statutes of Québec, 2012, c 20.

[17] *Système d'information et de gestion* (n 10).

[18] Interview by E Biland and C Rainville (Albanel Court, June 2011).

[19] Divorce agreements (under federal provision) are the only ones that have to be approved by judges.

[20] Fiss, OM, 'The Bureaucratization of the Judiciary' (1983) 92 *The Yale Law Journal* 1442, 1463.

'take a heavy burden' off them.[21] As a result, in 2008, about half of child support orders were made by proto-notaries instead of judges.[22] Finally, starting in April 2014,[23] a new public service introduced a novel way to settle family law decisions. With the *Service administratif de rajustement des pensions alimentaires pour enfants* (SARPA), legal aid lawyers are entitled to recalculate most child support orders. The child support amount does not need to be recalculated in court any more. Only the first amount should be set down by court officials. Although the scope for these administrative orders is still limited compared to judicial orders, this last reform opens the way to diversion: some family law cases can be settled out-of-court—though not outside of law and intervention by legal professionals.

Compared to the French position, these policies look quite proactive, offering several new services to families. However, the main features of the Québec justice system, ie adjudication through the courts (which is expensive in money and time) are also affected by legal tradition and uses of the justice system. Because of the length of adversarial hearings, counsel and legal fees[24] are much higher in Québec than in France and delays to hearings on the merits are longer.[25] As in other common law countries, access to justice is then a major issue. The public funding of Alternative Dispute Resolution is a way to improve access to family law—rather than to the judiciary. From 1982 to 2005, income eligibility cut-offs for legal aid services were no longer indexed[26] so that lower middle-class couples were encouraged to use mediation services, owing to the cost of judicial proceedings. In fact, our observations of court hearings show that middle-class parents are seldom heard in adversarial trials, which mainly involve low-income parents (especially women) and well-off ones (especially men). Of the 21 hearings that lasted three hours or more, only two women and four men earned about the

[21] Lipsky, M, *Street Level Bureaucracy: Dilemmas of the Individual in Public Services* (New York, Russell Sage Foundation, 1980) 20.

[22] Biland, E, Gollac, S and Schütz G, *Les barèmes de pension au Canada: incidences sur le niveau des pensions et le travail des juges*, paper presented at the conference La Justice au 21e siècle (Paris, January 2014) 10–11.

[23] Statutes of Québec, 2012, c 20. The fee for this service is $275.

[24] Counsel fees for contested divorces are close to $10,000 on average for each spouse (as compared to $1500 for agreements): Todd, R, 'The going rate' June 2011, available at: www.canadianlawyermag.com. In France, fees for consensual divorce are about 500 Euros (about $750) for each partner. In contested divorces, the fees vary from 1800 Euros (about $2600) to 3500 Euros (about $5200), according to the lawyers we met in Dormont. The fee for filing a motion in family law is $129 in Québec (2012, G.O. 2, 5424) v about $46 (35 Euros) in France, with an exception for litigants eligible for legal aid (Decree no 2011-1202, 09/28/2011).

[25] According to the assistant to the senior associate chief justice, it can take up to two years to schedule a divorce trial on the merits in the courthouse of Montreal. In France, the average duration of family proceedings is about nine months: www.justice.gouv.fr/statistiques.html.

[26] Moreau, P, *Pour une plus grande accessibilité à la justice* (Québec Department of Justice, 2005) www.justice.gouv.qc.ca/francais/publications/rapports/pdf/aide-jur0505.pdf.

However, unlike legal aid cuts in other jurisdictions, major improvements in eligibility cut-offs have been made for the last three years: Règlement sur l'aide juridique, 2014, c 4, r 2.

average wage. Moreover, unequal couples—in which the male partner earns far more than the female one—are over-represented in such proceedings. So the trend towards private ordering is far from complete: intrusive trials still occur, and their likelihood depends on individuals' social and economic status. Changes in legal processes have affected professionals' services as well as inequalities among families, both on a gender and social basis.

In France: Courts for All

In France, too, consensual divorce has increased in recent years, contributing to the trend towards private ordering. But this change has not been accompanied by the same partial withdrawal of judges from family litigation as in Québec. The consensual divorce procedure, introduced in the French Civil Code in 1975, has allowed couples who so agree to divorce without mentioning fault. When litigants resort to this procedure, French family judges deal only with the consequences of their separation, and not with its causes. This has reduced the potential exposure of private matters in French courts.[27] Moreover, this trend has been strongly reinforced over the past decade. The proportion of fault divorces has continued to fall, from 42 per cent of divorces in 1996 to 37 per cent in 2004, and to only 8 per cent in 2011.[28] This is the result of the 2004 national reform, which made fault-divorces less attractive for litigants,[29] while a lighter and simpler procedure was created for consensual divorce. The renewed 'mutual consent' procedure is well known to be the cheapest way of obtaining a divorce in France as it allows both spouses to use the same lawyer in court. It is also the quickest way, with an average of only three months between the filing of the motion and the judgment.[30] In 2011, this procedure accounted for more than 57 per cent of all divorces,[31] compared to only 40 per cent in 1996.[32] In 2011, 39 per cent of decisions issued by family judges dealt with unmarried couples;[33] as in Québec, it is only in matters linked to the children (parental authority, child custody, child-support) that judges may intervene, which limits their insight into the causes and circumstances of unmarried couples' separations.

However, this trend towards private ordering of separations does not follow the same pattern of family litigation as in Québec. In France every case is still adjudicated and heard—very briefly—by a judge. With public funding

[27] Théry, I, *Le démariage. Justice et vie privée* (Paris, Odile Jacob, 1993).

[28] Prioux and Barbieri, 'L'évolution démographique récente en France' (n 3).

[29] Since 2004, it takes only two years of physical separation to get a divorce without the other spouse's consent, even if he or she is not recognised to be guilty of any fault, while it took six years before. Loi n°2004-439 du 26 mai 2004.

[30] Chaussebourg, L, Carrasco, V and Lermenier, A, *Le divorce, Rapport de la sous-direction de la Statistique et des Études* (Paris, Ministère de la Justice, 2009) 18.

[31] Prioux and Barbieri (n 3).

[32] Belmokhtar, Z, 'Divorces: une procédure à deux vitesses' [2012] *Infostats Justice* 117.

[33] Data from the French Department of Justice (2011).

of the justice system in the lower range among European states,[34] French justice policies since the 1990s have focused on speeding up adjudication in order to cope with the increasing caseload in certain kinds of litigation, for example in criminal courts.[35] In family courts, targets set by the Department of Justice and monitored by the President of each court also focus on the number of judgments issued yearly by judges and on delays between the filing of an application and the closing of a case. Judges are supposed to issue as many cases as they can over a period of time, which means that they have to shorten the length of hearings and of deliberations. The average length of the 330 hearings that we observed is as short as 18 minutes, and no hearing lasted more than one hour and a half.

This focus on the quantity of judgments is explained by the choice to keep every case under the judiciary's jurisdiction. Indeed, contrary to Québec, judges still hear at least once from all divorcing couples, and also all unmarried parents who file a motion relating to their children. Even couples resorting to consensual divorce who agree on all the outcomes of their separation are heard in court by a judge. This means that settled solutions have not been turned into written procedures, and that the path of delegation to 'sub-judges' has not been taken in France to cope with the heavy load of family litigation. The possibility of entrusting other professionals—notaries—with consensual divorces was discussed in 2007 but finally rejected.[36] In January 2014, a judge of the Court of Cassation (the French Supreme Court for private law) recommended that the Minister of Justice should allow court clerks to process 'mutual consent' divorces,[37] but this proposal has not been endorsed by political authorities. In fact, the Bar (considering that court work is essential to its professional prestige) opposed these two proposals; so far its view that the judiciary's intervention is necessary for fairness and the protection of the weakest parties has been accepted.

Finally, out-of-court dispute resolution is far less encouraged than in Québec. Mediators seldom contribute to the building of agreements,[38] being involved in only 3 per cent of the 330 cases that we observed in court.

[34] Commission for the Efficiency of Justice, *Report on European Judicial Systems—Edition 2014 (2012 data): Efficiency and Quality of Justice* 25, available at: www.coe.int/t/dghl/cooperation/cepej/evaluation/2014/Rapport_2014_en.pdf.

[35] Vauchez, A, 'Le chiffre dans le "gouvernement" de la justice' (2008) 125 *Revue française d'administration publique* 111; Christin, A, *Comparutions immédiates: Enquête sur une pratique judiciaire* (Paris, La Découverte, 2008); Bastard, B, Delvaux, D, Mouhanna, C and Schoenaers, F, 'Maîtriser le temps? L'accélération du traitement judiciaire du divorce en France et en Belgique' [2014] *Temporalités* 19, available at: http://temporalites.revues.org/2795.

[36] Guinchard, S (ed), *L'ambition raisonnée d'une justice apaisée, rapport de la Commission sur la Répartition des contentieux remis au Garde des Sceaux* (Paris, La documentation française, 2008).

[37] Delmas-Goyon, P, *Le juge du 21ème siècle. Un citoyen acteur, une équipe de justice, rapport à la garde des sceaux* (2013) www.justice.gouv.fr/publication/rapport_dg_2013.pdf.

[38] Bastard, B, 'Family Mediation in France: a New Profession Has Been Established, but Where are the Clients?' (2010) 32 *Journal of Social Welfare and Family Law* 135.

The differential cost of accessing justice in court probably makes mediation services less attractive in France than in Québec. Although disputed divorces are also likely to generate higher counsel fees in France, the cases involving unmarried parents or already divorced parents who want to establish and revise judgments on child support or custody can access court with almost no direct cost for the litigants, as no lawyer is necessary to file and defend such motions. On the other hand, clients have to pay for mediation services, unless they are eligible for legal aid. These multiple factors account for a striking quantitative trend: contrary to their counterparts in Québec, in recent years French family judges have issued an increasing number of decisions, rising from 322,000 in 2004 to 376,000 in 2013.[39] Their average caseload is also much heavier: in the French courthouses that we studied, each family judge deals annually with 885 new family cases. In comparison, each judge of the Superior Court in Québec issues on average 170 decisions relating to family litigation. Even if family cases usually account for only half of their workload, the quantitative gap is substantial compared to France.

Because every case leads to a judge's intervention, the social polarisation observed in Québec between litigants who go to court and those who do not is not observed as such in France. The judiciary hear middle-class, working-class and upper-class couples. However, the individuals' social background affects the type of procedure they use. The middle classes are over-represented in consensual divorce procedures, whereas the working classes are more likely to resort to disputed than to consensual divorce, and are more visible in non-divorce cases (Table 2).

Table 2: Litigants' social background according to each judicial proceeding

	Working-class Men/Women (%)	Middle-class Men/Women (%)	Upper middle Men/Women (%)	Other status Men/Women (%)
Mutual consent divorce (N=110)	39/56	33/27	18/14	10/3
Contested divorce (N=110)	63/60	10/7	15/12	12/21
Unmarried or already divorced (N=176)	54/53	17.5/13	13/12	15.5/22

Source: Database of 396 cases selected randomly among the cases closed in 2007 in the four French courts studied by our research team.

[39] Sous-direction de la statistique et des études, French Department of Justice: www.justice.gouv.fr/statistiques.html.

Because undisputed proceedings are given priority by the courts, working-class couples experience a longer delay from the filing of the motion to the judgment. In the context of the French objective of short delay, their access to justice is less effective than that of middle-class couples. Differences in procedures also have consequences for the way litigants' privacy is exposed in court. Working-class couples, who are more often engaged in disputed cases than middle classes, are also the main targets of social inquiries ordered by family judges.[40]

To conclude, two differences between Québec and France can be seen with ambivalent consequences for privacy in the family court. French judges are still entrusted with all motions filed by ex-partners. Consequently, they are not specialised in major issues involving typical litigants. However, this does not mean that French judges are more likely to prevent the private ordering of separations. Because of the brevity and style of the hearings, the potential for in-depth examination of cases is more limited than in Québec for the most disputed cases, as we shall show below.

CHANGES IN PROFESSIONAL JURISDICTIONS AND ROLES

Whereas it is necessary to analyse institutional features in considering the various shifts towards private ordering, the ethnographic study of courtrooms and lawyers' offices is useful for an in-depth understanding of professional roles and jurisdictions. The relations between lawyers and judges vary greatly from one jurisdiction to another, leading to different ways of dealing with people's private lives. In Québec, this is largely bounded by lawyers' work outside and inside courts. In the French inquisitorial system, judges usually have more leeway to decide how far litigants' privacy will be discussed, and mostly limit its exposure owing to their own time constraints.

In Québec: Marital Breakdowns Without Use of the Court?

In Québec, lawyers play a major part in encouraging clients not to go to court. First, they disapprove of those who fight over what they consider to be minor issues, such as small amounts of child support, underlining the cost

[40] Minoc, J, *Évaluer des mœurs. L'enquête sociale et l'expertise médico-psychologique dans le traitement judiciaire des séparations conjugales*, mémoire de Master (2012) 2 PDI, ENS/EHESS.

of judicial proceedings. As Sylvie Lavergne, a 35-year-old non-specialised female lawyer, practising in the Albanel district asserted:[41]

> People don't have a lot of money. Even so, they want to fight. So we try to explain to them that sometimes to save $100 of child support per year, if they give it to us, it's not any better. We try to make them understand that it is in the best interest of their children.

Secondly, even when the issues at stake are considered more substantial, they warn their clients about the exposure of privacy, as well as the emotional burden of hearings and the uncertainty of the judicial outcome. Louise Lafrénière, a female lawyer from Québec City with more than 30 years of experience, described how she persuades her clients to settle in order to preserve their family life:[42]

> Sometimes we settle because the family could explode. (…) We really draw the picture, we say: 'Going to court, we have a chance to lose, we have a chance to win, we have a chance of being in the middle. On the other side we are offered X dollars to settle. So to avoid war and to avoid losing, we may not have the maximum, but let's go for something in the middle'. We realize that it helps the families a lot.

Thus lawyers play their part in the development of Alternative Dispute Resolution, putting forward the benefits of a settlement for their clients. Most of the attorneys we met estimate the proportion of out-of-court settlements as between 75 and 80 per cent of their cases.

As Darbyshire observed in English family courts,[43] judges are also involved in this process. Apart from trials, they encounter parties in order to make or to extend interim orders. Those simple hearings last from five minutes to three hours, according to our observations, and are not adversarial: litigants usually do not speak, but their lawyers make representations. In such cases, judges encourage separating couples to use opportunities for alternative conflict resolution as their case proceeds. As lawyers, judges make litigants aware that a trial is costly in terms of both money and time. Justice Gabriel Forest, a 48-year-old male judge, explained to divorced parents (the father was a truck-driver with a limited income) who wanted to challenge a previous decision on alimony for their three teenage daughters that he disapproved of the parents' persistent disagreement:

> You have to try to talk to each other to avoid going to court. With your yearly income, you can't afford to go to court. I think it is a shame. (…) Put your pride aside and talk to each other, or your legal bills are going to mount up.[44]

[41] Interview by M Mille and H Zimmermann (March 2013).

[42] Interview by E Biland and M Mille (February 2013).

[43] Darbyshire, P, *Sitting in Judgment: The Working Lives of Judges* (Oxford, Hart Publishing, 2011) 267–69.

[44] Hearing at the Albanel Court, observed by E Biland and C Rainville (June 2011).

Such examples illustrate that lawyers and judges, when presented with a case in its early stages, always have in mind the potential trial it may result in. As McEwan, Mather and Maiman pointed out 20 years ago in the US,[45] lawyers' practice is still based on a reference to trial as a possible avenue of family disputes. Lawyers anticipate the likely outcomes of a trial to direct clients as to a particular course, whether adjudicated or not. For example, Denise Mourneau is a female lawyer in her sixties with more than 30 years of practice in family law in Albanel. She met for the first time with a woman in her thirties who was asked by her ex-partner for a change in the custody and in the school of their 8-year-old daughter.[46] She explained to this new client what her options were in reference to an adjudicated solution. According to her, they should rather find an agreement with the father because judges do not like to rule on the choice of a school, giving her client an example where parents ended up in court arguing about this matter without a good outcome for either of them.

As a whole, lawyers do their own 'triaging' with the client to evaluate each case and its chances of being settled. When discussions with clients lead to a court-oriented strategy, they intervene by choosing which aspects of their client's life will be discussed during the hearing.

During a day-long meeting, Marie-Josée Bénard,[47] a Montreal lawyer in her forties specialising in wealthy clients, prepared for an emergency procedure called by the client's wife to modify their former agreement to share their two children's custody. Re-writing the affidavit, this lawyer decided to mention 'the troubled times' her client had been through after the break up, rather than stating that he indeed had had a nervous breakdown. This investment manager in a large company, in his thirties, read numerous text messages and emails sent by his ex wife and showed several children's pictures, but his lawyer decided not use them in the proceedings. Thus she acted as a filter, selecting which aspects of her client's life she would develop (like his involvement as a hockey-coach in his son's school) and which she would minimise (his personal difficulties).

Besides clients and lawyers' characteristics (wealthy clients are more likely than low- and middle-income clients to afford a trial; some lawyers are more court-oriented than others), the kind of topics ex-partners are arguing about matters in the kind of proceeding they experience. Disputes about family patrimony and child physical custody are the most likely not to settle before the trial. Such issues are not frequent. Disputes over patrimony amounted to 7 per cent of the 130 cases we have observed in courts; those about child custody constituted 14 per cent, but they account for all the 22 trials that we attended (15 disputes on child custody, nine disputes of patrimony). Their likelihood of going to trial is linked to the severity of the issue

[45] McEwen, C, Mather, L and Maiman, R, 'Lawyers, Mediation, and the Management of Divorce Practice' (1994) 28 *Law & Society Review* 149, 156.

[46] Observed by M Mille (May 2013).

[47] Observed by M Mille (September 2013).

that both professionals and families acknowledge and also to their coincidence with serious issues in the individuals' lives. Three-quarters of child custody disputes that we observed included accusations of abuse, which were regularly associated with other problems, such as abuse of alcohol or drugs, as well as parents' or children's illness or disability.

Because of the adversarial proceedings and the very nature of the allegations, those trials are quite intrusive, exposing the litigants' privacy to the court. Oral testimonies (lawyers' questioning of litigants and witnesses) and written documents (bills, pictures, emails, Facebook profiles etc) which are regularly added to the file, are all narratives about family life, on which judges have to arbitrate. Since the legal culture of common law countries, and especially the adversarial procedure, requires a passive role from judges and devotes a more active one to lawyers,[48] the latter play a key part in displaying family life in court.[49] They typically ask their clients to detail their daily routine with their children in order to confirm or to rebut that they are 'good' parents. During cross-examinations, litigants are likely to be asked about difficult events in family life (violent episodes, illness, substance abuse) that may make them cry. However, lawyers may choose not to address some topics and may even counter their client's will to expose them, because they do not believe in the allegations and want to preserve credibility in front of the court or because they are not sufficiently prepared to address such topics. Hence the way privacy is exposed during trials reveals power relations between professionals and litigants, and between professionals. Although judges speak far less than their French counterparts during hearings, they regularly reframe the lawyers' examinations. This often concerns the way the latter ask litigants about their private life. When lawyers argue, judges decide whether the lawyers' strategy on privacy exposure is accurate or appropriate. They are entitled to decide between the two lawyers' positions, and therefore to define the extent and limits of individuals' scrutiny. In this example, a judge sides with an experienced lawyer to prohibit the evocation of sexual matters that a novice attorney wants to underline.

At the Québec City Court, another hearing opposes a young African male lawyer (ML) against an experienced Québec female lawyer (WL), who counsel a man and a woman of African origin respectively.[50] Paul Emond, a 58-year-old male judge, regularly scolds the male lawyer, considering that his questions are inappropriate:

[48] Resnik, J, 'Managerial Judges' (1982) 96 *Harvard Law Review* 374.

[49] Although it is possible to go to family court without a lawyer, in practice, this is rare. Among the 130 cases that our research team observed, only one quite short case (20 minutes) did not involve any lawyer. In more than one case out of two (55%), each former partner was represented by a lawyer.

[50] Observed by G Schütz and C Rainville (September 2011).

ML [to the woman]: Why did you have a polygamous spouse? WL [shocked]: Mr. Justice! Look, it's not relevant! It is Québec, Québec laws are applicable to the situation! Judge [to ML]: I'd like to avoid this trial turning into an exercise in mutual satisfaction. The objective of this trial is the best interests of children. We are in Canada, the law prohibits polygamy. Ms. is not remarried, so the question of marital life is superfluous. I understand your question aims to intimidate Ms., but this it is not the objective.

The promotion of undisputed divorce and of Alternative Dispute Resolution has undoubtedly changed the role and the jurisdiction of judges and lawyers, giving the latter a crucial role in the promotion of settled agreement between ex spouses and in the definition of ways and places in which private issues are exposed. Trials are less frequent, partly because they lead to a thorough examination of people's lives. When they do occur, judges monitor how lawyers investigate litigants' privacy. In contrast, in France, this is less closely scrutinised, partly because every case goes to court. And, because of the inquisitorial system, judges play a more direct part in examining individuals' privacy.

In France: Frontline Judges and Trial Lawyers

Indeed, despite the trend towards private ordering, a court hearing in France is still a mandatory step in every family case, and remains the core of divorce professionals' practice. French judges hold a frontline position in this massive quantity of litigation, since they hear all motions filed in family law. During these court-oriented proceedings, the distribution of roles between judges and lawyers is quite different from what we observed in Québec, with consequences for the way they handle the exposure of private issues.

Time-allocation is a permanent concern for French judges. Their heavy caseload and targets imposed on them by their hierarchy means that they are constantly careful to maintain a quick rhythm during hearings and when deliberating.[51] Mathilde Tabares, a female judge in her late thirties, sitting in the large court of a French city, described her function by putting the emphasis on the quantitative targets she has to meet:

> We have to pay a constant attention to our organisation, we are like stock-managers [...] there is a statistical pressure from the hierarchy. If I was falling too much behind my targets, I would be summoned by the President of the Court.[52]

According to our observations, judges hear on average nine cases in half a day and they have to shorten the time of their deliberations along with

[51] Bastard et al, 'Maîtriser le temps?' (n 35).
[52] Interview by E Biland and R Audot (March 2010).

the quantitative indicators implemented by the Department of Justice. This break-neck speed is first made possible by the form of proceedings in French courts. Under the inquisitorial system that characterises the civil law tradition, the judge, and not the lawyers, leads the hearing. Every hearing starts with the judge recalling the situation of litigants sitting in front of him or her, after which only the judge allows them or their lawyers to speak. They can also cut short litigants, and even lawyers, when they take too long to present their arguments. Although the intensity of judges' interventions varies between individuals, with some remaining more silent and neutral and others intervening more frequently, they have more latitude to control the debates than their Canadian counterparts. Consequently, French judges have the means to quicken the pace when they wish or have to do so.

Without doubt, 'mutual consent' divorces are the proceedings where the judges can work quickly. During hearings that are on average eight minutes, they clearly have a rubber stamping attitude. Judges almost never reject an agreement reached by the litigants,[53] even if, in some cases, their short encounter with the litigants leads them to suspect that the agreement is fragile or unfair. Judges seldom go counter to the private ordering of consensual separations and it is clearly outside the court where the main decisions are made in such cases. The lawyers' work is then decisive in mutual consent procedures, especially when spouses share the same counsel.

In disputed divorces, the proceeding also encourages the shift towards private ordering. Moreover, the judges' behaviour tends to restrict the matters that are likely to be discussed thoroughly in court. Following the 2004 reform, all disputed divorces start with a 'conciliation hearing' in front of a judge. At this stage, spouses and lawyers are not supposed to discuss the causes of their separation; they must only testify whether or not they agree to obtain a 'no-fault' divorce. First, judges strongly encourage the spouses to sign the document by which they relinquish any possibility of a further discussion of conjugal offences. Secondly, in a more or less abrupt way, they tend to cut short the litigants when they try to talk about the circumstances of the separation at this stage of the proceedings. For example, during her one-to-one encounter with Justice Pierre Terreau,[54] a retired female farmer confirmed she wanted a divorce. At that moment, she took a piece of paper and said: 'I have prepared something to explain the reasons for the separation'. But the judge cut her short: 'Today, I am not supposed to study the motives; it is not the place'. The woman put her paper back in her bag: 'I understand'.

[53] Of the 52 'mutual consent' divorce cases that we observed in court, the judge turned down only one agreement.

[54] Hearing at the Marjac Court, observed by E Biland and P de Larminat (February 2009).

The refusal of this judge is linked to the legal definition of this conciliation hearing's purpose, but also to the necessity of getting through the list of the many cases scheduled for the day. As Pierre Terreau put it in interview:

> If it is 2 pm and I still have 10 cases to hear, I will tell them to stop immediately, that it is not possible. Otherwise, I let them say the big thing they want to say, and then I say 'Listen…'. When I saw her with 3 or 4 pages, I had to intervene immediately, because, afterwards, it would have been even more difficult to cut her short.[55]

Once through this first hearing, the further steps of French divorce proceedings are entirely written. Consequently, there will be no other moment when this woman will be allowed to talk about the circumstances of her separation in court. Contrary to the situation in Québec, litigants do not testify in court; they are not cross-examined by the opposing lawyer. It is only through written statements and counsel's conclusions that judges make further decisions. It is rare for lawyers to plead on the merits in front of judges during divorce hearings. As a result, the exposure of private issues linked to the circumstances of the separation is potentially more limited than in Québec. More generally, the form of French procedures and the judges' lack of time limit the attention devoted in French courts to issues between the spouses and not related to children. Also the question of fault and litigation about patrimony is handled in a limited and mostly written way. At the time of the 'conciliation hearing', the division of patrimony as well as the potential compensation of the poorer spouse in economically unequal couples is not a relevant issue. It is again in the written part of the proceeding that these questions are handled. Moreover, judges do not deal directly with patrimony division; they entrust it first to notaries, implicitly encouraging litigants to reach private agreements outside the court.[56]

However, as in Québec, disputes linked to children are the most likely to be more thoroughly investigated in French courts. But such hearings are far shorter than in Canada. Even when both parents are represented, they last 27 minutes on average. Whatever the legal process chosen by litigants and the matter at stake, judges lead the hearing, and use hearing-time sparingly. How they set limits to privacy exposure even in cases involving children's best interests can be seen from the example of a case about the custody of an 11-year-old girl, whose parents had been divorced for several years.[57] She had been living with her father since 2007, when her mother had an accident leaving her a quadriplegic. In March 2010, Coline Bouilly,

[55] By E Biland and P de Larminat (February 2009).

[56] It is only after the divorce that former spouses can return to the court if they still disagree on this issue.

[57] Hearing at the Valin Court, observed by M Mille and J Minoc (March 2010).

a female judge in her early forties, was presented with a motion filed by the mother, who claimed that the living conditions at the father's house were inadequate, and asked for custody. The hearing lasted an hour, which is 'long' according to Justice Bouilly. It was indeed one of the six longest of our 330 observations. Despite this unusual length, the arguments of the mother's lawyer and of the father, who had no lawyer, were strictly managed by the judge. She played an active part in this sensitive case without losing time, and avoided hearing details of their family history that she deemed unnecessary. After a short introduction by the judge, the mother's lawyer, a young and talkative woman in her thirties, presented the case, a 'peculiar one', for a few minutes, and challenged the conclusions of a previous social inquiry which gave a positive perspective of the child's living conditions at her father's house. Describing the lack of hygiene and of proper food at the father's house, the lawyer argued that, despite her heavy handicap, her client was able to take better care of her daughter. The judge interrupted the lawyer's speech several times to remind her that the social inquiry, which was 'very recent' and was conducted 'in depth', contradicted her arguments. Before the lawyer had finished her representations, the judge took control of the debates and started questioning the mother directly about her ability to take care of her daughter, before turning to the father. When the man started describing the acute family conflicts which followed the mother's accident, the judge strictly advised him not to recall the whole family history. 'We start from 2009, with the claims that you don't pay the rent, that your flat is dirty, that you do not take your daughter to the doctor, that you do not give her enough food'. On all these points, Coline Bouilly did not let the father talk freely, but went through a list of concrete questions to which the man answered with one or two sentences. These answers obviously confirmed the judge's impression that the child was not in danger with her father and, when the mother expressed her wish to add some more details about the precarious economic situation of the man, the judge answered: 'I think I have already many elements'.

From this example, we see that the leading part French judges play in the hearing as well as their time-constraints dictate the exposure of intimate details in court. On the whole, they play a more active and visible role than their Canadian counterparts to limit the exposure of litigants' private issues during trial hearings, and French lawyers have less leeway to decide which matters deserve a deeper investigation in court.[58] To sum up, court adjudication of marital breakdowns does not necessarily imply a strong control over privacy and is not incompatible with private ordering.

[58] Since the study in lawyers' offices has just begun in France, our analysis is not yet complete regarding their role outside courts.

CONCLUSIONS

Certainly the rise in 'undisputed' family procedures has changed the adjudication of marital breakdowns in both France and Québec. Judges are less involved than they used to be in decision-making. However, our comparative study demonstrates a nuanced response. First, changes in adjudication have been more important in Québec than in France. To that extent, comparative socio-legal research provides insight into the importance of national paths in judicial reforms. Moreover, out-of-court dispute resolution is not synonymous with self-decision: lawyers (as well as mediators in Québec) play a great part in designing agreements and, therefore, they frame individual expectations. Besides, the withdrawal of the judiciary is subject to limitations. When the child's 'best interests' (and/or large amounts of money) are considered to be at stake, privacy is most likely to be exposed and controlled, in both jurisdictions. Finally, the entanglement of negotiations between ex-partners and between professionals and separating couples is not neutral as to social and gender inequalities. Our in-depth study of French family justice has shown that when they approve private negotiations, judges tend to acknowledge and make enforceable decisions that may be unequal between men and women.[59] How can we ensure equality when priority is given to negotiations between individuals and when the judiciary and/or the litigants do not have enough resources to guarantee the protection of the most vulnerable, usually women and children? In two different ways, each jurisdiction is facing this dilemma.

[59] Le Collectif Onze, *Au tribunal des couples. Enquête sur des affaires familiales* (Paris, Odile Jacob, 2013).

6

Family Justice in Bulgaria: The Old System and New Demands

VELINA TODOROVA

THE WORLD OF justice in Bulgaria has been dominated for the last 15 years by the rhetoric of reform. Despite the efforts presented in strategy papers,[1] statutory amendments[2] and institutional and individual changes,[3] the reforms to the judicial system remain incomplete.[4] The system constantly generates uncertainty, disgrace and high levels of distrust that damage the principle of the rule of law. Above and beyond these national efforts, ongoing reform has become a constant issue of concern for the EU over the past eight years. To address the need for real and profound judicial reform in Bulgaria a special tool was constructed: the Mechanism for Cooperation and Verification (CVM) invoked by the European Commission (EC) on the accession of Bulgaria to the European Union on 1 January 2007.[5]

[1] Two strategies have been adopted to provide paths to reform: the first lasted from 2003 until 2008. The next, beginning in June 2010, aims to continue the reform in the new context of full membership for Bulgaria in the European Union. In addition, other strategic papers such as the National Strategy for the Child (2008–18) and the Concept for Public Policy on Justice for Children (2011) strongly recommend the establishment of a Family Court. All strategies are available in Bulgarian at the site of the Ministry of Justice: https://mjs.bg/107/.

[2] Important amendments were made in 2006–07 to the Constitution related to the management of the judicial system. A Judicial Power Act was passed in 2007.

[3] The Supreme Judicial Council was created under the Judicial Power Act to represent the system, to communicate with other powers and to manage the system (art 16).

[4] Neither of the reform strategies is realistic or concrete: see a speech by Y Grozev at the forum 'Rule of Law: a Major Principle for a Sustainable Business Environment' organised by the President of the Republic of Bulgaria on 8 July 2014; more at: www.legalworld.bg/37536.ogromnoto-nedoverie-kym-sydebnata-sistema-e-zaradi-nachina-po-kojto-tia-se-upravliava.html. The Minister of Justice, on resigning on 23 July 2014, declared that judicial reform had never been an actual political priority: https://mjs.bg/117/5197/.

[5] Commission Decision of 13 December 2006 establishing a mechanism for cooperation and verification of progress in Bulgaria to address specific benchmarks in the areas of judicial reform and the fight against corruption and organised crime [2006] OJ L 354/56. The legal basis for the CVM, as a measure against Bulgaria for not implementing its commitments in the

In such a context, not surprisingly, the family justice system has not been identified as a separate issue of concern except for the long-lasting debate among experts about the need to establish a specialised Family Court. Nevertheless, traditional family justice is experiencing change as a result of being part of a justice system undergoing transformation. Financial constraints, however, have not so far been a major concern. As a result of the ongoing transformative efforts, governments have been rather generous in the provision of public funding to the justice system.[6] The pressure comes instead from other factors:

— legislative changes that resulted in expanding family justice to include private and public law cases as well as in modifying some principles of dispensing justice to families and children (routinising proceedings and promotion of mediation); and
— administrative changes that resulted in the establishment of a separate governing structure following constitutional amendments: a Supreme Judicial Council (SJC) empowered to manage the system and to reach certain benchmarks imposed by the CVM (to improve the integrity of magistrates, management of caseloads and career development in the profession).

As a result, family justice is becoming increasingly underestimated and so are the judges dealing with family cases. Family law and family cases are thought to be of little complexity and thus of limited value in the career prospects of judges. Experienced, motivated and able family judges are therefore pushed towards working on other areas of legal disputes considered to be more prestigious and advantageous for them—eg contract law and commercial law. The enthusiasm for mediation changes the focus from the delivery of justice to enhancing private ordering. The legal aid system is immature and functions under constant fiscal constraints. This chapter explores the evidence of change in the family justice system that appears to come from both statutory innovations and from the management of the judicial system.

area of Freedom, Security and Justice, is art 38 of the Accession Act for Bulgaria: 'If there are serious shortcomings ... in Bulgaria in the transposition of *Acquis communautaire* relating to mutual recognition in the area of criminal law ... and ... civil matters..., the Commission may, until the end of a period up to three years after accession, ... take appropriate measures ... These measures may take the form of temporary suspension of the application of relevant provisions ... in the relations of Bulgaria and any other Member state.... The measures shall be lifted when the shortcomings are remedied. They may however be applied beyond the period of three years as long as the shortcomings persist'.

[6] A trend coming to an end: on resigning on 23 July 2014, the Minister of Justice questioned the financial appetite of the system declaring future funding conditional on visible reforms and accountability. This view was supported by the active NGOs: http://legalworld.bg/38019.oshte-dve-organizacii-napuskat-grajdanskiia-syvet-kym-vss.html.

FACTORS AND TRAJECTORIES FOR CHANGE

Any current commentator on the Bulgarian judicial system cannot avoid the influence of the CVM. It is an instrument of the EU Commission designed for Bulgaria (and Romania) in order to structure and discipline their judicial reforms. The overall objective is to ensure the rule of law in both countries. Initially the tool was planned to last for a period of three years. However, eight years later it is still in place. Briefly, the CVM sets out benchmarks[7] to provide a framework for monitoring progress in the area of justice.[8] It functions on the basis of periodic reports (14 so far, the last one dated January 2015) produced by the Commission. Each of them contains critical comments and proposals for future steps. However, despite some positive outcomes, the CVM has not proved to be an effective tool for overall reform.

The CVM has, however, been effective in placing the issue of justice reform high (but not at the top) of the political agenda, thus pushing forward several legislative, institutional and administrative changes.[9] Being an instrument for political pressure, the CVM is popular. Society has however remained sceptical because the reform has not achieved the desired results: transparency and objectivity in the management of the system by the SJC including the career development and promotion of judges, the integrity of magistrates, the length of proceedings and the quality and the

[7] The benchmarks are: (1) Adopt constitutional amendments removing any ambiguity regarding the independence and accountability of the judicial system. (2) Ensure a more transparent and efficient judicial process by adopting and implementing a new Judicial System Act and the new Civil Procedure Code. Report on the impact of these new laws and of the penal and administrative procedure codes, notably on the pre-trial phase. (3) Continue the reform of the judiciary in order to enhance professionalism, accountability and efficiency. Evaluate the impact of this reform and publish the results annually. (4) Conduct and report on professional, non-partisan investigations into allegations of high-level corruption. Report on internal inspections of public institutions and on the publication of assets of high-level officials. (5) Take further measures to prevent and fight corruption, in particular at the borders and within local government. (6) Implement a strategy to fight organised crime, focusing on serious crime, money laundering as well as on the systematic confiscation of assets of criminals. Report on new and ongoing investigations, indictments and convictions in these areas.

[8] 'To ensure that measures are taken to provide assurance to Bulgarians and to the other Member States that administrative and judicial decisions and practices in these areas in Bulgaria are in line with the rest of the EU': see *Report from the Commission to the European Parliament and the Council on Bulgaria's Progress on Accompanying Measures Following Accession*, Brussels, 27 June 2007 COM (2007) 377.

[9] The EC defines the objectives of the reform as: 'This involves making certain fundamental changes, which takes time and also requires broad political support across the political spectrum as well as in society at large. At the same time, these changes are an indispensable investment in the future of Bulgaria—an effective administrative and judicial system is necessary for sound public finances and well rooted socio-economic development. It is also necessary to enable Bulgaria to play its full role as a member of the EU in areas such as justice and home affairs'. *Report from the Commission to the European Parliament and the Council on Progress in Bulgaria under the CVM* {SEC (2011) 967 final} Brussels, 20 July 2011 COM (2011) 459.

predictability of court decisions.[10] Thus, the level of confidence in the justice system remains very low compared with other Member States—only 20 per cent say they trust the national judiciary, compared to an average of 48 per cent for EU25 in 2008.[11] Public perceptions of the judiciary have fallen according to similar research carried out in 2012: only 12 per cent of respondents consider the system as effective.[12] The reasons suggested are: corruption, political influence, cumbersome and incomprehensible procedures and lack of transparency; in short, the justice system is perceived as corrupt and ineffective. According to the same research the judges differ in their opinion about the reasons for the ineffectiveness of the system. They blame the dependence of the system on the executive power, the low quality of legislation, the management of caseloads, human resources policies, the capacity building of judges, and court administration and the development of e-justice.

Both the CVM and national justice reform strategies address all these issues. This chapter will discuss in more detail those relevant to the changes in family justice only. The first issue as set out as a benchmark in the CVM relates to the *quality of procedural legislation*: '2. *Ensure a more transparent and efficient judicial process by adopting and implementing a new Judicial System Act (JSA) and the new Civil Procedure Code (CPC)*'. The concern is both the structural reform of the judicial system and a new litigation framework not so much in civil but rather in criminal justice because it is linked to other benchmarks addressing the fight against corruption and organised crime. These are the main concerns of the EU Commission. The need for enhancing the quality of justice and achieving European standards of justice and the rule of law is a benchmark in the national strategy too. To reach it, the document focuses on access to justice, application of the standards of the European Convention on Human Rights and the promotion of mediation as a type of accessible, cheap and conflict-restraining method for dispute resolution.

[10] The effectiveness of the CVM has been recently problematised by Bulgarian scholars. Their research proves that CVM has not accelerated progress towards the rule of law but has rather resulted in steps back in the development of the Bulgarian judicial system. The main reason is suggested to be inadequacy between the monitoring tool and the Bulgarian milieu. The national circumstances summarised as 'specifics of the Bulgarian civilisation process' hamper the rule of law in becoming a stable societal feature. It is proposed that the CVM should be adjusted to fit the Bulgarian context; see Dimitrov, G, Haralampiev, K, Stoychev, S and Metodieva, L, *CVM—A Shared Political Irresponsibility between the EU Commission and the Bulgarian Governments. (Outcomes from Analytical Monitoring of the July Reports on Bulgaria)* (Sofia, University 'Kl Okhridski' Press, 2014). Also Ivanova, I, 'Five Years CVM: A Time for Judgment' (2012) 8 *Advokatski pregled* 31.

[11] Alegre, S, Ivanova, I and Denis-Smith, D, *Safeguarding the Rule of Law in an Enlarged EU: The Cases of Bulgaria and Romania* (CEPS Special Report/April 2009) 24.

[12] *Citizens, Clients and Judges about the Judicial Reform, Quality of the Service and Justice in Bulgaria*: Research of the 'Judicial System Development Programme' and Alpha Research Sociological Agency (2012) 10 *Advokatski pregled* 3. Available also at: www.prss-bg.org.

The second direction for the reforms targets the *internal problems of the judicial system:* its structure, management, workload and human resources policies, as a whole: the *capacity* of the system to deliver justice. Since the attempt to deal with these issues in a fragmented way failed, the Constitution was amended and a new JSA was enacted in 2007.[13] The new framework allowed for going further with the next benchmark set out in the CVM: '3. *Continue the reform of the judiciary in order to enhance professionalism, accountability and efficiency. Evaluate the impact of this reform and publish the results annually*'. This target was interpreted by some NGOs active in the promotion of judicial reform by creating additional tasks as to 'release the judicial system from routine and administrative activities as well as from light cases that need little legal knowledge in order to leave a space for important disputes that consist of valuable legal consideration'.[14] It should be noted that family cases perfectly fit the definition of being 'light and easy' in terms of legal thought, as described by the Chief of one of the busiest courts. As a way to do this the NGOs have proposed 'to develop and enlarge the scope of application of ADR, including mediation; and the creation of motivation for the parties to refer to mediation'. Another short-term objective has been projected to enhance the capacity of public administration to dispense legal information to citizens especially as far as access to social services is concerned. The view is that it could restrain the development of related legal disputes. NGOs have raised another point on how to ensure public support for the high level of public expenditure on the judicial system.[15] The first proposal is to increase the efficiency of the system of management and the second is to raise revenues from court fees. As a measure to avoid limiting access to justice it is proposed to broaden the space for ADR in the majority of cases and to improve access to initial legal aid and legal information for citizens.[16]

The above quotations demonstrate that judicial reform in Bulgaria does not have a clear leadership. Various actors are involved, motivated by their own interests and embedded in their strategies. The CVM articulates

[13] Thus the first benchmark of the CVM was reached—'1. Adopt constitutional amendments removing any ambiguity regarding the independence and accountability of the judicial system'.

[14] Open Society Institute, *Evaluation of the Implementation of the Strategy for the Reform of the Judicial System in Bulgaria, 2003–2008* (Sofia, Legal Programme, 2009) www.osi.bg 70–77.

[15] The share of expenditure for justice from the total state budget has increased considerably. While in 1998 it was 0.69%, in 2010–11 it rose to 2.11%, which is 3 times the former level. For the same period (1998–2011) the public costs for the judicial system increased by 800%, compared to health care (269%) and social expenditure (285%): Open Society Institute *The Price of Justice in Bulgaria: Assessment of the Public Expenditure on Justice and Home Affairs, 2009–2010* (Sofia, Legal Programme, 2011) available at: www.osi.bg 14–15. Bulgaria is leading among Member States on justice costs as a share of GDP: 7%, compared to: 6% in the UK, 3% in Sweden and 2% in Denmark (Eurostat, 2008)—see above, *The Price of Justice in Bulgaria* 35.

[16] ibid 136.

the general framework for ensuring compliance of the Bulgarian justice system with EU law and principles that is in the interests of the EU and EU citizens as a whole (general predictability of the system and rule of law). Then come the claims of the judiciary, focused on independence from the executive and increased resources but not so much on accountability and transparency. Active NGOs share quite liberal views on the system, seeing it primarily as securing the needs of the free market and combating corruption and organised crime. These NGOs are eager to support the claims of the system, ignoring important details resulting from fragmented legislation and knowledge. And finally the government becomes responsible both to the EU and a society that desires quick and accessible justice. The needs of the family justice system are somehow lost or pushed aside in such a patchwork of actors and interests. Most of the reforms are focused on the internal problems of the system and not so much on its role in delivering justice to ordinary people. For instance, structural issues addressed as a priority by the SJC, such as balancing the workload, personal evaluations of judges as a basis for their career development and remuneration, do not motivate able judges to stay in the family justice system. The ranking of family cases is low because it is based on purely legal criteria but not on additional factors such as stress, capacity in fields other than law, working with vulnerable people and so on. The Family Court is considered as a last resort if mediation or other ADR have not been able to resolve the dispute. The administration is positioned to provide legal advice and information. As a result people do not go to court, but this is not because their problems have been resolved but because they do not trust the system and equally do not have access to relevant information.[17] In such circumstances the idea of a separate Family Court remains unfeasible.

STRUCTURE AND RECENT DEVELOPMENT OF THE BULGARIAN FAMILY JUSTICE SYSTEM

Bulgaria keeps the traditional court-centred way of dispensing family justice. Family cases are administered by the common civil courts. Only in the big cities is there any division by subject matter: ie into a so-called 'family division' within the common court where a certain number of judges are assigned to deal with family cases. The court of today though, is under pressure from new demands: to deal with various sources of expertise, with an increasing number of international cases; to adjust to the promotion of private ordering and speeding up of the process, as well as with the inconsistent actions of the management of the judicial system.

[17] See more in Gramatikov, M, *Research on the Legal Problems in Bulgaria Applying the Method of Justiciable Events* (Sofia, Open Society Institute, 2010).

Some 15 years ago only disputes between family members under the Family Code were considered as family cases: eg divorce and its consequences, parental disputes over children, affiliation, adoption and maintenance. These were entirely private law cases. 'Family cases' today include not only private but also public law cases that come under the Child Protection Act of 2000 (CPA) and the Protection against the Domestic Violence Act of 2005 (DVA). The majority of cases are still divorce and child support but the share of childcare and domestic violence cases is increasing. All these are dealt with by one judge who has graduated in law sitting as a first instance court, excluding the cases of affiliation and adoption, which are heard by the second instance court. All the first instance decisions are subject to appeal—one or two instances, depending on the type of the case (public law family cases can be appealed at two instances).

The enactment of both the CPA and DVA challenged the family justice system. It faced the need to adjust to dealing with new litigation parties—public bodies—as well as with new types of evidence produced by the civil servants of the child protection administration.[18] The newly established child protection system also experienced difficulty caused by the lack of litigation experience and resources. This created tension between the two systems addressed initially by the elaboration of a large body of guidelines and training for family judges and social workers to work together. Two years ago new legislation was drafted to supply the family justice system with court-based social workers. The draft has not yet been taken forward. In summary, the child legislation has made the necessary link between the family judge and other professionals. This opened the system to families and to the public at large that had formerly interacted mainly with legal professionals. The wide participation of social workers and psychologists provoked the need for a new professionalism for the family judges too thus providing a strong argument for the need for specialisation in family justice.

The new CPC of 2008 made another transformation to the family justice system. The major goal of the reform in civil procedure was to discipline and speed up process. Lengthy proceedings have been one of its drawbacks demonstrated by a number of cases before the European Court of Human Rights as well as by public discontent.[19] The new Code abolished the reconciliation stage at divorce proceedings. It was thought to be extending the duration

[18] The CPA, as well as the amendments to the Social Protection Act of 2003 and consequent legislation, situated the source of expertise for the administrative system in Social Protection Departments within the Ministry of Labour and Social Policy.

[19] The ECtHR statistics shows that 30% of Bulgarian cases are under art 6 of the ECHR—violation of the right to due process in reasonable time. The issue was targeted by various means: legislative reform that included the CPC and amendment to the Judicial System Act (and created a special structure to the Inspectorate to the Supreme Judicial Council and an administrative procedure to compensate parties in proceedings taking unreasonable time), the elaboration of a concept paper and legal amendments to promote e-justice, as well as close monitoring of the length of cases by the Inspectorate to the Supreme Judicial Council.

of litigation and as an unnecessary attempt to protect marriage via divorce regulation. Instead of a conciliation stage, the judge was obliged to refer the spouses to mediation (CPC, art 321, para 2). Referral to mediation, if successful, comes with some incentives for the parties—refunding of half of the fees and conversion to the much easier procedure of consensual divorce where the role of the judge is more or less to register the dissolution of the marriage.[20] The new Family Code of 2009 included the same rule (art 49, para 2). Neither statute clarifies what type of outcome the spouses are encouraged to agree on—either termination of the marriage or on the consequences of divorce. The mixed regulation suggests that the legislator has not departed from the idea of using divorce proceedings as a means to save the marriage; however, the efforts in this direction are now transferred to the parties, not to the court.

The reform also provided more incentives for consensual divorce. The three-year waiting period after contracting the marriage has been abolished and the contents of the mandatory agreement on divorce consequences have narrowed.[21] The restructuring of the divorce process could be interpreted as a step to privatise marriage dissolution without an explicit and overall policy in this direction. What is missing is a plan to develop out-of-court services available to parties to reconcile or negotiate their relationship after marriage breakdown. Mediation appears as the only similar service but its quality and prospects could be questioned in a culture ignorant of family conciliation services.

ACCESS TO FAMILY JUSTICE

It is also hard to find a coherent policy relating to access to family justice. During the socialist past, access to courts had not been a problem. The state provided legal aid only for criminal cases.[22] Family cases were considered as strictly private matters with no access to support. Cheap justice[23] in terms of low or no court fees for the litigants was and still is the means to secure access to the court. The court can still exempt the petitioner from court fees if it is proved he or she is economically disadvantaged. In addition, certain claims are legally exempt from fees such as labour disputes and child support claims. Any claim against the administration costs 10 BGN (5 Euros). Therefore liberal commentators consider justice to be cheap: 'the general 4% court fee on valuable claims would be a burden only for business but

[20] The share of consensual divorce increased rapidly to 68% of all divorces in 2012.

[21] As per art 51 of the Family Code, spouses ought to agree only on post-divorce parenting and maintenance but no longer property matters.

[22] The budget for legal aid used to be part of the justice system budget.

[23] Justice is cheap for litigants but very expensive for the public: see n 15.

not for ordinary people'[24] but there may be difficulties in access because of the political dependence and mismanagement of the system in terms of workload and lengthy proceedings.[25] Costs for litigants however, started to rise due to increases in fees for legal services from April 2014. The possible increase of court fees is also under debate but the past two governments were hesitant to take action.

New legislation (the Legal Aid Act (LAA) of 2005 and the Mediation Act (MA) of 2004) was enacted as part of the intensive process of top-down legislative modernisation during the accession to EU. The LAA makes support available irrespective of the type of case but strictly dependent on the eligibility of persons to social assistance.[26] Aid to children in public care and child support claims is not conditional. Against the lack of any tradition and still relatively cheap access to court the legal aid scheme remains insignificant in creating real demand either from the needy population or from the community of lawyers as potential beneficiaries. A research study from 2011 identifies numerous statutory, administrative and management problems that prevent the system reaching its objectives as set out in the law.[27] The system constantly operates under financial constraints.[28] Criminal justice still remains its focus.

Legal aid comprises: (1) pre-litigation advice with a view to reaching a settlement prior to bringing legal proceedings or to start litigation; (2) preparation of documents for litigation; (3) court representation (LAA, art 12). Two-thirds of the claims for legal information or pre-litigation advice on civil cases go to family cases. There are 9000 cases yearly, which is only one third of the claims submitted.[29] A very small minority of beneficiaries

[24] Ivanova, I, Interview in Bulgarian before DW: Cheap but Inaccessible Justice, 3 August 2013.

[25] See also at: www.euinside.eu/bg/analyses/the-path-toward-article-7-is-now-cleared.

[26] The threshold established in the Social Assistance Act is very low and that hampers the access to legal aid for a large share of the needy population. The basis for calculation of the eligibility for aid is the amount of guaranteed minimum income, which is 65 BGN (32 Euros per month).

[27] *Report on the Assessment of the Implementation of the Legal Aid Act 2007–2011*. Available in Bulgarian at: www.osf.bg/?cy=10&lang=1&program=1&action=2&news_id=464.

[28] The state budget allocation for legal aid is about 0.01% annually of the GDP (it is about 10 million BGN equal to 5 million Euros per annum); annual state budget per capita allocated to legal aid in 2010 in Bulgaria was 0.5 Euros as against 45.7 Euros in the UK; 568 cases per 100,000 inhabitants were granted legal aid with 95 Euros per case (1286 cases per 100,000 inhabitants/3551 Euros per case in the UK); 80% of legal aid goes to criminal cases, which suggests the system remains unfamiliar to the needy population. See *Report: Judicial Systems of the European Union Countries Analysis of Data by the European Commission for the Efficiency of Justice (CEPEJ) Council of Europe* (2013). Available at: http://www.coe.int/t/dghl/cooperation/cepej/evaluation/2012/CEPEJ%20pays%20UE%20rapport%20JPJ-HJ%20V%20finale%2025%20juin%202013_arial10_final_en.pdf.

[29] *Report of the Director of Legal Aid Directorate at NLAO*, delivered on 26 June 2014 Seminar, Sofia. More at: www.nbpp.government.bg/images/documents/Otcheten%20doklad_2012.pdf.

(around 150 per year) receive aid for civil litigation compared with 45,000 for representation in criminal cases. Access to information for legal aid is limited via practising lawyers or via the web site of the National Legal Aid Office (NLAO).[30] The web access is extremely bureaucratic—applicants have to obtain the forms, fill them in and provide the necessary evidence of eligibility. Usually the applicants are poorly educated and are not users of e-technologies. The quality of aid is presumed to be low due to the low fees paid to lawyers (60 Euros per case and 15 Euros for legal advice and case preparation) and the lack of service-monitoring mechanisms. Another problem is the lack of established specific criteria for lawyers to enter the public register of legal aid lawyers. The lawyers are generally specialised in criminal or civil matters. But there is no specialisation, for example, in family cases.

Similar drawbacks were identified again in 2013 by a team of experts as appointed by the Ministry of Justice to assess the progress in implementation of the Judicial Reform Strategy. The assessment strongly recommended improving access to legal aid by the wider population, to enlarge the share of support for civil law cases and to raise its quality. The NLAO has recently started a project funded by a Norwegian cooperation fund that aims to increase the outreach of the NLAO via a permanent hotline, local offices and prioritising initial legal information and advice.[31]

The prospects for family mediation could be defined on the basis of the common judicial reform strategies. There is it seems a consensus that mediation is useful both for the court system and people. The initial resistance articulated by an MP during the parliamentary discussions on the Mediation Bill in 2004, who defined the mediation as 'dangerous' because it is the way to 'privatise' the function of dispute resolution, which belongs to the state, has been overcome.[32] Nowadays mediation is usually defined as a cheap, quick and effective tool to avoid litigation. This outcome is highly desirable as a means to resolve the internal problems of the system such as the heavy workload and lengthy proceedings. For instance, a strong personal and institutional commitment to mediation was expressed by the President of the Supreme Court of Cassation.[33] He stressed the Bulgarian concept of promoting mediation and other means for ADR via 'an evolutionary approach,

[30] www.nbpp.government.bg/%D0%B8%D0%BD%D1%84%D0%BE%D1%80%D0%BC%D0%B0%D1%86%D0%B8%D1%8F/%D0%B4%D0%BE%D0%BA%D1%83%D0%BC%D0%B5%D0%BD%D1%82%D0%B8.

[31] See Table 1, 'Assessment of the level of implementation at May 2013 of part of planned measures of the Judicial Reform Strategy'. Available in Bulgarian at the website of the Ministry of Justice: https://mjs.bg/107/.

[32] See minutes of the discussions on the Mediation Bill (no 402-01-9 of 16.02.2004), Kornezov, L.

[33] *Report of the President of the Bulgarian Supreme Court of Cassation* before the International Conference 'Judges and ADR' organised by the Italian Supreme Court in Rome (February 2012).

slowly but steadily, based on the training of judges and raising the awareness of citizens of its advantages and making use of various incentives'. For him, a key factor to promote is the readiness of the judges to become familiar with mediation, to be convinced about its benefits and to support it. The personal view of the Chief Justice is that mediation is to be encouraged because of its certain benefits, namely the speed of dispute resolution and relieving pressure on the court system as well the feeling of the parties coming out of the dispute as winners. In addition, the government received a considerable incentive being praised by the European Parliament as having 'achieved essential outcomes in encouraging ADR in civil and commercial cases'.[34]

Mediation in Bulgaria is organised as a private service monitored by the Minister of Justice via regulations setting out the minimum standards for the profession (mandatory training and its curriculum; procedural and ethical rules for mediators) and entry to the public registry. The early capacity to train mediators and to promote the service was built with support mainly from US donors and organisations of mediators. Currently the number of registered mediators is over 1200. The quality of training is entirely the responsibility of its providers. Experts recommend the Minister of Justice to develop standards for trainers, for specialisation of mediators related to the subject of the dispute as well as to keep statistical data on the number of mediators and mediations.[35] Another proposal is to address the low level of demand for the service through promotion of mediation via public campaigns and involvement of other relevant ministries and the SJC. The judicial reform strategy also foresees promotion of mediation and other means of ADR with the aim of decreasing the workload of the court system, increasing access to justice and reducing the conflicted nature of legal disputes. The following measures are planned to take place: additional incentives to the parties to refer to mediation, integration of mediation into the legal aid system and debate about making it mandatory.

The rhetoric about mediation does not correspond to the low level of demand for it. Despite lawyers enthusiastically entering the profession and training for many judges, referral is scarce and a tension exists between lawyers and mediators.[36] Mediation is still cheap and even free if practised in the Centre for Judicial Mediation in Sofia District Court.[37] It does not prevent proper legal advice: parties use the service accompanied by lawyers.

[34] See Resolution of 13 Sept 2011 on the implementation of the EU Directive 2008/52 on mediation of the EU Parliament.

[35] Open Society Institute, *Evaluation of the implementation of the Strategy for the Reform of the Judicial System in Bulgaria, 2003–2008* (n 14) 70–77.

[36] Sofia District Court developed the most successful Centre for Agreements and Mediation (Centre for Judicial Mediation). It started in 2009 with the training of 15 judges who acted as trainers to other judges. The Centre started to function in January 2010 and nowadays reports numerous successful mediations: over 200 cases in 2011, 40% of cases conclude with agreement. More at: http://srs.justice.bg/srs/images/mediaciq_buletin.pdf.

[37] The Centre still relies on external funding but this will soon expire.

This may change if the parties in future have to cover mediation costs as well as the increasing costs of access justice.

ADMINISTRATIVE PRESSURE OVER THE FAMILY COURT

Statistical data proves that family justice is far from being a burden for the justice system. The Supreme Judicial Council[38] statistics suggest that the share of family cases among all civil disputes brought before the first instance courts in Bulgaria during 2010–2012 was 9–10 per cent (9.55 per cent in 2012, 9.05 per cent in 2011, and 9.57 per cent in 2010). This makes around 37,000 to 38,000 family cases compared to around 400,000 civil cases per year.[39] The majority of them were divorce and child support cases as well as parental disputes in regard to children under the Family Code.

The workload of judges is one of the key issues under the scrutiny of the SJC. Its management is one of the measures for reaching the reform's benchmarks—to increase the efficiency of the judicial system. The workload differs considerably from court to court.[40] The busiest are the first instance courts in Sofia and in other big cities (Varna, Plovdiv, Burgas). In Sofia District Court one judge hears 70–80 cases per month, in Varna—60 cases, Plovdiv—55 cases. At the same time there are courts with five to six cases per judge per month. The SJC deals with the issue via transfer of workplaces to bigger courts, and closing down courts in small cities.

The lower workload of the family judges is one of the reasons for reducing their number in the family divisions. For example, by the end of 2013 the family division in Sofia District Court consisted of 13 judges, the same division in Sofia City Court of six judges, and the approximate number of family judges in other busy courts is three to four. A family judge in Sofia District Court had 35 cases per month in 2013 compared to 70 for a common civil judge. This arithmetical difference provided a good reason for the Head of the Sofia District Court to decrease the number of family judges from 13 to six starting from January 2014.[41] In addition to the lower workload of the family judges and the need to strike a balance with the workload of other judges, the Chief of the Court (a criminal law judge) explained his decision in the following way:

> the factual and legal simplicity of the majority of family cases, the need to avoid the loss of qualification of family judges and the possible following loss of competitiveness for their future career development, is at risk at the moment.

[38] www.vss.justice.bg/bg/start.htm.
[39] The population of Bulgaria as per 2011 census is 7.2 million inhabitants.
[40] www.vss.justice.bg/bg/start.htm.
[41] http://courtnewsbg.info/index.php/vss/90-court-news/6860-namalyavat-napolovina-broya-na-sadiite-v-brachnoto-otdelenie-na-srs.

Such a statement requires no comment. It clearly articulates the pressure on the family justice system within the frame of overall justice reform. The criteria for the success of the reform have turned out to be a burden for family justice.

Another example of mismanagement of the family justice system is the application of common criteria for ranking judges in attestation procedures as a basis for their career development and remuneration. The use of pure arithmetical standards (number of cases, and their legal complexity) lowers the status and salaries of family judges. Therefore the SJC should elaborate another set of standards reflecting the complexity of cases and the specific work of the family judge (eg the stress caused by the emotional involvement) and the need for constant learning. This is what family judges share as a main motivation either to stay or to leave the system.

The reform in the family justice system needs to involve the views of other professionals concerned with the well-being of children and other vulnerable family members. For the time being they are excluded on the basis of education—the reform is a job for lawyers only. It is extremely difficult to discuss specialisation of the Family Court in the context of such thinking. The need for specialisation of judges on family matters is already grounded in several political documents considering it from the perspective of the best interests of the child. It is supported by some acting judges, conditional on balancing of their status as judges and managers of cases together with social workers and other professionals dealing with vulnerable family members.

CONCLUSION

The ongoing judicial reform in Bulgaria is a factor in maintaining extensive public funding for the justice system. Politicians are failing to initiate reforms that would change the traditional system.

Nevertheless pressure is coming as a result of incoherent legislation, mismanagement and lack of specialisation. Reforms do not reflect the specifics of family justice in terms of its internal peculiarities and social functions. Rather, family justice is pushed to the back of the system since its part in upholding the market and its actors is not a direct one. The possible defenders of a proper family justice system have not been empowered yet: clients still have access to the system, lawyers have never utilised generous funding for legal aid, judges are not motivated to deal with family cases. The prospects for family justice in such a situation strongly depend on the modernisation of the justice system possibly linked to its marketisation.

7

Family Courts and Family Cases in Poland and other Post-Communist Countries

MAŁGORZATA FUSZARA AND JACEK KURCZEWSKI

FAMILY COURTS IN POLAND

FAMILY COURTS WERE first introduced in Poland experimentally in 1974. Contrary to the stereotypes, the communist Ministry of Justice was in some periods interested in innovations and that was the case with then Minister Professor Jerzy Bafia who was sometimes open to suggestions of reformist lawyers and sociologists of law. The so-called 'family courts', formally the family departments, were established in only a few selected common courts, and had been formed out of the former juvenile courts, which had had a tradition in Poland since 1919. The juvenile courts had originally been set up as part of the Europe-wide trend towards restructuring the judiciary's role with respect to minors in a manner that would be less about punishment and more about 'assisting children in need'.

As the tendency towards establishing family courts gained momentum, separate divisions for common courts were founded in Poland. They were called 'family and juvenile courts'. Initially set up as an experiment, they were later introduced to all courts in 1977. The rationale (widely accepted across Europe at the time by lawyers and other specialists working with families) was that investigation of family matters requires a special approach and special qualifications. Family cases therefore should be organisationally separated from other cases, and family courts should employ judges with specialist qualifications, allowing for the kind of cooperation with other experts (eg pedagogues, psychologists etc) which is crucial in this area. Proponents of the separation also argued that issues within a single family are often interrelated, with one problem leading to another, so that formally combining them and assigning them to one judge should be beneficial. At the outset, the jurisdiction of family courts in Poland covered all family-related matters, ie divorce, maintenance claims and parental responsibility. However, it also included legal incapacity, forced medical treatment and similar cases (previously in the remit of civil courts), as well as issues related to violence in the family, which were previously the remit of the criminal courts, and juvenile issues, previously the remit of juvenile courts. It became apparent very soon that violence-related cases were so numerous and so specific that they were returned to the jurisdiction of criminal courts.

The family courts survived in this form until the end of the 1980s and of the People's Republic. Then in the aftermath of the major change of political system in 1990, their jurisdiction was changed. Divorce cases were moved to the jurisdiction of courts of a higher instance (then labelled *voivodship* courts and now called regional courts). The official explanation for this decision was that cases as complex as divorce should be examined by older judges with more experience. Unofficially, it was explained as an attempt to reduce the number of divorces by making access to courts more difficult (as was the case in all the other countries where a similar decision was made) following the anti-divorce stand taken permanently by the now much more influential Catholic Church. Family courts lost part of their jurisdiction as a result. However, the biggest consequence of the change was that access to courts became more difficult, in particular for residents of smaller towns and rural areas. This is clearly demonstrated by the data that show how varied the decrease in the divorce rates was: the decrease was largest where there was no *voivodship* court in the main city of the *voivodship*, which made access particularly difficult. It was alarming because the impact was mainly on the poorest people, particularly female victims of domestic violence living in areas far from *voivodship* courts.[1] The process was nevertheless an element of the wider political project supported by the Catholic Church.

> Catholic sexual ethics represent the old idea of putting sex under moral control represented by the power of the Church. The vitality of the debate on contraception, birth control, sexual ethics, etc., represents, according to this theory, the Church's attempts to safeguard the last area of its direct control over the individual. Where the State has step by step retreated and removed itself, leaving the body for private use by citizens, the Church establishes, or rather continues, its jurisdiction.[2]

The struggle continues even today and the family laws and justice are not immune to it.

For several years now attempts have been made to abolish family courts in Poland. For example, there have been voices to the effect that family

[1] Fuszara, M, 'Divorce in Poland' (2011) 2(12) *Societas/Communitas* 222–23.

[2] Kurczewski, J, '"Family" in Politics and Law: In Search of Theory' in J Kurczewski and M Maclean (eds), *Family Law and Family Policy in the New Europe* (Dartmouth, Aldershot, 1997) 4.

law is not a separate branch of the law. In the opinion of the judiciary, such claims effectively amount to challenging the rationale for the existence of family courts. Whether family law is a separate branch of the law or whether it is a part of civil law has been a subject of debate for years. Yet the newest challenge to the separate status of family law comes in the form of the Green Book on the potential new Civil Code for Poland, drafted by the Codification Committee of Civil Law (*Komisja Kodyfikacyjna Prawa Cywilnego*) in 2006. The Green Book proposed that the family code (now outlining the separate legal regime of family law) should be incorporated into the civil code. Legislative tradition was invoked, and the following explanation was provided:

> [F]ifty years of tradition shaped under communist pressure should not determine the legal order of the Republic of Poland. The move away from this tradition, evident in several post-communist states, suggests that a return to European, democratic concepts is considered more attractive.[3]

The Committee planned to implement the change in 2010, but it has been unsuccessful so far. The Committee failed to engage in a process of consultation on the issue, and so the Association of Family Judges mailed a survey questionnaire to judges and received 956 responses. It is impossible to say whether the sample was representative, but nevertheless the responses are interesting. The respondents included judges sitting on the bench in family courts (527 respondents, 56 per cent) and in civil courts (411 respondents, 43 per cent); the remaining respondents worked in different types of courts.

The prevalent response was in favour of a separate family law regime: 671 respondents (70 per cent) supported a separate family code. Only 157 respondents (16 per cent) supported the incorporation of family law into civil law. The remaining respondents either cited arguments both in favour and against both options without taking a clear stand (8 per cent) or chose to give no clear answer (6 per cent). A separate regime was preferred by a clear majority of family court judges (81 per cent) and by a majority—although a smaller one—of civil court judges (56 per cent). The following arguments were invoked: family law is systematically separate from civil law; family cases have a unique nature and thus require a separate judicial track, to which separate regimes are conducive; the separation of the regimes makes it easier for the persons to whom the provisions of family law pertain to read and understand these provisions; reasons of tradition; reasons of convenience; and other practical considerations.[4]

[3] Codification Committee of Civil Law, *Green Book* (2006) 31–32.

[4] Elżbieta. Holewińska-Łapińska, 'Opinia sędziów na temat przedstawionego w "Zielonej Księdze" usytuopwania prawa rodzinnego w przyszłej kodyfikacji. Wyniki badania ankietowego' (2008) 6 *Prawo w działaniu* 177.

In the study, the judges clearly referred to the need for a separate judicial track for family cases. Yet one of the changes proposed recently was considered among the members of the judiciary to be another attempt to eliminate outright the separate family court structures. In 2010, a new bill on the organisation of common courts was proposed. The bill abolished the mandatory requirement to establish a family and juvenile division in every court, and only stipulated that such divisions could be established in courts that have a large proportion of such cases. The bill was drafted in the Ministry of Justice. The Ministry explained that in many small courts there were few cases and few judges, and the requirement to establish a separate division was counterproductive. There was also a cost-cutting aspect, as a separate division requires a number of management and administrative positions. After the change of the Minister with the new Cabinet led by Ms Ewa Kopacz, PM from the same Civic Platform (*Platforma Obywatelska*) party since September 2014, this policy was revoked and soon the abolished courts will be at least partially restored.

Family judges felt that the bill attempted to eliminate separate family courts. They noted that in regional (ie higher level, second instance) courts, where the establishment of family and juvenile courts is not mandatory, they only exist in 12 out of 45 courts, and the continued existence of several is uncertain. In total in 2012 in Poland there were 330 family and juvenile courts (ie court divisions). The judges were afraid that many of these courts would disappear once district courts (lower level first instance courts) are also freed from the obligation to have them.

In response to a parliamentary question on the issue, the deputy Minister of Justice then said: 'The implementation of the solutions proposed in the bill would automatically trigger neither a change in the structure of the judiciary nor the elimination of a specific number of divisions'. He also stated that the divisions would only be omitted where the number of cases is low and the small number of judges on the staff prevents judges from developing a specialisation in any given type of cases. In all other courts, the idea was not to eliminate the specialisation of judges, but only of court divisions.

The plans of the Ministry of Justice led to protests by family judges. The strongest protest came in 2010, when family judges gathered at a congress passed a resolution demanding that the requirement to establish family courts should remain in force. The following reasons were cited: the unique nature of family cases, and the correspondingly unique manner of operation of both family judges and family courts. The resolution also read: 'The track record of family courts so far in over 30 years of history demonstrates that it is not only reasonable to maintain them as separate courts, but it is actually necessary'. The resolution protested against the elimination of family courts and criticised the previous narrowing of their remit by removing from it divorce and legal separation cases. In the opinion of judges, this had failed to generate the intended consequences and also, to make matters worse, had

had unexpected negative side effects. The removal of divorce cases from the jurisdiction of family courts was assessed as a clear mistake:

> Notably, the jurisdiction of family courts was recently restricted in that divorce cases first, and then also legal separation cases, were placed in the jurisdiction of regional courts as first instance courts. It was expected that the number of effective reconciliations would rise and the number of divorce rulings would fall considerably. These effects failed to materialise, and the change was deemed a mistake by scholars, judges, and the Ministry of Justice alike. Yet to reinstate the previous situation appears so expensive that the Ministry has not decided to do so.

The position of family judges gained widespread support. There was the above-mentioned parliamentary question. Family law practitioners voiced their support. Even the NGO Committee for the Protection of the Rights of Children (*Komitet Ochrony Praw Dziecka*) took a stand in support of the judges. Nonetheless, the protest was unsuccessful. While family law was not incorporated into civil law, in 2011 the statute on the organisation of common courts was amended, abolishing the requirement to establish family and juvenile divisions in district courts. Yet in 2013 the Ministry of Justice stated that it was working on another amendment to the same statute, this time intended to reinstate mandatory family courts (divisions) in district courts. The proposed amendment does not, however, re-establish the mandatory character of family courts. On 25 September 2014 the Association of Family Judges again demanded 'the accelerating of the legislative drafting that would lead to re-establish the mandatory family and juveniles departments in the court structure and the judiciary specialized in family cases at all levels of common court system'.

The history of family courts in Poland is thus mostly a history of their gradual elimination after an early period of enthusiasm for the idea of concentrating all family and juvenile cases in a separate court in the hands of one judge who has insight into the situation of the whole family. The process of elimination has progressed from narrowing down the jurisdiction of the courts and taking certain categories of cases out of their remit, through the reduction in the number of these courts, to attempts at their complete liquidation. As discussed below, this process also encompasses the reduction of the remit of these courts in favour of private agreements and out-of-court mediation.

THE POWER OF THE COURTS VERSUS PRIVATE AGREEMENTS, AS ILLUSTRATED BY FAMILY LAW CASES

After the 'thaw', when Stalinism was renounced, and after the rule of law was announced in 1956 (even though it was a 'socialist' rule of law), the courts were generally believed to be relatively independent and the level of trust in courts was very high. Sociological research at the time demonstrated that courts were believed to be the best remedy for a great number of social ills. At the same time, the courts had immense power: the parties' contributions and control over the dispute were minimal, with very few exceptions. The courts of all jurisdictions, including family courts, were mandated to determine the truth of the case. Divorce cases provide a good illustration of how far this obligation was taken. The option of no-fault divorces was implemented in Poland relatively early. Yet the Supreme Court ruled that even in these cases, it was the court's duty to determine whether an irrevocable and complete disintegration of marriage had occurred. The parties' declarations to this effect were insufficient. The courts were thus obliged to seek 'the truth' and to determine what the truth was, even if the parties unanimously requested a divorce and provided concordant explanations as to the state of the marriage and the reasons for its disintegration. A contradiction was inherent in the procedure. On the one hand, the regulations allowed the court to limit the proceedings to the parties' explanations if the couple had no children and requested a no-fault divorce. On the other hand, the court was obliged to find the truth. As a consequence, divorce proceedings were often prolonged and overly focused on detailed information, despite concordant declarations of the parties that they indeed wished to divorce.

The obligation to find the truth also gave the courts considerable leeway in terms of their own initiative. The proceedings were therefore not completely adversarial. For example, with regard to the determination of parental responsibility after the divorce, the court could take the parents' requests into consideration, but its primary obligation was to act for the benefit of the child. At least theoretically the court had therefore to decide whether the proposed solution was in the child's best interest. There was no assumption that the parents would make the decision that would be best for the child; it was always for the independent court to determine. In practice, courts accepted the arrangements proposed by the parents. Yet formally, it was a ruling of the court which was not bound by the parents' suggestions.

The tendency to leave decisions in the hands of the court rather than of the parties was also clear in the design of conciliation proceedings, which survived throughout the communist period in a variety of forms. The heavy focus on bringing the parties to reconciliation was apparent both in civil and in criminal procedural regulations. The judge was either obliged or allowed to act as a mediator. In selected types of cases, it was mandatory for the judge to make an attempt at reconciling the parties. In the 1970s, the judge had the option of referring the case to social mediators (social reconciliation committees).[5] Yet a great majority of conciliation proceedings were conducted by judges as an inherent part of court proceedings.

[5] See Kurczewski, J and Frieske, K, 'The Social Conciliatory Commissions in Poland: a Case Study of Nonauthoritative and Conciliatory Dispute Resolution as an Approach to Access to Justice' in M Cappelletti and J Weisner (eds), *Access to Justice, vol 1, bk 1, Promising Institutions* (Milan, A Giuffrè; Alphen an den rijn: Sijthoff & Noordhoff, 1978) 156.

It is not easy to determine whether the level of trust in courts remains high in Poland. Eurobarometer studies demonstrate that it is lower in Poland than in many EU countries, but this lower level is consistent with the levels of trust in other post-communist countries, among which Poland ranks in the middle of the scale of trust towards the justice system.

Table 1: Overall, would you say that you tend to trust or not to trust the justice system in your country?

Country	Tend to trust (EU 53%)	Tend not trust (EU 43%)
Finland, Denmark	85	13
Austria	78	20
Luxembourg, Germany	77	19, 21
Sweden	76	20
Netherlands	70	23
Ireland, Great Britain	61	36, 31
Belgium, France	59	37, 40
Hungary	58	39
Estonia	56	21
Latvia, Greece	48	45, 49
Malta	45	47
Portugal, Romania	44	51, 54
Poland	42	54
Croatia	37	57
Bulgaria, Cyprus	35	59, 62
Spain	34	64
Italy	33	63
Lithuania	31	62
Czech Republic, Slovakia	25	72, 66
Slovenia	24	73

Source: Authors' own compilation of data from Flash Eurobarometer 385

Importantly, post-communist countries are generally characterised by low levels of trust towards institutions. Trust in the justice system is lower in Poland than in most 'old' EU countries, but higher than trust towards other institutions. This conclusion is supported by European Social Survey studies in the last decade, by means of comparing the highest- and lowest-evaluated institutions in Poland. Owing to methodological constraints (respondents ranked their trust level on a 0–10 scale) the tables present only the most extreme opinions.

Table 2: Proportion of respondents expressing a total lack of trust in selected institutions in Poland in the last decade (respondents who chose 0 on a 0–10 scale, in %)

Institution	2002	2004	2006	2008	2010	2012
Political parties	—	27.94	27.82	23.74	21.62	26.35
Politicians	17.41	33.76	28.51	24.25	20.02	25.88
Parliament	11.57	27.54	21.82	17.22	11.59	18.72
Legal system	10.05	18.71	10.22	9.27	6.32	11.22
European Parliament	7.21	8.99	6.36	6.47	6.69	9.67
Police	5.51	8.12	6.03	4.98	3.71	5.03

As the data demonstrate, opinions with regard to local politicians tend to fluctuate the most, with opinions on the police and the European Parliament—the least. Data on the highest ranking institutions show a reverse order.

Table 3: Proportion of respondents expressing complete trust in selected institutions in Poland in the last decade (respondents who chose 10 on a 0–10 scale, in %)

Institution	2002	2004	2006	2008	2010	2012
Police	5.51	8.12	6.03	4.98	3.71	5.03
European Parliament	2.01	1.66	2.19	0.85	1.44	1.63
Legal system	0.57	0.92	1.04	0.49	0.83	1.13
Parliament	0.88	0.51	0.79	0.18	0.53	1.05
Politicians	0.11	0.12	0.34	0.05	0.27	0.27
Political parties	—	0.12	0.29	0.05	0.18	0.12

The studies demonstrate a general lack of trust towards institutions. Yet the 'legal system' is consistently in the middle rank. It generates less trust than the police and the (remote and generally unknown) European Parliament, but clearly more than politicians, political parties and political representatives.

The recent changes to Poland's court procedures across a variety of cases demonstrate not only that institutions are changing, but so is the philosophy with regard to understanding the roles of the parties to the dispute and the role of third parties such as mediators. This in turn means a redefinition of the role of the court. Private agreements dividing responsibility, the abolition of conciliation proceedings, replacement of these proceedings with the option of referring the case for mediation—all of these changes contribute to a broader change in the relationship between the institution (court) and its 'clients' (litigants, defendants, etc). This broader change may be perceived in a number of ways. It may be viewed as a departure from a totalitarian, omnipotent model of the courts, a departure which only became possible after the totalitarian political system collapsed (despite the fact that in that system, the courts generated a great deal of trust, because they were perceived as relatively independent, compared to the totalitarian bureaucracy and its officials). It may also be viewed as a crisis of trust in the courts, which in the postmodern world no longer aspire to the role of a sole truth-finder and no longer have the monopoly for suggesting optimal solutions. Finally, it may be viewed as a part of an even greater global tendency towards 'unburdening' the courts, of limiting their role, and of cutting the costs of court proceedings. Relying on private agreements, requiring only that they must be approved by a court, is much cheaper than lengthy court proceedings. Most likely, all three of these aspects motivate the changes that occur in Poland to a certain extent.

CHANGING FAMILIES AND CHANGING FAMILY LAW, AS ILLUSTRATED BY DIVORCE

It is interesting to study the increase in divorce rates in post-communist countries. In all of them, divorce had become possible after World War Two (if it had not been possible earlier). In Poland as it emerged in 1918 divorce was available before religious courts of non-Roman Catholic denominations and before common courts in the former Prussian-ruled region when Poland was partitioned by its neighbours between 1777 and 1918, resulting in the variety of legal regimes. The Codification Committee drafted a very progressive proposal allowing for divorce before World War Two. However, the proposal met with fierce opposition from the Catholic Church, and consequently the government decided not to send it on for a parliamentary reading. Yet the proposed regulations came into force immediately after World War Two. In the pre-war debates on allowing divorce, the USSR was cited as negative example. In the Soviet Union, the procedure to obtain divorce was administrative in nature. Conservative voices in Polish debates have been invoking this for years (even recently) as a negative model leading to the collapse of the institution of marriage and a cause of many social problems, including in particular the problem of children left without parental care (*bezprizornoje*). Despite the 50 years of relatively liberal divorce laws, the countries of the region vary in terms of the proportion of divorced persons in their populations.

Table 4: Proportion of divorced persons in the population of post-communist countries

Country	% of divorced men in the population	% of divorced women in the population
Montenegro	1.3	2.6
Croatia	2.3	3.5
Bulgaria	3.3	4.7
Poland	3.5	5.0
Romania	3.6	5.3
Slovenia	4.2	5.5
Ukraine	4.6	7.6
Belarus	5.2	7.8
Slovakia	5.6	7.2
Russia	6.1	9.3
Hungary	7.6	10.1
Estonia	8.0	10.9
Lithuania	8.6	11.6
Czech Republic	8.9	10.9
Latvia	9.9	13.7

Source: Central Statistical Office (GUS),*The International Yearbook 2013*, p 95

The explanations typically offered for these data are hardly useful here. Divorce rates vary widely among post-communist countries. They are very low in some, although never as low as in Malta or Spain (which used to have very restrictive legal regulations concerning divorce). There is a group of countries where the proportion is 3–4 per cent of men; this group includes Catholic Poland and Orthodox Bulgaria. The highest proportion of divorced persons in the population is noted in the Baltic states (which interestingly include the predominantly Catholic Lithuania) and the mostly atheist Czech Republic. The typical sociological explanations, which tend to link the divorce rate with religiosity, have very limited applicability here.

All the countries in the region have gone through a transformation. In part, this transformation has pertained to courts and court procedures. And institutional changes are accompanied by shifting social attitudes. It is interesting to see whether this is reflected in divorce statistics.

Table 5: Divorce in Central and Eastern Europe in 2010

Country	Divorces per 1000 residents, 2000	Divorces per 1000 residents, 2008	Divorces per 1000 residents, 2010	Divorces per 1000 newly solemnised marriages, 2010
Macedonia	0.7	0.6	0.8	122
Montenegro	0.8 (2005)	0.7	0.8	142
Croatia	1.0	1.1	1.1	238
Slovenia	1.1	1.1	1.2	372
Romania	1.4	1.7	1.5	282
Bulgaria	1.3	1.9	1.5	453
Poland	1.1	1.8	1.6	269
Slovakia	1.7	2.3	2.2	473
Latvia	2.6	2.7	2.2	531
Estonia	3.1	2.6	2.2	590
Hungary	2.3	2.5	2.4	672
Czech Republic	2.9	2.8	2.9	659
Ukraine	3.9 (2005)	5.3	2.8	412
Lithuania	3.1	3.1	3.0	535
Belarus	3.1 (2005)	3.8	3.9	476
Russia	4.2 (2005)	5.0	4.5	526

Source: Central Statistical Office (GUS), *The International Yearbook 2013*, p 99

The lowest divorce rates can be found in the ethnically and religiously diverse countries of the former Yugoslavia. In Macedonia, the obstacles to divorce resulting from Islamic regulations could be invoked (approximately a third of the population is Muslim), but this explanation does not apply to Croatia and Slovenia.

In several post-communist countries the divorce rate must be considered high primarily due to the high proportion of divorces in relation to the number of newly solemnised marriages. Even though the proportion of divorced persons in the population is not growing in, for example, Hungary or the Czech Republic, the proportion of marriages ending in divorce is very high (more than 600 in 1000 marriages). Furthermore, the number of marriages has fallen sharply in these countries in the last decade (Hungary: from 4.7 to 3.6 per 1000 persons; Czech Republic: from 5.4 to 4.4 per 1000 persons). Ukraine is an exception. In 2008, the number of divorces rocketed (from 3.9 to 5.3 per 1000 persons), and then promptly fell back to the previous level (3.2 in 2009 and 2.8 in 2010).

MEDIATION AND OTHER OUT-OF-COURT METHODS OF DISPUTE RESOLUTION

The Eurobarometer (November 2013 report) asked the residents of all EU countries whether they would use an out-of-court alternative to going to court. The study revealed great differences between EU countries in terms of willingness to use alternative methods of dispute resolution. Overall, a clear majority of EU residents would prefer not to go to court if an alternative was available. In all countries, only a minority would go to court despite the availability of alternatives.

Table 6: Imagine you are seeking a solution to a dispute with a company, another citizen or an administration. If you could use an alternative instead of going to court, would you prefer to go to the court anyway?

Country (Total EU—8%)	Go to court anyway
Bulgaria	23%
Denmark	18%
Lithuania	17%
Croatia	13%
Cyprus, Latvia	12%
Sweden	11%
United Kingdom, Netherlands, Hungary	10%
Italy, Slovakia, Romania	9%
Czech Republic, Greece, Spain, France	8%
Malta, Estonia, Luxemburg	7%
Germany, Belgium, Ireland, Slovenia	6%
Poland	5%
Austria, Portugal	4%
Finland	2%

Source: Authors' own compilation of data from Flash Eurobarometer 385

Less than a tenth of respondents (8 per cent) said they would go to court even if there were alternatives. Approximately nine out of ten respondents (89 per cent) would seek an agreement out-of-court. The respondents were presented with two different options of Alternative Dispute Resolution. The first option was a private agreement.

Table 7: Imagine you are seeking a solution to a dispute with a company, another citizen or an administration. If you could use an alternative instead of going to court, would you prefer to find an agreement with the other party directly?

Country (Total EU—43%)	**Find an agreement with other party directly**
Estonia	70%
Slovenia	60%
Latvia	57%
Poland, Hungary	56%
Portugal, Czech Republic	54%
Romania, Belgium, Lithuania, Malta	53%
Bulgaria, Slovakia, Croatia	51%
Finland	50%
Italy	49%
Greece	46%
Netherlands, Austria, Luxemburg	45%
Spain, Cyprus	44%
Sweden	42%
Germany	38%
France	36%
Denmark	35%
Ireland	34%
United Kingdom	26%

Source: Authors' own compilation of data from Flash Eurobarometer 385

The data demonstrate that residents of the EU countries differ greatly in their attitudes to private agreements. The difference between Estonia, where the attitude is most enthusiastic, and the United Kingdom, where it is most sceptical, is 46 per cent. Private agreements are a popular option in post-communist countries, which have a larger proportion of their proponents than the EU average. Private agreements tend to be less popular in the 'old' EU states, all of which have a smaller proportion of proponents of private agreements than the EU average.

Another option was to approach an institution acting as a mediator. In this scenario too there are differences between the countries.

Table 8: Imagine you are seeking a solution to a dispute with a company, another citizen or an administration. If you could use an alternative instead of going to court, would you prefer to find an agreement with the other party with the help of a non-judicial body that has a mediation role?

Country (Total EU—46%)	Find an agreement with the other party with the help of a non-judicial body that has a mediation role
United Kingdom	60%
Ireland	59%
France	55%
Germany	52%
Austria	49%
Finland, Spain	47%
Luxembourg	46%
Greece, Netherlands	44%
Cyprus, Denmark, Sweden	42%
Belgium, Portugal	40%
Poland, Slovakia	38%
Malta, Romania	37%
Czech Republic	36%
Italy	35%
Hungary	33%
Slovenia	32%
Croatia	31%
Latvia	28%
Lithuania	24%
Bulgaria	21%
Estonia	19%

Source: Authors' own compilation of data from Flash Eurobarometer 385

In eight countries, finding an agreement with the help of a non-judicial body that has a mediation role was the most popular course of action. Over 50 per cent of people would do this in four countries: the UK (60 per cent), Ireland (59 per cent), France (55 per cent) and Germany (52 per cent). Relatively few people would take this option in Estonia (19 per cent) and Bulgaria (21 per cent). The differences of opinion here to a large extent mirror the situation with regard to private agreements. In most general terms, the countries with sceptical attitudes towards private agreements register enthusiasm for institutionalised mediation. The difference with regard to mediation as the best instrument of conflict resolution between the most enthusiastic Great Britain and the most sceptical Estonia is again very large, standing at 41 per cent.

Table 9: Three European legal cultures?

	Direct agreement favoured by more than 50%	Direct agreement favoured by 50% or less
Administration of justice trusted by more than 50%	Belgium 59/53, *Estonia 56/70*	NWEurope: Denmark 85/35, Germany 77/38, Ireland 61/34, France 59/36, Luxemburg 77/45, *Hungary 58/56*, Netherlands 70/45, Austria 78/45, Finland 85/50, Sweden 76/42, UK 61/26
Administration of justice favoured by 50% or less	Mostly *CEEurope: Bulgaria 35/51, Czech Republic 25/54, Latvia 48/57, Lithuania 31/53*, Malta 45/53, *POLAND 42/56*, Portugal 44/54, *Romania 44/53, Slovenia 24/60, Slovakia 25/51, Croatia 37/51*	Southern Europe: Greece 48/46, Spain 34/44, Italy 33/49, Cyprus 35/44

Source: Data from Flash Eurobarometer 385 'Justice in the EU'
Former communist countries are shown in italics.

These research results are fascinating. North-Western European countries, whether traditionally Protestant or Catholic' show more trust more in the administration of justice and the alternative of institutionalised mediation. In former Communist Europe, informal direct agreements are more often trusted and institutions less often. In Southern Europe, the prevalent pattern is that of general distrust both in reference to the institutions and to the people. Mediation, typically viewed as an alternative to the courts, is revealed to be more of an alternative to private agreements. It may mean that in post-communist countries, where alternative institutionalised methods of dispute resolution are less well known, the awareness of them is lower, leading to lower acceptance. Yet the results are surprising particularly because other studies have demonstrated that post-communist countries have very low levels of general social trust.[6] 'This study thus indicates that countries that have transitioned away from a communist state should focus on increasing trust first rather than setting up complex institutions that require trust to work in the first place'.[7] That would apply to institutionalised mediation as well. But what about Southern Europe? And what about the fact that in the post-communist Poland and other European countries private agreements are found to be preferable? These two facts appear contradictory, but they may suggest that trust towards mediators (a profession which is relatively unknown) is even lower. Another explanation might be that some memories continue to survive of institutionalised mediation in communist times, such as for instance Social Conciliation Committees (*Społeczne Komisje Pojednawcze*). There is certainly little knowledge of these concepts now, but they appear to be remembered as 'a communist idea'. On the other hand, as Ekiert and Foa noted, the overall critical depiction of the post-communist societies as lacking in social trust and civil society might be erroneous:

> Using a wide range of data from various available sources and tracing the stages of civil society transformations, we show that civil societies in Central and Eastern European countries are not as feeble as is often assumed. Some post-communist countries possess vigorous public spheres and active civil society organizations strongly connected to transnational civic networks and able to shape domestic policies.[8]

In 1964 Adam Podgórecki[9] undertook the first Polish representative survey on attitudes towards law and justice. He asked the question that in the light of later debate might be called the question on trust in the law: do you consider that law should be obeyed even if you consider it unjust? To this question in 1964 he received 45 per cent affirmative answers while 22 per cent answered that the unjust law should be obeyed in appearance only and 20 per cent rejected abiding by the law. In 2014, we repeated this question in the nation-wide representative survey of 1059 people and the distribution was almost the same: 45 per cent, 17 per cent, 20 per cent. However, one

[6] See Bjørnskov, C, 'Determinants of Generalized Trust: A Cross-country Comparison' (2004) 130 *Public Choice* 1.

[7] Traps, L, 'Communism and Trust' (2009) *Journal of Politics & International Affairs* Spring 63–76.

[8] Ekiert, G and Foa, R, 'Civil Society Weakness in Post Communist Europe: A Preliminary Assessment' Carlo Alberto Notebook (January 2011) 1, available at: www.carloalberto.org/working_papers.

[9] Podgórecki, A, *Prestiz prawa (Prestige of Law)* (Warsaw, KiW, 1966).

should know that in 1988, that is in the last year of communist dictatorship, Kurczewski was collecting a different set of frequencies using the same type of sample and the same question: trust in law was as low as 27 per cent and since the transformation it had risen to 28 per cent in 1990, in 1992 to 33 per cent and in 1993 up to (or rather back to) 43 per cent. Thus the fact that in 1964 21 per cent answered that one should trust everybody until they fail and that in 2014 26 per cent answer this way while 19 per cent in 1964 and 21 per cent in 2014 opt for full lack of trust by saying that one should not trust the others at all (49 per cent and 51 per cent respectively say that one should trust only those whom one knows) does not exclude the fall in the trust during the toughest years of the communist dictatorship after introduction of martial law in 1981. Still those who trust others more tend to favour direct compromise and not institutionalised justice. So trust has different social effects than in the North-West.[10]

Statistical data on the (un)popularity of mediation in Poland support this conclusion. Mediation in criminal cases and juvenile cases was introduced in the late-1990s (in juvenile justice, first as experiment in 1996–99, and in the criminal code in 1997). Before that, a settlement was only possible under Polish regulations in private prosecution cases. Eventually in 2005 mediation was also introduced in civil cases. This development is significant because the Code of Civil Procedure regulates proceedings in family cases, for example divorce proceedings. There are two forms of civil mediation: either the case may be referred for mediation by the court, or the mediation takes place on the initiative of the parties. In the latter scenario, mediation is divided into mediation requested by both of the parties and mediation requested by one party and accepted by the other.

Referring a case for mediation is not the only option for conciliation in a family dispute in Poland. In many post-communist countries, there are general clauses in the legislation stipulating that an amicable resolution of any dispute is possible. In several of them, the courts are actually obliged to try to persuade the parties to settle. These regulations had (or, in some cases, have) been in force for decades. In Poland, this general option of settling was found for many years in regulations which made it mandatory for the court in a divorce case to conduct a separate session designated as a conciliation session. The session was run by a judge who was obliged to encourage the parties to reconcile, and preceded actual divorce proceedings. The quality and efficiency of these attempts were dubious and judges themselves were sceptical.[11] In 2005, the mandatory conciliation session was replaced by the option of referring the case for out-of-court mediation.

[10] Kurczewski, J, 'Trust in Administration of Justice and Trust in Others', presentation at Vietnamese-Polish Conference on Social Trust in Societies Under Transition (Vietnamese Academy of Social Sciences/Institute of Philosophy and Sociology, Polish Academy of Sciences, Hanoi, 29 October 2014).

[11] Górecki, J, *Divorce in Poland: a Contribution to the Sociology of Law* (The Hague, Mouton, 1970); Fuszara, M, *Rodzina przed sądem (Family at Court)* (Warsaw, ISNS UW, 1994).

There are no statistics to address the question of how many divorce cases and legal separation cases are referred for mediation. Because these cases are heard by civil courts, the numbers merge with the data on all other civil cases. Furthermore, family cases include (in terms of official statistics) juvenile cases, which makes it even more difficult to determine the proportion of family cases referred for mediation. Nonetheless, the data that are available make it very clear that the number of cases referred for mediation in Poland is tiny.

Table 10: Number of civil and family cases in courts and referred for mediation

Year	Number of civil cases	Civil cases referred for mediation	Number of family cases	Family cases referred for mediation
2006	5,040,201	1448 (0.29%)	1,123,860	270 (0.24%)
2007	5,608,180	1399 (0.25%)	1,191,934	326 (0.27%)
2008	6,214,982	1455 (0.23%)	1,296,387	427 (0.33%)
2009	6,701,686	1842 (0.27%)	1,325,816	716 (0.54%)
2010	7,591,387	2196 (0.29%)	1,315,246	988 (0.75%)
2011	8,058,791	2514 (0.31%)	1,321,993	1149 (0.87%)
2012	8,277,470	2844 (0.34%)	1,347,716	1342 (1.00%)

The proportion of cases which proceeded through mediation to a successful resolution is even lower. Overall, only 6.42 per cent of the cases referred for mediation in 2006 and 8.86 per cent of the cases referred for mediation in 2012 ended in discontinuation of the court proceedings as a result of the mediation. Academic literature on the subject notes that this can hardly be used as a measure of effectiveness of mediation. Instead of leading to a specific solution, mediation may be transformative. In this case, it helps the parties change their relationship and the way they communicate, thus contributing to a solution, although in a manner which is less tangible than a settlement.

There has been no research in Poland into mediation, and the attempts to explain why so few cases are referred for mediation are scarce.[12] The explanations that are given tend to focus on three groups of reasons why judges

[12] The Ministry of Justice has recently commissioned a research project 'Diagnosis of the State of Implementation of Mediation' which is currently in progress.

choose not to refer cases for mediation often enough. First, judges tend to believe that they have superior negotiating skills, and that they themselves are the best mediators. Consequently, they believe that in a situation where they cannot see the potential for a settlement, a mediator would be equally unable to do so. This attitude shows the symptoms of the former philosophy of an omnipotent judge who is most competent to resolve a dispute. Secondly, there are no connections between judges and mediators, which means that mediators' skills and competencies are not well known, and that there is a general absence of trust towards them. Thirdly, there is the issue of the length of proceedings. Referring a case for mediation prolongs the proceedings. Yet the courts are accountable on a number of indicators, and the number of cases closed, speed and lack of backlog are decisive factors here. The effectiveness of the solutions reached and the benefits of conciliation are not taken into account. All of these reasons prevent the judges from referring cases for mediation more often. Parties to litigation on the other hand rarely request mediation, because they are unfamiliar with this option. Moreover, once a case is taken to court, the litigants are motivated to win and to assert their claim, rather than to reconcile.

Since 2010, the Ministry of Justice has been taking steps to popularise mediation. A Social Council for ADR was established in the Ministry. Mediation coordinators have also been appointed. Their task is to facilitate contracts between judges and mediators. Training sessions on mediation are being offered to judges and other court employees. Information campaigns are also planned, both general TV and radio campaigns and more in-depth campaigns for various target groups. One aspect, however, has not changed and is not going to change in the near future: the state does not provide funding for mediation. Yet the financial burden of mediation is likely one of the main reasons why it is not more popular among parties to disputes.

INSTEAD OF CONCLUSIONS

Options for amicable dispute resolution are available in all post-communist countries. In Poland, the Code of Civil Procedure stipulates: 'where a settlement is allowed, the court should at all stages of the proceedings aim for a conciliatory resolution of the case. In these cases, the parties may settle in front of a mediator' (art 10). Article 223 of the Code of Civil Procedure requires that the court must make an effort towards reconciling the parties. In divorce cases and in legal separation cases, at any stage of the case the court may refer the parties for mediation in order to agree on issues of, for example, maintenance, parental responsibility, child visitation, etc. In this model, there is a good range of options, but they were implemented in a specific manner: the powers that the courts held previously were upheld, while mediators were added to the status quo, alongside the judges who are also required to encourage conciliation. In Ukraine, there is only a general regulation to the effect that a judge is required to make an attempt to reconcile the parties (art 111 of the Ukrainian Civil Procedure Code). The few judges and clients from city of Drohobych we interviewed were sceptical of the procedure. In Macedonia, the provisions on reconciliation in divorce cases have been expanded. A procedure of reconciliation is now mandatory. In cases of marriages with no children, the procedure is conducted by the court, unless the court decides it would be better if the Centre for Social Work were in charge. If there are children involved, the procedure is always conducted by the Centre for Social Work (art 237 of the Macedonian Law on Family 1992/80). There is no single model shared by all post-communist countries, even though these countries share a reluctant attitude to out-of-court mediation. In Poland, while the courts are still obliged to encourage the parties to settle, and mediators have been introduced, the use of their services is voluntary. In Ukraine, the issue of reconciliation is within the remit of the judges. In Macedonia, apart from the courts, there is a duty to go through a reconciliation procedure at the Centre for Social Work. What these three countries have in common is the strong position of courts and judges even where mediation is possible which illustrates the paradox found in the overall attitudes towards the dispute settlement. The post-communist group of European countries strongly differ internally as to the frequency of divorcing and do not form a specific group as for this criterion. In the majority they remain at a level of distrust of the courts similar to the southern European countries without communist pasts while the level of trust for institutionalised mediation in this group is even lower than in most of the latter and that makes them distinct from other European countries.

Part III

Current Context of Practice and Policy

Sub-part I

Bypassing Courts

8

Paths to Justice in Divorce Cases in England and Wales

ROSEMARY HUNTER, ANNE BARLOW,
JANET SMITHSON AND JAN EWING

INTRODUCTION

THIS CHAPTER CHARTS the landscape of family dispute resolution in England and Wales, drawing on the results of a three-year, ESRC-funded research project on out-of-court resolution options in private family law cases.[1] Although the chapter title refers to 'divorce' cases, not all of the cases we were concerned with involved a divorce. We were interested in what happens when separating couples are in dispute about arrangements for their children and finances following separation. In relation to disputes over children, it did not matter whether or not the parents were married since the relevant law and legal processes are the same. In relation to financial disputes, however, we did focus on divorcing couples, since the law relating to property division differs between former spouses and former cohabitants.

The study focused on three forms of out-of-court family dispute resolution: solicitor negotiations, mediation and collaborative law. Solicitor negotiations describes the process in which each party instructs their own solicitor and the solicitors attempt to broker a resolution of the dispute through correspondence without resorting to court proceedings. Mediation involves the parties meeting with a neutral third party, who facilitates a discussion of the issues in dispute to assist them to arrive at a resolution. Collaborative law is a kind of hybrid of the two, in which the parties each

[1] *Mapping Paths to Family Justice* (2011–15) Economic and Social Research Council Grant number ES/I031812/1. The project was led by Anne Barlow with Rosemary Hunter and Janet Smithson as co-investigators, and Jan Ewing as Research Associate. We would also like to acknowledge the contributions of Kate Getliffe and Paulette Morris to qualitative data gathering. For a full summary of findings, see Barlow, A, Hunter, R, Smithson, J and Ewing, J, *Mapping Paths to Family Justice: Briefing Paper and Report on Key Findings* (University of Exeter, June 2014) http://socialsciences.exeter.ac.uk/law/research/frs/researchprojects/mappingpathstofamilyjustice/about/.

have their own solicitors, but the parties and solicitors negotiate face-to-face in four-way meetings, with the aim being to reach a resolution which is in the best interests of the family as a whole, and without resort to court proceedings. We began with the hypothesis that one size does not fit all: that some cases will best be resolved out-of-court while others may require court proceedings; and that for those cases where out-of-court resolution is most appropriate, different dispute resolution processes may work better for different kinds of cases and parties. One of our research questions, therefore, was to see whether we could identify cases and parties most suited to one form of dispute resolution or another.

The study methods consisted of three phases. First, we undertook a national survey of awareness and experiences of the three forms of out-of-court family dispute resolution. The survey asked a small number of questions at a high level of generality of a nationally representative sample of just under 3000 respondents, as part of an omnibus survey conducted by the research firm TNS-BMRB. This was supplemented by inclusion of the same questions about awareness of family dispute resolution processes on a second survey, the Civil and Social Justice Panel Survey conducted by Ipsos MORI on behalf of the Legal Services Research Centre, which involved a further 3700 respondents.

In the second phase we undertook in-depth qualitative interviews with 95 parties who had undergone one or more of the dispute resolution processes since 1996, and with 40 solicitors and mediators. The majority of the solicitors interviewed were trained and practised in all three dispute resolution processes. Just over half of those practising solely as mediators had come from a legal background with just under half from a non-legal (therapeutic/social work) background. Some of the parties interviewed were recruited via follow-up contacts from the two surveys, but the majority were recruited via law firms and mediation organisations, including (but not confined to) the practices of our practitioner interviewees. Consequently, the majority of parties interviewed had experienced family dispute resolution relatively recently (with the earliest mediation experiences dating from 2002).

The third phase of the study involved recording a small number of examples of each dispute resolution process and analysing the transcripts to understand the dynamics of the process and the interactions between the parties and practitioners, and to triangulate the interview data. We recorded five mediation processes (four concerning children's matters and one financial; four sole and one co-mediation; involving a total of nine separate sessions) and three collaborative law processes (all concerning divorce and financial matters; involving a total of 11 separate sessions—with one case running to seven sessions). Recording solicitor negotiations posed more of a challenge, both due to the difficulty of trying to record all meetings between both parties and their solicitors, and because much of the negotiation takes place by correspondence rather than face to face. Accordingly, we made the pragmatic decision only to record lawyer-client first interviews, since this was the point at which the client would be explaining the issues in dispute, the solicitor would be giving advice and explaining dispute resolution options, and (ideally) together they would be deciding the course of action to take. We ultimately recorded five lawyer-client first interviews: two concerning children's matters, two divorce and finances and one focused primarily on divorce; four privately funded and one legally aided. The recordings, although few in number, provided a rich source of data for analysis and brought alive much of the interview data and theoretical material on the different processes.

The project had the all-too-familiar experience of researching a moving target due to changes in policy and practice, both during the overall period covered by the study (1996–2014), and particularly during the three years in which the study was conducted (2011–14). The study period commenced in 1996, when mediation first became widely available in England and Wales and first began to garner significant policy support.[2] Collaborative law, however, was only introduced in England and Wales in 2003, and remains a somewhat niche area of practice. Unlike in some other jurisdictions (such as the Republic of Ireland), collaborative law has never been supported by legal aid funding in England and Wales.[3] By the time we began the study in 2011, arbitration had recently been added to the range of available out-of-court resolution methods for financial disputes. We did not include it in the study, however, because of its novelty and its exclusive focus on finances.

By contrast, from the early-2000s, mediation was increasingly seen as a money-saver for the legal aid budget, and legally aided clients were subject to increasing levels of 'encouragement' to consider and subsequently to undertake mediation as a condition of receipt of public funding.[4] In April 2011, the mandate to receive information about mediation—via a Mediation Information and Assessment Meeting (MIAM)—was extended to all prospective court applicants, regardless of funding status.[5] This requirement was not widely enforced, however, and has now been enshrined in primary legislation.[6] As a consequence, everyone lodging a court application in respect of children or finances must now demonstrate either that they have

[2] Mediation formed a central element of the proposed reforms to the divorce process introduced in the Family Law Act 1996, pt II.

[3] Legal aid for collaborative law was set to be introduced from November 2011, but was withdrawn prior to commencement.

[4] As specified in the former Legal Services Commission Funding Code. See also National Audit Office, *Legal Services Commission: Legal Aid and Mediation for People Involved in Family Breakdown* (HC 2006–07, 256); House of Commons Public Accounts Committee, *Legal Services Commission: Legal Aid and Mediation for People Involved in Family Breakdown* (HC 2006–07, 396); Legal Services Commission, *Publicly Funded Mediation: The Way Forward* (LSC, 2008).

[5] Family Proceedings Rules, Practice Direction 3A—Pre-Application Protocol for Mediation Information and Assessment (in force 1 April 2011).

[6] Children and Families Act 2014, s 10.

attended a MIAM, or that their attendance is not required because they fall within one of the specified exemptions. Respondents are not subject to the same legislative mandate, although if the applicant contacts a mediation service, the service will in turn contact the respondent and encourage them to make an appointment. In the meantime, on 1 April 2013, legal aid ceased to be available for court proceedings and out-of-court solicitor negotiations in most children's and financial cases, but it remains available for mediation.[7] This effectively means that clients who are unable to pay privately for a lawyer now have only one out-of-court family dispute resolution option available to them: mediation. This provided a sharper edge to our research questions: would the evidence support this exclusive policy emphasis on mediation, or would it support our working hypothesis that one size does not fit all?

AWARENESS OF DISPUTE RESOLUTION OPTIONS

Our survey data indicated that those who had experienced divorce or separation were, unsurprisingly, more aware of family dispute resolution options than the general population.[8] Further, older members of the general population (aged 45–54) were more aware of family dispute resolution options than younger people—no doubt because if they had not experienced divorce or separation themselves, they would have discussed the experience with friends and family members who had done so. The same trends in awareness of the three different dispute resolution processes were evident among both the general population and the divorced/separated population, however, with mediation attracting the highest levels of awareness, followed by solicitor negotiations, followed by collaborative law.

Low levels of awareness of collaborative law are not surprising given its status as a relative newcomer in the field and the fact that it has come to occupy a particular niche. Lower levels of awareness of solicitor negotiations were more surprising, given the findings of Hazel Genn's earlier legal needs survey showing that people with family disputes were more likely to go to a solicitor than for other kinds of legal problems.[9] However, it is probably necessary here to distinguish between awareness of solicitors as the first port of call for advice in family disputes, and awareness of solicitor negotiations as a form of family dispute resolution. Quite a few of the parties we interviewed had been unaware that solicitors engaged in out of

[7] Legal Aid, Sentencing and Punishment of Offenders Act 2012.

[8] For a more detailed account of the survey findings, see Barlow, A et al, 'Mapping Paths to Family Justice: A National Picture of Findings on Out-of-Court Family Dispute Resolution' (2013) 43 *Family Law* (March) 306.

[9] Genn, H, *Paths to Justice: What People Do and Think about Going to Law* (Oxford, Hart Publishing, 1999).

court dispute resolution, tending instead to associate solicitors with going to court. This persistence of the adversarial image of family lawyers has arguably been reinforced and perpetuated by government policy-makers over a number of years,[10] despite the fact that codes of practice for family solicitors eschew adversarialism,[11] and all the research evidence on the practices of family solicitors demonstrates that their 'default setting' is to take a conciliatory approach.[12]

Interestingly, sources of awareness of family dispute resolution methods differed substantially between the general population and the divorced/separated population. The two major sources of information about all family dispute resolution methods for members of the general population were family and friends and the media/internet. Solicitors came a distant third, followed closely by work/education/personal experience. For the divorced/separated population, however, solicitors were the major source of awareness of dispute resolution options, with family and friends figuring much less prominently, and the media/internet even less so. This is consistent with the notion that people experiencing divorce or separation during the period covered by the study would tend to visit a solicitor, who would them inform them of the range of dispute resolution options available to them. It is also consistent with the fact that after the recent legal aid reforms, the number of publicly funded MIAMs and mediation starts in England and Wales plummeted.[13] Since people no longer had access to a solicitor funded by legal aid, the pipeline of solicitor referrals to mediation was cut off. This precipitated frantic efforts by government and by the mediation community to raise awareness of and promote mediation,[14] but our research suggests it

[10] See eg Lewis, P, *Assumptions About Lawyers in Policy Statements: A Survey of Relevant Research* (Lord Chancellor's Department, 2000); Eekelaar, J, Maclean, M and Beinart, S, *Family Lawyers: The Divorce Work of Solicitors* (Oxford, Hart Publishing, 2000); Ministry of Justice and Family Mediation Council, *Family Mediation: Sorting out Family Disputes without Going through Court* (2014) www.justice.gov.uk/downloads/courts/mediation2/family-mediation-leaflet.pdf.

[11] Resolution Code of Practice, available at: www.resolution.org.uk/site_content_files/files/code_of_practice_22.2.07_final.pdf.

[12] See Ingleby, R, *Solicitors and Divorce* (Oxford, Clarendon Press, 1992); Davis, G, Cretney, C and Collins, J, *Simple Quarrels: Negotiating Money and Property Disputes on Divorce* (Oxford, Clarendon Press, 1994); Eekelaar et al, *Family Lawyers* (n 10); Wright, K, 'The Role of Solicitors in Divorce: A Note of Caution' (2007) 19 *Child and Family Law Quarterly* 481.

[13] Ministry of Justice, *Legal Aid Statistics in England and Wales: Legal Aid Agency Apr to June 2014* (September 2014) 24. The number of publicly funded MIAMs fell from approximately 30,000 in the year April 2012–March 2013 to approximately 13,000 in the year April 2013–March 2014. The number of publicly funded mediation starts fell in the same period from approximately 13,500 to approximately 8000.

[14] See eg Family Mediation Task Force, *Report of the Family Mediation Task Force* (Ministry of Justice, June 2014); The Rt Hon Simon Hughes MP, Press Release: 'More Free Mediation Sessions for Separating Couples' (20 August 2014) www.gov.uk/government/news/more-free-mediation-sessions-for-separating-couples. Further research on family mediation is currently being undertaken by the Ministry of Justice.

will be difficult to do so in the absence of an obvious first point of contact such as solicitors provided. Indeed, it may now be the court application form or the court counter which has become the first point of contact. Application forms for parenting orders now include a front page encouraging mediation and certifying attendance at a MIAM, and court counter staff are supposed to divert would-be applicants to a MIAM if they have not already attended one or claimed an exemption.[15] The difficulty is that a client visiting a solicitor for advice about post-separation arrangements may be more amenable to considering mediation than someone who has got to the point of issuing court proceedings.

Only around 10 per cent of our national survey sample (n=315) had experienced separation or divorce since 1996. Of these, almost half (47 per cent) did not seek any kind of legal advice, and presumably sorted out their post-separation arrangements on their own. Those who were divorcing were more likely to seek legal advice (62 per cent) than those who had been in a cohabiting relationship (45 per cent). Of those who sought legal advice, two-thirds said they had been offered at least one of our family dispute resolution processes. Solicitor negotiations and mediation were reported to have been offered in roughly equal proportions of cases, with, unsurprisingly, very few reporting having been offered the option of collaborative law.

Since for most of the period of our study people's first port of call for family disputes was a solicitor, it was mainly solicitors who offered the various dispute resolution options. Since April 2011, mediators conducting MIAMs are also required to explain the various dispute resolution options available. What we found from our interviews with both parties and practitioners, however, was that it was not very common for parties to be offered a genuine choice of dispute resolution options, by either solicitors or mediators. Rather, the client's options tended to be circumscribed by a combination of their own circumstances and practitioner preferences. Prior to the legal aid reforms, many of the legal aid clients we interviewed were clearly under the impression that legal aid required them to attempt mediation (not just attend an information meeting about mediation). Whether or not this was what their solicitors actually said, we did get the impression that legal aid solicitors fairly routinely referred clients directly for mediation and would only pursue the matter if mediation failed or the case was assessed by the mediator as being unsuitable for mediation. Likewise, some practitioners said that there had been little point telling legal aid clients about collaborative law, since legal aid was not available for that process and clients would not be able to afford to pay privately (although one practitioner admitted to

[15] HM Courts and Tribunals Service, *Revised Guidance for HMCTS: Practice Direction 3A—Pre-Application Protocol for Private Law Proceedings: Attendance at a Mediation Information and Assessment Meeting (MIAM) Prior to Issue of Application* (1 December 2012).

having done two collaborative cases on Legal Help, the legal aid grant paid for initial legal advice). Following the legal aid reforms, as stated earlier, there is realistically only one dispute resolution option available to a client lacking private means, and that is mediation.

Even for privately paying clients, the range of options available tended to be offered with a strong steer from the practitioner towards one option or another. Sometimes this was based on an assessment of appropriateness, but sometimes less objective reasons came into play. In some cases, the practitioner was a passionate advocate for a particular form of dispute resolution—typically mediation or collaborative law. They were convinced that this was the best way to resolve family disputes or particular kinds of disputes, and thus would attempt to convince the client to the same view. For example, one mediator, Laura Gurney,[16] said in interview that although in MIAMs she would explain the pros and cons of each dispute resolution process, she felt that it was the mediator's role to 'sell' mediation to the client, while Sally Fenton said she would feel she had failed if the client chose another process over mediation. Conversely, some practitioners were sceptical of particular forms of dispute resolution, which was often based on lack of familiarity with the process. Thus, some mediators were sceptical of solicitor negotiations and some solicitors were sceptical of mediation. Both mediators and solicitors could be sceptical of collaborative law and not really understand how it worked. Indeed, on the basis of our interviews and recorded sessions, we concluded that those practitioners who had experience in the collaborative process were best placed to explain it as an option, while those who were not collaboratively trained were less able to articulate its potential benefits. Finally, the presentation of dispute resolution options could be driven by vested interests. Both law firms and mediation practices could be under financial pressure, and in those circumstances, there was a strong desire to hang on to business rather than see it walk out the door and into a different process.

EXPERIENCES OF DISPUTE RESOLUTION PROCESSES

In the national survey there was a substantial difference in the take-up rate of the dispute resolution processes offered, with 89 per cent who said they were offered solicitor negotiations taking up the offer, while only 58 per cent of those who said they were offered mediation took it up. The take-up rate for collaborative law was difficult to judge, owing to small numbers and some questions about the reliability of the data (for example, people claiming to have done collaborative law before 2003). The main reasons

[16] In order to preserve anonymity, all names of interviewees are pseudonyms.

for not taking up solicitor negotiations were that people preferred to handle the matter on their own (after having some initial legal advice) or did not feel they could afford the cost. The reasons given for not taking up mediation were more varied, including the ex-partner not wanting to participate, not feeling able to talk to the ex-partner, and a history or fear of violence or abuse.

The interviews yielded many further reasons for taking one track rather than another, ranging from actively choosing a particular option (for example, wanting to keep solicitors out of it or wanting the support of a solicitor; wanting to resolve matters as quickly and amicably as possible or wanting to maintain a clear distance from the other party and a buffer in between them); to resisting or refusing to engage with whatever process the other party wanted to pursue; to feeling pressured into mediation or collaborative law by their ex-partner. The combination of circumstances necessary to launch a collaborative law process seemed the hardest to achieve, requiring two agreeable parties, both of whom had engaged or were willing to engage collaboratively trained lawyers, both willing to take the risk of the participation agreement, which requires a commitment from all four participants not to go to court, and from both solicitors to cease acting if either party issues court proceedings, and who had enough money to be able to afford to pay for what could be an expensive process. The dearth of collaborative cases and the failure of collaborative law to really take off in most areas of the country was a persistent refrain among the collaboratively trained practitioners we interviewed.

A number of parties experienced more than one form of dispute resolution, usually some combination of mediation and solicitor negotiations. This might be different processes for different issues (for example, solicitor negotiations for finances, mediation for children), or one followed by the other (unsuccessful or partially successful mediation followed by solicitor negotiations, or initial solicitor negotiations followed by mediation). In many cases there was also an element of direct negotiation between the parties in combination with one or more dispute resolution processes. For two parties, Tracy and Sheila, the collaborative process broke down, to be followed by mediation in Tracy's case, or solicitor negotiations and court proceedings in Sheila's.

There was a noticeably different resolution rate for all three dispute resolution processes between children's matters and financial matters, although the number of collaborative law cases was too small to enable meaningful separate comparisons. Only 43 per cent of children's matters overall were resolved by one of the three processes, compared to 67 per cent of financial matters. Mediation was very much better at resolving children's disputes (55 per cent) than solicitor negotiations (20 per cent), and somewhat better at resolving financial disputes (71 per cent mediation vs 58 per cent solicitor negotiations). It should be stressed that these figures relate only to the fact of resolution and not the parties' levels of satisfaction with the outcomes they achieved.

A substantial number of parties ended up in court after attempts at out-of-court dispute resolution failed, particularly in children's matters. Of the 27 parties who failed to resolve children's matters by out-of-court dispute resolution, 19 (70 per cent) commenced court proceedings. Of the 22 parties who failed to resolve financial matters by out-of-court dispute resolution, just over half (13) commenced court proceedings. For both types of matters, court proceedings were more likely to be initiated following failed solicitor negotiations than following failed mediation or collaborative law.

Of the 19 children's matters that went to court, proceedings were still ongoing in six cases at the time of the interview. Of the 13 that had finalised, seven were resolved by adjudication while six were resolved by negotiations in the course of proceedings. Of the 13 financial matters that went to court, three were still ongoing at the time of the interview, eight were resolved by negotiation in the course of proceedings, and only two were adjudicated.

The overall picture gained from the experiences of the parties we interviewed was that attempts to resolve matters out of court were a rather random, hit-or-miss process. While some parties actively and mutually chose mediation or collaborative law and were willing and able to resolve their post-separation issues in that way, others were subject to the vagaries of funding requirements or the preferences of the adviser they saw, as well as their own relationship dynamics. In financial matters, it seems that the choice of dispute resolution route did not make such a difference. Solicitors and mediators were similarly capable of resolving these matters, especially when collaborative law was included in the picture. And if matters did not resolve, solicitors in particular were ready to issue court proceedings and generally succeeded in brokering an agreement in the context of proceedings. On the other hand, in children's matters while many people felt more comfortable with or were more willing to agree to solicitor negotiations than mediation, people who did go to mediation were more likely to reach some kind of resolution, whereas those who engaged in solicitor negotiations were more likely to end up in court.

There are two possible inferences which may be drawn from these findings. One is that it is about the process: mediation is more conducive than solicitor negotiations to the settlement of children's matters. The other is that it is about the people who engage in the process: those who go to mediation are generally more willing and able to reach an agreement, while those who have no capacity to mediate end up with solicitor negotiations as the default option (sometimes after a fruitless attempt at mediation) and often find themselves going to court. In other words, mediators and solicitors are dealing with different kinds of parties, and solicitors see those who are less able to reach an agreement between themselves and, indeed, tend to need a court order to determine their dispute.

This brings us back to the questions posed earlier: is the government's promotion of mediation in almost all cases justified? And, if not, can we identify from the outset the parties and cases which are more or less suited to the different dispute resolution processes, so that advisers have a less subjective basis for steering parties down a particular track?

MATCHING CASES AND PARTIES WITH DISPUTE RESOLUTION PROCESSES

As a general proposition, parties' suitability for any form of out-of-court dispute resolution process is determined by their capacity, in the words of practitioner David Leyton, to 'do a deal'.[17] As discussed below, there are many factors which may limit parties' capacity to 'do a deal', but one which affects almost everyone is the rawness of emotions in the first few months after the breakdown of a relationship. At this point, it may be possible to do no more than put in place interim arrangements for the children, certainly not to make any significant decisions about money or finances. But with the lapse of time—or, in some cases, with the aid of therapeutic intervention—parties are likely to become more emotionally equipped to negotiate. As Rebecca put it:

> My overall feeling, even looking back now, that it was all too soon. But in hindsight the mediation was a good thing, but if there was some statutory time limit. Obviously you've got children, you've got to sort out some care arrangement quite quickly, but I feel looking back there should be a temporary arrangement made quickly, and then you need a minimum of, I don't know, three to six months before you can start talking about anything else. Because when you're an emotional wreck obviously you can't make good decisions, and that was really the position that I was in.

Similarly, Jason conceded that:

> when emotions are running high … certain people are not ready to negotiate, especially my ex, who was very bitter and very sore. I think initially she wouldn't have listened to sense and at that point she never listened to sense so erm, I would have liked to have thought yes, definitely, you know, it would have certainly suited me if we could have negotiated sooner and an outcome had happened sooner, but as far as getting anything out of my ex, I don't think so.

Once parties have reached the point of emotional readiness, there are a range of indicators which would appear to make them suitable for a

[17] See also Hunter, R, Barlow, A, Smithson, J and Ewing, J, 'Mapping Paths to Family Justice: Matching Parties, Cases and Processes' (2014) 44 *Family Law* (October) 1404.

party-interactive process, either mediation or collaborative law. These include the parties:

— being willing to engage in the process, including willing to sit around a table with each other;
— having an element of trust and respect between each other;
— being relatively amicable or low conflict, and wanting to maintain cordial relations with each other;
— wanting to achieve the best outcome for their children;
— being committed to financial transparency and willing to make full financial disclosure;
— being on a relatively equal footing in terms of resources, information and power, such that any imbalances can be redressed by a mediator or co-mediators;
— either communicating well, or wishing to improve their future communication;
— being willing and able to listen to and appreciate the other party's point of view;
— not starting from widely divergent positions; and
— being open-minded and willing to compromise

In these cases, when choosing between mediation and collaborative law, relevant factors would include:

— whether the dispute is about arrangements for children or all issues (in which case mediation is likely to provide a better option) or finances only (which could go either way). For example, Sandra used mediation for children but a solicitor for finances:

> I think the security of solicitors because you have the law behind you, certainly because it's very much more fact based and so therefore it worked for me financially.... I didn't feel there was a place for emotion in the finances because to me it was cut-throat. Whereas with the children, the mediation, there was a big place for emotion, you know. So that's how I felt it worked, that's my personal level.

— the complexity of financial issues involved (with practitioners generally—though not universally—agreeing that complex financial cases involving high net worth individuals, companies, overseas assets, multiple pensions, trusts, tax issues, and needing expert input from actuaries, financial advisers, pension advisers and so on are better suited to collaborative law than mediation);
— the parties' eligibility for legal aid (for mediation but not for collaborative law);
— cost considerations for privately paying clients; and

— the nature of the dispute and the type of assistance needed by the parties (if they need help communicating and generating options, mediation may be more appropriate, but if they need legal advice about what a court might decide, collaborative law would be a better choice).

Parties who need the support, advice and guidance of a lawyer throughout the dispute resolution process are not suitable for mediation, but require a lawyer-led process, either collaborative law or solicitor negotiations. The circumstances in which the ongoing support, advice and guidance of a lawyer may be needed include:

— a significant disparity between the parties in psychological/emotional terms (for example, one is stuck in the past, the other has moved on);
— a significant power imbalance between the parties (including disparities in intellectual capacity, disparities in knowledge and understanding of the parties' finances, where one party has been dominating and the other subservient in the relationship, or a party is timid or feels bullied or intimidated by the other party's control or financial resources); or
— one of the parties is vulnerable in some way (examples given in practitioner interviews included those who are 'their own worst enemies', too guilty about the breakup, overwhelmed by financial information, nervous about making major decisions alone or unable to make decisions at all, or thoroughly uncomfortable with their ex-partner)

In addition, complex financial cases involving technical legal issues such as the scope of the marital acquests or the applicability of a pre-nuptial agreement are likely to require a lawyer-led process. When choosing between collaborative law or solicitor negotiations in these cases, factors to be taken into account would include:

— whether both lawyers are collaboratively trained;
— whether the parties otherwise fit the indicia for collaborative law set out above;
— cost considerations (in the past, legal aid eligibility would also have been a factor, but that is no longer an option for solicitor negotiations);
— whether the weaker/more vulnerable party feels able to face the other party in the same room and able to speak out in their presence (with or without therapeutic intervention), or whether they need to be shielded from any direct contact with their ex-partner;
— whether the weaker/more vulnerable party is able to make rational decisions;
— whether it would be helpful for the more powerful party to hear the advice being given to the weaker/more vulnerable party—which, as Kirsty Oliver noted, would occur in collaborative law but not in solicitor negotiations; and

— whether, as Jeremy Hutchings observed, the power imbalance creates a risk that the collaborative law process may break down, which would have an adverse impact on the weaker/more vulnerable party.

Practitioner interviewees further identified a series of circumstances in which neither mediation nor collaborative law would be appropriate as the matter is too complex for a party-interactive process, or there is a need for a buffer between the parties. These cases are only suitable for solicitor negotiation, with the strong possibility that they may end up in court. These include:

— cases involving third party disputes;
— where one or both parties are unwilling to listen to the other or to understand their position;
— where one party is very controlling; in the words of Caroline Underwood: 'domineering characters ... who want to run the show', who 'come to the ... table with their spreadsheets and try to dictate the process';
— where one or both parties has fixed ideas of what they want to achieve in negotiations, is entrenched in their position and not prepared to compromise (Jane Davison estimated this accounted for 20–30 per cent of family disputes), is clinging to a fixed position based on their rights rather than their children's needs (such as fathers who will not budge from a demand for formal shared care), or is looking for vindication of their position;
— where one or both parties wants to fight to the bitter end on a point of principle;
— where one or both parties is seeking vengeance or determined to defeat the other party. This was Monica's experience:

> It [mediation] depends on both parties being reasonable and you cannot mandate that. And just because a legal form is forced on people, doesn't mean that they won't treat it as adversarial. I mean, my ex-husband came into it with all guns blazing, determined to destroy me. Now that is not what mediation is about but you were never going to stop him feeling like that.

— where one or both parties are intent on securing the best deal for themselves in negotiations; or
— cases in which there are concerns or issues about non-disclosure.

In these cases, if both parties share these characteristics, there is little or no prospect of any out-of-court resolution. If only one party displays these characteristics, the only possible outcomes of mediation are that the other party will be forced to accept the entrenched party's position, or the process will break down. The former would be unjust (and potentially not in children's best interests) and the latter would be a waste of time.

Finally, there are the cases which appear to have no prospects at all for out-of-court resolution and should go straight to court:

— if there is a need for an emergency injunction
— cases involving child abduction, child safety concerns, child abuse or neglect with police or social services involvement, vulnerable children or sex offenders;
— cases involving absolute conflicts of fact which need to be determined by a court, such as paternity disputes;
— leave to remove (relocation) disputes where there is no scope for compromise. As Glenys explained:

> I wanted the Leave to Remove and go back to [home country] and it was … You know, neither of us were going to back down on our position, really…. Unfortunately … there is no negotiation with moving to [another (distant) country]. It's not like saying, 'Well, shall we settle on [third country] as a halfway point?', you know? It's not … there wasn't an awful lot that … that could be negotiated.

— where one party refuses to disclose their financial position;
— where one party will not accept that the relationship is over, and therefore has no interest in agreeing post-separation matters;
— where one party is determined to play the victim and not prepared to take responsibility for decision-making; or
— where one party is entrenched in a strategic position and has nothing to gain and everything to lose by engaging in negotiation and compromise (for example, a residence mother in 'possession' of the children and controlling contact, or a husband in 'possession' of the assets and unwilling to divide them).

Having distilled from our data this series of indicators for matching parties and cases with processes, it should also be noted that the most advanced thinking we encountered among the practitioners interviewed focused not on suitability for discrete dispute resolution processes, but upon tailoring creative combinations of processes to meet the needs of individual cases. Such combinations may often involve collaborative work between practitioners, such as the notion of 'lawyer-supported mediation',[18] or referring clients to counselling or parenting programmes, or bringing financial advisers and/or child consultants into the mediation or collaborative process. These possibilities certainly deserve to be explored further, although under current policies they appear available only to the relatively wealthy and well out of reach of legal aid clients.

[18] See http://lawyersupportedmediation.com/.

PARTICULAR ISSUES IN MEDIATION

Three further categories of case need to be addressed in terms of their suitability for mediation. The first is high-conflict children's cases. Although they do not fit the criteria for mediation set out above, some practitioners considered that these cases—variously described as 'thorny' children's issues, or couples with 'significant anger issues'—are suitable for mediation, on the basis that mediation can potentially help to reduce the conflict and improve communication between the parties by getting them to focus on the interests of their children. This was usually accompanied by a caveat that such cases require a high level of skill and experience on the part of the mediator, and are better suited to co-mediation or shuttle mediation. The co-mediation process we recorded fell into this category, and did indeed succeed in making progress with contact and communication after the very angry mother took the opportunity to vent her anger at length in the first mediation session. But it might be expected that in some proportion of these cases mediation will be unsuccessful and the case may end up in court.

Secondly, in some situations, practitioners noted that specialist mediators might be able to handle a case that would otherwise be considered unsuitable for mediation. For example, complex financial cases could be handled by specialist financial mediators, or by co-mediation with a mediator trained as an independent financial adviser, or through caucusing with lawyers. Or international child abduction cases could be mediated with a specialist Reunite mediator.

Thirdly, there was a considerable variety of views among practitioner interviewees as to the suitability for mediation of cases involving domestic violence, mental health conditions, or drug or alcohol problems. The best approach, as articulated, for example, by Martin Appleby, appeared to be to consider such cases as raising a question of risk to an adult party and/or to the children concerned which needs to be addressed and managed. This first requires careful identification of the nature of the risk. Thus, in the case of domestic violence, the nature of the violence needs to be understood, as well as its effects on the victim and on the children. Unfortunately, the evidence from our own and other research is that mediator training on screening for domestic violence has not always been adequate to this task, and the amount of time devoted to the question of violence in MIAMs is minimal.[19]

Once the nature of the violence and its effects have been identified, the indicia set out above can be applied to the specific circumstances of the case. If the perpetrator has acknowledged his violence, expressed contrition and sought to make amends, and the victim accepts this as genuine, then mediation is likely to be appropriate. If one party is making allegations which

[19] Morris, P, 'Mediation, the Legal Aid, Sentencing and Punishment of Offenders Act of 2012 and the Mediation Information and Assessment Meeting' (2013) 35 *Journal of Social Welfare and Family Law* 445.

are denied by the other party and their truth or otherwise is central to the issues in dispute, then it is a factual issue which needs to be adjudicated by a court. Likewise, if there is a need to assess whether the alleged perpetrator poses a risk to the children's safety, in England and Wales this requires court proceedings to commission a Cafcass report. If there is an ongoing threat of harm to the victim or the children, or ongoing controlling behaviour on the part of the perpetrator, the victim requires the support of a lawyer and mediation (including shuttle mediation) is not appropriate, since intimidation and control still exist whether or not the parties are brought face to face. If the effect of the violence has been to create a significant power imbalance between the parties such that the victim is unable to participate effectively without lawyer support or protection, again, mediation is not appropriate. Two of our party interviewees, Charlotte and Sara, made particular note of this fact:

> if they're in a situation where you feel ... that your partner dominates you or, you know, there's been a bit of violence or anything of that kind, I would say, be cautious ... Because I think there's always a danger that, um, you'll agree to something that, you know, you don't want to agree to just because you're going along with it. Do you know what I mean? That's one situation where I'd feel ... Especially if the mediator didn't pick up on it.

> The problem is that if you're in an abusive relationship, you have ... Mediation is just not going to work because ... you're not dealing with a reasonable, fair person ... Fortunately I've met a lot of people now [laughs] through all this and everyone that has, um, been in an abusive relationship ends up going to court because they're not going to get ... He's not a decent person they're dealing with ... He can't do the mediation.... And the thing is, when they come across, these type of men, they're very charming and polite and they're very ... you know, so ... Yeah. You just should never be put in that situation, anything like that, basically. No.

If the victim of abuse considers that she is capable of mediating and wishes to attempt it, the nature of the violence, its effects and the nature of any ongoing risk (to the children as well as the adult party) should still be independently assessed, together with the likely effectiveness of available safety measures. In summary, participating in mediation should constitute an 'occasion of respect' for the victim of violence. If it would, instead, constitute a further 'occasion of oppression' then mediation is not appropriate.[20]

People with serious mental health conditions which render them unable to participate effectively or safely in the process are also unsuitable for mediation. This is likely to be more than a rare occurrence. Seventeen of the 95 parties we interviewed mentioned mental health issues for themselves

[20] Hunter, R, 'Consent in Violent Relationships' in R Hunter and S Cowan (eds), *Choice and Consent: Feminist Engagements with Law and Subjectivity* (Abingdon, Routledge, 2007).

or their ex-partner or both. In some cases this was reactive depression, for which a few received counselling, but in the majority of cases the issues were more serious and chronic. Again, the nature of the condition and its effects need to be clearly understood. If the party can participate safely and effectively in mediation because their condition is controlled and/or they have sufficient professional support to do so, it must still be considered whether there are any risks to the other party or to the children. If there are concerns about child safety arising from the party's mental health condition, or if the severity and consequences of the condition are matters in dispute, then court proceedings are required. The same is true for people with drug and alcohol problems. In the latter case, there is the possibility of voluntary drug or alcohol testing prior to mediation (as there is also the possibility of voluntary paternity testing), but in the absence of agreement to testing, a court order will be required.

CONCLUSION

As the above discussion makes clear, our research suggests that one size does not fit all when it comes to family dispute resolution, and that the absolute policy preference for mediation is not justified. There are a number of circumstances in which mediation is unlikely to be an appropriate method of resolution for the particular parties or the particular dispute, and these circumstances extend well beyond the narrow categories of exemption from attending a MIAM and continued eligibility for legal aid for legal representation and court proceedings.[21] If a party needs the support of a lawyer, if the parties do not meet the indicia for successful mediation, if there are unassessable or unmanageable risks to the safety of a party or child, or if it is a case which requires a court decision, then mediation (and sometimes other forms of out-of-court dispute resolution) is likely to be at best futile and at worst dangerous. It is all very well to say this, however, in an ideal world in which the options of mediation, collaborative law, solicitor negotiations or court proceedings are genuinely open to everyone. But many parties in England and Wales do not live in that ideal world. If they cannot afford a lawyer and do not fall within the legal aid eligibility criteria, their only options are mediation or going to court as a self-represented litigant.

A number of mediators we interviewed took the view that as between mediation and court, mediation would always be the best option because it is less costly, time-consuming and traumatic, and the parties are more in

[21] Essentially confined to situations where a party has independent evidence of recent, serious domestic violence or child abuse: Family Procedure Rules, Practice Direction 3A—Family Mediation Information and Assessment Meetings; Legal Aid, Sentencing and Punishment of Offenders Act 2012, sch 1, ss 12–13; and Civil Legal Aid (Procedure) Regulations 2012, reg 33.

control, than the court process. There are two problems with this view. One is that it focuses only on the process and ignores the outcome, particularly the possibility of an unfair or unjust agreement, or one which is not in the best interests of any children involved. Secondly, the evidence from some of our party interviewees makes clear that they did find the process of mediation traumatic, and far from being in control, felt they were being controlled and intimidated.

These findings suggest that in order to cater adequately for people with no real alternatives, mediation cannot rest on its laurels but needs to rise to the challenge. This would require more work being put into developing mediator skills and specialisations, and developing new models of mediation, including hybrid models incorporating lawyer and other forms of support,[22] specifically to address the kinds of parties for whom and cases for which 'classic' facilitative mediation was not originally designed. Such developments would be a valuable consequence of the amount of faith and public funding invested in mediation, and would potentially be of benefit to everyone seeking to resolve family disputes out-of-court. Otherwise, the family dispute resolution pathway in England and Wales is likely to remain fraught, uncertain and obstructed.

[22] See eg Australian Institute of Family Studies, *Evaluation of a Legally Assisted and Supported Family Dispute Resolution in Family Violence Cases* (December 2012).

9

Family Lawyers and Multi-agency Approaches

Why Don't Lawyers Work with Other Service Providers?

ANGELA MELVILLE, KAREN LAING AND FRANK STEPHEN

MULTI-AGENCY SOLUTIONS INVOLVE a range of service providers, often located across different professional backgrounds, working together in order to address a client's problems. In England and Wales, multi-agency approaches are at the heart of welfare policies aimed at tackling complex social problems such as gender violence, social exclusion, crime prevention, child protection and community health. For supporters of multi-agency approaches, clients benefit from being offered integrated, holistic and innovative solutions, which are more likely to address the root causes of problems. Despite this, family lawyers often work alone rather than work with other service providers.

First, this chapter examines previous work into the advantages and barriers of family lawyers being involved in multi-agency approaches. Secondly, we look at evaluations of two initiatives implemented by the Legal Services Commission (LSC) in England and Wales, namely the Family Advice and Information Network (FAInS) pilot; and Community Legal Advice Centres and Networks (CLAC/Ns). These initiatives both attempted to involve lawyers in providing a holistic service to address clients' overlapping legal and non-legal family issues.

Both FAInS and CLAC/Ns have been discontinued and the demise of the LSC means that similar initiatives now face a bleak future. However, this does not mean that it is impossible for lawyers to work with other service providers to tackle family law problems. Our analysis identifies two main barriers to the lawyers working with other service providers: lack of financial incentives; and unequal power relations. The loss of legal aid funding for family law matters will force lawyers to look for new ways to survive in a shrinking market. One survival mechanism, and one which also addresses the barriers of funding and uneven power relations, may be to become employees for not-for-profit (NfP) organisations who provide a holistic and joined-up service to their clients.

INVOLVING LAWYERS IN MULTI-AGENCY APPROACHES: ADVANTAGES AND BARRIERS

Multi-agency approaches involving lawyers are not common. However, they have gained prominence in the form of medical-legal clinics in the US. Medical-legal clinics were founded by Zuckerman, a paediatrician working in Boston, who was frustrated by only being able to resolve a narrow aspect of a child's illness rather than the underlying social issues that often cause childhood disease. Zuckerman set up a clinic involving doctors referring patients with potential legal problems to lawyers.[1]

For Zuckerman, medical-legal clinics promote a preventative approach to social problems, which involves tackling a problem before it reaches a crisis point, which may in turn produce long-term outcomes. The clinics encourage a culture of advocacy, and assist the most vulnerable members of society who are also the most likely to experience multiple problems. These clients are also the most likely to find it difficult to access multiple services, and do not necessarily realise that their problems may have a legal solution.

Despite the growth of medical-legal clinics, there are few evaluations aimed at testing how the involvement of lawyers in multi-agency approaches works in practice.

The evaluations that have been done have highlighted advantages as well as potential barriers. For instance, Lynch examined efforts by lawyers providing services to homeless clients in an Australian legal clinic to engage with social services providers in order to address their clients' non-legal issues.[2] The clinic offered outreach services, so that clients did not have to come in to the service, and lawyers were then exposed to the clients' lives. The main problem faced by the clinic involved obtaining ongoing funding, and the service was dependent on lawyers working free of charge.

Another Australian example consists of Noone's evaluation of efforts by a Community Legal Centre and Community Health Service at providing a holistic service for clients with legal, health and welfare problems.[3] The service's success relied on referrals being appropriate and mutually beneficial,

[1] Zuckerman, B, Sandel, M, Lawton, E and Morton, S, 'Medical-legal Partnerships: Transforming Health Care Medical-legal Partnerships' (2008) 372 *Lancet* 1615.

[2] Lynch, P, 'Human Rights Lawyering for People Experiencing Homelessness' (2004) 10(1) *Australian Journal of Human Rights* 4.

[3] Noone, MA, 'Towards an Integrated Service Response to the Link between Legal and Health Issues' (2009) 15 *Australian Journal of Primary Health* 203.

the referral process being understood by both agencies, and checking that clients followed up on referrals. An integrated approach reduced the anxiety experienced by clients who were facing a cluster of problems, and improved client satisfaction also increased lawyer satisfaction.

Noone's evaluation also identified a number of barriers. Funding was insufficient to allow for organisational integration, and there was a lack of overarching policies. In order to be successful, there needed to be willingness across providers to share resources, providers needed to have agreed goals, planning to be integrated, and for there to be trust between providers. Professional boundaries were found to create barriers, and service provision was hampered by differences in communication and decision-making styles, professional identities, levels of commitment, willingness to recognise the expertise of others, and levels of management support.

These barriers are similar to those identified by Moorhead and Robinson, who compared the advice provided by legal firms and NfP agencies based in England and Wales.[4] Clients experienced clusters of complex housing, debt and benefit problems which required integrated solutions. The provision of an integrated service was limited by financial constraints, lack of organisational skills and capacities and lack of information about what other services provided. Some clients ended up being confused by instructions, and instead of resolving issues before they reached a crisis point, problems were allowed to escalate.

The barriers identified by these evaluations would potentially hamper the delivery of multi-agency approaches regardless of the service providers involved. However, there are additional barriers that are specific to lawyers. The first such barrier involves regulation. Multi-agency approaches in the form of multidisciplinary practices (MDPs) were only allowed in England and Wales with the passage of the Legal Services Act 2007, and are still banned in some jurisdictions such as the US.[5] The medical-legal clinics sidestep regulations as they are non-profit organisations and clients are referred, and therefore there are no fee-sharing arrangements.[6] Opponents of MDPs argue that they undermine the core values of the legal profession, namely protecting client privilege and confidentiality, avoiding conflicts of interest, and ensuring the profession's independence.[7] However, it has been

[4] Moorhead, R and Robinson, M, *A Trouble Shared—Legal Problem Clusters in Solicitors and Advice Agencies*, Department for Constitutional Affairs, Research Series 8/06. http://webarchive.nationalarchives.gov.uk/+/http://www.dca.gov.uk/research/2006/08_2006.pdf.

[5] Paton, PD, 'Multidisciplinary Practice Redux: Globalization, Core Values, and Reviving the MDP Debate in America' (2010) 78 *Fordham Law Review* 2193.

[6] Brustin, SL, 'Legal Services Provision through Multidisciplinary Practice—Encouraging Holistic Advocacy while Protecting Ethical Interests' (2002) 73(3) *University of Colorado Law Review* 787.

[7] Garcia, JR, 'Multidisciplinary Practices: What is Wrong with the Legal Profession's Ethics Rules' (2000) 44(2) *Saint Louis University Law Journal* 629; Paton, 'Multidisciplinary Practice Redux' (n 5).

argued that ethical issues can be dealt with, for instance extending privilege. Referrals also bypass restrictions arising from lawyers' ethical codes.[8]

It has also been argued that the legal profession's opposition to MDPs arises from a desire to protect their monopoly over the legal services market.[9] In England and Wales, the lifting of the ban on MDPs followed from a report by the Office of Fair Trading[10] which found that the restriction was anti-competitive and could be used to unfairly increase legal fees. This was followed by a report by Sir David Clementi which suggested abolishing the legal profession's self-regulation.[11] Clementi argued that MDPs would provide an impetus to improve services, allow for greater innovation, increase efficiency, lower costs and provide a more integrated service that would better address clients' needs. Clementi's recommendations are partly reflected in the Legal Services Act 2007. The Act permits lawyers and non-lawyers to provide legal services on an equal footing. Part of the opposition against MDPs had been based on the difficulties in implementing regulation across different professionals. The Act attempts to resolve this issue by moving regulation from the individual profession to the 'economic unit' in which the service provider operates.[12]

Regulatory barriers are not the only reason for lawyers' reluctance to work with other service providers. Prior to removal of the ban on MDPs, lawyers could have drawn on the services of non-lawyers through referrals, and yet lawyers have been reluctant to recommend their clients to other services.[13] As we discuss below, the main service that family lawyers refer to consists of mediation, and research has consistently demonstrated that many lawyers have been reluctant to refer. Pilot information meetings about mediation in anticipation of proposed mandated meetings under the Family Law Act 1996 failed to enhance enthusiasm for mediation. Consequently the proposal was dropped except for clients in receipt of legal aid funding, although as the LSC could not insist that parties paying privately should attend, referrals to mediation continued to remain relatively low.[14]

[8] Wyrda, H, 'Keeping Secrets within the Team: Maintaining Client Confidentiality while Offering Interdisciplinary Services to the Elderly Client' (1993) 62 *Fordham Law Review* 1517.

[9] Dzienkowski, J and Peroni, RJ, 'Multidisciplinary Practice and the American Legal Profession: a Market Approach to Regulating the Delivery of Legal Services in the Twenty-first Century' (2000–01) 69(1) *Fordham Law Review* 83.

[10] Office of Fair Trading, *Competition in Professions* (London, HMSO, 2001).

[11] Clementi, D, *Review of the Regulatory Framework for Legal Services in England and Wales: Final Report* (2004) www.aiga.it/old/pdf/doc-57-871.pdf, ch F.

[12] Stephen, F, *Lawyers, Market and Regulation* (Cheltenham, Edward Elgar Publishing, 2013) 113.

[13] Davis, G, *Monitoring Publicly Funded Family Mediation: Report to the Legal Services Commission* (London, Legal Services Commission, 2000); Melville, A and Laing, K, 'Closing the Gate: Family Lawyers as Gatekeepers to a Holistic Service' (2010) 6(2) *International Journal of Law in Context* 167.

[14] Davis, ibid; Davis, G and Bevan, G, 'The Future Public Funding of Family Dispute Resolution Services' (2002) 24(2) *The Journal of Social Welfare & Family Law* 175.

In May 2010, a Coalition government formed by the Conservative and Liberal Democrat parties came to power. The new government has reinstated mandatory attendance at a mediation intake session for applicants to the court in family matters (known as Mediation Information and Assessment Meeting) whether parties are legally aided or not. However, there is no requirement upon parties to attend mediation beyond the MIAM, and parties not in receipt of legal aid are required to pay. Previous experience would suggest that referrals for mediation will not increase, although the government appears determined to ignore previous empirical evidence and instead rely on popularist beliefs that lawyers promote an adversarial culture, mediation is always effective and that there is unmet demand for mediation.[15]

The lack of referrals may not be entirely due to lawyers protecting their market. It may partly reflect lawyers' desire to protect their client's interests. Lawyers have criticised the NfP sector for lacking adequate training and skills, providing inappropriate advice and having long queues and erratic opening hours.[16] They may not refer as they are not aware of what other services are available,[17] or feel that other services do not provide anything that they do not already offer.[18] According to Moorhead and Richardson, lawyers largely see the NfP sector as being supplementary to legal services, rather than offering something that is valuable in its own right.[19]

Research has also shown that lawyers are often aware of their client's non-legal problems, but feel that exploration of these issues is beyond their professional remit.[20] Lawyers may be reluctant to discuss non-legal issues as they feel that this is beyond their expertise, or that to do so does not assist their client to 'move on'.[21] Sherr argues that lawyers' ability to examine

[15] Dingwall, R, 'Divorce Mediation: Should we Change our Mind?' (2010) 32(2) *Journal of Social Welfare and Family Law* 107.

[16] Mather, L, McEwan, CA and Maiman, RJ, *Divorce Lawyers at Work: Varieties of Professionalism in Practice* (Oxford, Oxford University Press, 2001) 75; Moorhead, R, Paterson, A and Sherr, A, 'Contesting Professionalism: Legal Aid and Non-lawyers in England and Wales' (2003) 37 *Law and Society Review* 765; Neilson, LC, 'Solicitors Contemplate Mediation—Lawyers' Perceptions of the Role and Education of Mediators' (1990) 4 *International Journal of Law, Policy and the Family* 235; Richardson, CJ, *Court Based Divorce Mediation in Four Canadian Cities: An Overview of Research Results* (Ottawa, Department of Justice, 1988).

[17] Smart, LS and Salts, CJ, 'Attorney Attitudes toward Divorce Mediation' (1984) 6 *Mediation Quarterly* 115.

[18] Davis (n 13); Feldman, M, 'Political Lessons: Legal Service for the Poor' (1995) 83 *Georgetown Law Journal* 1529; Felner, RD, Terre, L, Farber, SS, Primavera, J and Bishop, TA, 'Child Custody: Practices and Perspectives of Legal Professionals' (1985) 14(1) *Journal of Clinical Child and Adolescent Psychology* 27; Smarts and Salts, ibid.

[19] Moorhead and Richardson, *A Trouble Shared* (n 4).

[20] Eekelaar, J, Maclean, M and Beinart, S, *Family Lawyers: The Divorce Work of Solicitors* (Oxford, Hart Publishing, 2000).

[21] Mather, L, Maiman, RJ and McEwen, CA, '"The Passenger Decides on the Destination and I Decide on the Route": Are Divorce Lawyers "Expensive Cab Drivers"' (1995) 9 *International Journal of Law, Policy and the Family* 286; Trinder, L, Firth, A and Jenks, C, '"So Presumably Things have Moved on since then?" The Management of Risk Allegations in Child Contact Dispute Resolution' (2010) 24(1) *International Journal of Law, Policy and the Family* 29.

non-legal issues is hampered by deficiencies in communication.[22] Lawyers tend to treat their clients as 'exam questions' rather than as people with complex problems. Moorhead and Richardson argue that lawyers generally work within narrow specialisations with little overlap between areas of law, and the trend towards increased specialisation has been accelerating in recent years.[23]

MULTI-AGENCY INITIATIVES: EVALUATING FAINS AND CLAC/NS

While there are still few efforts at involving lawyers within multi-agency approaches, the Legal Services Commission in England and Wales had been at the forefront in providing initiatives. Two such initiatives consisted of the Family Advice and Information Network (FAInS) pilot, and more recently Community Legal Advice Centres (CLACs) and Community Legal Advice Networks (CLANs). These initiatives followed earlier research by Genn into the types of legal problems encountered across the community and what people do once they encounter a justiciable problem.[24] Genn found that problems frequently 'cluster', and that legal problems are often accompanied by an array of complex and overlapping non-legal problems. This research created a framework for understanding legal needs that stressed that dealing with a trigger problem before it evolves into clusters may reduce overall legal need, and in turn reduce social and economic costs and improve clients' lives.[25]

The FAInS pilot commenced in 2001 and closed in 2007. One of its primary aims was to have family law practitioners identify client's non-legal issues and refer to other service providers where appropriate, so that clients received a holistic service that dealt with their entire problem cluster. Lawyers were provided with additional funding in order to explore their client's non-legal issues more fully in the first meeting. However, an evaluation of FAInS showed that approximately a quarter of clients were not provided with any information about another service or were referred. When a referral was made, clients were usually left to their own devices to make an appointment. The most common service signposted by lawyers was family mediation, and even then half of the lawyers interviewed were sceptical of the value of mediation.[26] A number of reasons were given for this reluctance

[22] Sherr, A, 'Lawyers and Clients: the First Meeting' (1986) 49(3) *The Modern Law Review* 323.

[23] Moorhead and Robinson (n 4).

[24] Genn H, *Paths to Justice: What People Do and Think About Going to Law* (Oxford, Hart Publishing, 1999).

[25] Moorhead and Robinson (n 4) 2.

[26] Melville and Laing, 'Closing the Gate' (n 13).

to refer. Lawyers were not necessarily aware of what other services were available. Some also claimed that the services required by their clients were unavailable or had long waiting lists, lawyers were unsure of the quality of services offered by other agencies, and they did not want their clients to feel as if they were being passed off to another service rather than having their problems addressed.[27]

In order to save clients from having to recount their story each time they saw a different service provider, lawyers were encouraged to draw up a Personal Action Plan (PAP) for their clients. The PAP was intended to provide a 'travelling document' that summarised both legal and non-legal issues. However, Melville and Laing report that most PAPs contained insufficient information to provide another service with an understanding of the case.[28] Some lawyers were reluctant to use the PAPs as they felt that client confidentiality was breached, or that their clients would be upset if sensitive details were written down. Many lawyers also used the documents primarily to encourage their client to focus on legal issues and marginalise non-legal issues.

Melville and Laing argue that the main barriers to the provision of a holistic service through FAInS consisted of the lawyers' conceptions of their professional role.[29] For many family lawyers, their role involves separating their client's legal and non-legal needs, and then focusing on resolving the issues that are within their professional remit. Many clients present in a highly emotional state, and lawyers felt that dwelling on non-legal issues encourages clients to be irrational, unreasonable and distracted from thinking about their children's best interests. FAInS was discontinued in March 2007 when it was superseded by the FAInS Additional Modes of Delivery Pilot, although this pilot was also discontinued.

Following FAInS, the LSC commenced another initiative aimed at integrating services for clients: Community Legal Advice Centres (CLACs) and Community Legal Advice Networks (CLANs). CLACs brought together all services within a specified geographical area into a single entity, and CLANs brought together a consortium of difference organisations, including NfP agencies and private solicitor firms, under a lead provider. The services were funded jointly by the LSC and local authorities, and were delivered through a one-stop shop. CLAC/Ns covered a range of categories of law, focusing for the most part on welfare benefits, family law, community care, employment and debt, mental health and immigration issues. CLAC/Ns were also intended to meet a client's legal needs through the entire resolution process, starting with diagnosis and information, advice and assistance, through to legal representation in court. The LSC explained that CLAC/Ns were

[27] ibid.
[28] ibid.
[29] ibid.

intended to provide a seamless service that would address clients' clusters of non-legal and legal issues, reduce the problem of referral fatigue and join up services.[30]

The first CLAC opened in April 2007 in Gateshead. The Gateshead's CLAC used an initial 10 to 15 minute 'diagnostic' interview, after which the client was referred if appropriate to a specialist for further advice with the appointment arranged immediately during the interview. Further CLACs opened in Derby, Leicester and Portsmouth in 2008.[31] However, cuts to legal aid funding means that few cases could now be handled by CLAC/Ns. Consequently, contracts to CLAC/Ns were terminated in March 2012.

A comprehensive evaluation of CLAC/Ns conducted by the Legal Services Research Centre reported that the services were well received by clients. CLACs were seen to be accessible and efficient, clients appreciated having a range of advisers located in the one place, and felt that staff were more welcoming, professional, knowledgeable and better at resolving problems than other services they had used previously. It was important to clients that services were free, covered a range of issues and were flexible. From the providers' perspective, CLAC/Ns were successful when there were clear roles among advisers at each tier of the service. A client's multiple problems needed to be clearly defined and coordination between services well organised and supported by agreed procedures for sharing case management information. Services were also improved if there was appropriate aftercare and feedback.[32]

There were also some important differences between FAInS and CLAC/Ns. With FAInS, the initial diagnosis interview was conducted by a lawyer. However, as lawyers conceived their professional role as keeping the client focused on legal issues, this often prevented an exploration of other issues. The initial CLAC/N's interview was conducted by a generalist adviser. Advisers appeared to more fully explore their clients' multiple issues and identify future advice needs, although this did not occur in every instance. Advisers reported that they did not always have time to fully examine multiple problems, and one of the main themes was problems caused by over-demand. Identification of multiple issues was also often left to the diagnostic interview only, rather than occurring at all tiers of service provision.

[30] Buck, A and Curran, L, 'Delivery of Advice to Marginalised and Vulnerable Groups: the Need for Innovative Approaches' (2009) 3 *Public Space: The Journal of Law and Social Justice* 1; Legal Services Commission, *Making Legal Rights a Reality* (2006) www.legalservices.gov.uk/docs/civil_contracting/CLS-Strategy-final-15032006cover.pdf.

[31] Buck, A, Smith, M, Sidaway, J and Scanlan, L, *Piecing it Together: Exploring One-Stop Shop Legal Service Delivery in Community Legal Advice Centres* (Legal Services Commission, 2010).

[32] ibid.

As with FAInS, the CLAC/Ns did not always produce referrals. Some generalists did not refer as they were worried about deskilling and wanted to keep interesting cases. Some specialists also reported experiencing inappropriate referrals, inadequate paperwork and high client numbers. The way in which referrals were handled was also important for clients. Whereas FAInS asked lawyers to use the PAP as a means of informing a referral service of their client's issues, CLAC/N clients wanted opportunities to give their own narrative in order to establish trust with a service provider.

The majority of clients felt that CLAC/Ns provided a seamless service, although some reported having to see a number of people before obtaining specialist advice. This problem reflected over-demand, which also meant that some drop-in sessions were closed early, crowded waiting rooms and long waiting times due to a shortage of interview rooms. Although the evaluation investigated how services were joined up, internal performance monitoring was not particularly well matched to the programme's aims. There was little monitoring of how services addressed clients' clustering of problems or integrated services.[33]

Both FAInS and the CLAC/Ns were intended to 'tailor services' to clients, meaning that clients who were deemed capable were encouraged to take responsibility for resolving their own issues. Whereas FAInS lawyers rarely devolved tasks to clients, the CLAC/Ns advisers appeared more willing to recognise an appropriate division of labour. FAInS advisers also largely left their clients to follow up on referrals, whereas CLAC/N advisers tended to write down next steps and provide phone numbers. Tailoring services was not always successful, and some clients judged to be capable of resolving their own issues struggled to follow recommendations. Some lacked the financial resources to do so and could not cope with an unfamiliar situation. Tailoring services was also reported to be time-consuming and resource intensive.[34]

In addition, there were problems at a broader policy level. CLAC/Ns were jointly funded by the LSC and local authorities, and the aims of each organisation were not easily reconciled. Each CLAC/N provided a bespoke service that required collaboration between the LSC, local authorities and service providers. As such, planning resources was difficult, and timeframes were largely determined by political processes within each local area.[35] A further evaluation commissioned by the Local Government Association also reported tension between the different organisations. LSC funding is only available to clients who reach the threshold, and LSC objectives are not necessarily aligned with local government commitments to support the

[33] Fox, C, Moorhead, R, Sefton, M and Wong, K, *Community Legal Advice Centres and Networks: A Process Evaluation* (Legal Services Commission, 2010).

[34] Buck and Curran (n 30).

[35] See n 33.

NfP sector. The LSC also determined the specifications for contracts. Only some local councils were able to influence that contracting process and to specify their own objectives, and those that did needed to invest a significant amount of time and resources.[36]

Local authorities also expressed concern about the long-term sustainability of CLAC/Ns. They were concerned that contracts may not provide private providers with a sufficient caseload. The shift of funding towards large single contracts could also put smaller voluntary community organisations at risk.[37] Indeed, some of these concerns have proven to be well-founded. The LSC has now terminated CLAC/N contracts following the withdrawal of funding for most family law and social welfare matters. Considering that one of the main problems faced by CLAC/Ns was over-demand, the impact of this will mean that many people with complex, overlapping multiple needs will now not receive the service that they clearly need.

DISCUSSION: WHY WON'T LAWYERS WORK WITH OTHER SERVICE PROVIDERS?

Our review of FAInS and CLAC/Ns suggests two major barriers preventing family lawyers from becoming involved in multi-agency services: financing and unequal power relations. First, lawyers need to get paid, and as vulnerable clients often cannot afford to pay private fees, they are reliant on the NfP sector or the state for assistance. The fate of both FAInS and CLAC/Ns provides a stark example of what often happens to multi-agency approaches that are dependent on state funding during cutbacks.

Secondly, even when funding has been available, multi-agency approaches are often hampered by unequal power relations between agencies. This can lead to some services, in particular those from the voluntary sector, being marginalised. In relation to CLAC/Ns, this problem occurred when the objectives of the LSC were given priority over the aims of local authorities and local service providers. The problem of unequal power relations may also appear in another guise. Multi-agency approaches appear to work best when generalists refer to lawyers, as was the case for CLAC/Ns, and also for medical-legal practices and other examples cited in the previous literature. In contrast, FAInS involved lawyers referring to other services, and lawyers did not see that this was within their professional remit. Even when lawyers had been specifically tasked with signposting other services, they were reluctant to do so.

[36] Tribal Group, *Early Lessons from Changes to Legal Advice Provision and Funding: The Local Authority Experience. London* (Local Government Association, 2010) www.local.gov.uk/c/document_library/get_file?uuid=7680d321-6cd2-4235-90b4-92c69da45881&groupId=10180l.

[37] ibid.

Multi-agency approaches involving lawyers typically operate in a hierarchical manner, with lawyers at the apex. FAInS highlighted that lawyers do not necessarily understand that referring to other services could be useful. This suggests that lawyers do not see that their own skills set may be limited, and that other service providers may provide useful assistance to clients. Whereas some proponents of multi-agency approaches claim that they are a useful means for lawyers to learn new skills,[38] it seems that instead they reinforce lawyers' professional dominance over other service providers. A one-way referral system does little to encourage lawyers to recognise the skills of other professionals or to consider their client's non-legal problems.

This narrowness of focus on the part of lawyers working in the field of family law is an example of a wider phenomenon associated with the practice of law. Several researchers have pointed to the narrowness of experience of lawyers in private practice.[39] Lawyers are on the whole educated, trained and practise the law with other lawyers. Hadfield argues that this results in a relative lack of innovation by law firms and the adoption of relatively narrow business model.[40]

CONCLUSION: IS ALL LOST?

The elimination of legal aid for family law matters has resulted in the termination of CLAC/Ns, but even more worrying has been the rise of the number of litigants in person, and evidence that inappropriate cases are being referred to mediation. In some instances, practitioners have reported that referring to mediation is better than leaving a vulnerable client to cope alone at court.[41] Despite this, the Coalition government appears to have made an ideological commitment to the demise of legal aid funding. However, this does not necessarily mean that innovations such as FAInS and CLAC/Ns are confined to the past. It may be that as social problems arising from the failure to fund the resolution of family law problems continue to mount, the government will be forced to take action. However, efforts to address family law problems without recourse to re-establishing legal aid are likely to be ad hoc, unstable and vulnerable to changing political agendas.

A more coherent way forward, which addresses both the financial constraints and unequal power relations, may emerge from Alternative Business

[38] eg Anderson, A, Barenberg, L, Buck, A and Walker, H, 'Professional Ethics in Interdisciplinary Collaborates: Zeal, Paternalism and Mandated Reporting' (2007) 13 *Clinical Law Review* 659.

[39] Hadfield, GK, 'The Price of Law: How the Market for Lawyers Distorts the Justice System' (2000) *Michigan Law Review* 953; Stephen, *Lawyers, Market and Regulation* (n 12).

[40] Hadfield, ibid.

[41] Barlow, A, Hunter, R, Smithson, J and Ewing, J, *Mapping Paths to Family Justice: Briefing Paper and Report on Key Findings* (2014) 8 available at; http://socialsciences.exeter.ac.uk/law/research/frs/researchprojects/mappingpathstofamilyjustice/keyfindings/.

Structures (ABSs) which are permitted by Legal Services Act 2007. ABSs are providers of legal services owned, inter alia, by non-lawyers and may be able to provide welfare legal services more efficiently and effectively than traditional 'High Street' law firms. Stephen suggests that this will lead to a 'technological revolution in lawyering'.[42]

At present NfP organisations have a special status under the Legal Services Act 2007 which does not require them to be licensed under the Act. This is seen as a transitional arrangement, although the exemption will now continue until 2015 at the earliest. Nevertheless, given the reduction in public funding through legal aid for such services, socially motivated ABSs may provide a more viable and effective multi-agency model to provide such service in the future. The loss of legal aid funding means that lawyers must adapt to the new reality of a reconfigured legal market under the age of austerity, and one survival mechanism may be to become employees outside the traditional law firm.

[42] Stephen (n 12) 132–33.

10

Family Justice Without Courts

Property Settlement on Separation Using Contracts in Scotland

JANE MAIR, FRAN WASOFF AND KIRSTEEN MACKAY

> Family law is not all 'fluff and nonsense' ... We're not thought of as being contract lawyers, yet to a significant extent, that's exactly what we are. A surprising amount of our time is spent drafting and considering contracts.[1]

CONTRACTUALISATION OF FAMILY LAW

A KEY THEME in family law debate, particularly since the 1970s, has highlighted the unsuitability of the court as a forum for the resolution of issues arising from family breakdown. First the idea of 'private ordering'[2] and more recently the concept of 'contractualisation'[3] have been promoted as alternative, and better, ways of dealing with family-based disputes. Often this theme of private ordering is linked with a trend away from law and lawyers as the key players within the field of dispute resolution, with the emphasis shifting to alternatives such as mediation and collaboration.[4] In many jurisdictions, there have been significant attempts to shift family disputes out of the courts and into the arena of Alternative Dispute Resolution (ADR).[5] Various objectives underpin these attempts:

[1] Kelsey, R, 'Family law is not all fluff and nonsense' *The Scotsman* 27 February 2007 www.scotsman.com/news/family-law-is-not-all-fluff-and-nonsense-1-683601.

[2] A concept highlighted in Mnookin, RH and Kornhauser, L, 'Bargaining in the Shadow of the Law' (1979) 88 *Yale Law Journal* 950.

[3] A theme considered in Dewar, J, 'Family Law and its Discontents (2000) 14 *International Journal of Law, Policy and the Family* 59, 70–74. See also Swennen, F, 'Family (Self-) Governance at the Boundaries of a Privatized Family Law: a Belgian Exploration' (2011) 19 *European Review of Private Law* 209.

[4] Granberg, RS and Cavassa, SA, 'Private Ordering and Alternative Dispute Resolution' (2010) 23 *Journal of American Academy of Matrimonial Law* 287.

[5] For discussion of recent experience in England, see *Special Issue: Delivering Family Justice in Late Modern Society: in the Wake of Legal Aid Reform* (2013) 35(1) *Journal of Social Welfare and Family Law* 1–160.

relationship benefits, therapeutic consequences, client-centred focus and apparent cost saving potential have all been cited as motivating factors behind the promotion of non-court based settlement and the push towards an alternative way of delivering family justice.[6]

These themes are common in Scots family law, as in other jurisdictions, but in some respects their development in Scotland has been distinctive. Scots law is a mixed legal system[7] combining elements of both civilian and common law approaches, and to that extent it is something of an exception, particularly within the area of family law and matrimonial property.[8] While to the rest of Europe it looks rather like a common law system, lacking as it does a proper matrimonial property regime, when compared with England, its principled legislation and openness to contractual variation highlights its civilian roots. The quote above, from a leading Scots family lawyer, makes the point in very succinct and down-to-earth terms that drafting contracts is what family lawyers in Scotland do and, it might be added, this is nothing new. The precise purpose and terms of the contracts which modern solicitors draft may have changed from those written by their predecessors, with ante-nuptial contracts all but disappearing and separation agreements becoming much more common,[9] but broadly speaking there is a strong pattern of continuity. Unlike jurisdictions[10] where there have been and still are doubts about the legitimacy and suitability of contract within the domain of family law, in Scotland its legality is well settled and long established.[11] In Scotland, contemporary interest in contractualisation has its roots in long-established historical practice and, if there is a drive to promote it further, it is one which is largely motivated by legal practice: a bottom-up pattern of solicitor-led growth rather than a top-down intervention. While there may be a revived interest in marital agreements and contracts in recent years, and evidence of their increased use in practice, this development in

[6] See eg Singer, JB, 'Dispute Resolution and the Post-divorce Family: Implications of a Paradigm Shift' (2009) 47 *Family Court Review* 363.

[7] For discussion of Scotland as a mixed system and of mixed systems more generally, see Sellar, WDH, 'Scots Law: Mixed from the Very Beginning—A Tale of Two Receptions' (2000) 4 *Edinburgh Law Review* 3; Orucu, E, 'What is a Mixed Legal System: Exclusion or Expansion?' (2008) 12 *Electronic Journal of Comparative Law* 1.

[8] This can be seen, eg, in Boele-Woelki, K, Ferrand, F, Gonzalez-Beilfuss, C, Jantera-Jareborg, M, Lowe, N, Martiny, D and Pintens, W, 'Principles of European Family Law Regarding Property Relations Between Spouses' in *European Family Law*, vol 13 (Antwerp, Intersentia, 2013).

[9] Norrie, K, 'Money and your Life' (2009) 54(10) *Journal of the Law Society of Scotland* 24.

[10] The most obvious comparison is with English family law: for discussion of some of the differences, see Mair, J, 'The Marriage Contract: *Radmacher v Granatino*' (2011) 15 *Edinburgh Law Review* 265.

[11] There is an excellent overview of marriage contracts in Clive, EM, *The Law of Husband and Wife in Scotland*, 4th edn (Edinburgh, W Green, 1997) ch 17.

Scots family law did not require a marked change in attitude,[12] nor a policy 'transformation'[13] or 'paradigm shift'.[14]

When Scots family lawyers draft contracts now they are doing what lawyers have always done and while the attitudes and methods of contemporary solicitors may be strongly influenced and informed by the 'fluff and nonsense'[15]—family-centred practice, mediation and collaborative law[16]—private ordering in Scotland is quite definitely the work of lawyers. There might be a move away from court as the place for resolution of family disputes but there is little evidence of a shift away from lawyers. In stark contrast to England, for example, where policy-makers have been criticised for their 'steadfast refusal' to see options beyond a binary choice between 'mediation or courtroom adjudication',[17] the story of private ordering in Scots family law is embedded in solicitors' offices and shaped by legal practice.

What is understood by the terms 'private ordering' and 'contractualisation' ranges from a fairly limited perspective, providing simply for the privatised implementation of public norms, to a much broader model which encompasses individual contractual construction of publicly significant relationships.[18] In many legal systems, couples frequently regulate the consequences of separation and divorce through private agreement rather than by court action and such separation agreements are commonly regarded as being less problematic than other types of relationship contracts.[19] It is this type of contractualisation which is most evident within the Scottish context: privately negotiated separation agreements which to a large extent reflect an underlying statutory system of norms. While it is this particular form of contractualisation which currently dominates, the pattern of gradual development in practice, continuity with a range of marital contracts of the past and absence of detailed consideration or review of contracts as a matter

[12] Bix, B, 'Bargaining in the Shadow of Love: The Enforcement of Premarital Agreements and How We Think About Marriage' (1998) 40 *William and Mary Law Review* 145, 149.

[13] See generally, Dewar, J, 'Family Law and its Discontents' (2000) 14 *International Journal of Law, Policy and the Family* 28.

[14] Singer, 'Dispute Resolution and the Post-divorce Family' (n 6).

[15] While the quotation does not elaborate on what is meant—and the tone is quite clearly self-deprecating—it might be taken as a reference to the distinction between traditional legal skills such as drafting and the modern perception of family lawyers as mediators, counsellors and collaborative practitioners.

[16] See Myers, F and Wasoff, F, *Meeting in the Middle: A Study of Solicitors and Mediation Practice—Research Findings* (Edinburgh, Scottish Executive Central Research Unit, 2004); Nicholson, P, 'A Better Way to Talk' [2012] *Journal of the Law Society of Scotland* 149; Quail, TY, 'Keep CALM and Carry on' [2013] *Journal of the Law Society of Scotland* 24.

[17] Eekelaar, J, '"Not of the Highest Importance": Family Justice under Threat' (2011) 33 *Journal of Social Welfare and Family Law* 311, 313–14.

[18] For discussion of some of these variations, see Bix, BH, 'Private Ordering and Family Law' (2010) 23 *Journal of American Academy of Matrimonial Law* 219; Atwood, BA, 'Marital Contracts and the Meaning of Marriage' (2012) 54 *Arizona Law Review* 11.

[19] An issue explored in the US context in Atwood, ibid.

of policy means that there is little legal principle to restrict usage in this way. It is in essence a well-established but very *laissez-faire* system.

This chapter will look at the Scottish system of separation agreements within the context of a broader trend towards contractualisation; a term defined as meaning 'the ordering of the family by families and individuals through legally binding private instruments'.[20] It draws on recent empirical research which analysed a random sample of 600 agreements made across Scotland in 2010, with follow-up interviews with parties to agreements (30: 17 women and 13 men) and solicitors (13).[21] In Scotland, agreements between couples are frequently reduced to writing in the form of a minute of agreement. They are treated as legally binding contracts with no requirement of judicial scrutiny or approval, which become directly enforceable as a result of registration,[22] thus entirely bypassing the courts.

OPEN TO CONTRACTUALISATION

Scotland provides a legal setting, which is open to the possibility of private ordering in the regulation of family relationships, and in which negotiated settlements have been able to flourish. A number of factors can be identified which contribute towards this settlement-friendly environment: long-established legality and use of a range of marriage-related contracts; a statutory family law framework with clear principles and guidelines and a preference for consensus; an effective system of registration which provides for simple enforcement and limited scope for legal challenge. While there have been some specific initiatives aimed at encouraging individuals to reach agreement,[23] rather than seeking resolution of disputes through the courts, to a considerable extent the increasing prevalence of private settlement seems to have developed naturally within this friendly legal environment.

A Flexible and Familiar Form

Marriage contracts, of various kinds; ante-nuptial, post-nuptial, marriage settlements, separation agreements, have a long and well-established history

[20] Swennen, 'Family (Self-)Governance at the Boundaries of a Privatized Family Law: a Belgian Exploration' (n 3).

[21] *All Settled?* (ESRC 1-year funded project, ES/J004960/1). The Final Report: Mair, J, Wasoff, F and Mackay, K, *All Settled? A Study of Legally Binding Separation Agreements and Private Ordering in Scotland* (2013) is available at: www.crfr.ac.uk/assets/MinutesofAgreement20131.pdf.

[22] They are registered in a public register, the Books of Council and Session, and stored centrally in the National Records Office, Edinburgh.

[23] Key statutes make specific provision for agreements within the statutory framework: eg Family Law (Scotland) Act 1985, ss 10(6) and 16.

in Scotland.[24] While their purpose, form and relative popularity have changed over time, their legal enforceability has been constant. As a general rule, Scots law respects the private agreements of couples as enforceable and does not distinguish between different types of marriage contracts. Subject to standard legal principles regarding capacity and consent,[25] 'parties to a marriage contract ... are entitled to make such terms as they think fit'.[26] While an agreement may always be challenged on standard contractual grounds and might be reduced on the basis of, for example, undue influence, duress or misrepresentation, this is relatively rare and claims can be difficult to substantiate.[27]

There is continuity in terms of the use and enforceability of private settlement but over time the specific purpose has changed. In the nineteenth century, ante-nuptial agreements were used to avoid the common law rights of the husband over his wife's property during marriage and to provide for property and financial settlement if the marriage broke down. At a time when divorce was less accessible and less socially acceptable, separation agreements were also common as a non-judicial way of formalising the end of a couple's relationship 'at bed and board' and could be used to make provision for aliment and property settlement between spouses and in respect of children. Their original purpose was to signal the end of married life in practice without the final step of divorce. As divorce became easier, gained in social acceptability and became increasingly common, the use of 'separation' agreements continued but their purpose gradually changed. For many couples, separation, instead of a long-term status, became a relatively short-lived stage on the way to divorce and, therefore, increasingly separation agreements were entered into as preparation for divorce and with the intention of regulating its long-term consequences. In addition to Scots law's general openness to marriage contracts, their specific use in this context is explicitly approved:

> parties may by agreement oust the jurisdiction of the court ... It has always been the law that notwithstanding statutory provisions regulating the rights of parties, they may agree to certain terms, and if they do so they must receive effect.[28]

It is this type of contract—commonly referred to by solicitors as separation agreements—which has become widely used in modern family practice in Scotland.

[24] See Clive, *The Law of Husband and Wife in Scotland* (n 11) ch 17.
[25] eg, duress, undue influence, facility and circumvention. For discussion, see McBryde, WW, *The Law of Contract in Scotland*, 3rd edn (Edinburgh, Thomson/W Green, 2007).
[26] *Thomson v Thomson* 1982 SLT 521 per Lord Cameron at 526.
[27] For a recent example of a challenge concerning coercion, see *MacDonald v MacDonald* 2009 Fam LR 131.
[28] *Milne v Milne* 1987 SLT 45 at 47, per Lord Kincraig.

Where parties have reached agreement in respect of some aspect of their relationship, it is common for them to reduce that agreement to writing; often referred to as a minute of agreement. Such deeds are by no means specific to family law but their use has become particularly well established within that context and to a significant extent minutes of agreement have come to be regarded as the normal means for dealing with the consequences of relationship breakdown. As one solicitor put it: 'The minute of agreement was always around but I think it may have become a more popular way of taking things'. (Interview: Solicitor 12)

Broadly referred to as minutes of agreement, there is no requirement that they be entered into at the point of separation. Agreements might be made before or after marriage, at an early sign of relationship difficulty or at the courtroom door. Separation agreements are often a precursor to divorce reflecting the fact that if a separating couple reach an agreement, and if there are no dependent children of the marriage, they may also make subsequent use of a cheaper simplified divorce procedure.[29] In practice, the vast majority of agreements in our sample were separation agreements, with 10 having been made prior to the relationship[30] and nine during a subsisting relationship. In principle, however, there is no legal distinction in how agreements made at different points in the relationship are treated.

One of the strengths of the contemporary use of separation agreements is that it has developed organically with no major government initiative or policy drive. To a large extent it has grown out of the practice of family solicitors and as a result it is regarded as a very normal, settled and familiar process. As one of the solicitors we interviewed explained: 'My practice is based on the fact that I don't think the court should be used for family matters … the more they can sort matters out for themselves, it's better for everyone'. (Interview: Solicitor 1)

Agreements are flexible in form and in the process leading to their conclusion, not being required to conform to a set format or procedure. While there is often similarity between individual agreements, this is more a consequence of common drafting styles rather than the result of any requirement of uniformity. Whether positive or negative, there has been no systematic review of the process and little prescription as to the legal form which is in stark contrast to other systems.[31]

[29] The Scottish government recently consulted about the extension of the simplified divorce procedure to couples with dependent children who agree about the arrangements for the children. The great majority of divorces in Scotland (over 93% in 2012–13) use the two separation grounds to demonstrate the irretrievable breakdown of the marriage (one year with consent or two years otherwise): Civil Law Statistics for Scotland 2012–13, available at: www.scotland.gov.uk/Topics/Statistics/Browse/Crime-Justice/Datasets/DatasetsCJS/suptab1213.

[30] Of these, 5 were ante-nuptial agreements and 5 were pre-cohabitation.

[31] The Law Commission, *Matrimonial Property, Needs and Agreements: Execution of Qualifying Agreements* (Law Com No 343, 2014).

A Principled Framework

Although there has been no single legislative initiative to encourage or impose private ordering, statutory context is a key factor in its growth. The two principal statutes relevant to separation agreements are the Family Law (Scotland) Act 1985, dealing with financial provision on divorce, and the Children (Scotland) Act 1995 which regulates parental responsibilities and rights. Each statute establishes a very clear and detailed framework of orders, principles and guidance and each has an inbuilt preference for private agreement.

Although there is considerable freedom and flexibility in the form and execution of separation agreements, they are constructed around the statutory framework of the Family Law (Scotland) Act 1985. On application, the court may make a range of orders,[32] which must be justified by one or more of the principles set out in section 9. One of the key aims of the legislation was to provide clear guidance to the courts in terms of making financial provision orders and it was hoped that, with relative certainty as to what a court might do, couples would be encouraged to make their own agreement without resorting to court action. Section 8 provides the court with a range of orders for sharing and redistribution of property and finance on divorce: payment of a capital sum, transfer of property, periodical allowance and various orders related to the sharing of pensions.[33] According to section 8(2), the court may only make an order where it is justified by one or more of the section 9 principles and where it is reasonable with regard to the resources of the parties. The five principles that can justify the order of a financial award on divorce may be summarised as follows: fair sharing of matrimonial property; balancing of economic advantage or disadvantage; fair sharing of the ongoing burden of childcare in respect of children under the age of 16; provision for a period of readjustment (limited to three years) where one party has been substantially dependent on the other: relief of long-term financial hardship caused by the divorce where one spouse has been substantially dependent on the other. There is a statutory preference for orders for capital sum payment, property transfer or pension sharing with orders for periodical allowance (the Scottish term for post-spousal maintenance) being available only in respect of the final three principles and only where the other orders are not sufficient. In this way the Act states a preference for clean break settlements when possible and this is strongly reflected in separation agreements. As one of the solicitors we interviewed put it: 'The clean break principle is a very wise one, because you want to make, implement the terms of the agreement, relatively quickly, I would say, to stop any possibility of things going wrong'. (Interview: Solicitor 1)

[32] Family Law (Scotland) Act 1985, s 8(1).
[33] ibid.

The Children (Scotland) Act 1995 also sets out clear and detailed principles in the form of parental responsibilities and rights.[34] While all decisions concerning a child are subject to the guiding principle of the welfare of the child,[35] the explicit statement of what is expected of parents in respect of their children is likely to help them to reach private agreements about the care of children following the breakdown of an adult relationship. This is specifically encouraged by section 11(7)(a), which includes what is often referred to as the principle of minimal or non-intervention: the court shall not make an order in respect of a child unless it would be better to do so than to make no order. In other words, the preference is for the parties to make their own arrangements. The effectiveness and enforceability of agreements between couples concerning their children are obviously subject to different considerations from those concerning property and finance, but nonetheless the clear, detailed and agreement-focused provisions of the Act are likely to encourage parties to seek agreement rather than resorting to court action.

The statutory principles which govern the consequences of divorce and dissolution are key to understanding the development of separation agreements in Scotland. There has been no explicit pressure on parties to reach agreement but a system has been created which is so well settled and accepted that parties and their solicitors in many cases see no need to go to court: as one solicitor commented, 'we can predict what is likely to happen' (Interview: Solicitor 2). While modern separation agreements represent continuity with the past in terms of the form which is used, their relationship with the statutory or general rules of family law has changed significantly. Ante-nuptial contracts in the nineteenth century were made to avoid the application of the general rules of family law which had become unacceptable; contemporary separation agreements are made to reflect the general rules of family law which have become so widely accepted.

Effective Registration

There are no specific rules regulating the form or procedure for reaching agreement with regards to separation or divorce and parties are free to make their own informal arrangements. In practice, many couples who wish to regulate the consequences of the breakdown of their relationship will conclude a formal written agreement, usually with the assistance or advice of legal advisers. These minutes of agreement are commonly registered in a public register, the Books of Council and Session, as a result of which they become directly enforceable in the same way as a court decree. In order to

[34] Children (Scotland) Act 1995, ss 1 and 2.
[35] ibid, s 11(7)(a).

create a binding contract between the parties, no particular form is required but in order to have it accepted by the Keeper of the Registers, the deed must be self-proving according to the Requirements of Writing (Scotland) Act 1995; meaning that it must be signed by both parties and witnessed. The process of registration ensures the preservation or safe keeping of the agreement and, provided it includes consent to registration for execution, it will also result in the grant of warrant for execution of summary diligence. Herein lies the great benefit of the option of registration of such agreements, allowing the parties to enforce their agreements by means of summary diligence if the need should arise. This process of registration is a familiar and long-established aspect of the Scottish legal system, which has enabled separation agreements to develop as a simple and effective way of giving force to the outcomes of private settlement.

Limited Challenge

A significant factor, which contributes to the popularity of negotiated separation agreements in Scotland, is the fact that there is very little scope for these documents to be challenged or reviewed. Parties who have invested time and effort in reaching a settlement can be fairly confident that their agreed terms will be respected. These agreements or contracts are subject to the standard requirements relating to capacity and consent but provided that the parties are of full age and appropriate mental capacity and provided that there has been no coercion, undue influence or error, they will be regarded as binding and enforceable.

There is specific provision within the Family Law (Scotland) Act 1985 for challenge and review of agreements as to financial provision. Section 16 provides that the court may make an order setting aside or varying such an agreement in two situations. The first applies to any term of the agreement relating to periodical allowance but only where the agreement expressly includes a term providing for such review. This provision reflects the ongoing nature of periodical allowance, the possibility of changing and unforeseen circumstances and the power of the court to vary or recall a court order for periodical allowance.[36] The court may exercise this power to vary or set aside 'at any time after granting decree of divorce'.[37] While this provision does offer important scope for reconsideration of an agreement, its use is dependent on the parties including specific provision for its use within the agreement itself.[38]

[36] Family Law (Scotland) Act 1985, s 13(4).

[37] ibid, s 16(1)(a).

[38] See eg *Ellerby v Ellerby* 1991 SCLR 608. In our sample of 600 agreements, we did not find any such provision relating to spousal maintenance.

The other situation in which the court may set aside or vary an agreement, or any term of it, is 'where the agreement was not fair or reasonable at the time it was entered into'.[39] This is of limited application particularly in view of the requirement that the fairness of the agreement is considered at the time it was made rather than at the time of the application for review. There is also a very limited period during which a challenge can be made in terms of section 16(1)(b). It is specifically linked to the point of divorce and the court can only make an order 'on granting divorce or within such time thereafter as the court may specify on granting decree of divorce'.[40] It is important to note that the parties cannot agree to exclude the operation of section 16(1).[41]

Section 16 applies to 'an agreement as to financial provision to be made on divorce'[42] and this was held in *Kibble v Kibble*[43] to include an ante-nuptial agreement, which purported to provide for possible future divorce. This decision emphasises and confirms Scots law's openness to private settlement in the context of adult relationships and the lack of distinction between agreements made at different stages. Parties should think carefully, and be fully advised, whenever they enter into an agreement as it may have implications at a much later stage: a point which was highlighted in one of the interviews with a party who was shocked on separation to discover that an agreement made many years before about the proportions in which she and her partner were contributing to the purchase of their house would still have effect:

> because initially we had, my previous partner had put in a larger sum than me, so we'd agreed that should something happen, that she would get return of her amount and I would get return of mine. Now what I didn't foresee is that after 12 years that that would still stand, despite the fact that I had earned and put in, you know, that amount three times over into our house and, you know, just general living. (Interview: Party 7)

What the court must consider under section 16(1)(b) is whether the agreement was fair and reasonable at the time it was made rather than with the benefit of hindsight or at the point of challenge. It is clear that the courts have limited scope for interference and there are relatively few cases of successful challenge. Guidance was provided by Lord Weir in *Gillan v Gillan (No 3)* in the form of five principles[44] which make it clear that the court should not choose lightly to interfere with an agreement. The agreement is judged from the perspective of the parties rather than from any objective assessment

[39] Family Law (Scotland) Act 1985, s 16(1)(b).
[40] ibid, s 16(2)(b).
[41] ibid, s 16(4).
[42] ibid, s 16(1).
[43] 2010 SLT (Sh Ct) 5.
[44] 1995 SLT 678.

of what was fair and that might include taking account of motivations other than simply economic ones. For example, parties may be prepared to accept terms which, while relatively unfavourable in purely financial terms, have perceived benefits in other ways: such as early settlement. In *Inglis v Inglis*,[45] the sheriff rejected a woman's challenge to an earlier agreement stating that it:

> was entered into by the pursuer in the full knowledge that she had a potential claim on the defender's pension rights and she renounced that claim in order to achieve what appeared to her to be the immediate and significant advantage of the defender's departure from the matrimonial home.

The very limited scope for challenge which section 16 affords may be regarded as both the Scottish system's greatest strength and also potential weakness. While parties can be fairly confident that what they agree will be upheld, they should also be fully aware that they have little legal scope for reconsideration or regret.[46]

EVIDENCE OF CONTRACTUALISATION

In our recent research, we looked at a randomly selected sample of 600 agreements registered in 2010. Such agreements can be made at any point during the course of a relationship: ante-nuptial, post-nuptial, and on separation and can be made by spouses, civil partners and cohabitants.[47] However, in our study, of the 600 agreements examined, the great majority (590, over 98 per cent) were separation agreements. We were fortunate as researchers to be able to access the full sample from a single location, National Records of Scotland, that hold copies of all such agreements across Scotland, and also to be able to draw on an earlier study of minutes of agreement carried out in 1992.[48] The first allowed us to estimate the total number of agreements across Scotland in 2010 and the latter allowed us to infer the increased use of such agreements between 1992 and 2010. We found that agreements were commonplace and had become twice as frequent over that period, with an estimated 3000 minutes of agreement in 1992, when there were about 12,000 divorces, or a rate of one agreement for every four divorces,

[45] 1999 SLT (Sh Ct) 59.

[46] For further discussion of these issues, see Junor, JG, 'Challenging Separation Agreements' (1998) 24 *Scots Law Times* 185 and MacBride, G, Wedded to the Pact?' (2010) 55 *Journal of Law Society of Scotland* 10.

[47] Mair et al, *All Settled?* (n 21).

[48] Wasoff, F, McGuckin, A and Edwards, L, *Mutual Consent: Written Agreements in Family Law* (Edinburgh, Central Research Unit, The Scottish Office, 1997).

compared to a rate in 2010 of one agreement for every two divorces (an estimated 5000 agreements and 10,000 divorces).[49]

Who Makes Agreements?

Almost all agreements were made by parties who were separating, and the great majority of these were spouses (84 per cent). Despite the introduction of civil partnerships between same sex couples in 2004, only 1 per cent (5) of minutes of agreement were between same sex couples and three of these couples were cohabiting and not civil partners. However, the proportion of agreements entered into by heterosexual cohabitants had doubled since the 1992 study (from 7–15 per cent of all registered agreements) reflecting the growth in heterosexual cohabitation as well as the introduction of the right of cohabitants to claim some financial provision on separation from 2006.[50]

Agreements are primarily made by parties with some property to divide. Most of the agreements were made between parties who were owner-occupiers of their housing: 94 per cent, compared to a national average of 64 per cent.[51] Just under half of the sample of agreements referred to dependent children of the marriage (46 per cent; 270) and of these, 258 contained further information.[52]

What Did the Parties Agree?

The sample of agreements that was analysed showed that the vast majority dealt with property matters although a significant number also contained provisions relating to children as well. From the sample of 600 agreements, property was mentioned in almost all of them. Agreement about the family home was included in 83 per cent, with a range of provisions including transfer to one party or immediate or deferred sale. The most common agreement regarding the family home was that it be transferred to the female party (38 per cent), followed by sale of the property (33 per cent) and transfer to the male party in a quarter of agreements. Half of all minutes of agreement included a transfer of a capital sum and in half of these agreements the amount was equivalent to half the net value of the family home.[53]

[49] Mair et al (n 21) 28. It should be noted that registered minutes of agreement are stored in numbered boxes with a range of other deeds including wills and contracts. There is no index or record of the type of agreements registered and therefore the total number registered in any year can only be estimated.

[50] ibid 29.

[51] The Scottish government, *Scotland's People Annual Report: Results from the 2011 Scottish Household Survey* (2012) 17.

[52] Mair et al (n 21) 30–32.

[53] ibid, ch 4, for further discussion.

It is well established in statute that pensions may form part of the matrimonial property for the purposes of financial provision on divorce[54] and the Family Law (Scotland) Act 1985 contains a number of specific orders designed to facilitate pension sharing.[55] It was therefore not surprising that pensions were highly visible in the agreements, being mentioned in more than half of the sample (57 per cent). In the vast majority of these agreements, however, they were mentioned simply to confirm that neither party would seek a share of the other's pension. Pension sharing of some form was agreed in only 11 per cent of the total sample. While in interviews, solicitors stressed the significance of pensions as part of the fund of matrimonial property, and the importance of having them valued, it was acknowledged that parties were often reluctant to share. The point was also made that pension claims might be traded off for other property benefits and through the practice of 'offsetting' the value of the overall pot of cash might be shared in a variety of ways.[56]

The Family Law (Scotland) Act 1985 provides for the possibility of an order for periodical allowance but it is available only where justified by three of the five principles and where the other orders are not appropriate or sufficient.[57] The statutory preference is for one of the clean break options—a capital sum payment or property transfer order and this was clearly reflected in the agreements where provision for spousal maintenance by means of periodical allowance was agreed in only 5 per cent of the sample. This reflected a continuing trend from the earlier research in 1992, where periodical allowance was payable in 10 per cent of agreements.[58]

Overall, the agreements about property sharing reflected closely the preference of the 1985 Act for a clean break settlement and the principle of fair or equal sharing enshrined in the section 9 principles clearly underpinned what was agreed. While minutes of agreement do not necessarily disclose all relevant property and financial arrangements and in many it was not possible to calculate the value of the agreed shares, in interviews with both solicitors and parties the dominance of a 50:50 split was clear.[59]

Although the sample of agreements indicated very clearly that they were property-driven, children were mentioned in just under half (46 per cent) of agreements, with further information in 96 per cent of them.[60] Agreements are encouraged in respect of post-separation parenting, but such agreements cannot be treated as legally enforceable contracts because they are always subject to the supervisory jurisdiction of the courts and must give way to protection of

[54] Family Law (Scotland) Act 1985, s 10(5).
[55] ibid, ss 8 and 12A.
[56] For fuller discussion of the treatment of pensions within minutes of agreement, see Mair et al (n 21) ch 5.
[57] Family Law (Scotland) Act 1985, s 13(2).
[58] For further discussion, see Mair et al (n 21) ch 6.
[59] ibid 62–63.
[60] For full discussion of the provision for children in the sample of agreements, see ibid, ch 7.

the child's welfare.[61] These agreements are perhaps a good example of a trend in Scotland towards what might be described as the 'consensualisation'—if not always contractualisation—of family law. Nevertheless, in 73 per cent of those agreements which dealt with children, there was express agreement in relation to residence, with 90 per cent providing for residence with the mother and only 4 per cent with the father. In 5 per cent of agreements the phrase 'shared care' was used although the fact that child support in most of these continued to be paid to the mother questioned the extent to which there was shared responsibility in practical terms of residence. Child maintenance and contact arrangements were discussed in about two-thirds of agreements involving children. Contact was usually provided for in non-specific terms: 'as agreed between the parties' (80 per cent). Solicitors pointed out that the reason agreements usually omit to specify days and times for contact is that, unlike agreements over property, as already noted, an agreement over child contact is not enforceable, as in this solicitor's comment:

> If they stopped contact then I can produce the minute of agreement for the court and the court will say, that's lovely, I'm glad to see that in 2010 they thought that, but now contact has stopped, and we look at the present. So, you know, it's not really helpful but often people like it in. You know, it's a, sort of, it's a fall-back for them. (Interview: Solicitor 4)

Reaching Agreement

The agreements indicated little evidence of the prior use of ADR, though there is no requirement to disclose its use. A collaborative process was mentioned in one minute of agreement and by two interviewees, and there was no mention of mediation, although mediation can culminate in the making of an agreement. Five agreements provided for use of future mediation to resolve any major issues concerning children. In view of the frequent linkage between out-of-court settlement and ADR, this evidence is perhaps surprising but it offers further confirmation of the fact that in Scotland, private ordering is closely tied to legal practice.

Drafting Effective Contracts

When compared with formalities for execution of agreements in other European jurisdictions or, for example, the proposed 'Qualifying Agreements'

[61] Children (Scotland) Act 1995, s 11. The Scottish government sought to encourage parents to reach agreement by provision of a template: Scottish Executive, *Family Matters Parenting Agreement—The Plan* (2006) www.scotland.gov.uk/Resource/Doc/112200/0027302.pdf.

in England, Scottish minutes of agreement are relatively informal and unregulated.[62] While awareness of possible challenge and concern about subsequent negligence claims no doubt motivate careful drafting and advice, the form of separation agreements is largely in the hands of family law solicitors.

Clearly, the drafting of effective contracts is fundamental to the exercise. Parties who have invested time and effort in reaching a settlement must be confident that their agreed terms will be respected. Though agreements need not follow any prescribed form, it was not surprising that there was considerable standardisation across the sample. The vast majority had clearly been drafted by legal professionals (only three appeared to be DIY agreements). In particular, certain standard clauses were included in many agreements, which signalled the awareness of those who drafted the documents of the potential areas for challenge.[63] For example:

Table 1: Standard clauses

Parties warrant they have made full disclosure	30%
Parties agree terms are fair and reasonable	78%
MoA represents full and final agreement	91%
MoA is irrevocable and binding for all time coming, regardless of any change in circumstances	35%
Parties had the opportunity of obtaining independent legal advice	93%
Parties had the benefit of independent legal advice	73%
Relevant statutes have been fully explained to the parties	15%

Consensus and Satisfaction

In follow-up interviews with 30 parties to agreement three years after the agreements were made, most (75 per cent) reported they were either mildly or very satisfied with the agreement they had entered into.[64]

[62] The Law Commission, *Matrimonial Property, Needs and Agreements: Execution of Qualifying Agreements* (n 31).

[63] For further discussion of this, see esp Mair et al (n 21) chs 3 and 9.

[64] Interviewees were asked: 'Even though you probably had to compromise on some aspects of the agreement, how satisfied would you say you are overall with your MoA on a scale of 1–10, where 1 is "extremely dissatisfied" and 10 is "extremely satisfied"'?

Table 2: Party satisfaction with minutes of agreement (on a scale of 1–10)

9–10	43%
7–8	33%
5–6	21%
3–4	3%

Overwhelmingly the terms of the agreement had been put into effect which may be due in part to the fact that in a significant number there had been a clean financial break between the parties. They were glad of the certainty that their written agreements gave them and in allowing them to move on:

> if you've got it in black and white you can't go again and say, no that's not what was agreed. You know, and it's just protection for you. (Interview: Party 15)

> I would probably say 10 because, although it was horrible at the time, it allowed me to keep the property that I still live in and that I call my home and it allowed me to get divorced and move on with my life. (Interview: Party 17)

Or a slightly less satisfied assessment:

> it was a fairly hard knock to take to come out of this with less than half of the assets, but I think having knuckled down to that I think the nature of the minute of agreement was very fair and reasonable, so eight plus, maybe nine. (Interview: Party 28)

Solicitors too valued agreements, as this person summarised:

> It takes away the difficulties with court. The lack of certainty with court, the cost of court and it makes the settlement between the parties more likely to succeed because they have both worked towards that. It's not imposed from somebody else. (Interview: Solicitor 4)

The Cost of Agreement

The financial costs associated with going to court were obviously a significant factor for parties and solicitors but what of the cost of making an agreement? The cost of legal advice did emerge as an issue of concern in interviews with parties and those who did not qualify for legal aid typically stated their minute of agreement and divorce had cost between £1500 and £6000. Only one minute of agreement expressly mentioned the receipt of legal aid but in interviews seven of the 30 respondents had either been in receipt of legal aid or their ex spouse or partner had been.[65] Legally aided interviewees usually cited a smaller total cost for the advice they had received; ranging between £35–£500. These figures are however unreliable indicators of the cost of agreement itself as there was often some uncertainty about exactly what was included in the total bill or whether costs might already have been deducted in other ways.

Very limited detail about property values could be gleaned from the sample of agreements with specific values included in only 5 per cent. There was reference to investments in 19 per cent of the agreements[66] and, in a similar number, there was reference to debts and arrears. The fact that the vast majority of agreements involved owner-occupiers is a clear indication that agreements are principally used by property owners but it would be misleading to think of them as the preserve of the very wealthy.

THE LIMITS OF CONTRACTUALISATION?

What was already, in the early-1990s, a strong trend in favour of private settlement in the form of registered minutes of agreement,[67] has become even more pronounced. Not only in terms of the number of agreements registered, but also in the perspectives of parties and solicitors, the practice is well established and largely welcomed. The pattern which emerges in Scotland, reflects a legal framework which respects party autonomy, a style of legal practice which encourages and supports settlement and a system of enforcement which welcomes and gives effect to private agreement. There is long-standing legal certainty in respect of the enforceability of marriage contracts, defined broadly to include those made in contemplation of the relationship, during its subsistence and on its breakdown. Not only are they regarded as legally binding but there is subsequently very limited scope for challenge. What is also evident, however, is the significance of the underlying statutory framework. Willingness to settle, rather than to dispute, is informed by the confidence of both parties and solicitors that they can predict with relative clarity and certainty what the likely outcome would be if they did go to court. The current preference for private settlement rather

[65] During the year that the dataset MoA were registered (2010), anyone with a disposable income of less than £26,239 could qualify for legal aid. Where there was no court action, work would fall under the category of 'advice and assistance' in which case solicitors themselves are able to assess whether or not their client qualified. Further detail guidance on legal aid is available at: www.slab.org.uk.

[66] Investments other than pensions or bank accounts were mentioned in 19% of the total sample and of these 6% took the form of endowment policies which were probably linked to mortgages rather than being a sign of wealth.

[67] Wasoff, McGuckin and Edwards, *Mutual Consent* (n 48); Wasoff, F, 'Mutual Consent: Separation Agreements and the Outcomes of Private Ordering in Divorce' (2005) 27 *Journal of Social Welfare and Family Law* 237.

than court action when relationships break down, is a reflection of the combination of these various factors.

Perhaps because the system in Scotland has developed gradually and with little obvious intervention, there has been relatively little opportunity or need for review and reflection. Our research has confirmed that the practice is continuing to grow and broadly, whether by chance or design, it seems to work. There has been a significant increase in the use of separation agreements and, while there are no statistics available on the number of court applications for financial provision, there are certainly relatively few reported judicial decisions. The balance has shifted between private agreement and court adjudication. In reflecting on the provision of family justice we might ask what is the current Scots law on financial provision on divorce? Is it as set out in the principles of the Family Law (Scotland) Act 1985 or is it as contained in the minutes of agreement? To a large extent one maps onto the other and what we have is to some extent a system of contracted-out family law.[68] But there are gaps and it is in those gaps that we might highlight some concerns about the delivery of family justice and reflect on whether there should be clearer limits in Scots law on private ordering and contractualisation.[69]

A Clean Break?

Scotland has become associated with a clear preference for a clean financial break on divorce. The primacy of section 9(1)(a) of the 1985 Act, which is backward looking in its focus on the division of property acquired during the marriage, together with the limited availability of periodical allowance for ongoing payments, have in practice tended to lead the courts towards orders which create a one-off settlement between the parties. This is a tendency which is very strongly reflected in the minutes of agreement. While there is provision for ongoing support of children, ex-spousal maintenance has all but disappeared. The ideal of individual parties who are able to move on from a past relationship to independent new lives, which underpinned the 1985 Act, remains attractive but optimism must be tempered by the reality of, in many cases, a very limited fund of matrimonial assets, the continuing impact of childcare and other domestic caring responsibilities particularly on women and the disappointing experience of equal pay and sex discrimination legislation.[70] The relatively small funds of matrimonial

[68] In an English context, see Barton C and Jay, G, 'Outsourcing Justice on Family Breakdown: A Road to Consent Orders' (2013) 43 *Family Law* 840.

[69] Mnookin, RH, 'Divorce Bargaining: The Limits on Private Ordering' (1985) 18 *Journal of Law Reform* 1015.

[70] For further discussion, see Mair, J, 'An Ideal Balance?' (2013) 117 *Employment Law Bulletin* 2.

property which many agreements appear to involve, and the highly gendered nature of the arrangements for ongoing childcare with the probable effect that will have on earning capacity and career development, raise some concerns about the practicability and fairness of a clean break based on the sharing of matrimonial property. If the Scottish system for financial provision is not to be unduly harsh, particularly on the woman who has given up work or in other ways restricted her career in order to care for her family,[71] the full possibilities of the five section 9 principles must be considered rather than a simple focus on section 9(1)(a). Contracts which concentrate on early and full settlement are inherently a good thing: the opportunity for default is minimal. It is easy to understand why, in making an agreement, it might be preferable to focus on a simple, one-off sharing of assets but there may be later injustice.

Fair and Equal

Equality, in many forms and contexts, is a key driving force in modern family law and that is, to some extent, reflected in our research. Equal sharing of property is strongly endorsed but, while the language of equal responsibility in respect of children is quite widely used, the extent to which this formal equality leads to equality in practice is less clear. Issues of gender-based difference emerge both from the agreements themselves and from the interviews.

Section 9(1)(a) of the 1985 Act is sometimes misquoted as providing for equal sharing of matrimonial property. The starting point is in fact 'fair' sharing but it is presumed, unless special circumstances apply, that equal shares will be fair.[72] Leaving aside the niceties of the legal language, the headline message is equal shares and it is that message which is strongly reflected not only in the sample of minutes of agreement but also in the interviews with parties and solicitors. Although the written agreements themselves provide incomplete snapshots, equal sharing is a key objective in the words of many of the parties and solicitors who were interviewed. Section 9(1)(a) is, of course intended to be only the starting point for financial provision but if the other principles have been relatively rarely used in reported cases, they are even less evident in private settlements.

The dominance of equality as a guiding principle has become so strong that it can seem difficult to question its fairness. The interaction between equal and fair is particularly highlighted by what these minutes of agreement

[71] A possibility highlighted by Lord Hope in *Miller v Miller: McFarlane v McFarlane* [2006] UKHL 24 although strongly refuted elsewhere, eg in Norrie, K, 'Clean Break under Attack' (2006) 51 *Journal of the Law Society of Scotland* 16.

[72] Family Law (Scotland) Act 1985, s 10(1) and (6).

disclose about day-to-day responsibility for the care of children. The gender inequality of arrangements for the residence of children is stark. There are of course many possible explanations behind why parties agree what they do in these formal agreements and it certainly cannot be concluded that individual fathers are not or do not wish to be actively involved in the ongoing care of their children but the evidence is nonetheless very strong that primary responsibility for children remains with the mother in 90 per cent of these agreements. Against that background, it should be questioned whether equal shares are fair and, even where there is sharing of property in some other proportions, the overall 'fairness' of the agreements merits consideration.

This issue raises much broader questions about the purpose of financial provision itself. Fairness, as a guiding principle in this context, has been questioned by some[73] and it is clear that what is appropriate depends to a great extent on our understanding of the purpose of family law. Is the aim in this context to provide for the welfare of parties, to protect their rights or to respect their autonomy?[74] Minutes of agreement are, by definition, private arrangements between two parties and the focus is unsurprisingly on what is fair and appropriate between them. Any wider, social objectives are to a large extent lacking. If agreements are simply a private mechanism for implementation of the social norms laid down in family statute then it can be assumed that they continue to achieve social objectives. Whether the growth of separation agreements is viewed as a success or not is very much dependent on what family law and family policy seeks to achieve. One obvious example for concern from a broader social policy perspective is the very limited evidence of pension sharing. From what is known of gender differences in employment, family responsibilities and pension provision, while these agreements may satisfy immediate tests for individual satisfaction, they may give cause for concern about longer term alleviation of poverty in later life.

In the Shadow of the Law

Our research would tend to suggest that, in various ways, private ordering in Scotland does take place in the shadow of the law. But what is the shadow of the law? In terms of financial provision on divorce, the meaning and impact of the statutory provisions is generally perceived as being clear

[73] Herring, J, 'Why Financial Orders on Divorce Should be Unfair?' (2005) 19 *International Journal of Law Policy and the Family* 218.

[74] For discussion of a shift in judicial approaches to English ancillary relief, to reflect these different objectives, see Diduck, A, 'What is Family Law For?' (2011) 64 *Current Legal Problems* 282.

and relatively consistent and therefore separation agreements by and large reflect what a court would be likely to do in the circumstances. What is agreed tends to be a shadow of the orders which a court might make in terms of the Family Law (Scotland) Act 1985. It might be argued that in some cases what is agreed is slightly 'under' the shadow of the law as the threat of 'ending up in court' may temper what are perceived as more controversial or demanding claims. In respect of arrangements for children, the position is less clear. The shadow of the Children (Scotland) Act 1995 is reflected to the extent that the language of shared and continuing parental responsibilities and rights is widely used but the formal legal equality of mothers and fathers is not reflected in the details of the agreements which are made for residence. Social perceptions, and to some extent expectations, of increased equality of parenting are starkly at odds with what is agreed in these private arrangements in respect of residence of children.

As the balance between formal legislation and private ordering shifts, the question may become less one of 'bargaining in the shadow of the law' and more one of the extent to which the legislation is 'overshadowed' by private arrangement. Scots family law prides itself on a modern and coherent system of largely codified rules but to what extent are those rules being used by families? While the statutory provisions are not being enforced directly through the courts, it can be argued that they underpin the private arrangements which are reduced to written form in minutes of agreement. This research has demonstrated a considerable level of match between the law in the statute books and the law in individual practice but there may be some areas for concern. The detailed provisions of the 1985 Act, and associated regulations, for pension sharing are clearly not being used to any great extent in private settlements. Of the five statutory principles set out in section 9 only the first, which provides for fair sharing, appears to be used to any great extent. And while it is perhaps no great surprise, there is relatively little evidence that, in reaching these agreements, the guiding principle that children should be consulted[75] is being put into practice.

All Settled?

That parties and solicitors favour settlement is clear from our research and there is considerable evidence of its benefits, but why do they settle and what do they settle for? Settlement is perhaps always about compromise and the point at which parties will compromise appears in many cases to be gendered. While it was common for men to focus on the preservation of their pension, for women it was about stability, children and the family home.

[75] Children (Scotland) Act 1995, ss 6 and 11.

Whether this is merely an insight into human nature or a cause for concern is again dependent on what we perceive as the purpose of family law.

For solicitors, the benefits of settling rather than going to court were consistently highlighted and, undoubtedly, the recent history of minutes of agreement, as a means of coping with the consequences of relationship breakdown, is positive. For the continued development of family law, however, and for the effective delivery of family justice, it is important to guard against complacency. A sense emerged from interviews that agreement was achievable in many cases but sometimes only where the parties settled for what was relatively straightforward: terms that fell within the range of 'settled' law. In areas that were more legally controversial—whether or not business assets constitute matrimonial property; more practically time consuming or costly—the valuation of pensions, or more socially challenging—departures from formal equality, there was a tendency simply to settle for the easier option. As more couples settle and fewer take the risk of court action, there is a danger that the level at which parties compromise may stagnate. A fear of court should not be the key driver of negotiation. As fewer cases reach court, there is a danger that precedent will be fixed and possibilities limited with 'the impact of inhibiting family law practitioners to push the boundaries'.[76] What parties agree in private is clearly influenced by judicial precedent and, while court may not be the best place to resolve relationship matters, the role of judicial decisions in driving law forward and opening its application to public scrutiny should not be overlooked.

[76] Mair, L, 'Whither Whittome?' (2013) 58 *Journal of the Law Society of Scotland* 27.

Sub-part II

Reducing Public Funding

11

Access to Justice in Spain in Times of Austerity, with Special Reference to Family Justice

TERESA PICONTÓ-NOVALES*

INTRODUCTION

LAW AND POLITICS cannot be divorced from the context in which they develop. Thus the reforms in the system of justice currently taking place in Spain cannot be explained without reference to the severe financial crisis which has so deeply affected economic, social and political affairs in Europe since 2008. With the demands of the crisis on the horizon, or rather with the pretext of the crisis, austerity policies are producing a clear reversal in the rights and services hitherto provided by the state to its citizens.[1] Areas related to family justice have not escaped the dictates of the 'neoliberal context'.[2] It has already been pointed out that family law is experiencing 'hard times'.[3] Many chapters in this book demonstrate this reversal in several countries, and we are undoubtedly experiencing a generalised crisis in legal assistance and protection in the area of family law.

Not only is Spain no exception in this respect, it has in fact experienced greater setbacks owing to the cuts in public services across the board. Obviously the cuts in the administration of justice have had the most obvious impact on legal protection together with the increase and extension of court fees implemented under the Law 10/2012, 20 November, regulating

* This work has been undertaken within the Consolider Ingenio 2010 project 'El tiempo de los derechos' (CSD2008-00007).

[1] Ferreira, AC, *Sociedade da Austeridade e direito do trabalho de exceção* (Porto, Vida Económica, 2012).

[2] Sommerlad, H, 'Some Reflections on the Relationship between Citizenship, Access to Justice, and the Reform of Legal Aid' (2004) 31(3) *Journal of Law and Society* 345; Treloar, R and Boyd, SB, 'Family Law Reform in (Neoliberal) Context: British Columbia's New Family Law Act' (2014) 28 *International Journal of Law, Policy and The Family* 77.

[3] Maclean, M, 'Family Law in Hard Times' (2011) 33(4) *Journal of Social Welfare and Family Law* 309.

specific fees in the area of the administration of justice, and the Organic Law 8/2012, 28 December, covering budgetary efficiency measures in the administration of justice. It should be emphasised that these laws come within a wide-ranging strategy involving the complete reform of the justice system as a whole[4] which, of interest in this context, includes a bill currently being debated relating to legal aid which, in the words of legal professionals, 'diminishes the citizens' right to defence'.[5] In the light of these developments, perhaps it is more than anecdotal to mention that the 'dejudicialisation' and the proposal to privatise the Civil Registry are contained in the provisions of the Royal Decree Law (RD-L 8/2014, 4 July) for approving urgent measures for growth, competitiveness and efficiency.[6]

The Spanish justice system is undergoing far-reaching reform. This reform follows the general pattern of public policy in Spain: cutting public services and making the public pay more. The problem is that justice is not just another service. The regression in this field reduces fundamental rights such as the right to effective legal protection and consequently diminishes 'the fundamental content of citizenship'.[7] Family justice and the associated rights to protection are particularly sensitive to such retrograde reforms. The repercussions of these policies on the rights of especially vulnerable groups could be especially serious. These include those who resort to the courts in cases of family breakdown, child custody claims etc.

This chapter examines the consequences of the increase and extension of court fees from the point of view of the fundamental right to effective legal protection and concludes with some final reflections on specific repercussions in the area of family justice. First of all, we study the reforms introduced in 2012 under which court fees were increased and extended while at the same time financial cuts were imposed on the justice system. The resulting strong criticisms as well as the widespread political and social repudiation provoked

[4] The *Anteproyecto de Ley Orgánica del Poder* (Draft Bill for the Organic Law of the Judiciary) passed in April 2014 aims, according to the Ministry of Justice, to reduce litigiousness and to reorganise and abolish some courts (available at: www.mjusticia.gob.es/). A further step in the 'dejudicialisation' of the Spanish system will involve developments in mediation and the *Anteproyecto de Ley de la Jurisdicción Voluntaria* (Draft Bill for the Law of Voluntary Jurisdiction) which has been strongly criticised by the General Council of the Judiciary (2014) in its report on the draft bill (available at: www.poderjudicial.es/).

[5] *Proyecto de Ley de asistencia jurídica gratuita* (Free Legal Aid Bill) (121/000084), Boletín Oficial de las Cortes Generales, Congreso de los Diputados, Series A No 84-1, 7 March 2014. The General Council of Spanish Legal Practitioners considered at the outset that this bill 'diminishes the citizens' right to defence'. Available at: www.abogacia.es/.

[6] The 'Decree Law' enables the government to introduce extraordinary measures or legislation in cases of extreme urgency. These decree laws have to be approved by Parliament but debate is usually very limited owing to the urgency procedures. The current Conservative government, relying on its overall parliamentary majority, frequently uses this measure, eg the case of the Royal Decree Law 8/2014, 4 July, for *approving urgent measures for growth, competitiveness and efficiency*. This is an omnibus law which includes mainly economic measures and labour reforms, but it also includes privatisation of the Civil Registry.

[7] Sommerlad, 'Some Reflections on the Relationship between Citizenship, Access to Justice, and the Reform of Legal Aid' (n 2).

the Spanish government to take a step backwards with its Royal Decree Law 3/2013, but the 2012 reforms continue to have serious consequences, especially for family justice. After all these developments, there are loose ends which need to be tied up, requiring a deeper analysis of the consequences of the reforms. After providing an initial assessment of the significance of this set of legal reforms and enquiring into whether or not the promise to extend legal aid will materialise, we focus on the problems posed by the reforms in the area of family justice.

CONTENT AND SCOPE OF THE REFORM FOR FINANCING THE JUSTICE SYSTEM IN SPAIN BY MEANS OF FEES

The Law 10/2012, 20 November, regulating specific fees in the area of the administration of justice, and the Organic Law 8/2012, 28 December, covering budgetary efficiency measures in the administration of justice, seek to directly involve those who resort to the justice system in the financing of the services they use by means of paying fees in civil, administrative and social proceedings. In other words, initially, in the reform of 2012, all areas were included except for criminal proceedings. Resorting to fees in the justice system is similar to the use of fees paid under general tax law. The idea is to defray the costs of using a public service by making the person who benefits from the service pay. Consequently, as stated in the Preamble of Law 10/2012, 'the setting of the charge is not made according to the user's ability to pay, but to the cost of the service used' (clause II).

The Law 10/2012 sought to find justification in the decision of the Constitutional Court 20/2012, 16 February, referring to the National Law 53/2002, 30 December, which introduced in a limited manner some specific fees for profit-making organisations in civil and administrative litigation proceedings. The decision confirmed that imposing such fees was constitutional. In the opinion of the Spanish Constitutional Court[8]

> the requirement to pay civil court fees does not in itself infringe the right of access to a court, a right protected by article 6.1 of the Rome Convention. However, the amount of the fees should not be excessive in the light of the circumstances of each case such that the essential right of access to justice may be impeded (fto jco 10).

[8] STC 20/2012, 16 February 2012. Plenary session. Question of unconstitutionality 647-2004. Raised by the Court of First Instance No 8 of A Coruña in relation to the second clause of art 35.7 of the Law 53/2002, 30 December, on fiscal and administrative and social order measures (BOE No 61, 12 March 2012). Numerous decisions of the Spanish Constitutional Court resolving questions of constitutionality have been followed (STC 79/2012, 17 April 2012 (BOE No 117, 16 May 2012); STC 85/2012, 18 April 2012 (BOE No 117, 16 May 2012)) and appeals of 'amparo' in relation to the law 53/2002 (STC 116/2012, 4 June 2012 (BOE No 159, 4 July 2012); STC 125/2012, 18 June 2012 (BOE No 163, 9 July 2012); etc). The abbreviation 'ftc jco' refers to the paragraphs in which the legal arguments of the judgment are listed.

It is clear from this that the Constitutional Court expressly recognises the viability of a model under which part of the costs of the administration of justice is borne by those who 'most benefit from it' (fto jco 8), but it goes on to establish a clear note of caution in order to avoid any resulting detriment to the access to justice. Furthermore, it is clear that those who pay are those who benefit from the administration of justice, and in this context it must be remembered that the fees referred to in the Law and which are discussed by the Constitutional Court in decision 20/2012 are paid by 'profit-making legal persons subject to corporate taxes and with a high annual turnover' (fto jco 12). Obviously, this is quite a different situation from that of family court proceedings. If we ask ourselves who benefits from the administration of justice in family cases, the answer is not obvious: the parents as those liable to pay the fees? the children? society in general?[9] In our opinion, the Spanish government has made a tendentious interpretation of these constitutional rights and of the jurisprudence of the Constitutional Court. Its reading goes against the spirit of the Court's decision.

On the other hand, the legitimacy of court fees has also been reinforced by a paradoxical decision of the Spanish Constitutional Court that has ratified the court fees imposed by the regional government of Catalonia. This recent decision means that Catalan citizens may end up paying two sets of court fees: the national fees imposed by the state and the regional fees imposed by the regional government (fto jco 4 and 6). The Constitutional Court considers that the two sets of court fees are payments in respect of different things: the national fees are in respect of access to justice whereas the Catalan regional fees are payments towards the costs of court materials and personnel.[10]

Behind the attempts of the government to justify this measure and the rhetoric about reducing litigiousness which it has described as 'artificial'[11] the aim of the court fees imposed by the legal reforms of 2012 is clear: to dissuade people from going to court, *thus renouncing their rights*, and to introduce private financing of the justice system. The measure is an attempt to relieve the saturation of a system of justice lacking the necessary resources and whose situation is exacerbated by the public expenditure cuts resulting from the austerity measures imposed by the Spanish government.

The problem is that beyond the economic policy objectives, the reforms will result in a clear restriction of access to the system of justice and will

[9] Castillo Aynat, E, 'Tutela judicial "en efectivo" de los procedimientos de familia' (2013) 858 *Actualidad jurídica Aranzadi* 5. Available at: www.aranzadidigital.es/.

[10] STC 71/2014, 6 May 2014. Plenary session. Appeal of unconstitutionality 7208–2012. Filed by the Prime Minister (BOE No 135, 4 June 2014).

[11] A report by the Ministry of Justice to the Cabinet and the Preamble to the law itself states that the aim of this initiative is to avoid 'the *artificial* litigiousness that is currently saturating the courts' (sn). This categorical statement is not supported by any rigorous study. Increasing the fees plainly and simply results in the renouncing of rights.

consequently diminish the right to legal protection. This 'blocking' appears at an early stage as it is necessary to prove that payment has been made before filing a claim or any other procedural measure that initiates judicial proceedings. This is not merely symbolic. We are facing a considerable increase in the costs of using the justice system. Many people will be unable to afford the fees and will not therefore be able to go to court, regardless of whether the promised increase in legal aid materialises (see further below).

To assess the scope of these reforms, it is of interest to look at some specific data.[12] The amount of the court fee is made up of a fixed sum according to the type of procedure or jurisdiction in question together with a variable sum. The fixed sum for the civil jurisdiction, which includes the family courts, ranges from 150 Euros to 1200 Euros for a cassation appeal or an extraordinary appeal for breach of procedure (Table 1).

Table 1: Fixed court fees under civil jurisdiction in euros

Category	Amount (€)
Hearing	150
Ordinary proceeding	300
Appeal	800
Cassation or extraordinary appeal for breach of procedure	1200

Source: Website of the justice administration. www.administraciondejusticia.gob.es/

A variable fee is added to the fixed amount. This variable fee is different for individuals and legal entities. It is calculated by applying a charge to an established tax base. This can result in as much as 10,000 Euros for legal entities. For individuals, there is a single variable fee of 0.10 per cent of the base with a ceiling of 2000 Euros (art 7.3, after the reform made by the R-D Law 3/2013). The tax base coincides with the cost of the procedure fixed by procedural rules. In cases where the amount is undetermined, the base is 18,000 Euros. It is important to emphasise that the procedures regulated in chapter IV, title I of book IV of the Code of Civil Procedure (Procedures relating to marriage and children) which are not exempt from payment of fees are considered as procedures of an undetermined amount (art 6.2, after the reform made by the R-D Law 3/2013).

It can be appreciated that there has been a considerable increase in the costs of going to court. The costs of legal representation and other professional services also have to be factored in, except in cases where legal aid

[12] See website of the Justice Administration, available at: www.administraciondejusticia.gob.es/.

is available. In short, it appears that the lack of resources available for the Spanish judicial system is being addressed by limiting access to the system and levying fees on those who 'benefit from justice'. As stated above, the obvious question, particularly in the area of family justice, is 'who benefits?' Family justice has clear social implications and minors are often affected. Putting obstacles in the way of access to justice in family conflicts cannot be said to be in the 'interest of minors' and for their essential protection, juridically and socially speaking. The 2012 reforms described above immediately attracted a great deal of criticism. Several criticisms placed special emphasis on the repercussions in the area of family law.

GENERAL CRITICISMS AND PARTIAL RECTIFICATION IN THE AREA OF FAMILY JUSTICE

The Draft Bill on Fees in the Area of the Administration of Justice *(Anteproyecto de Ley sobre tasas en el ámbito de la Administración de justicia)* became the object of harsh criticism from the moment it appeared in April 2012. To begin with, the new fees were considered excessive and consequently a deterrent for many citizens. Moreover, the new court fees were criticised for causing inequalities in the access to justice and considered to be possibly economically discriminatory. The introduction of these laws was said to represent an attack on the constitutional rights of citizens, in particular the right to effective judicial protection established in Article 24 of the Spanish Constitution of 1978.

The attack on free justice for all and in particular the extension and increase in court fees militate against the progress towards effective legal protection made in Spain since the introduction of democracy. The first consequence is reducing the fundamental rights of citizens. It should be borne in mind that after the coming into force of the 1978 Spanish Constitution, many existing court fees that had been imposed in civil, litigation, administrative and criminal proceedings by Decree 1035/1959, 18 June, were abolished (by Law 25/1986, 24 December, on the abolition of court fees). This 1986 law sought to follow the constitutional principle recognised in Article 24 of the Spanish Constitution which states 'Every person has the right to obtain the effective protection of the judges and the courts in the exercise of their legitimate rights and interests, and in no case may a person go undefended'. The right to justice should be independent of the financial situation or social position of any parties.[13]

[13] The abolition of court fees suffered its first blow with the passing of the National Law 53/2002, 30 December, on fiscal, administrative and social order measures which in a limited manner introduced court fees specifically for profit-making organisations in the civil and administrative-litigation areas. This is the Law considered by the Constitutional Court decision 20/2012, 16 February, already referred to above.

The right of access to the courts and effective legal protection was a creation of the constitutionalism of the second half of the twentieth century. The aim was to elevate a requirement of the rule of law to the category of a fundamental right. In other words, all legitimate interests and rights must be able to be defended before a genuine judicial body in such a way that justice cannot be denied in any case.[14] Furthermore, according to extensive interpretation by the Constitutional Court, Article 24 of the Spanish Constitution of 1978 recognises not only the right of access to the courts but also, once a judicial process has been started, a set of rights including the right to a full and substantial resolution, the execution of such resolutions, and access to appeal processes provided for by the law. The first of the rights articulated in Article 24 of the Constitution, effective judicial protection in its strictest sense, means above all the right to access to justice. All legitimate interests and rights should be able to be defended by a judicial process. Any denial of justice is prohibited under the Constitution.

The importance of access to justice is such that any attempt to limit this fundamental right must be very closely examined. It is a right which confers full citizenship under the rule of law. In this context, Jeremy Bentham[15] had already criticised the 'mischievousness' of court fees as long ago as 1795. A recent author, addressing the 2012 reforms, has emphasised that they not only represent a backward step in social terms but also in terms of the state under the rule of law.[16]

Funding the system of justice by means of fees has been questioned from the point of view of constitutional principles and the rights of citizenship as well as from the technical point of view. This is especially so when a resource ceases to become exceptional and converts into something disproportionate.[17] Many civil organisations and institutions have also severely criticised the 2012 reforms, insisting that they represent a step backwards in terms of effective judicial protection.

The General Council of Spanish Bar Associations (*Consejo General de la Abogacía*, CGA) approved a report on 8 November 2012 which questioned the constitutionality of the Bill on Fees in the Area of the Administration of Justice. Part of this report was read as a manifesto in many of the demonstrations held in November 2012 protesting against the new law of court fees, many of which were called by lawyers' associations in several Spanish

[14] Díez-Picazo, L, *Sistema de Derechos Fundamentales* (Valencia, Tirant Lo Blanch, 2008) 426, 428.

[15] Bentham, J, (1795), A de la Oliva Santos *Una protesta contra las tasas judiciales: en la que se demuestra la peculiar malignidad que entrañan todos estos impuestos como coste añadido al de acudir a la Justicia* (1795), A de la Oliva Santos (ed) (Cizur Menor, Thomson-Aranzadi/ Civitas, 2013).

[16] Pérez Ron, JL, 'El nuevo estado de derecho' (2014) 4 *Quincena fiscal* 97 available at: www.aranzadidigital.es/.

[17] Ruiz Garijo, M, 'La financiación de la justicia a través de tasas' in *Alternativas a la financiación en época de crisis* (2014) available at: www.aranzadidigital.es/.

cities. The General Council of the Spanish Bar also organised an opinion poll about the new regulation of court fees.[18] About 83 per cent of respondents considered that there was no justification for having to pay a fee in advance for having access to the justice system, and a similar percentage, 79 per cent, also believed that the fees were excessive.

The Governing body of the Spanish Judiciary (*Consejo General del Poder Judicial*, CGPJ) published a report approved by its council on 31 May 2012 criticising and questioning the draft bill. In its report, the Governing body stated that

> while the legislator argues for the need to rationalise the Administration of Justice in the sense of reducing litigiousness (...) the system of fees which it wishes to introduce is totally alien to the mechanisms for extra-judicial solutions to conflicts within the different procedures (conciliation, agreement and mediation).

This body went on to conclude that

> the [Spanish] legislator is attempting to introduce a system in which use of the Administration of Justice is selective, that is to say having regard to whether or not users have sufficient financial resources, funding such services at the expense of the current public system of free justice.[19]

Specifically, the Governing body of the Spanish Judiciary considered that this represents a substantive modification to the philosophy of legal practice to date (Law 53/2002 and Law 1/1996) as regards the system of free justice.[20] In short, in the opinion of this body, the legal reform relating to court fees 'is governed by motives of political and economic opportunism which seek to alleviate the effects of the economic crisis'.[21]

During its progress through Parliament, the Bill of Law 10/2012, on fees in the area of the administration of justice, was also criticised and rejected by many associations of judges, lawyers and prosecutors, as well as associations of citizens, consumers and trade unions. Some of these organisations radically opposed the Bill. For example, the Platform for Justice for All (*Plataforma Ciudadana por una Justicia para todos*), with representatives

[18] The opinion poll was carried out by Metroscopia at the request of the Consejo General de la Abogacía (CGAE): CGAE—METROSCOPIA, 'Sondeo de urgencia a la población española sobre la nueva Ley de tasas judiciales' (*Urgent Survey of the Spanish People on the New Law of Court Fees*) (2012) www.abogacia.es/wp-content/uploads/2012/11/METROSCOPIA-INFORME-TASAS.pdf.

[19] CGPJ, *Informe del Consejo General del Poder Judicial sobre el Anteproyecto de Ley por el que se regulan determinadas tasas en el ámbito de la Administración de Justicia y del Instituto Nacional de Toxicología y Ciencias Forenses* (Madrid, 2012) 17, available at: /www.poderjudicial.es/cgpj/es/Poder_Judicial/Consejo_General_del_Poder_Judicial.

[20] ibid 17–18.

[21] ibid 12.

from the legal profession, the council of consumers and users, and various Spanish trade unions (UGT, CCOO, USO and CSI-F) firmly repudiated the so-called Law of Judicial Fees on the grounds that it hindered access to justice of many social groups.[22] Other legal organisations and associations made similar criticisms, including those representing judges, prosecutors, lawyers, clerks, secretaries and court assistants.

The Ombudsman also criticised the initiative and made written representations to the Ministry of Justice in February 2013 concerning the Law 10/2012, recommending a substantial modification to the system of court fees.[23] Specifically, the Ombudsman considered that the amount of the fees should be reduced for civil first instance courts and administrative courts, and that the amounts should generally be more moderate to facilitate access to appeals in various processes. Like the governing body of the Spanish Judiciary, the Ombudsman also considered that fees already paid should be refunded to those benefiting from legal aid. The European Commission has also expressed criticism of the new Spanish law on court fees. In particular, it has expressed its disagreement with the excessive nature of the court fees in Spain on the grounds that this could have a damaging effect on the fundamental right of citizens to effective judicial protection, that is, to be heard in court (European Charter of Fundamental Rights, art 47; European Convention on Human Rights, art 6(1)). The reaction of the Spanish government to the criticisms, and to the widespread social and political rejection by both the general public and the main institutions connected with the Administration of Justice, was to pass the Royal Decree Law 3/2013, 22 February, which amended the rules on fees within the justice system and the legal aid system. It also established certain distinctions that have important consequences in the area that concerns us most: family justice. Thus, the new Royal Decree Law includes a modification to Article 2 of the Law 10/2012 and provides for exemptions from the payment of court fees for, among others, proceedings relating to filiation, capacity and minors; matrimonial proceedings concerning custody, care and child support; proceedings initiated by mutual consent or which are initiated by one of the parties with the consent of the other;[24] for victims of gender violence; for claims for visiting rights by grandparents and other relatives; and for proceedings and appeals against decisions in matrimonial proceedings relating only to custody and care or child support. However, the high court fees still apply in proceedings of annulment, separation and divorce not involving minors or people with

[22] See Plataforma Ciudadana por una Justicia de Todos 2012, *Manifiesto*, available at: http://porunajusticiadetodos.wordpress.com/manifiesto/.

[23] DEFENSORÍA DEL PUEBLO, *Recomendaciones para modificar la Ley de Tasas Judiciales* (Madrid, 2012) www.defensordelpueblo.es/es/Prensa/Notas/Documentos/Recomendaciones_tasas_judiciales.pdf.

[24] In other cases the exemption from payment of court fees is granted only when the sought measures relate to minors.

disabilities. In addition, as regards legal assistance, certain people are eligible for the right to free legal aid. Such aid is available to especially vulnerable groups including victims of gender violence and minors, irrespective of their financial resources. However, as pointed out by Eekelaar,[25] any person whose legal rights are at stake in the area of family justice is potentially 'vulnerable', not only minors or victims of gender violence, given the serious personal and social consequences that can result from family conflicts.

The amendments introduced by the Royal Decree Law 3/2013, 22 February, modifying the rules on fees in the justice system and the free legal aid system, are not sufficient to overcome the limitations placed on the right to effective judicial protection resulting from the legal reforms of 2012. For this reason, several appeals of unconstitutionality have been presented and accepted which are currently in progress.[26]

AN INITIAL ASSESSMENT OF THE SIGNIFICANCE OF THE REFORMS

A preliminary assessment of the reforms can be found in a report presented by the President of the CGPJ (the General Council of the Spanish Judiciary) to the Spanish Parliament in June 2014. The report, *La justicia dato a dato: año 2013*,[27] reveals a stabilising in the total number of cases, and increases in the number of cases brought before the family courts (approximately 2 per cent), the commercial courts (about 20 per cent) and labour courts—*juzgados y tribunales de lo social*—(also 20 per cent). These figures reflect the effects of the economic crisis on court activity. The report also states that family mediation saw an increase of about 65 per cent compared to the previous year (from 3056 mediation referrals to 5116), with agreement being reached in 49 per cent of cases as compared to 31 per cent in 2012.

Although it is too early to draw conclusions, the available statistics do provide one significant fact: the revenue from court fees has increased

[25] Eekelaar, J, '"Not of the Highest Importance": Family Justice under Threat' (2011) 33(4) *Journal of Social Welfare and Family Law* 311.

[26] The Spanish Constitutional Court still has to hear several appeals pending against the new law on court fees. Specifically, appeals on the constitutionality of the reform of court fees introduced by the government have been presented by the Socialist Parliamentary Group and the regional governments of Andalusia and Catalonia. These have been accepted and are currently in progress. The first two appeals argue that the reform is abusive and unjust, and represents a direct attack against equality rights and the right to effective judicial protection. Subsequently, the Socialist Parliamentary Group and the regional government of Andalusia presented appeals against the Royal Decree Law 3/2013, 22 February, which amends some of the excesses of the initial reform but is insufficient from the point of view of the appellants to fully guarantee constitutional rights.

[27] CGPJ, *La justicia dato a dato: año 2013* (Madrid, 2014) (*The Spanish Judiciary in Figures: 2013*) www.poderjudicial.es/stfls/CGPJ/ESTADÍSTICA/JUSTICIA%20DATO%20A%20DATO/FICHERO/20140616%20Justicia%20dato%20a%20dato%202013%20Ingles%20v_1.pdf.

considerably. Table 2 shows that income in 2013 is practically double that of 2012. In certain autonomous regions the income has almost tripled. It must be remembered that the legislative changes came into force during 2013, so data for this period needs to be treated with caution.[28] Moreover, for more precise data about the repercussions in the area of family justice, a more specific statistical analysis is required given that the figures provided in the CGPJ report are global.

Table 2: Income from court fees (2012–13, in thousands of Euros)

	2012		2013	
	Gross	Net	Gross	Net
Andalucía	9,551	9,471	33,423	33,070
Aragón	3,323	3,299	7,305	7,214
Asturias	864	855	5,443	5,371
Balears	1,658	1,637	6,587	6,552
Canarias	1,006	988	9,853	9,810
Cantabria	13,218	13,142	19,264	18,991
Castilla y León	965	954	10,430	10,341
Castilla-La Mancha	3,076	3,068	8,694	8,607
Cataluña	33,936	33,803	59,742	58,113
Comunitat Valenciana	16,030	15,894	21,021	20,785
Extremadura	342	338	3,163	3,114
Galicia	5,174	5,102	13,675	13,579
Madrid	63,750	63,318	88,359	87,387
Murcia	505	488	5,362	5,334
Navarra	588	588	2,500	2,475
País Vasco	18,888	18,779	24,306	24,006
La Rioja	69	68	1,402	1,386
Ceuta	4	4	232	227
Melilla	3	3	180	174
Total	**172,950**	**171,799**	**320,941**	**316,536**

Source: CGPJ 2014, from figures provided by the Spanish Treasury for 2013. (www.poderjudicial.es/)

[28] It is probably true that after the corrections made by the Royal-Decree Law 2013, 22 February, regarding the increase in fees introduced by the 10/2012 Law, family justice is one of the areas least affected by the increase in court fees but it is still too early to know.

In an attempt to justify the imposition of the new court fees, the Spanish government has defended its legal reforms on the grounds that they will result in an increase in resources which will be reflected in an improvement in legal aid. The link between court fees and legal aid was first questioned by the Bar Associations.[29] Even the autonomous regions governed by the Conservative Party have protested against the delays and cuts in legal aid funding.[30]

In general, applications for legal aid substantially increased while funding was reduced in 2013. The introduction of court fees resulted in the Bar Associations receiving 18 per cent more applications for free representation than in 2012. The total investment in legal aid by the Spanish public administration in 2013, supported by the Bar Associations, was reduced by 4 per cent compared to 2012, a year which had already seen cuts of 8.7 per cent compared to 2011.[31] As regards the allocation of available legal aid, duty lawyers from the Bar Associations account for 67.3 per cent of the total costs while legal advice for people arrested by the police accounts for 20 per cent. Legal advice for victims of gender violence accounts for 3.3 per cent of the total. Within the duty lawyer service, criminal cases account for 58.5 per cent of the costs, followed by civil cases with 28.2 per cent. Administrative cases account for about 4 per cent while labour disputes account for 2.4 per cent.[32]

The legal aid available for family justice obviously represents a minimal part of the 28.2 per cent allocated under the civil jurisdiction, and it remains to be seen how the figures evolve after the 2013 reforms. Moreover, in addition to the question of legal aid there are other issues to be considered in relation to the protection of the rights of access of individuals to the justice system and the right to effective legal protection in family justice, including

[29] In its rejection of the legal aid reform, the Spanish Bar Association stated that 'the link between legal aid and the law of court fees [...] deserves the unanimous rejection it has received (96%) from lawyers with legal aid experience. As the General Council of Bar Associations has stated, legal aid is a constitutional right—as established in Article 119 of the Constitution, linked with Article 24—and should be paid for by the Public Administration without depending, therefore, on any fee revenue': General Council of Spanish Bar Associations, *Legal Aid Observatory* (2014) 165, available at: www.abogacia.es/.

[30] The Regional Minister for the Presidency and Justice of the Madrid regional government sent a letter to the Spanish Minister for Justice, Alberto Ruiz-Gallardón, requesting that the Law of Court Fees be complied with in relation to the provision that fee revenue should revert to the funding of legal aid in the autonomous regions. It should be noted that applications for legal aid have increased significantly as a consequence of the new fees. In 2013, the Madrid region dealt with 129,969 applications for legal aid, an increase of 48.79% over the previous year when 84,041 applications were made: www.eleconomista.es/.

[31] CGAE, Observatorio de la Justicia Gratuita CGAE-La Ley 2014, *VIII Informe del Observatorio de la Justicia Gratuita CGAE-La Ley: Justicia gratuita: Estadística completa 2010–2013* (Madrid, 2014) 17. Editorial La Ley, available at: www.abogacia.es/repositorio/viii_observatorio_justicia_gratuita/.

[32] ibid 17–18.

the need for social assistance or psychological help in judicial proceedings. If family justice in Spain already suffered significant deficiencies, the successive expenditure cuts of the last two years will further endanger the advances made since the establishment of democracy.[33]

FINAL REFLECTIONS FROM THE PERSPECTIVE OF FAMILY JUSTICE

To conclude, this chapter provides a brief analysis of some of the debates and controversies arising over the last year resulting from new Spanish laws which have introduced substantial increases in court fees, a requirement to pay such fees in advance, and various cuts in the budget leading to a reduction in the already limited facilities and resources of the Spanish justice system. In certain areas such as family justice, this represents a serious setback in terms of the right of access to justice in cases of separation, divorce and child protection. The subsequent urgent reforms introduced by the government in the face of a general rejection of the new legislation, which correct some of the most criticised excesses in this area, have done little to resolve the outstanding problems. Given the characteristics of family jurisdiction, the cuts in the budget and the consequent reduction in personnel working in the justice administration, in particular social workers who provide technical assistance to the family courts, could have devastating consequences for the judicial protection of rights in the family area. In relation to the family area, courts are a crucial tool for the protection of rights in family issues and conflicts.[34] Therefore, from a general perspective and from the family viewpoint we are speaking of legal reforms that affect fundamental rights. Furthermore, these are rights protected by the international system of human rights and by the Spanish Constitution of 1978.

The reasons behind this attack against effective judicial protection and in particular against the legal protection of family rights appear to be economic. Within the general context of cuts in social services, both the system of justice and the right of Spanish people to effective judicial protection have borne their share of the burden. However, this perspective is hard to justify in terms of rights, and seems especially narrow-minded when it affects the family jurisdiction and the protection of the rights of children. Such a policy only contributes to encouraging discrimination in an area where the imbalances in power are marked and accentuate the inequalities and vulnerability

[33] According to sources from the Ministry of Justice, the budget for 2014 was again reduced, this time by 2.31% from the previous year.

[34] Maclean, 'Family Law in Hard Times' (n 3) 310.

of women and children in the family environment. Access to the law and justice in the family area is a fundamental right in itself, but it is also a necessary right in order to compensate for existing inequalities and to make progress towards social change.

By imposing significant budgetary cuts, the Organic Law 8/2012 is having serious consequences for the means and resources of the system of justice. Beyond corporatist perspectives, combining an increase in court fees with a reduction in resources will affect the essence of the fundamental right of citizens to effective judicial protection. In particular, this is bound to be felt in the area of family law and the protection of the rights of children. Other measures taken under the guise of legal reforms include a reduction in the number of judges and of professional court officials.

The legal reforms begun in 2012 treat court fees more like a traffic fine than a family issue. If the idea is to dissuade people from unnecessary or excessive use of the justice system, it does not seem fair to put recourse to the courts on the same level as paying a traffic fine considering the problems that can occur in the area of family justice. It may be true that in many cases it is desirable to resort to alternative or other 'appropriate' means to resolve family conflicts, but it must not be forgotten that in our society the imbalance of power is an important issue in the relations between partners,[35] not to mention the unsuitability of these alternative procedures in cases of gender violence.[36]

As had been explained above, many civil organisations and institutions have severely criticised the legal reforms. These include criticisms made by the General Council of Spanish Bar Associations, the General Council of the Spanish Judiciary and the Public Ombudsman. Many associations of judges, lawyers and public prosecutors as well as consumer associations and trade unions have added their voices to these criticisms.

If it hadn't been for the political and social opposition of institutions and citizens, it is highly probable that the Spanish government would have gone further in its restrictions on the fundamental right to effective judicial protection and the right of access to justice in the area of family law. However, in the face of the avalanche of criticism, particularly from the main institutions concerned with the administration of justice, the government adopted the Royal Decree Law 3/2013, 22 February, which modified the court fees and legal aid regulations established by the 2012 reform.

The reform brought about by the Royal Decree Law 2013, 22 February, is in essence a response to pressure on the government which shows its lack of focus with respect to family justice and the associated interests at stake ranging from the interests of minors to the protection of the family, an

[35] Treloar and Boyd, Family Law Reform in (Neoliberal) Context (n 2) 81.
[36] Hunter, R, 'Exploring the "LASPO Gap"' (2014) 44(5) *Family Law* 660.

institution of undeniable social relevance. However, it must not be forgotten, as pointed out by Eekelaar, that any person may be considered 'vulnerable' from the moment at which his or her rights are at stake in a family justice process. That is to say, from the moment mothers or fathers put themselves at risk of winning or losing 'visiting and communication rights', 'shared custody arrangements', 'sole custody' etc. It is therefore necessary in the area of family justice to assess critically to what degree the vulnerability of individuals can go beyond the cases recognised by the law: minors and victims of gender violence.

POSTSCRIPT

As a consequence of the general repudiation of the court fees and the pressure from citizen's groups, legal professionals and institutions during the last two years, the Spanish government approved a Decree Law at the end of February 2015 abolishing the court fees for private individuals.

12

Legal Aid, Fundamental Rights and Family Issues

ENCARNA ROCA TRÍAS

THIS CHAPTER PROVIDES some thoughts on the constitutional problem of so-called legal aid in Spain. It is only since the constitutional review of 1978 when access to legal aid became a basic right for citizens that the Constitution has provided a double principle: (1) the right to effective judicial protection and (2) the right to free access to justice. As one might imagine, these two rights are not absolute.

Article 24 of the Constitution refers to the right to effective judicial protection and states that '1. All persons are entitled to obtain effective judicial protection from judges and courts to exercise their rights and legitimate interests and in no case may they go undefended'. The Constitutional Court has warned that this right may not be exercised directly but it is the legislator who must regulate the way citizens may exercise this. Despite this limitation, it must be said that this provision has caused a great change in Spain's judicial scene, since it has been used widely by the Constitutional Court, through recourse to constitutional protection (*recursos de amparo*).[1]

Yet one of the limits to effective judicial protection is precisely the cost of access to justice. Article 119 of the Spanish Constitution establishes that 'justice shall remain free when thus provided by law, and shall in any case be so in respect to those who have insufficient means to litigate'.[2] Here the Constitution includes two limits which will be seen later: (1) justice is not always free, but only when established in the law; and (2) a system of legal aid exists for those who lack sufficient economic resources.

This contribution deals with how these issues are organised.

[1] Rebollo, M, *Constitución española (texto y contexto)* (Navarra, Editorial Aranzadi, 2012) 112.
[2] ibid 179.

THE RIGHT TO LEGAL AID: CONSTITUTIONAL COMMENTS

In 1930, the future President of the Second Spanish Republic wrote a small book, today a classic, entitled *Orders to Pay Judicial Costs*.[3] The book referred to one of the issues of legal aid: the case where the losing parties to the suit or appeal are ordered and obliged to pay judicial costs. At a certain point in the book, the authors complained of the unfairness of not granting legal aid to any party proving insufficient solvency for litigation.[4] Throughout Spanish history, no constitution had recognised the right to litigate cost-free until the 1931 Constitution of the Second Republic, where Article 94 established that 'The Republic will guarantee legal aid to any litigating parties with economic needs'.

Does this mean that before 1931 cost-free litigation did not exist in Spain? Such a conclusion would be mistaken. Articles 10 to 30 of the 1881 Civil Procedure Act established how those parties with insufficient means could address the courts in order to uphold their rights. These rules have remained in force until very recently, when they were repealed by Legal Aid Act 1, of 10 January 1996, acknowledging a right to receive advice, legal counsel and defence and cost-free representation during court proceedings by 'any individuals whose resources and economic income, calculated annually for all items and per family unit, are less than twice the minimum salary established by law for each professional category'.

CURRENT REGULATIONS: ARTICLE 119 OF THE SPANISH CONSTITUTION (CE)

According to the current 1978 Constitution, 'legal aid will be granted whenever this is provided for by law and, in any case, in favour of those who are able to accredit insufficient resources for litigation' (art 119 CE). This article entails various consequences, as access to legal aid involves different issues.

The first thing to note is that Article 119 CE does not proclaim that all justice is cost-free, but that the law may determine whether or not to grant legal aid and to what extent. According to various authors who have examined this provision, the Constitution establishes legislative intermediation, which is why the legislator will always be the one to decide whether or not to apply judicial rates (see below). The organisation of justice, entailing a right to address the courts in order to uphold the interests inherent to a litigating party, may require the payment of certain rates, and this is the matter referred to here. We will return to the topic below, given that judicial rates evolved in a complex manner.

[3] Alcalá Zamora and Alcalá Zamora Castillo, *La Condena en Costas* (Madrid, Librería Jiménez, 1930).

[4] ibid 99 ff.

The second consequence derived from Article 119 CE is related to the fundamental right to effective judicial protection and defence. Article 24.1 CE provides that 'everybody will be entitled to obtain effective judicial protection from the courts and tribunals when exercising their rights and legitimate interests, without ever generating a lack of protection'. According to the authors who have examined this article, 'this means that any right or legitimate interest, ie any legally relevant situation, must be able to be eventually upheld in a suit before an actual judicial body. Any refusal to grant justice is therefore constitutionally forbidden'.[5] For instance, the Constitutional Court has granted standing as party to an adoption suit to the provisional foster parents of an unprotected minor[6] and the Supreme Court has also granted standing to the female partner of a biological mother who was claiming her right to interrelate with her partner's child.[7]

The right to effective judicial protection raises a second issue: the right to be defended and assisted by a lawyer (art 24.2 CE). According to legal scholars,[8] Article 119 CE also includes the right to a defence lawyer which, ultimately, is the main cost facing anyone who intends to address the courts seeking protection of his or her rights.[9] Both decisions raise issues concerning legal aid and constitutional doctrine, and demonstrate that the right to legal aid is directly related to the right to effective judicial protection held by low-income persons. STC 10/2008, of 21 January, states that

> (legal aid) is instrumental with respect to the right to access the courts, given that its direct object is to enable anyone with insufficient economic resources to act in a suit in order to uphold or refute petitions, ie ensuring that nobody is left without procedural protection due to insufficient litigating resources.

As a result, legal aid has the following characteristics: (1) it is a legally configured right, given that it is the legislator who will determine its content and the specific terms in which to exercise it; (2) it is a service, given that when certain circumstances are met, the aid established will be provided; (3) it is universal, as it also covers foreigners;[10] and (4) it is related to the rights to effective judicial protection and defence.

[5] Giménez, DP, *Sistema de Derechos fundamentales*, 4th edn (Navarra, Thomson Reuters-Civitas, 2013) 406.

[6] Constitutional Court Judgment (STC) 124/2002.

[7] Supreme Court Judgment (STS), of 12 May 2011.

[8] Llobregat, G, 'Comments on Art. 119 CE in Casas Baamonde-Rodríguez Piñero' in Maria Emilia Casas Baamonde and Miguel Rodríguez-Piñero Y Bravo-Ferrer (coordinators), *Comentarios a la Constitución española* (Madrid, Fundación Wolters Kluwer, 2009) 1858.

[9] STC 114/1998, amongst others. In the absence of a professional lawyer, an appointment will be made ex officio; proceedings will be suspended until a lawyer is appointed; the right to effective judicial protection will be actually infringed if there is evidence that the defence is detrimental to the litigator.

[10] STC 236/2007, of 7 November 2007.

JUDICIAL RATES AND LEGAL AID

In relation to legal aid, there is a tendency to confuse two separate issues: (1) the costs incurred by the litigator when filing suit or when seeking to defend in a suit filed by another party (referred to as *judicial costs*). The constitutional reference to the cost-free nature of this justice focuses on this point, also referred to by the rights foreseen in Article 24.1 CE, indicated above; and (2) *judicial rates*, viz the amounts payable by litigators in order to use the public services offered by the judicial system, basically access to the courts. This is the matter we will refer to now.

Act 25 of 24 December 1986, on the cancellation of judicial rates, repealed the former legislation that required the payment of certain amounts in order to access the courts. Article 1 stated that 'all judicial rates are hereby cancelled'.[11] However, Article 35 of Act 53 of 30 December 2002[12] subsequently reinstated these former judicial rates and imposed a rate 'to exercise jurisdictional competence in the civil and contentious-administrative courts'. As a result, a rate was levied on the filing of any claim, remedy of appeal or motion to vacate. Article 35.3 of Act 53/2002 declared as exempt from the payment of this rate 'the filing of a claim and subsequent appeals in matters related to succession, family law and individual civil status'. Consequently, all proceedings related to divorce, separation and changes in measures related to children and others were excluded from payment of the rate.

However, the current economic crisis has made it necessary to find new sources of income and the traditional idea of legal aid for all has given way to new judicial rate regulations, affecting family proceedings. Consequently, Act 10/2012, of 20 November 2012,[13] considers that all judicial rates levied on civil proceedings (art 2) are excluded when

> (a) Filing a claim and subsequent appeals related to legal capacity proceedings, filiations and minors, as well as marital proceedings that exclusively examine the guardianship and custody of underage children or alimony claimed by one parent from the other on behalf of minors.

The Act 10/2012 has been modified by the Act 1/2015, of 27 February; in this Act, no rates will accrue in proceedings between parents that examine any measures affecting under-age children, including divorce proceedings not involving minors.

[11] The Preamble of the Act states that 'further to the Administration of Justice, constitutional values are evidenced in the right to obtain effective judicial protection for any rights and legitimate interests, acknowledged in Art. 24 of the Spanish Constitution. In addition to justice, there is also a right to freedom and equal treatment, which should all be actual and effective, as intended by the Constitution; this requires that all citizens be able to seek justice irrespective of their economic situation or social status'.

[12] On Tax, Administrative and Social Measures (Official State Gazette no 313).

[13] Regulating certain rates related to the Administration of Justice and the National Institute of Toxicology and Forensic Science (Official State Gazette no 280).

The reinstatement of these rates is justified on the following grounds: (1) STC 20/2012, of 16 February, upheld the constitutionality of judicial rates; (2) judicial rates should not affect the right to address the courts, 'as a basic component of the fundamental right to effective judicial protection', ie they should not affect the legal aid enjoyed by those with insufficient economic means for litigation, who are excluded from payment of the rates; and (3) the idea is for administration of justice costs to be borne by those who will benefit from the same.

STC 20/2012 is therefore significant, where the Constitutional Court affirms that 'legal aid may be foreseen [...]. However, justice is evidently not free', because

> insofar as a guarantee of the rule of law, which entails collective advantages that surpass a citizen's individual interest, it is a fact that any financing that is exclusively tax-based will always mean that those citizens who do not address the courts would be helping finance the proceedings examined by the Courts and Chambers of justice to the benefit of others applying for justice once, several or many times. In a democracy, such as the one foreseen by the Spanish Constitution, it is up to the legislator to decide whether to establish a financing system for civil justice that is tax-based or otherwise, whereby citizens are obliged to subsidise any costs generated by their request for justice in the form of rates or duties, or through other semi-private models where the operation of Civil Courts is partly financed with tax and rates paid by those benefiting from judicial assistance, in varying proportions.[14]

JUDICIAL RATES AND FAMILY MATTERS

To judge from the statistics published by the General Council of the Judiciary in March 2014,[15] all jurisdictions have registered a fall in litigation rates. Consequently, as regards the civil jurisdiction, which is relevant here, 9.2 per cent fewer suits were filed in 2013 compared to the previous year. Global figures for settled and unsettled divorces/separations and decrees of nullity are provided below:

— 2012: 109,841
— 2013: 160,382

This indicates a 2.3 per cent increase in family litigation, as opposed to less general litigation, supposedly due to excluded payment of judicial rates.[16]

[14] See also STC 16/1994, of 20 January; 79/2012, of 17 April; and103/2012, of 5 June.

[15] www.poderjudicial.es/cgpj/es/Temas/Estadistica_Judicial/Informes_estadisticos/Informes_periodicos.

[16] www.poderjudicial.es/cgpj/es/Temas/Estadistica_Judicial/Informes_estadisticos.

I would like to point out two different types of cases related to family matters, according to the statistics published by the National Council of the Judiciary:

1. Cases in which a marriage is dissolved, including its economic effect on any children, particularly if under-age. A judge is necessary in these cases, given that according to law the dissolution of a marriage and its effects need to be agreed in judicial proceedings.
2. Cases where a judge is required in order to protect minors or other unprotected persons. This may happen in situations prior or subsequent to a divorce, or separately.

Given these two scenarios, the need for a judge would only be justifiable in the first, given that it is the law which requires that a judge determines when and how a marriage will end.[17] I am, however, doubtful about other cases. In my opinion there are other more suitable measures to settle a disagreement between parents holding parental responsibility, given that a judicial solution generates a winner/victim scenario that is very detrimental to minors. I believe it is not wrong to assume that the judge should be the last resort when parents are unable to reconcile their differences. But it should be taken into account that minors do not live in static situations. They evolve with age and according to their needs, which is why it is not only inappropriate, but also detrimental, to speak in terms of legal rules.

So it may be deduced from the above that currently in Spain the private methods of dispute resolution and legal aid are not seen as alternatives. Legal aid is also available when mediation is used as the means to solve the dispute, which is quite common in family cases. However, if one wishes to focus on whether private or public systems are better for families involved in cases that affect minors, the issue requires another approach. The question would then be: is it better for families to be constantly litigating, or is it preferable to resolve disputes concerning minors through less complex ways, basically private systems? The advantage of the private model is the greater ease of reaching an agreement; this can be seen when mediation is used. However, an argument against this is the need to protect minors, for if private methods are used, this may exclude court control. In Spain there is court control because the court must approve the agreement reached by the parties through mediation

John Eekelaar's chapter raised a series of thoughts:

1. When the parties, ie the parents, have to reach a new agreement because there has been a change in the circumstances of the minor, one must not forget that a legal system exists that often provides adequate solutions.

[17] The Ministry of Justice is contemplating the future possibility of notaries public being able to attest a marital breakdown, if a divorce application is mutually agreed by the spouses and there are no under-age children.

Even when the parties choose private solutions, law must not be excluded.

2. Mediation, at least in Spain, is not exactly an alternative to court proceedings. The solution reached by parents through mediation must be controlled by the judge when the agreements affect minors.
3. The cost of mediation is regulated in the same way as court costs, ie people who may request legal aid may also request it for mediation. Legal aid is available for judicial proceedings as well as for mediation.
4. Under Catalan civil law, an agreement must be reached between parents in separation and divorce proceedings regarding various aspects in the relationship between parents and minors which will arise following the divorce or separation. Non-compliance with the agreements in this plan may be challenged through court proceedings as well as mediation. The parents can agree that disagreements arising from how the plan is applied or the suitability of changing it to adapt it to the different stages of each child's development will be solved through mediation.[18]
5. Judges must be able to offer litigants in family matters the chance to use mediation before judicial proceedings start. This offer does not imply that judges will be substituted by mediators when agreements affect minors. However, it would be possible for the judge to intervene only to control the contents of the agreements, again, when minors are affected.

[18] Catalan Civil Code, art 233–9.3.

13

Taking Responsibility? Legal Aid Reform and Litigants in Person in England

LIZ TRINDER

INTRODUCTION

IN APRIL 2014, the Legal Aid, Sentencing and Punishment of Offenders Act 2012 (LASPO) introduced sweeping reforms to legal aid in England and Wales. The impact was felt most severely on private family law cases, that is, divorce or civil partnership dissolution, property and finance and arrangements for children. Since April 2013, legal aid has only been available for a restricted range of private family law cases, primarily for victims of domestic violence.[1]

The severe cuts to family legal aid reflect a combination of both financial and ideological drivers. On the financial side, the Ministry of Justice was seeking to reduce its budget by almost a quarter following the global economic crisis.[2] Public funding was therefore to be strictly targeted at 'the most serious cases in which legal advice or representation is justified'.[3] In current terms that meant the continuing availability of legal aid for victims (but not alleged perpetrators) of domestic violence, and subject to strict evidential criteria. A 'safety net' in the form of an exceptional funding scheme was also made available, again reiterating the residual nature of the state's role.

The reforms also reflect a particular neoliberal ideology towards the state's role in relation to families, emphasising individual responsibility rather than state intervention. Thus whilst the LASPO reforms restricted funding for litigation of family disputes, at the same legal aid remained available for mediation.[4] Looked at more closely, however, this is not a straightforward

[1] Eligibility is set out in LASPO, sch 1. Applicants must also satisfy a means and merits test.

[2] Ministry of Justice, *Proposals for the Reform of Legal Aid in England and Wales* Consultation Paper, CP12/10 (Cm 7967, 2010) para 1.4.

[3] ibid, para 2.2.

[4] Subject to a means test.

withdrawal of the state, but one that reinforces norms of behaviour by other means. In this case, it is an example of what Diduck refers to as family law assigning responsibility for responsibility.[5] The government's consultation paper on the legal aid reforms made this quite explicit, referring to 'the desire to stop the encroachment of unnecessary litigation into society by encouraging people to take greater personal responsibility for their problems, and to take advantage of alternative sources of help, advice or routes to resolution'.[6] The withdrawal of legal aid and emphasis on ADR significantly extends long-standing trends in family law towards what has been variously termed 'dejuridification'[7] or 'delegalisation'.[8] In other words, a shift away from formal legal rules and norms to regulate the family and towards processes like mediation that simultaneously promise greater autonomy or responsibility for individuals but at the same time regulate the form that that responsibility should take, both in the processes used and in the guiding norms. Taking personal responsibility is therefore now mandatory as long as responsibility means opting for mediation rather than court.

In practice, however, the public have not exercised their responsibility quite as the government had intended. Rather than turning in large numbers towards mediation, the cuts in legal aid have prompted a significant increase in the numbers of litigants in person (LIPs) in the family courts.[9]

This outcome was not entirely unexpected. The government's consultation paper did anticipate that the legal aid reforms would be likely to lead in an increase in litigants in person.[10] At the same time, the government recognised the possible negative consequences of an increase in LIPs envisaged in terms of 'delays in proceedings, poorer outcomes for litigants (particularly when the opponent has legal representation), implications for the judiciary, and costs for Her Majesty's Courts Service'.[11] It noted, however, that there was little 'substantive evidence' on the conduct and outcome of proceedings.[12] Others were less sanguine. The authors of the Family Justice Review, a major government-appointed but independent analysis at the time, expressed concern about the potential increase in LIPs and suggested that procedural reforms such as diversion to mediation were not a full answer.[13]

[5] Diduck, A, 'What is Family Law for?' (2011) 64 *Current Legal Problems* 287.

[6] Ministry of Justice, *Proposals for the Reform of Legal Aid in England and Wales* (n 2) para 2.11.

[7] Diduck, A, *Law's Families* (London, Butterworths, 2003) 2.

[8] Dewar, J, 'The Normal Chaos of Family Law' (1998) 61 *Modern Law Review* 467, 476.

[9] The details are presented below.

[10] Ministry of Justice (n 2) para 4.266.

[11] ibid, para 4.266.

[12] ibid, para 4.268.

[13] Norgrove, D, *Family Justice Review: Final Report* (Ministry of Justice, 2011) paras 4.180–4.183.

In this chapter I explore what the consequences of an increase in LIPs might mean. It explores why people self-represent, what impact self-representation has and what supports are available. Whilst clearly not the government's preferred mechanism by which people can exercise responsibility, how able are litigants to exercise responsibility as self-representing parties? What support is available to help them and how effective is it in facilitating access to justice? If LIPs are able to secure access to justice for themselves, what impact does their presence have on other court users? Do LIPs result in delays for and blockages, frustrating access to justice for other litigants?

Answering these questions is challenging as the government has not conducted or commissioned any systematic analysis of the reforms, despite earlier commitments to do so.[14] In the absence of robust independent evaluation data we are forced to rely on other sources to understand how LIPs and the courts might be coping currently in a post-LASPO world. The sources available include administrative data from the court service that maps trends in applications and representation. There is an existing body of empirical research on the experiences and impacts of litigants in person in family law conducted in England and Wales some time before the introduction of legal aid reforms[15] as well as other recent international studies.[16] Whilst this research is not a substitute for detailed analysis of the impact of LASPO, the consistency of the findings from diverse jurisdictions does provide some clear indicators of what may be happening on the ground now. In addition, there are some clear themes emerging from a range of surveys of professional opinions and from published judgments since the implementation of legal

[14] 'We are undertaking further research into this area, and we will report our findings as part of the government's response to this consultation. We will also be conducting a full post-implementation review of the impact of those reforms we decide to pursue following this consultation: Ministry of Justice (n 2) para 4.269. The Ministry of Justice did commission a study of how LIPs were faring *prior* to the implementation of LASPO. It was intended that this pre-LASPO research would provide evidence that would assist in mitigating any of the issues that might arise post-reform. The fieldwork for the study was carried out by a very experienced team led by the author between January and March 2013, prior to the implementation of LASPO. The fieldwork included observation of 151 private law children and financial remedy hearings across 5 different courts. For each of the 151 observed cases, the team also analysed the court file and conducted interviews with the parties (and any supporters), any lawyers and Cafcass. Focus groups were also held with judges, court staff, lawyers and Cafcass in each of the 5 courts. The report was not published until late November 2014, unfortunately too late to incorporate into this chapter. See Trinder, L, Hunter, R, Hitchings, E, Miles, J, Moorhead, R, Smith, L, Sefton, M, Hinchly, V, Bader K and Pearce, J, *Litigants in person in private family law cases* (Ministry of Justice, 2014) https://www.gov.uk/government/uploads/system/uploads/attachment_data/file/380479/litigants-in-person-in-private-family-law-cases.pdf.

[15] Moorhead, R and Sefton, M, *Litigants in Person* (Ministry of Justice, 2005).

[16] Notably Macfarlane, J, *The National Self-Represented Litigants Project* (University of Windsor, Canada, 2013) is a large recent study based primarily on interviews with LIPs in Canada. There are also two large-scale Australian studies: Dewar, J, Smith, B and Banks, C, *Litigants in Person in the Family Court of Australia* (Family Court of Australia, 2000) and Hunter, R et al, *The Changing Face of Litigation: Unrepresented Litigants in the Family Court of Australia* (Law and Justice Foundation of NSW, 2002). There is also a very comprehensive review of the international evidence conducted by the Ministry of Justice: Williams, K, *Litigants in Person: a Literature Review* (London, Ministry of Justice, 2011).

aid reforms.[17] This practitioner material is not a substitute for systematic evaluation and is likely to over-emphasise the problematic nature of LIPs. Nonetheless, whilst it cannot give any indication of prevalence of LIP-related problems, it does give an illustration of the range of problems being experienced on the ground.

POST-LASPO TRENDS: SELF-REPRESENTATION NOT MEDIATION

We start by examining trends in the pattern of applications following the introduction of LASPO in April 2014. What is immediately evident is that the changes have meant a very significant and immediate drop in the number of publicly funded private law cases. These dropped from 60,000 cases in the (pre-LASPO) second quarter (April–June) of 2011 to 10,000 cases in the second quarter of 2013. The number of publicly funded cases has not recovered and remained at 10,000 cases for April–June 2014.[18]

The question then arises as to what alternatives individuals have pursued to address their dispute now that legal aid has been so severely curtailed? What is evident is that mediation has not picked up the slack. There has been no major diversion of potential litigants from court to mediation. Indeed, the number of referrals to legally aided mediation and the number of mediation starts dropped by more than half between April–June 2012 to April–June 2014.[19] Mediation agencies have also reported drops in privately funded mediation although reliable data is not available.

At the same time, there has also been a drop in those going to court. Private family law applications remained fairly steady immediately post-LASPO but have since declined. The number of applications dropped by 41 per cent between April–June 2013 and April–June 2014,[20] although recent figures published by Cafcass suggest that the numbers of applications may be starting to increase again.[21] At present, though, the numbers are down. It is unclear at present whether individuals have indeed found their own private solutions to family problems without professional help from

[17] The material includes submissions to the Justice Select Committee inquiry on the impact of changes to civil legal aid under the LASPO 2012, available at www.parliament.uk/business/committees/committees-a-z/commons-select/justice-committee/inquiries/parliament-2010/laspo/?type=Written#pnlPublicationFilter.

[18] Ministry of Justice, *Legal Aid Statistics in England Wales: Legal Aid Agency April to June 2014* (Ministry of Justice Statistics Bulletin, September 2014) 23.

[19] ibid 24. Further measures have been introduced subsequently to encourage mediation, including extending legal aid funding beyond mediation assessment to a mediation session.

[20] Ministry of Justice, *Court Statistics Quarterly April to June 2014* (Ministry of Justice Statistics Bulletin, September 2014) 13.

[21] The Cafcass private law demand statistics for October 2014 are running at a similar level to the October 2011 and 2012 figures. Cafcass: 'Cafcass Private Law Demand: October 2014 Statistics from Cafcass' (Cafcass, November 2014).

the courts or whether they represent an unmet legal need of individuals who have given up without resolving their problems.[22]

That said, the drop in numbers of applications is far less than the reduction in cases eligible for legal aid. The gap is being made up by litigants in person. As widely predicted, and anticipated by the pre-LASPO Green Paper,[23] there has been a significant increase in the numbers of LIPs in England and Wales. Whilst LIPs have been fairly numerous in private family law cases in England and Wales for a while, they were given a significant boost by LASPO. Thus, in the first quarter of 2013, 42 per cent of private law Children Act cases disposed of nationally had one party unrepresented, and 11 per cent had both parties unrepresented. By the first quarter of 2014 this had increased significantly to 47 per cent with one party unrepresented and 26 per cent with both parties unrepresented, leaving just 27 per cent with both parties represented.[24] A request to the Ministry of Justice under the Freedom of Information Act also indicated that over 30 per cent of parties to financial remedy cases were now unrepresented.[25]

TAKING RESPONSIBILITY? REASONS FOR SELF-REPRESENTATION

What does the increase in LIPs mean? Are LIPs choosing rationally to self-represent, as a new form of exercising responsibility? As yet there are no data on the reasons for self-representation post-LASPO. However, the message from previous studies is that it is more common for LIPs to self-represent primarily because they cannot afford legal representation, than because they think they can do a better job than a lawyer or because the task appears relatively straightforward. The Australian study by Dewar[26] and Canadian study by Macfarlane[27] both found between 75 and 80 per cent of litigants self-represented owing primarily to an inability to pay for legal representation. Moorhead and Sefton similarly concur that self-representation is primarily

[22] Genn's large-scale study of civil justice distinguished between the 'self-helpers' who took action privately and the 'lumpers' who did nothing at all to address a justiciable problem: see Genn, H, *Paths to Justice: What People Do and Think about Going to Law* (London, Bloomsbury, 1999) 69, 72.

[23] Ministry of Justice (n 2) para 4.266.

[24] Ministry of Justice, *Court Statistics Quarterly April to June 2014* (n 20) Main tables. Table 2.4, available at: www.gov.uk/government/statistics/court-statistics-quarterly-april-to-june-2014. Note that the main report does not include a breakdown of representation rates, rather these must be calculated from an excel spreadsheet available on the Ministry of Justice (MoJ) website. The MoJ data refers to completed cases. It is not possible to tell from the MoJ data whether or not the parties were represented (or not) for the entire duration of the case.

[25] Reported in *Family Law Week* 13 October 2014: www.familylawweek.co.uk/site.aspx?i=ed133862.

[26] Dewar et al, *Litigants in Person in the Family Court of Australia* (n 16) 33.

[27] Macfarlane, *The National Self-Represented Litigants Project* (n 16) 49.

about necessity in the absence of an alternative rather than autonomy.[28] It seems highly likely therefore that the sudden increase in the number of LIPs following legal aid reform reflects an inability to pay for legal representation rather than a positive choice to self-represent.

CAPACITY TO SELF-REPRESENT

Whether a matter of choice or not, previous research has also raised issues about the potential capacity of LIPs to self-represent. That said, LIPs are not a homogenous group and will have varying capacity to self-represent. The Judicial Executive Board[29] noted in a submission to a parliamentary select committee inquiry that some LIPs are 'competent and able', but at the same time that many LIPs have little or no knowledge of their legal rights or of key processes and procedures.[30] This observation largely accords with the international research evidence. In a review, Williams notes a consistent finding that some LIPs were able to participate effectively in proceedings but that there were widespread difficulties with understanding legal and evidential processes.[31]

There are particular concerns about the minority of LIPs who are particularly vulnerable, or as itemised by the Judicial Executive Board, those with learning difficulties, psychological or psychiatric problems and/or dysfunctional lifestyles.[32] Williams' review of previous research concluded that LIPs are more likely to be younger and have lower levels of education and income levels than represented parties.[33] Moorhead and Sefton found that 15 per cent of LIPs in Children Act cases showed evidence of vulnerability, including a background of domestic violence, drug and alcohol use and depression.[34] The latter study was conducted in England and Wales in the mid-2000s when it could be presumed that at least a proportion of vulnerable litigants would at that time have been represented through legal aid and therefore would not have featured in the 15 per cent of vulnerable LIPs.

[28] Moorhead and Sefton, *Litigants in Person* (n 15) 64.

[29] The Judicial Executive Board is chaired by the Lord Chief Justice and includes the most senior judges in England and Wales, including the Master of the Rolls and the President of the Family Division.

[30] Judicial Executive Board, *Written Evidence—Justice Committee Inquiry: Impact of Changes to Civil Legal Aid under the Legal Aid, Sentencing and Punishment of Offenders Act 2012* (2014) http://data.parliament.uk/writtenevidence/committeeevidence.svc/evidencedocument/justice-committee/impact-of-changes-to-civil-legal-aid-under-laspo/written/9472.pdf.

[31] Williams, *Litigants in Person* (n 16) 5.

[32] Judicial Executive Board, *Written Evidence—Justice Committee Inquiry: Impact of Changes to Civil Legal Aid under the Legal Aid, Sentencing and Punishment of Offenders Act 2012* (n 30).

[33] Williams (n 16) 5.

[34] Moorhead and Sefton (n 15) 70.

It seems highly likely that post-LASPO a higher proportion of LIPs will display these vulnerabilities than Moorhead and Sefton's 15 per cent and thus possibly precluding effective participation in proceedings.

LASPO introduced two safeguards to protect vulnerable litigants: continuing eligibility for legal aid for victims of domestic violence and an exceptional funding scheme. There are, however, concerns about the effectiveness of the safety net under both schemes. Legal aid remains for victims of domestic violence but the criteria are tightly drawn and evidential requirements stringent.[35] Research by Rights of Women (ROW) suggests that they have been tightly interpreted as well.[36] The ROW research found that around half of women surveyed did not have any of the prescribed forms of evidence, while others had been charged considerable sums to obtain copies of the required evidence, or had difficulty finding a legal aid solicitor specialising in family law to take their case.

Section 10 of LASPO also provides for an exceptional funding scheme to make legal services available in order to avoid a breach of their rights under Article 6 (right to a fair trial), Article 8 (right to respect for family life) or Protocol 1, Article 1 (right to protection of property) of the European Convention on Human Rights. The number of grants of exceptional case funding in family law to date has been very low,[37] with the number of applications and awards less than expected. The scheme has been subject to widespread criticism, including from the Joint Committee on Human Rights.[38] The government, however, insists that the scheme is working effectively.[39]

Without systematic research it is not possible to identify how common vulnerable LIPs are or to assess the numbers of LIPs who are not able to conduct their cases effectively. What is clear, however, from some of the reported cases is that there are examples of highly vulnerable litigants, including those who have not qualified under the current exceptional funding scheme. A very stark example is the respondent mother in *Re H* who was described by the judge as having hearing, speech and intellectual difficulties and was unable to read or write. The mother had been refused exceptional funding to oppose the father's residence application. The father was

[35] The evidence requirements are set out in the Civil Legal Aid (Procedure) Regulations 2012, reg 33.

[36] Rights of Women, *Evidencing Domestic Violence: A Barrier to Family Law Legal Aid* (August 2013).

[37] In the year April 2013–March 2014, 821 applications for exceptional case funding were made in the area of family law, only nine of which were granted: Ministry of Justice, *Legal Aid Statistics in England Wales: Legal Aid Agency April to June 2014* (n 18) 27.

[38] Joint Committee on Human Rights, *The Implications for Access to Justice of the Government's Proposals to Reform Legal Aid, 7th report of session 2013–14* (2013–14, HL 100, HC 766).

[39] Lord Faulks, Minister of State for Civil Justice and Legal Policy, in response to a parliamentary question, noted that there had been fewer applications than the 5000–7000 that had been expected but denied that the application process was too onerous: HL Deb 11 February 2014, vol 752, cols 529–31.

represented. The local authority was also represented and also supported the father's application. The judge concluded that the mother had physical but not intellectual access to the court[40] in clear breach of her Article 6 rights to a fair hearing, not least as a vulnerable person against two advocates.[41]

IMPACT ON INDIVIDUAL CASE OUTCOMES

How does self-representation impact on case outcomes? Are LIPs necessarily disadvantaged or can judges ensure a level playing field? Based on detailed analysis of court files, Moorhead and Sefton concluded that LIPs were more likely than lawyers to make mistakes, including serious mistakes, and also found it difficult to cope with both substantive law and procedure.[42] The types of problems that LIPs were reported to experience spanned almost every aspect of proceedings, including pursuing both a misconceived case and misconceived remedies, not understanding the substantive law, difficulties coping with evidence, difficulties in identifying relevant facts, poor or limited advocacy skills, not understanding court orders, not following directions, not appreciating the importance of negotiation and not understanding the purpose of appeals.[43]

It is relatively easy to identify problems, particularly procedural problems, which LIPs might experience. It is more difficult, however, to identify whether or not those problems actually result in adverse outcomes for LIPs, in other words whether LIPs did worse than they would have done if they had been represented. There is no recent UK research evidence addressing the issue of impact. There are, however, examples of reported cases where clearly things had gone against the LIP at first instance where, on appeal, the lack of legal representation at an earlier stage of proceedings was flagged as an issue. In *Re C*,[44] for example, an appeal against an order for indirect contact was upheld, with Ryder LJ identifying a string of procedural irregularities at first instance that an LIP would have been unlikely to either to spot or to challenge without the benefit of legal advice.

Elsewhere some attempt has been made by researchers to quantify the extent of poorer outcomes for LIPs. In a review of the international literature on representation across case types, Williams concluded that 'case outcomes were adversely affected by lack of representation'.[45] Specifically in relation to family law, Dewar's Australian study noted that that only 34 per cent of judicial officers reported that, in their view, the LIP had handled

[40] *Re H* [2014] EWFC B127 at [4].
[41] ibid at [6].
[42] Moorhead and Sefton (n 15) 130.
[43] ibid, ch 7.
[44] *Re C* [2013] EWCA Civ 1412.
[45] Williams (n 16) 6.

the case competently.[46] Drawing on post-hearing ratings by judicial officers, Dewar reported that more than half (59 per cent) of LIPs were thought to have been disadvantaged by their lack of representation.[47]

More research is needed to understand why LIPs may be disadvantaged. Williams notes that existing studies provide different explanations as to why represented parties might do better, including their lawyer's knowledge of the law or knowledge of procedures. That said, there are likely to be a range of factors that shape whether or not the LIP is disadvantaged or not in proceedings, including both the competence and capacity of the LIP and the approach or supportiveness of the court.

On the latter point, the support that LIPs receive from the judiciary in court appears to be quite variable, with some judges offering more information and explanation to LIPs than others.[48] Aside from possible pressures of time, part of the explanation for this variation might reflect ethical dilemmas about the judicial role. Moorhead and Sefton note that English judges recognise that the traditional 'passive arbiter' model is not necessarily appropriate in an LIP case, but judges vary in how interventionist they should become as a result.[49] Judges have the difficult task of striking a balance between supporting LIPs and being fair to any represented party, in other words ensuring a level playing field but without showing favouritism to LIPs.[50] Getting that balance right can be difficult. It is interesting to note that the judicial officers in Dewar's study also considered that 41 per cent of *represented* parties were reported to be disadvantaged by one party's lack of representation. Whether that was as a result of the judicial officer trying to support the LIP or the LIP's lack of representation causing additional tasks or delays for the represented party was not clear.

The balance between 'neutral arbiter' and substantive justice is particularly acute where either the LIP or the represented party is especially vulnerable. An example of the former is the mother in *Re H*, described above. There are also several examples of recent private family law cases where the LIP has been accused of sexual violence against the represented party. In these cases, judges are understandably reluctant to allow the LIP to cross-examine the alleged victim, but at the same time consider that the judge cannot do justice to the LIP's case by attempting to cross-examine on their behalf. In *Q v Q; Re B; Re C*[51] the President of the Family Division suggested, rather provocatively, that if Article 6 and 8 rights risked being breached and the court could not deal with the matter justly and fairly then

[46] The judicial officers were reporting after the hearing: Dewar et al (n 16) 2.
[47] ibid 2.
[48] Williams (n 16) 7; Macfarlane (n 16) 95–107.
[49] Moorhead and Sefton (n 15) 192–93.
[50] Lawyers for represented parties can also face a moral dilemma.
[51] [2014] EWFC 31.

the state should fund legal representation, if not through the exceptional funding mechanism then through the court service.

IMPACT OF LIPS ON THE COURT

Aside from whether LIPs are able to secure justice for themselves, there are issues about whether LIPs cause delays and consume a disproportionate amount of court resources, thus raising issues of justice for other litigants.

LIPs face two main challenges in trying to conduct litigation. The first is overcoming a lack of the knowledge and skills required to undertake the range of tasks needed for effective litigation. Examples of tasks include form completion and complying with evidential requirements (including preparing bundles). The second challenge is overcoming a lack of professional distance from the issues. Whilst LIPs have the advantage of knowing what has happened, they may find it more difficult than a lawyer in identifying the legally rather than the personally relevant. The lack of knowledge and skills and professional distance may mean either that essential tasks are not completed by the LIP or that essential tasks are attempted by the LIP but less efficiently and effectively than by a lawyer. In both situations, it may well mean that tasks (and costs) are displaced onto others, especially judges, opposing lawyers or court staff as they attempt to either coach the LIP through the task or have to assume responsibility for a task.

There is a strong perception amongst family justice professionals that LIPs add to their workloads owing to either lack of understanding or lack of professional distance. In its evidence to the Justice Select Committee, the Judicial Executive Board suggested that proceedings could be lengthened owing to judges having to take time to explain procedure and substantive law to LIPs, judges having to undertake their own research in the absence of lawyer-prepared skeleton arguments and judges having to draft orders rather than being able to rely on lawyers to do the drafting.[52] The Judicial Executive Board also identified additional tasks for judges (and court staff). These included having to deal with extensive correspondence from LIPs and also LIPs not understanding the importance of negotiation, leading to more cases resulting in trials rather than settling before or during the course of proceedings.[53] The latter point was also identified in Maclean and Eekelaar's small observation study of LIPs pre-LASPO. They noted examples of (unnecessary) applications that had been made without having been filtered out by initial legal advice as well as cases where LIPs were less

[52] Judicial Executive Board (n 30) 5.7, 5.9, 5.21.
[53] ibid.

willing to settle in court, based on misunderstandings of what was legally possible.[54]

Three recent Court of Appeal judgments provide further case studies of the types of delays caused by LIPs' lack of knowledge or skills and the task- and costs-shifting onto other professionals within the system. The case of *Re C*, noted above, resulted in an appeal that may not have been necessary if the applicant had been represented at the earlier hearing. In his judgment, Ryder LJ identified that in the absence of lawyers it was up to the judge to provide both the legal analysis as well as maintaining 'both the reality and perception of fairness and due process'. He acknowledged that was not an easy task without preparation or any additional time-allocation.[55]

Two judgments by Lady Justice Black have highlighted the particular challenges faced by the Court of Appeal in LIP cases.[56] In *Re O-A*, the judge noted the difficulties the Court of Appeal had in understanding the case or 'marshalling the arguments into a logical and readily intelligible form' if there had been no lawyers present in earlier proceedings to provide a summary of what had occurred.[57] In the absence of a summary, the result was the court 'inching forward' rather than proceeding robustly. In *Re R*,[58] Black LJ noted that LIPs were often not aware that it was their responsibility to prepare bundles or, if they did know, their bundles were often incomplete. The result was that the burden of preparing bundles was picked up by others, including the court office or, if it was involved, the local authority.

In addition to the extra tasks being undertaken by judges and court staff that the Judicial Executive Board identified, lawyers also perceive that LIPs place additional burdens on them as well as causing delays. A recent Bar Council survey identified a range of issues that lawyers reported when acting against a LIP, including the court's expectation that the lawyer would undertake all the administration in the case instead of it being shared by both parties.[59] There is also a perception amongst family justice professionals that LIPs lengthen cases. Thus 80 per cent of respondents to the Bar Council survey[60] reported increased delays following legal aid reform. These perceived delays were attributed to the action or inaction of LIPs, including non-disclosure, a lack of focus on the relevant issues, a reluctance

[54] Maclean, M and Eekelaar, J, 'Legal Representation in Family Matters and the Reform of Legal Aid: A Research Note on Current Practice' (2012) 24 *Child and Family Law Quarterly* 223, 232.

[55] *Re C* [2013] EWCA Civ 1412.

[56] The Judicial Executive Board (n 30) also raised the issue of LIPs not understanding the appeals process or having sufficient knowledge of the law required to substantiate an appeal (at para 5.22).

[57] *Re O-A* [2014] EWCA Civ 1422, at [40].

[58] [2014] EWCA Civ 597.

[59] The Bar Council, *The Legal Aid, Sentencing and Punishment of Offenders Act 2012 (LASPO): One Year On. Final Report* (The Bar Council, 2014) 29.

[60] ibid.

to negotiate, and failure to adhere to court directions and court timelines.[61] The Judicial Executive Board[62] suggested that private law cases with two LIPs can take 50 per cent longer.[63] A survey by the Magistrates' Association reported that 62 per cent of its members thought that LIPs had a negative impact on the court's work most or all or the time and raised concerns about delays.[64]

It is more difficult, however, to find hard quantitative data on whether LIPs do indeed result in longer proceedings, and even harder to quantify the amount of court resource used by represented and self-represented litigants. Williams, summarising the international research on case durations, notes that there is not a straightforward relationship between representation type and the length of proceedings. Her review highlights that the impact of LIPs on case duration is influenced by the type of case, the representation type (full, partially represented and unrepresented) and the level of involvement or participation of the LIP in the case.[65] That said, Williams concludes that specifically for family cases the weight of evidence is that self-representation is associated with longer durations as cases were less likely to settle.[66]

In contrast, the only recent data on timeliness and representation that is in the public domain suggests that full representation is associated with longer case durations. Ministry of Justice data for concluded cases between January and March 2014 reports the longest case durations where both parties or only the respondent are represented (25 weeks and 22 weeks respectively) and the shortest durations for unrepresented applicants and neither party represented (15 weeks).[67] The difficulty with interpreting these figures is that they do not give any indication of the nature and severity of the cases. Full representation cases are now very much in the minority and are more likely to involve domestic violence and safeguarding issues that might be

[61] ibid 29.

[62] Judicial Executive Board (n 30) 5.4.

[63] The emotional toll on judges from having to support LIPs whilst ensuring a fair process cases should also not be overlooked: Maclean and Eekelaar, 'Legal Representation in Family Matters and the Reform of Legal Aid' (n 54) 232.

[64] The survey of 461 magistrates was undertaken by the Bureau of Investigative Journalism in partnership with the Magistrates' Association: McClenaghan, M, 'Family Courts: Self-representation Hinders Justice say Magistrates' (The Bureau of Investigative Journalism, 1 June 2014) www.thebureauinvestigates.com/2014/06/01/family-courts-self-representation-hinders-justice-say-magistrates/.

[65] Williams (n 16) 6.

[66] ibid 6. Williams relies here on the UK study of Moorhead and Sefton (n 15), and the two Australian studies led by Hunter (n 68) and Dewar et al (n 16).

[67] Ministry of Justice, *Court Statistics Quarterly April to June 2014* (n 20) 20. It should be recognised that case duration is a partial indicator of court resource consumed. It does not indicate the number and length of hearings or the number of adjournments in sets of proceedings. Maclean and Eekelaar (n 54) noted that adjournment and relisting was required when LIPs did not attend a hearing and had not given any instructions for anyone to act on their behalf. They also noted that litigants were less likely to fail to attend if they had an adviser.

expected to take longer. It is worth noting that the average duration of fully represented cases has increased since the introduction of legal aid changes, quite possibly reflecting a greater concentration of domestic violence issues in the full representation population. The same may be said for the respondent only representation cases given that most respondents in private family law cases are women who are most likely to raise safeguarding issues. It is also worth noting that short proceedings are not necessarily a sign of success. In one large Australian study, fully unrepresented cases were more likely to end by being withdrawn, resolved by directions or interim orders, a default judgment or dismissal.[68] This suggests that greater effort should be put on diverting cases from court or that more support is needed for LIP cases during proceedings. More detailed and systematic analysis of current cases in England and Wales is clearly needed to understand what accounts for variation in case durations.

THE SUPPORT NEEDS OF LIPS

It is unlikely that there will be a major restoration of legal aid in England and Wales. As a result we can expect the current high levels of LIPs to continue. If LIPs are to continue in large numbers then there is an urgent question of how they can be best supported, not just to ensure fair outcomes for themselves but also to minimise their impact on the court system. Providing effective support for LIPs is going to be a significant challenge, not least because the family justice system has been designed and developed based on a full representation model.[69] It is clear from previous research that LIPs have a wide range of support needs, although these will be at different levels of intensity given varying capacities and vulnerabilities. At minimum, Dewar identifies these support needs as a need for information (eg about court procedures), advice (eg document preparation, rules of evidence), and support (emotional and practical).[70] Similarly, Macfarlane suggests a requirement for orientation, education, emotional support, coaching and legal advice.[71] However, it is clear that meeting these lists of needs is very challenging. Macfarlane's large Canadian study suggested that LIPs typically start the litigation process with diverse expectations, ranging from confidence to trepidation. She reports that most LIPs rapidly become disillusioned and frustrated with the process, and some become entirely overwhelmed.[72]

[68] Hunter, R, Genovese, A, Chrzanowski, A and Morris, C, *The Changing Face of Litigation: Unrepresented Litigants in the Family Court of Australia* (Law and Justice Foundation of NSW, 2002) 71.
[69] Judicial Executive Board (n 30) 1.
[70] Dewar et al (n 16) 45.
[71] Macfarlane (n 16) chs 8, 9.
[72] ibid 50–55.

There are a range of reasons why that might be the case. The first is the awareness of what support services are available. Dewar notes that in Australia few LIPs seek advice but that most LIPs were not aware of what advice or support was available.[73] Moorhead and Sefton also concluded that English courts were not confident at signposting LIPs to what help was available.[74]

The second reason relates to the availability and accessibility of support services, or what Macfarlane identifies as a mismatch between the wide-ranging needs of LIPs and the supports that are available. Support services are typically limited in scope and availability and are not necessarily available in a form that all LIPs can utilise. This is a particular problem in England and Wales where, until recently, there was comparatively little demand for advice, support and orientation from support services as these were generally provided by family lawyers. The sudden removal of legal aid has provided relatively little time to allow the system to adapt in response to the dramatic rise in LIPs. There is a particular shortage of access to free legal advice for family cases. The most well-known advice agency in England and Wales is the Citizens Advice Bureau (CAB) but only four of the hundreds of bureaux offer a specialist family law advice service to deal with family legal issues in-house. Prior to the introduction of legal aid reforms the CAB was already expressing concerns about an increase in enquiries on family issues that they considered that they did not have the resources or expertise to deal with.[75] More recently the Law Centres Network has reported that one in six of their centres have had to close due to legal aid cuts. They also noted that their members have had a surge in enquiries on family issues but that there have been few if any alternative sources to refer enquiries onto.[76]

The third problem with support services relates to their effectiveness or their ability to meet the clients' needs. In many respects, support services are trying to replace the advice and guidance offered by lawyers, based on many years of training, tailored to a specific client and typically delivered face to face. That is quite a formidable task. Not surprisingly it can prove difficult to achieve.

Considerable weight is being placed on the potential for online resources to provide effective information for LIPs. However, the multiplicity of sources available on the internet has both the potential to confuse and mislead as well as inform. Macfarlane's Canadian study suggests that LIPs often

[73] Dewar et al (n 16) 46.

[74] Moorhead and Sefton (n 15) 259–60.

[75] Citizens Advice Bureau, *Breaking up is Never Easy: Separating Families' Advice Needs and the Future of Family Justice* (CAB, 2011) 14.

[76] Law Centres Network, *Written Evidence from the Law Centres Network* (LAS 57) http://data.parliament.uk/writtenevidence/committeeevidence.svc/evidencedocument/justice-committee/impact-of-changes-to-civil-legal-aid-under-laspo/written/8956.html.

find online resources less helpful than they had anticipated. Information was reported to be incomplete and inconsistent. It was also difficult for LIPs to judge the reliability of information available online.[77] Many commentators, including Macfarlane in Canada and Zorza[78] in California, therefore recommend the creation of a single authoritative official website as the primary internet source that LIPs will know immediately can be trusted as a provider of accurate, comprehensive and unbiased information.

The California court website[79] and its self-help centre provide a useful model as a virtual one-stop-shop. This is in contrast to the court service website in England that appears to be oriented primarily towards lawyers and has no visible pathway for LIPs.[80] The Sorting out Separation website commissioned by the government is equally limited from an LIP perspective. Indeed a recent evaluation of the effectiveness of the site found that 'users were often unclear about the purpose of the site and the range of information it offers'.[81] A complementary analysis of traffic indicated that the app had attracted a fairly modest 91,469 unique users over a 13-month period, only 13 per cent of whom went beyond the home page.[82]

Even if the English and Welsh websites could be brought up to the standard of the best available internationally, it is important to note that they are not a panacea. It should be recognised that not all LIPs are digitally literate or have regular access to online services. There are also limitations in making material accessible to all users. What might appear to be the more straightforward task of redesigning court forms to make them more accessible has proved difficult. Macfarlane, for example, found LIPs had difficulties with form selection and completion even with specially redrafted online forms, and that is assuming that litigants are literate.[83]

[77] Macfarlane (n 16) ch 7.

[78] Zorza, R, 'An Overview of Self-represented Litigation Innovation' (2009) 43 *Family Law Quarterly* 519, 525.

[79] At: www.courts.ca.gov. It is notable that the link to the online self-help centre is the first item on the homepage.

[80] The court service home page is entirely directed at professionals: www.justice.gov.uk/about/hmcts. The home page for the 'family court guide' also appears to only address professionals given that its opening page requires visitors to choose between public and private law matters without any explanation of what the terms mean www.judiciary.gov.uk/related-offices-and-bodies/advisory-bodies/fjc/guidance/familycourtguide/. The court service form-finder http://hmctsformfinder.justice.gov.uk/HMCTS/FormFinder.do presents a dropdown list with no signposting for LIPs. If the LIP is sufficiently informed to select 'Children Act' from one of 77 categories they are then presented with a list of 51 different forms. A 'Guide for separated parents' (CB7) is listed at the very bottom of the long list of forms and accompanying leaflets.

[81] Connors, C and Thomas, A, *Sorting out Separation Web App: Evaluation of Effectiveness* (Research Report no 863, DWP, 2014) 59.

[82] Department for Work and Pensions, *Sorting Out Separation Web App: Analysis of Management Information* (DWP, 2014).

[83] Macfarlane (n 16) ch 6, app H.

LOOKING AHEAD

How might LIPs be better supported in future in a way that facilitates their access to justice and does not impinge on the rights of others? Rosemary Hunter[84] has very usefully identified three strategies that could be used to enable LIPs to function more effectively. The first consists of making available more tailored and accessible information and resources of the type identified above to help LIPs to represent themselves. In effect these types of resources are geared towards helping LIPs to become their own lawyers or what the Legal Services Consumer Panel calls rather optimistically 'self-lawyering'.[85] Improved information will doubtless meet the needs of some but, as noted above, will not address all the needs of all litigants.

Hunter's second element is to provide free or low-cost legal services, including law centres, pro bono and duty lawyer schemes, and unbundled and fixed price packages. Again, this is likely to make a contribution but it is very unlikely that the free legal advice in the form of law centres and pro bono schemes could ever meet demand. There are also doubts about whether pro bono schemes can provide the continuity required. Recent research[86] revealed that a pro bono advice scheme for family and civil proceedings was of limited effectiveness in terms of having a discernable impact on the progress of proceedings. Much was contingent on the ability of the LIP to follow up on advice and on factors beyond the control of the LIP and the pro bono adviser.

There has been something of a push recently to develop unbundled[87] and fixed price[88] legal services in England and Wales. There is some evidence that the summary advice model may not provide an adequate substitute for full representation. Albeit on housing cases, Greiner et al's randomised controlled studies in the US suggest that full representation offers significantly better outcome for clients than unbundled services, at least in some circumstances.[89] Macfarlane also cautions against over-reliance on a summary legal advice model. She reports that LIPs who accessed brief advice sessions could end up feeling more confused and stressed afterwards.[90]

[84] Hunter, R, 'Access to Justice after LASPO' [2014] *Family Law* 640.

[85] Legal Services Consumer Panel, *2020 Legal Services: How Regulators Should Prepare for the Future* (LSCP, 2014) 2.

[86] Sefton, M, Moorhead, R, Sidaway, J and Fox, C, *Unbundled and Pro Bono Advice for Litigants in Person: One Study* (ILAG Conference Paper, 2013).

[87] The Law Society has recently issued a practice note on unbundling: www.lawsociety.org.uk/advice/practice-notes/unbundling-family-legal-services/.

[88] There is also a push for fixed pricing in financial remedy cases. See remarks by Mostyn J in *J v J* [2014] EWHC 3654 where the legal costs of £920,000 represented 32% of the parties' assets.

[89] Greiner, J, Wolos Pattanayak, C and Hennessy, J, 'The Limits of Unbundled Legal Assistance: A Randomized Study in a Massachusetts District Court and Prospects for the Future' (2013) 126 *Harvard Law Review* 901.

[90] Macfarlane (n 16) 122.

Hunter's third strategy is to modify the court process and, in particular, to move away from a traditional adversarial system predicated upon lawyers to a more inquisitorial approach.[91] Such an approach would require significant changes in the role of the judge, most notably in cases where only one side is represented. The current President of the Family Division is in favour of a more inquisitorial approach.[92] What that might look like in practice is yet to be fully elaborated. A move to an inquisitorial process would not be resource free. It would require a considerable expansion in the number of judicial hours.

All of these strategies, if well thought through, are likely to bring some benefit, at least to those LIPs who are able to take advantage of the support offered. However, these types of interventions, particularly those offering to train LIPs to represent themselves, are predicated on a rational actor model requiring not just taking responsibility for one's own case but also taking responsibility appropriately by researching and utilising legal information as if one were a lawyer. That may be an appropriate model for some individuals, but it assumes an emotional readiness, intellectual and linguistic competence and organisational and logistical capacity that many LIPs may not possess. It also makes an assumption that some of the ethical issues about the appropriate role of the judge and court staff in supporting, but not advising LIPs, can be overcome.

In the meantime, there is little sign in England of a sustained policy response to the growth of LIPs. There were very little, if any, additional services put in place as LASPO was implemented other than a modest amount of extra funding for mediation services.[93] Rather belatedly, the government announced a new package of support measures in late 2014, but amounting to just £2 million. The package included a range of services—better online information, a six-month pilot telephone helpline run by Cafcass (the court social work service), funding for some local support services, a named person in each court to manage the 'new service' and an appointed judge in each centre with particular responsibility for LIPs. Whilst none of those measures is likely to be unhelpful, they fall far short of what is likely to be needed. What is missing especially is any funding to make initial legal advice more widely available,[94] not least to enable people to resolve issues out-of-court either through solicitor negotiation or to encourage uptake of mediation.

[91] See also Zorza, 'An Overview of Self-represented Litigation Innovation' (n 78).

[92] Sir James Munby, 'View from the President's Chambers (12) The Process of Reform: Next Steps' (2014) www.judiciary.gov.uk/publications/view-from-presidents-chambers/.

[93] Even that additional funding was not used as the number of mediation starts halved, apparently due to the lack of family lawyers who had previously been the main supply/referral route to mediation.

[94] The funding included Personal Support Units which do not offer advice, just information and support.

What appears to be developing instead, whether by design or default, is a free for all in the supply of information, advice and 'legal services' in the broadest sense. Mavis Maclean[95] has identified, in particular, a multiplicity in the range of online sources springing up. These range from lawyers adopting new methods to attract and support clients, to not-for-profit organisations providing assistance, unqualified but nonetheless fee-charging McKenzie Friends together with other services charging a fee for a 'lawyer-managed' service the nature of which is not clear. Maclean notes that such diversification, fragmentation and (for some) lack of regulation is offering greater consumer choice, but at some risk. Prices for advice may go down as a consequence but there is little evidence of quality control or consumer protection. One of the newcomers to the field is the 'Society of Professional McKenzie Friends' whose Director stated in November 2014 that 'Now that legal aid has all but gone from family proceedings, the consumer is king. The consumer now pays the piper personally out of his own pocket and is starting to call the tune'.[96] The problem, of course, is that the piper in this instance has very little information to go on to be sufficiently informed to shop around and make the most informed decisions.

CONCLUSION

Since the introduction of legal aid reform, individuals (or at least applicants) have increasingly taken responsibility for their disputes, but not quite as the government intended. Individuals have not been diverted to mediation to conduct a 'good divorce' but instead have accessed the courts in increasing numbers as litigants in person.

How well that is working, both for litigants and other court users, is not clear in the absence of systematic research. However, there are very clear indications from family justice professionals of problems being experienced on the ground, some raising very concerning issues about access to justice for the most vulnerable. We can also extrapolate from the findings from a body of international research on the likely support needs and impact of LIPs post-LASPO. The combined message from both bodies of evidence is that LIPs have a wide range of support needs, but that it is very difficult to provide accessible, consistent and effective support for all LIPs that will enable them to put their case forward effectively. It is even more difficult to provide support for LIPs without also disadvantaging represented parties or shifting tasks and costs that LIPs cannot shoulder to already stretched judges and court staff.

[95] Maclean, M, 'The Changing Professional Landscape' [2014] *Family Law* 177.

[96] 'McKenzie Friends' trade association introduces new rules' *Family Law Week* 16 November 2014 www.familylawweek.co.uk/site.aspx?i=ed136795.

The difficulties that LIPs and justice systems have in adjusting to each other is perhaps not surprising given that justice systems have developed based on a full representation model that is now relevant to only a minority of cases in England and Wales. What is of particular concern is how little the government has done to ensure that the courts and LIPs can accommodate each other. There was very little preparation by the government before the introduction of legal aid reforms and a very limited response subsequently other than a reliance on mediation and the marketplace. As John Eekelaar[97] has pointed out, this frames the issues arising from individual decisions about partnering and parenthood as personal (and not very important) choices rather than matters concerning rights and justice of both social and individual significance. In the meantime a brave new world of an increasingly deprofessionalised and unregulated advice and support sector is developing rapidly to supply legal consumers. The caveat emptor message that development brings sits uneasily with ideas about justice, fairness and the protection of the vulnerable that have long been the purpose of family law.

[97] Eekelaar, J, '"Not of the Highest Importance": Family Justice under Threat' (2011) 33 *Journal of Social Welfare and Family Law* 311.

14

Access to Justice in Hard Times and the Deconstruction of Democratic Citizenship

HILARY SOMMERLAD*

INTRODUCTION

IT IS COMMON ground that the attacks of the last three decades on post war social citizenship in the UK—fundamental to which was access to justice[1]—are attributable to neoliberalism.[2] However, the breadth and plasticity of the concept reduces its explanatory power.[3] As a result of its coincidence as a rationale and form of governance with the intensification of globalisation and policies of economic liberalisation, monetarism and privatisation, it is sometimes framed as a primarily economic project.[4] Certainly, governments typically underplay the ideological drive behind their policies of welfare cuts and state retrenchment, emphasising the efficiency of the market and, especially over the course of the last few years, the necessity of extreme fiscal prudence in the face of crisis.

This economistic interpretation is belied by the juxtaposition of state withdrawal from responsibility for many of the functions identified by Weber as basic to its role—such as administering to citizens' 'hygienic, educational,

* I would like to express my gratitude to Rosemary Hunter for her invaluable comments on the draft of this chapter.

1 TH Marshall, one of the visionaries of the welfare state, argued that post war socialised citizenship had initiated a transformation of the formulaic equality of liberal legalism into more responsive, policy-oriented forms of law and lawyering: Marshall, TH, *Citizenship and Social Class* (Cambridge, Cambridge University Press, 1950); Sommerlad, H, 'Some Reflections on the Relationship between Citizenship, Access to Justice and the Reform of Legal Aid' (2004) 31(3) *Journal of Law & Society* 345.

2 See eg Crouch, C, *The Strange Non-death of Neo-liberalism* (Cambridge, Polity Press, 2011) and Treloar's chapter in this volume.

3 Hall, S, 'The Neo-liberal Revolution' (2011) 25(6) *Cultural Studies* 705.

4 See eg Comaroff, J and Comaroff, JL, *Millennial Capitalism and the Culture of Neoliberalism* (Durham NC, Durham University Press, 2001).

social and cultural needs'[5]—with discourses which depict individual responsibility as a moral value. As Wendy Brown argues, neoliberalism should therefore not be viewed as 'the result of leakage from the economic to other spheres but rather as a 'form of political reasoning that articulates the nature and meaning of the political, the social, and the subject'.[6] This drive to re-make the nexus of state, market and citizen

> entails a host of policies that ... produce citizens as individual entrepreneurs and consumers whose moral autonomy is measured by their capacity for 'self-care' and governance criteria of productivity and profitability, with the consequence that governance talk increasingly becomes market speak.[7]

However, Brown also notes how, in the US, neoliberalism works in symbiosis with its seeming opposite—neo-conservatism—which 'identifies the state, including law, with the task of setting the moral-religious compass for society'.[8] Although informed by a radically different theoretical perspective, Wacquant similarly highlights this meshing of market-driven discourses with those which draw on older, including religious, rationalities.[9]

The influence of both rationalities can be discerned in the social policies of the UK Coalition government.[10] Legitimation for its dismantling of the welfare state, including legal aid,[11] has been sought in its depiction of

[5] Weber, M, *Economy and Society* (Berkeley, University of California Press, 1978) 2, 905; and see West, R, 'Tragic Rights: The Rights Critique in the Age of Obama' (2011–12) 53 *William and Mary Law Review* 713.

[6] Brown, W, 'American Nightmare: Neoliberalism, Neoconservatism, and De-Democratization' (2006) 34 *Political Theory* 690.

[7] ibid 694.

[8] ibid 697.

[9] Wacquant, L, *Punishing the Poor: The Neoliberal Government of Social Insecurity* (Durham and London, Duke University Press, 2009). See also Harvey, who argues that both neoliberalism and neo-conservatism are a project of the corporate class aimed at rescuing and consolidating upper-class political and economic power from its decline in the latter part of the twentieth century: Harvey, D, *Brief History of Neoliberalism* (Oxford, Oxford University Press, 2005).

[10] The policies of the previous New Labour administration (1997–2010), despite the claims to represent a 'third way', were similarly informed by neoliberal and neoconservative discourses of enterprise, managerialism and 'benefit dependency'. For instance, in 2006 the Department of Work and Pensions announced that benefits trap people into a lifetime of dependency. The clear policy intention in the later years of the New Labour government was to move towards a form of workfare, in which virtually all unemployed benefit claimants would have personalised 'support' into employment, backed by compulsory work-related activity and sanctions. This approach was strengthened with the Welfare Reform Act 2007, which introduced the employment and support allowance (ESA), a tougher medical test and increased engagement with personal advisers and work-related activity. The Welfare Reform Act 2009 aimed to further weaken automatic entitlement to benefits by enacting the 2008 review of conditionality, which separated claimants into a work-ready group; a progression to work group; and a no-conditionality group: Gregg, P, *Realising Potential: A Vision for Personalised Conditionality and Support* (Department of Work and Pensions, 2008).

[11] A strong anti-legal aid discourse began in the early-1990s, which propagated an image of the vexatious client who pursued unmeritorious claims (at taxpayers' expense), exemplified by Gary Streeter, Conservative Under-Secretary of State at the Lord Chancellor's Department ('Streeter Confirms Legally Aided Litigants are Rottweilers' [1996] *New Law Journal* 1378, 1378).

welfare as 'out of control' and, as a prime cause of what has been reconfigured as a fiscal crisis,[12] in need of immediate and drastic surgery. This strategy has entailed the mobilisation of the discourse of the lean state, at the centre of which is the free, possessive individual who meets his needs through consumption in the market. This discourse has been complemented by that of the 'Big Society', grounded in a re-moralised, active citizenry, both individual and communal,[13] which is threatened by the moral weakling, whose dependency has been produced by the 'bloated' 'nanny state'.[14] The evocation of these two ideal types—the responsible citizen and the welfare parasite—highlights the fact that the task of reconfiguring a social order requires work at both the material and symbolic levels. In this instance, this entails: first, practical policies which build on the work of previous governments of stigmatising and penalising the poor and excluding them from state-sponsored dispute resolution in the courts;[15] secondly, a re-making of people's subjectivities and hence their 'common sense' views on social reality.[16] This second objective is exemplified by the re-conceptualisation of keywords like liberty as the freedom to acquire commodities, the construction of taxation of income as immoral[17] and the prioritisation of such norms as 'self-reliance and self-sufficiency'.[18]

The recent reconstruction of the family justice system through its reforms of both public law by the enactment of the Children and Families Act 2014 and of access to private law remedies through the Legal Aid, Sentencing and

[12] Clarke, J and Newman, J, 'The Alchemy of Austerity' (2012) 32(3) *Critical Social Policy* 299.

[13] In the form of the not-for-profit sector; see eg Philip Blond, one of the leading neo-conservative ideologues, who summarised the 'project of radical transformative conservatism' as 'nothing less than the restoration and creation of human association', arguing that the cure for Britain's 'atomised' and 'broken' society are the twin strategies of liberating those currently 'trapped in welfare' by shifting the burden of dispensing social services onto the 'third sector': Blond, P, *Red Tory* (London, Faber and Faber, 2010). This proved a point of conflict between the two rationales, as the neoliberal wing of the Coalition government favoured opening up the outsourcing of public services to businesses as well as the not-for-profit sector.

[14] See eg the writings of Charles Murray and Lawrence Mead who recommended 'autonomization and responsibilization' to counter the moral hazard of the welfare state: Murray, C, *Losing Ground: American Social Policy 1950–1980* (New York, NY, Basic Books, 1984); Mead, L, *Beyond Entitlement: the Social Obligations of Citizenship* (New York, NY, Free Press, 1986).

[15] However, since mediation represents a key plank in the government's drive to privatise dispute resolution, legal aid remains available for this, governed by the usual eligibility requirements; each case is also screened by mediators.

[16] Wacquant, in his studies of the penal state which neoliberalism has constructed, argues for a 'materialist vision of the political economy of punishment to capture the constitutive power of symbolic structures reverberating roles of the criminal justice as cultural engine and fount of social demarcations, public norms, and moral emotions': Wacquant, *Punishing the Poor* (n 9) xviii.

[17] At the end of October 2010, Prime Minister David Cameron said that he felt it a 'moral duty' to cut taxes: see www.dailymail.co.uk/wires/pa/article-2813464/PM-feels-moral-duty-cut-taxes.html.

[18] Cabinet Office, *Building the Big Society* (London, Cabinet Office, 2010).

Punishment of Offenders Act 2012 (LASPO) and Civil Legal Aid (Procedure) Rules 2012,[19] works at both these levels. Beginning with the material level, this legislation has transformed the practical arrangements for dealing with private family disputes—particularly for people who had previously qualified for legal aid, since it has ended automatic financial eligibility for those on benefit[20] and removed from scope the majority of private family law matters, including applications for child arrangement orders.[21] And while legal aid for these matters remains, in theory, available where the applicant has suffered, or is at risk of suffering, domestic violence, or where a child is at risk of abuse from a partner, this is conditional on the production of strictly prescribed evidence.[22] Mediation is offered in place of court processes, but where this is deemed unsuitable (which includes the situation where one party refuses to participate) or there is a failure to reach settlement, then, unless the applicant can fund legal advice, the only option is self-litigation, which the Ministry of Justice has itself acknowledged is likely to produce adverse effects for the parties.[23]

This push to private dispute resolution through mediation is fundamental to the reforms' symbolic work of eroding the very idea of state responsibility for private justice, and instantiating a new moral compass or truth criteria for society,[24] work which is clearly infused with both neoliberal and neo-conservative rationalities. Whereas welfare state policies were generally directed towards constructing a social morality based on solidarity, the reforms are mechanisms for furthering the atomisation of social relationships and establishing poverty as a personal, moral responsibility/deficiency unrelated to social structure.[25] The point is underlined by the fact that

[19] See Civil Legal Aid (Procedure) Regulations 2012, reg 33.

[20] Those in receipt of the following benefits will no longer automatically be eligible for legal aid: Income Support; Income Based Job Seekers' Allowance; Income Based Employment and Support Allowance or Guarantee Credit. Applicants will also now have to meet the capital limit for savings and other capital including equity in property. Applicants who have more than £8000 in capital will not be eligible for legal aid. Other changes include deep cuts to lawyers' fees.

[21] From 1 April 2014, Child Arrangement Orders replaced applications in relation to children for contact, residence, prohibited steps or specific issue orders and child maintenance and applications under Children Act 1989, sch 1.

[22] See the Ministry of Justice website at: www.justice.gov.uk/legal-aid-divorcing-separating-abusive-partner; and for a valuable critique when the measures were at the Green Paper stage, see Hunter, R, 'Doing Violence to Family Law' (2011) 33(4) *Journal of Social Welfare and Family Law* 343.

[23] Miles, J, Balmer, N and Smith, M, 'When Exceptional is the Rule: Mental Health, Family Problems and the Reform of Legal Aid in England and Wales' (2012) 24 *Child and Family Law Quarterly* 3, 24.

[24] Brown, 'American Nightmare' (n 6) 693.

[25] This neoliberal narrative has been described as misrepresenting 'the effects of social relations and institutions as if these were generated by individual choice ... a large cast of contrasting individuals have been conjured up around which to build stories of equality, responsibility or choice', the effect of which is 'to encourage us to think that our chance talents and aspirations really do explain how and where we end up, drawing us into a discourse of

they, together with a raft of other benefit reforms, have been instituted at a time when rising unemployment has increased levels of debt, homelessness, mental health problems and family breakdowns, intensifying the need for specialist legal advice and assistance.[26] Further, the government has itself acknowledged that 'legal aid recipients are amongst the most disadvantaged in society, reflecting both the nature of the problems they face as well as their eligibility for legal aid'.[27] However, responsibility for the reforms, the inhumanity of which this statement implicitly acknowledges, is then generalised and the reforms normalised through the refrain that they are a response not only to the 'crisis' but also to the lack of public support for legal aid.

Fundamental to this new common sense is the (re-)establishment of the family as a strictly private sphere, and the irresponsibility of either the state or market for any role in social reproduction.[28] This in turn is contributing to the erosion of the 'social' law which developed as a result of legal aid: this socialised, or 'responsive' law[29] created by the actions of those who were once only the objects of law had generated new legal functions[30] and norms. However a neoliberal social order has no need for abstract debates over rights (which in any event are reduced to conditional entitlements largely in the gift of, frequently private sector, administrators). Private law has thus been re-constituted as a commodity, concerned only with matters for which people are 'prepared' (and able) to pay.[31] The reforms therefore are key

individual variation that has less and less purchase on the larger issues of inequality ... in a world where the three hundred wealthiest individuals control assets equivalent to those of the poorest three billion, the distribution of resources is clearly about something more than the distribution of tastes or talents or the propensity for hard work'; Phillips, A, 'Defending Equality of Outcome' (2004) 12(1) *Journal of Political Philosophy* 1, 15.

[26] Law Centres Federation, *Weathering the Storm* (London, Law Centres Federation, 2011); Morris, D, 'Charities and the Big Society: a Doomed Coalition?' (2012) 32(1) *Legal Studies* 132.

[27] Ministry of Justice, *Impact Assessment, Cumulative Legal Aid Reform Proposals* (London, Ministry of Justice, 2010) 13, para 39.

[28] This is of course the continuation of a process which began in the 1990s, when the neoliberal move to re-construct the state/citizenship was extended to family law through, for instance, the Family Law Act 1996.

[29] Arthurs, HW and Kreklewich, R, 'Law, Legal Institutions and the Legal Profession in the New Economy' (1996) 34 *Osgoode Hall Law Journal* 1 speak of welfare statist responsive law; see also Selznick, P, *The Moral Commonwealth Social Theory and the Promise of Community* (Berkeley and Los Angeles, UCLA Press, 1992).

[30] Such as regulatory functions which of course contrast starkly with the neoliberal ideal of the market as the primary source of allocation; see eg Prosser, T, 'Regulation and Social Solidarity' (2006) 33(3) *Journal of Law and Society* 364.

[31] Lacey argues that the implicit premise of LASPO together with the package of family law reforms is that only those who are well resourced and/or made the right 'choices' in the past should be given full access to justice: Lacey, N, 'Justice Redefined—or Justice Diluted' (2014) 2 *Family Law* 593; see also Crouch, *The Strange Non-death of Neo-liberalism* (n 2) 64. This restriction in access to justice is extending beyond family law and increasingly affecting private citizens in general, as courts close and other (cheaper) forms of dispute resolution such as the Ombudsman are pushed forward in their place.

components in the reconstruction of the common law as the preserve of the wealthy and, in particular, corporate interests, so that, while still framed by the liberal fiction of equality and universality, it will in practice be increasingly constituted by elite discourses and norms. Correspondingly, the effective extinction of poor people's access to civil justice both expresses and affirms the hierarchical form of citizenship implicit in neoliberalism's naturalisation of inequalities and differential valuation of citizens on the basis of their property ownership and capacity for self-care. And since it is women who are primarily affected by the reforms,[32] they can also be interpreted as part of a wider misogynist turn which, drawing strength from archaic patriarchal representations of women, is reversing the gains of the last 30 years, and silencing women,[33] especially working-class and non-white women. Finally, the contempt conveyed by the reforms for such core liberal ideals as equality of arms and the dignity of the individual contributes to the process by which neoliberalism is producing a general corrosion of the rule of law and democratic governance.[34]

In the discussion that follows, I consider these issues through data generated by a small number of interviews, conducted as part of a wider qualitative study,[35] supplemented by parliamentary debates, NGO reports and the press. Respondents were primarily concerned with the withdrawal of legal aid for private family law disputes, and I therefore pay less attention to the changes to public law matters. Five themes emerged strongly from the data: the increase in litigants in person (LIPs); domestic violence and exceptional funding; expert reports; the particular impact of the reforms on women; the

[32] This is so for several interrelated reasons: women continue to be the primary caregivers and despite the supposedly gender-blind individualisation of neoliberal society, still earn on average considerably less than men, with their relative or absolute poverty being exacerbated by irregular participation in the labour market; thus, recent statistics published by the Centre for Economic and Social Inclusion show that 'men get more jobs through the Work Programme than women, and the gap is increasing'. Furthermore, a range of austerity policies implemented by the Coalition government is also starting to affect these same women in a disproportionate manner. For instance, the Women's Budget Group notes that Universal Credit could signal a return to a 'male breadwinner model' in which men do paid work and women stay at home to look after children and other dependents: Women's Budget Group, 'Impact on Women of Budget 2014: No Recovery for Women', available at: http://www.wbg.org.uk/wp-content/uploads/2014/03/FINAL-WBG-2014-budget-reponse.pdf. See also Women's Resource Centre, *The Impact of Public Spending Cuts on Women's Voluntary and Community Organisations in London* (London, Women's Resource Centre, 2013); Scott, J and Dex, S, 'Paid and Unpaid Work. Can Policy Improve Gender Inequalities in Relationships?' in J Miles and R Probert (eds), *Sharing Lives, Dividing Assets* (Oxford, Hart Publishing, 1990) 55; Fawcett Society *Cutting Women Out* (2013) http://uat.fawcettsociety.org.uk/cutting-women-out/#sthash.L7N9MA9z.dpbs.

[33] See Mary Beard's recent genealogy of women's silencing, in response to the threats and abuse she has received: Beard, M, 'The Public Voice of Women' (2014) 36(6) *London Review of Books*, 20 March, 11–14.

[34] Harvey, *Brief History* (n 9); Brown (n 6); Wacquant (n 9); Crouch (n 2).

[35] The study is being conducted with Linden Thomas and Lesley Griffiths, Centre for Professional Legal Education and Research (CEPLER), Birmingham Law School.

quality of, and access to, justice. Before I do this, I provide a brief outline of the research study.

THE STUDY

The interviews which I draw on in the discussion which follows were conducted between March and May 2014; the study is ongoing. The final sample is projected to include representatives from most groups which were once involved in the delivery of family legal aid: solicitors, paralegals, barristers, barristers' clerks, mediators, judges, court clerks and ushers and spokespeople from both local law societies and the Law Society and Bar Council.[36] The practitioner sample is primarily drawn from one community—a large urban centre—but in order to gauge the differential impact of locality it also includes individuals from other centres (including London and a small market town). It is anticipated that the final sample will comprise 30 to 35 respondents, selected as far as possible to ensure a range in terms of both demographic characteristics and experience. This chapter draws on interviews with nine respondents: one circuit judge (white British male); four solicitors: a British African-Caribbean woman who is a partner in a small firm, two white British females and a white male partner of a market town practice, just retired; three senior barristers: two white females (one based in London) and one British South Asian; and a white British barristers' clerk.

The research has several objectives including assessing how the size and structure of the family legal aid market in the main urban centre under study has changed over the last 18 years. However, its primary aim is to elicit practitioners' views on the significance of LASPO for the quality of, and access to, justice. The breadth of this aim meant that interviews were relatively unstructured in order to give the respondent the space to discuss whatever particular issues about LASPO have concerned them. In order to mitigate the influence on respondents' accounts of the emotional investment

[36] The legal profession in England and Wales is divided into two main branches with different functions and routes to qualification: barristers who were the legal specialists and had exclusive rights of advocacy in the higher courts but no direct access to clients, and solicitors who enjoyed monopolies over certain practice areas such as transactions in land (conveyancing), had direct contact with clients, and were more likely to be general practitioners. Today these divisions are less clear-cut—for instance solicitors can acquire advocacy rights in the higher courts—and the financial pressures which LASPO has accentuated is blurring the distinction further, as, for instance, barristers seek direct access to clients. Traditionally, the profession has also encompassed legal executives and paralegals; again, the use of these lower status and therefore cheaper forms of labour is increasing. Barristers' clerks manage chambers and the division and loading of work for barristers; ushers work in the courts, by, for instance, bringing clients into court. The solicitors' representative body is the Law Society, but local law societies also exist.

they have in the previous system, they were asked to give examples of particular cases to illustrate their concerns.

The interviews were conducted in locations chosen by the respondent, which were generally their places of work, and in one case by telephone. They lasted from between an hour and two hours and were all recorded, but notes were also taken.

THE IMPACT OF THE REFORMS

Litigants in Person

The central importance, discussed above, to neoliberal ideology that citizens be re-constituted as rational economic actors in all spheres of life, whatever the consequences for the individual, family group and social fabric, is clearly evident in Coalition government policy. For instance, in the debates which preceded the enactment of LASPO government ministers and agencies repeatedly emphasised the need for individual responsibility and choice, exemplified by the statement that 'issues' that arise from a person's 'own personal choices' were not likely to be considered 'of the highest importance' for legal aid, and that not everyone involved in such disputes is entitled to 'a particular outcome in litigation'.[37] Further, this argument was made in disregard of the strong evidence of the unfavourable outcomes for what would be a growing number of LIPs[38] and, secondly, that such LIPs are more likely to have mental health issues, learning difficulties and other problems.[39] The government also ignored independent evidence that

[37] Ministry of Justice, *Proposals for the Reform of Legal Aid in England and Wales*, Consultation Paper CP 12/10 (London, Ministry of Justice, 2010) para 4.19.

[38] Bevan, C, 'Self-Represented Litigants: The Overlooked and Unintended Consequences of Legal Aid Reform' (2013) 35 *Journal of Social Welfare and Family Law* 43; and see Hunter, R, De Simone, T and Whitaker, L, *Women and Legal Aid: Identifying Disadvantage: Final Report* (Brisbane, Legal Aid Queensland and Socio-legal Research Centre, Griffith University, 2006) 201, 208.

[39] Civil Justice Council, *Access to Justice for Litigants in Person (or Self-Represented Litigants): A Report and Series of Recommendations to the Lord Chancellor and to the Lord Chief Justice* (2011) available from Civil Justice Website at: www.judiciary.gov.uk/about-the-judiciary/advisory-bodies/cjc/. This is borne out by research conducted by Trinder et al for the MOJ which found that around half of those observed experienced one or more vulnerabilities which added to their difficulties in self-representation: This is borne out by research conducted by Trinder et al for the MOJ which found that around half of those observed experienced one or more vulnerabilities which added to their difficulties in self-representation: Trinder, L, Hunter, R, Hitchings, E, Miles, J, Moorhead, R, Smith, L, Sefton, M, Hinchly, V, Bader, K and Pearce, J, *Litigants in Person in Private Family Law* (Ministry of Justice Analytical Series, November 2014) www.gov.uk/government/uploads/system/uploads/attachment_data/file/380479/litigants-in-person-in-private-family-law-cases.pdf.

LASPO would cost rather than save money,[40] while objections raised by its high-profile opponents, including experts in family law,[41] that it would damage core legal and democratic norms,[42] were countered with business speak, such as that 'the reform ... would deliver better value for money'.[43]

The impact that an increase in LIPs was likely to have on perceptions of fairness and hence the legitimacy of the legal system was a particular concern for Lord Scott of Foscote:

> a plethora of litigants in person is not an ornament to a civil justice system but a reproach ... every judge must bear in mind that one party is going to lose and must leave the court feeling that he or she has had justice. Where there is a litigant in person, the judge cannot avoid appearing to be on the side of that party.[44]

For Lord Pannick, it was the democratic process which was likely to be damaged: 'legal aid is a vital element in securing access to justice and ... without

[40] In an independent report commissioned by the Law Society, it was noted that LASPO could not make its savings target if it generated substantial knock-on or consequential costs to the public purse, but that 'the Government's own impact assessment indicated that the reforms could generate knock-on costs including reduced social cohesion, increased criminality, reduced business and economic efficiency, increased resource costs to other Departments, and increased transfer payments from other Departments', and found that these costs could be 'in the region of £139 million per annum, realising a net saving of significantly less than half (42%) of the Government's prediction within the areas of law under study': Cookson, G, *Unintended Consequences: the Cost of the Government's Legal Aid Reforms: a Report for the Law Society of England and Wales* (London, King's College, 2011); see also Sir Alan Ward in *Wright v Wright* in which he argued that saving expenditure in one public department simply increases it in the courts [2013] EWCA Civ 234.

[41] The opposition to LASPO was not only overwhelming numerical (less than 3% of respondents to the government consultation paper supported the proposals to remove large numbers of matters from scope); Ministry of Justice, *Reform of Legal Aid in England and Wales: the Government Response* (Cm 8072, 2011) Annex B, para 2. It also included some of the highest level judges such as Baroness Butler-Sloss.

[42] The website of a legal aid solicitors in Liverpool predicted that the system would comprise a 'hotch-potch of procedures and legislation held together by an inadequate budget, which, more often than not, will have to be navigated by the parties themselves with no legal representation ... A good family justice system is one that supports families with practical and legal help at (what is often) the most traumatic times of their lives. The ideal resolution is, of course, one that ensures that the difficulties are addressed and resolved with as little conflict as possible. But the fact of the matter is we do not live in a world where most people are emotionally equipped on their own to deal in a practical and rational way with the implications of family breakdown': Kate Gomery, 'Get a Grip—Reform of Family Justice' 6 July 2011, available at: http://www.boydcarter.co.uk/Legal-Aid-Changes.php. The vindication of this prediction has generated criticism even from quarters generally sympathetic to Conservative policy; this, for instance, was the view of a *Daily Telegraph* columnist: 'The slashing of legal aid in cases heard in the family courts has resulted in an explosion of "litigants in person" attempting to argue complex points within a system they don't fully understand—an outcome fully predicted by the judges' council in 2011—and costing ever more expensive court time', available at: http://blogs.telegraph.co.uk/news/jennymccartney/100262545/legal-aid-chris-grayling-is-now-inextricably-entwined-with-from-the-disaster-he-has-created/.

[43] Ministry of Justice, *The Government Response* (n 41) Annex B, para 3.

[44] Lord Scott of Foscote (former Lord of Appeal in Ordinary) in a Debate in Committee in House of Lords 16 January 2012.

access to justice, the rights and duties which we spend time creating in this Parliament by legislation are reduced in value and effect'.[45] Underlying these objections is a normative view of government as responsible for providing the primary institutions of adjudication and for issues affecting the welfare of its citizenry and particularly that of children, a view implicit in human rights jurisprudence (and in particular Article 6 of the European Convention on Human Rights (ECHR)).

The predictions that self-representation would increase following the implementation of the changes to legal aid in April 2013 have been vindicated,[46] and the concerns outlined above about the consequences have recently been reiterated by Thomas CJ and Black CJ.[47] These concerns also featured strongly in respondents' accounts; for instance, a senior Family Law barrister began by noting the increased time which cases run by LIPs take:

> when you are represented your barrister or solicitor will often do a short position statement, outlining the issues quickly so the court can understand them and deal with them quickly. An LiP will turn up without having had the papers, not having produced a bundle, often arriving with plastic bags of papers for the judge to look at. It is a concern for judges because it brings the system to a halt. They have to give those people priority ... if you have two lawyers you can often bring a hearing to conclusion in half an hour, but with an unrepresented party it can take all day.

Several worried about unfairness where one party was represented and the other was an LIP. In articulating it as a breach of the 'fundamental principle of equality of arms', the Circuit Judge gave an example of a dispute over residence he had recently heard which involved an East European couple:

> the man speaks English and is working and was therefore able to afford a lawyer. The woman speaks no English at all. I was presented with an order by the father's solicitor but there is no way she could understand the order. However his solicitor said that she had agreed it. When I asked how she could have done so, given her lack of English, she said that husband had translated it for her. So the woman clearly needed legal representation but under LASPO could not get it.

[45] Debate in Committee in House of Lords 20 December 2011.

[46] In the quarters following the implementation of LASPO there has been a drop of 41% in the number of disposals for private family law cases where both parties were represented and a doubling in disposals where neither party was represented: Ministry of Justice, *Court Statistics Quarterly April to June 2014 Ministry of Justice Statistics bulletin* (London, Ministry of Justice, 2014) 21, available at: www.gov.uk/government/uploads/system/uploads/attachment_data/file/358230/court-statistics-quarterly-april-to-june-2014.pdf.

[47] Hyde cites Thomas CJ as saying 'There has been a significant increase [in LIPs]. I find that out when I talk to district judges and it's having an effect on the bottom rung. It is particularly acute in family cases as two people are required to be adversarial': Hyde, J, 'Litigants in person putting pressure on courts system—LCJ' (2014) *Law Society Gazette* 3 April; Hyde, J, 'Litigants in person make life "infinitely more difficult"'—CoA judge' (2014) *Law Society Gazette* 9 May.

However a solicitor noted that there could be unfairness to the represented party too because 'you cannot make the points, put the questions—or at least not in a forceful way as you would to another lawyer, because the judge has to protect the LIP', and argued that as a result the reforms were producing a complete 'unravelling of the rules of the system'.

A further consequence of the state's retreat from its role in the provision and regulation of justice has been the emergence of a plethora of new forms of legal services[48] including an unregulated advice market in 'McKenzie friends'.[49] While some of these advisers gave free support, respondents spoke of a growing trend towards charging, and expressed concern about the dangers they posed to 'highly vulnerable, often damaged individuals who feel they have nowhere to turn' (barrister). A solicitor said:

> We now have a whole industry of unregulated paralegals; McKenzie Friends who charge for services with no insurance, no liability; DIY divorce and other IT platforms providing online advice; fixed fees and unbundling—all of which present challenging risk management issues.

Far from providing the 'filter, the management of expectations' which lawyers provide, McKenzie Friends could compound the emotion and hence unmanageability of proceedings, since 'a lot of them are ex-husbands whose experience of courts comes from their own contact cases; some are even from groups like Fathers 4 Justice and Families need Fathers'.[50] One barrister had found that her client's partner was being advised by an extremely prominent member of one of these groups.[51] As she pointed out, such 'representatives' had 'their own axe to grind', and this was particularly so in this instance, since she had represented the man's wife years before in his own long-running contact case:

> So I have to negotiate with this man who at one time, during his own case was driving round the streets of (name of town) broadcasting to the world, naming his own children … he carried out paint bombings … and he is now 'helping' my client's

[48] For a clear outline of on unbundled, fixed fee and other new legal services, see Maclean, M, 'Delivering Family Justice: New Ways of Working for Lawyers in Divorce and Separation' in H Sommerlad, S Harris-Short, S Vaughan and R Young (eds), *The Futures of Legal Education and the Legal Profession* (Oxford, Hart Publishing, 2015).

[49] A McKenzie Friend is someone—who need not be legally qualified—who assists an LIP in court. The term stems from *McKenzie v McKenzie* (1970] 3 All ER 1034, CA, which established the entitlement of the LIP to have assistance, lay or professional, unless there are exceptional circumstances. Their presence in the legal system has been endorsed by the Legal Services Consumer Panel: Legal Services Consumer Panel, *Fee-charging McKenzie Friends* (Legal Services Commission, 2014) www.legalservicesconsumerpanel.org.uk/publications/research_and_reports/documents/2014%2004%2017%20MKF_Final.pdf.

[50] Such groups, which sprang up in the early years of the century, aimed to gain public and parliamentary support for changes in UK legislation on fathers' rights, mainly using stunts and protests, often conducted in costume.

[51] The man in question had been an active protestor, frequently in costume.

> husband in proceedings for contact and financial remedy. This is dangerous. These people might well have been refused contact because of allegations of violence or abuse.

Domestic Violence and Exceptional Funding

The presumption of the benefit claimant's moral turpitude which pervades the legislation is evident even in cases of domestic violence;[52] although as a signatory to the ECHR the government was obliged to leave these in scope, the imposition of stringent requirements for evidence may mean that it is nonetheless in breach of the Human Rights Act.[53] As one barrister put it:

> if you're a victim of domestic violence, you get funding, (but) that's not the whole story because they've made it so difficult to get … victims have to obtain written evidence from their doctor (who often wants to charge for the report), from the Police, maybe they're ashamed and haven't been to their doctor, so they don't have that evidence.

A solicitor spoke of having to 'turn loads of cases away' and gave the example of

> a woman who was profoundly deaf and a long standing victim of domestic violence who couldn't access the police because they were unable to deal with her. So she couldn't mount a recent DV allegation because she couldn't provide the gateway evidence.

Support for these accounts comes from a report of two post-LASPO surveys conducted by Rights of Women, with Women's Aid England and Welsh Women's Aid, which found that over half respondents to both surveys who had experienced or were experiencing domestic violence did not have the forms of evidence required in order to access family law legal aid. This confirmed the findings of research they had conducted prior to the enactment of LASPO and reported on to the government, which showed that 16.7 per cent of respondents had to pay over £50 to obtain copies of the required evidence; 37.5 per cent had to wait longer than two weeks to get copies of their evidence; 60.5 per cent took no action in relation to their family law problem as a result of not being able to apply for legal aid.;

[52] Hunter, Doing Violence to Family Law' (n 22).

[53] The lawfulness of the evidence rules for domestic violence and legal aid is currently being challenged by Rights of Women supported by the Public Law Project; see www.publiclawproject.org.uk/news/43/press-release-high-court-to-hear-rights-of-womeneys-legal-challenge-to-restore-access-to-legal-aid-f.

23.7 per cent paid a solicitor privately and 15.8 per cent represented themselves at court.[54]

Even where applicants are granted funding, since those charged with perpetrating domestic violence are no longer eligible for funded representation, they can end up being 'taken to court by their partner who has assaulted them, for a contact order to see their children and can end up being cross-examined by their assailant'. Another solicitor shared this concern:

> if you are facing an allegation of domestic violence, you can't get legal aid to defend yourself. That's unfair for the person accused and ... also for the victim because if you've got a contested hearing, you're going to end up with the person who has beaten you up cross examining you in court.

Inevitably this was resulting in the general raising of emotional temperature in the court; in the words of another solicitor: 'It's extremely stressful ... I suspect you're going to end up seeing a lot more assaults taking place in the court'. Others spoke of the unmanageability of court proceedings 'you get more people kicking off in court. Whereas solicitors used to be there to manage situations and tell them to calm down, or keep parties apart, there isn't anyone there to do that now'.[55]

For those in particular difficulties or with exceptional problems, there is the possibility of obtaining a grant of 'exceptional funding' from the Legal Aid Agency (LAA): 'you have to provide very specific evidence in domestic violence cases. If you don't get it you are supposed to be able to apply for Exceptional Funding'.[56] However, in practice, the proportion of applications granted by the LAA has been tiny,[57] due, in the view of the Circuit Judge, to the fact 'that the LAA are terrified and so they are more restrictive in their interpretation of government provisions than they need be'.

[54] Rights of Women, *Briefing for Individual Women: New Legal Aid Rules for Family Law* (Rights of Women, 2013) http://rightsofwomen.org.uk/wp-content/uploads/2014/10/Evidencing-DV-a-barrier-2013.pdf.

[55] Trinder et al's report, *Litigants in Person in Private Family Law* (n 39), provides graphic descriptions of the unfairness (and or inefficacy) which can characterise hearings involving LIPs; they describe four types of cases/LIPs: 'hot potato' hearings which are chaotic with disruptive LIPs; those in which the judge is unable to restrict overconfident LIPs to legal matters; 'out of their depth LIPs' and 'unprotected LIPs'.

[56] Miles et al, 'When Exceptional is the Rule' (n 23) predicted that the Exceptional Cases Funding rules were too limited to alleviate this predicted increase in LIPs and that those litigants with lower levels of income and educational attainment could suffer. See too discussion in Hunter (n 22); the Legal Aid Agency's implementation of Exceptional Case Funding in immigration cases has recently been subject to a successful judicial review: [2014] EWHC 1840 (Admin).

[57] eg from 1 April 2013 to 18 June 2013 only 1 of the 89 family law applications which had been processed had been granted. The apparent breach of Art 6 represented by the difficulties which this statistic indicates and which suggests that applicants are encountering in obtaining assistance has led the Public Law Project to develop its Exceptional Funding Project: www.publiclawproject.org.uk/exceptional-funding-project.

The anti-democratic implications of substituting review by the LAA for court scrutiny of the merits of a case were evident in the fact that 'there is no transparency within the Agency as to how their officers are trained or their decision making process'. Yet there is no right of appeal against its opaque decision-making, and the growing trend to unaccountable governance is evident too in the changes to funding for judicial review: 'you now don't get paid as a practitioner and so you run a great risk with the result that we can't even challenge them administratively'.

Children

For several decades child welfare has been at the heart of government policy in its steering of family disputes. A recurring theme in respondents' accounts was the shift in this policy as a result not only of LASPO but also the Children and Families Act 2014. Respondents were united in the view that the emphasis on speed prioritised cost over justice; for example:

> the Public Law Outline is trying to rush everything through in 26 weeks without doing proper assessments. The Government wants cases completed within 6 months and it was thought this would lead to more adoption but the case of Re B-S, which came out last September, said there's been too much emphasis on adoption and courts weren't doing enough to give a child the chance of being brought up within its birth family. That came in at the same time as rushing through the new completion deadlines; the effect is lots of courts were returning children to unsuitable birth families to speed things up.

This solicitor then returned to the legal aid cuts:

> however the biggest danger is not in child care cases where you can still get representation, it's in the child contact disputes, where now a mother can put her foot down and refuse contact altogether. In reality, we know that parents use children as a weapon and the evidence is that children suffer if they don't have a relationship with both parents.

But as another respondent asked,

> how do you promote and safeguard safe contact? If someone has an injunction they may get a Prohibited Steps Order, but how are they going to sort out their child contact? If the perpetrator is a risk to them or the child where is that contact going to take place?

In her subsequent comments she reflected on the tensions between, on the one hand, the government's reiteration of the child first philosophy and, on the other, the privatisation of the family based on the presumption that children are to be the responsibility of both parents and the withdrawal of state support for the structures which had been in place to ensure that this would be a safe solution for the child:

> The basic jurisprudence of a child's right to see its parents is at odds with the whole Government philosophy of putting the child's welfare at the heart of the system because there is no resource. We have the National Association of Contact Centres but people can't pay and this, again, will put more pressure on the police.

Expert Witnesses

In 2000, the European Court of Human Rights[58] found that the refusal of a German court to order an independent psychological report in a contact dispute was a factor in finding that both Article 8 and Article 6 had been breached. In the UK too, for over two decades there has been increasing recognition of the importance of using expert evidence to clarify issues in both public and private law cases.[59] Evidently, the absence of legal aid means that it is no longer possible for a court to call on expert testimony in private law matters. At the same time, exemplifying its disengagement from involvement in public and individual welfare and its prioritisation of business norms over juridical principles, the government has significantly restricted the length of report and level of fee which can be paid in public law matters.[60] The resulting difficulties in obtaining expert evidence for public law matters was a general preoccupation, and one of the first issues raised by the Circuit Judge: 'a big concern of mine is expert reports', which he saw as vital since for his work since 'Circuit judges tend to get the most difficult Section 8 work—we get the sex abuse/ dumping abroad cases'.

One respondent spoke of the 'the hurdle of getting the LAA to grant funding for experts ... They've regulated the number of hours and the hourly rate for expert testimony, so those with the appropriate authority or experience are too expensive for the process'. As a result, it was reported to be 'very difficult, for example, to get a child psychologist' and 'those available (might) not be your first choice ... which could impact the outcome' (solicitor). The following account by the Circuit Judge illustrates precisely this danger:

> it was a trial where father represented himself and the allegation by mother was that father suffers from mental illness which includes paranoid symptoms, and

[58] *Elsholz v Germany* (2000) 2 FLR 486.

[59] See eg Masson, J, Bailey-Harris, R and Probert, R, *Cretney. Principles of Family Law* (London, Sweet & Maxwell, 2008) para 19.018 on courts' reliance on experts in child welfare (and hence public law cases).

[60] Civil Legal Aid (Remuneration) Regulations 2013.

> that this paranoia prevents him from perceiving the children's needs and handling them properly. Obviously such an allegation needed verifying so I wanted to request a psychiatric report—and in the past that would have happened as a matter of course. However, they cost £3000 and it was clear that this would not be possible. So I knew that we wouldn't get a psychiatric report. In the event, the father gave a clear indication in the course of his evidence that he did indeed have paranoid thoughts, but it's a matter of grave concern that had this not been the case I could either have been exposing the children to poor care or even danger by not making the order or committing an injustice against him by acting on her allegation in the absence of clear evidence. The allegation might be that a party posed a risk of sexually abusing a child—we should be able to investigate that.

Others also gave examples of public law cases where the involvement of an expert had been crucial; for instance, a solicitor recounted how, prior to the reforms, she had

> acted for two children who were removed from their parents' care. The community paediatrician said they had been abused. I was able to bring in an expert from another part of the country who determined that was not the case and the children were returned. That expert would not have been able to be instructed now because of fixed rates and those children could have become wards of the state … there now have to be sharply identifiable issues to determine the necessity of experts. If you have a complex sexual abuse or non-accidental injury case you need medical expertise, but they won't do it at the rate. An independent social worker would challenge local authority social workers in defence of parents, but the cuts mean that unless a solicitor is prepared to absorb the financial risk, these independent experts are unavailable to people.

The erosion of state commitment to the provision of public and private security depicted by these accounts is also evident in the business priorities which now guide the police: 'we've had a case where we needed police records. The police now charge for providing information in private law cases'. And, as this solicitor went on to explain, the lack of legal aid meant that she was unable to obtain the records:

> We couldn't get all of the information that we wanted because although our client had public funding because she was the victim of domestic violence, the Dad didn't have any [public funding]. The dad wasn't going to pay the half of the money that was necessary for this police information. He probably couldn't afford it. And of course the Legal Aid Agency wouldn't pay it all because you have to apportion.

The Intensification of Gender Injustice

There is extensive evidence that the resource differentials between women and men have increased as a result of the sustained neoliberal rhetorical assault on egalitarianism, underpinned by discourses of gender blindness and agency;[61] it is equally evident that women are the primary victims of the privatisation of the family and of violence. The particular impact of the reforms on women was a pervasive theme of the Circuit Judge's interview; he expressed particular concern 'about the provisions for disadvantaged parties, who are usually battered women'. He then recounted several cases in illustration of this exacerbation of gender injustice, such as the following which he described as a fairly typical case of the

> wealthy young businessman who picks up a girl in a nightclub—they have a couple of children and then he leaves her. He can afford silks and junior counsel to represent him in his application for residence and property orders but she has no legal aid and so has very little chance of success. In other words people—generally women—can and are getting bullied.

His concluding remark, underlining his view that the reforms therefore were almost certainly in breach of both the ECHR and EU equality provisions,[62] was that 'it would be interesting if someone applied to judicially review them and took it to Europe'.

Impact on Access to and the Quality of Justice

Many respondents moved from a concern with particular issues to reflect on the macro-level implications of the reforms.[63] The Enlightenment value

[61] Women experience a full-time pay gap of 14.9% and 64% of low-paid workers are women: Cooke, G and Lawton, K, *Working Out of Poverty: A Study of the Low-Paid and the 'Working Poor'* (London, IPPR, 2008) 10.

[62] He grounded his view in the fact that both the ECHR and the Equality Act, s 29 prohibit discrimination (whether direct or indirect) in relation to the provision of services, including the services of public authorities, and that the reforms are having a disproportionate effect on women. The Law Society has also argued that the residence test proposal is likely to be unlawful because 'it is likely to be in breach of Article 14, the anti-discrimination provision of the ECHR where Article 6 (right to a fair trial) issues are engaged. A change of this nature interferes with the common law rights of access to the courts and non discrimination. According to the now well-established common law principle of legality, the general words of the power to make regulations in LASPO are not apt to allow such a fundamental interference with constitutional rights, which can only be effected by primary legislation'. They further argue that it is highly likely to breach 'section 29 of the Equalities Act 2010 which prohibits discrimination in the provision of services including those provided by public authorities.' (Law Society: Legal Aid Sentencing and Punishment of Offenders Act 2012 (Amendment of Schedule 1) Order 2014 (civil legal aid residence test) Motion to approve—House of Commons 9 July 2014.) Equally, the International Covenant on Civil and Political Rights, art 14.3 recognises that a person should 'have legal assistance assigned to him, in any case where the interest of justice so requires, and without payment by him in any such case if he does not have sufficient means to pay for it'.

[63] Luban argues that 'legal aid offered to the poor ... Should be a fundamental right and, further, that failure to provide legal assistance impairs the legitimacy of the system': Luban, D, *Lawyers and Justice: An Ethical Study* (Princeton University Press, 1988) 237–66 and until

of the equal worth of all individuals and consequent right to respect is enshrined in human rights law; however, as, discussed above, in the discourse underpinning the reforms welfare recipients have been depicted as devoid of rationality and dignity, symbolised by the lack of 'respect for the privacy of clients, no consultation rooms, just standing around in corridors'.[64] Evidently there is a relationship between this disrespect and the quality of service which it is possible to offer:

> There are undoubtedly fewer conferences, solicitors undertake more of the work themselves and the first contact tends to happen at court. There are times when I've represented a client at a final hearing where the local authority wants to adopt their kids and that's the first time I've met them—that's really difficult. I think that will increase, you won't get to form those professional relationships and develop the trust that you would like.

The pressure on judges 'who now have so many cases and only 10–15 minutes allocated to each case, instead of the necessary 1–2 hours' flowing from the reforms to public law cases was leading, according to another barrister, to 'draconian decisions being made on behalf of children by judges that could impact them for the rest of their lives'. Her view is supported by Lady Justice Black's judgment in a care and placement order for four children (where the mother had been unrepresented). In her judgment she explained why an appeal against the care orders had been granted permission at a subsequent hearing overseen by Lord Justice Lewison. In her judgment Lewison LJ had stated that the original judge had not dealt with 'less draconian outcomes' than the orders that were made.[65] Such high-level concerns about the impact of government failure to provide legal aid for vulnerable parents in child custody cases were more recently voiced by Sir James Munby, President of the Family Division, when in his judgment in the case of two unrepresented parents battling to stop their child being put up for adoption he said that 'some state agency' should pay the costs of legal representation for

recently, the proposition that access to justice was a necessary prerequisite of any democracy based on the rule of law, equality and respect for human rights appeared uncontroversial; see eg Held, D, *Democracy and the Global Order* (Cambridge, Polity Press, 1995); Gavrilovic, B, *Legal Aid in Civil Proceedings: between Wishful Thought and Accomplished Fact* (2009) published PhD thesis, record number b1143362 (Central European University Legal Studies Department, ETD Collection Budapest).

[64] The progressive cuts to legal aid, which formed a central part of its reform through New Public Management, has meant that this has long been a feature of the service offered to legal aid clients; see eg Sommerlad, *Some Reflections* (n 1); Sommerlad, H, 'Reflections on the Reconfiguration of Access to Justice' (2008) 15(3) *International Journal of the Legal Profession* 179.

[65] Black LJ proceeded to comment sympathetically on the 'infinitely more difficult' task of dealing with LIPs in the family court: Hyde, 'Litigants in person make life "infinitely more difficult"' (n 47).

the parents: 'It is unthinkable that they should have to face the local authority's application without proper representation'. 'In the circumstances as I have described them, the parents' predicament is stark, indeed shocking, a word which I use advisedly but without hesitation'.[66]

A further concern for respondents was the 'pressure cooker' atmosphere of the courts, which another likened to a 'factory or A & E (Accident and Emergency) department'.[67] Reflections on the impact of this atmosphere on victims of domestic violence, especially on those with poor English, led one solicitor to compare the fees paid to interpreters and barristers: 'it's a disgrace that interpreters are paid £25 an hour—often unqualified, working for an unregulated agency—when the legal representative gets just £32.60'. For this respondent, these extremely low fees demonstrated government's lack of respect not only for poor people but also their lawyers: 'it's not right that in order to promote access to justice you get paid peanuts'. Others stated that the consequences of these extremely low fee levels together with the lack of 'volume ... because of the scope cuts' were leading people to 'cut corners, using unaccredited paralegals'. Another barrister said that she had seen 'some appalling court work by people who are sent along to do advocacy because of the fee structure being the same—paralegals can go along and do the work'. This was also a concern for a solicitor in his sixties, based in a small market town, who attributed the dramatic decline he had witnessed in the quality of service—such as divorce petitions littered with spelling mistakes—to the heavy use of poorly supervised paralegals by the few firms that continued to do legal aid.[68] Another result is the growing tendency for solicitors' firms to do their own advocacy, rather than instructing barristers; reflecting on his recent experiences of this in public law cases, the Circuit Judge argued that it was producing a decline in quality:

> solicitors are coming to court to do the cases themselves, often very unprepared and/or inexperienced in advocacy. I heard some care proceedings where one of the solicitors didn't appear to know what to ask or of whom. So, we're downgrading standards, doing things on the cheap. I understand that one firm in this city has forbidden its staff to instruct barristers. And because of the low rates, the work

[66] 31 October 2014; see www.telegraph.co.uk/news/uknews/law-and-order/11201620/Child-adoption-row-couple-win-judges-sympathy-over-legal-fees.html; and the report in *Upper Case The Anya Legal Journal* 2014 at: www.anyadesigns.co.uk/uppercase/senior-judge-condemns-governments-unprincipled-and-unconscionable-behaviour#sthash.7gQQvPMG.dpuf.

[67] This 'pressure cooker' atmosphere has been intensified by other changes to the court system such as reductions in court counter hours, while the complex procedural tasks which the litigant must manage have been largely unadapted to meet the needs of the LIP (Trinder et al (n 39)).

[68] As noted above with respect to the lack of privacy for clients, the ongoing programme of cutbacks to legal aid have made this delegation of work down to low-cost labour a feature of the work for many years: Sommerlad (n 1), 'Reflections on the Reconfiguration of Access to Justice' (n 64): see also Sommerlad, H, '"I've Lost the Plot", an Everyday Story of Legal Aid Lawyers' (2001) 28 *Journal of Law and Society* 335.

> is being pushed down further and further the chain of experience—so often the work is being done by the most poorly qualified, least experienced practitioners.

Along with other respondents he also spoke of firms making redundancies or collapsing, and a barrister predicted that there would be 'advice deserts—whole swathes of the country with no access to legal advice'.

This concern about the extinction of access to justice was a pervasive theme; respondents spoke not only of people being turned away, but of others

> not reporting incidents through the appropriate channels, there may be cultural factors at play with influence from religious leaders, there may be unregulated discussions outside the court sphere, people can't afford to pay the court fee, don't know how to fill in the forms. The frustration of practitioners is making the cases fit the LASPO regulations—issuing an injunction first before it can go to the private sphere.

Some articulated concerns about the general social fabric, because, for instance, 'Family law is the one type of law that will affect almost everyone, so do we want to live in a society without access to that good quality representation, both through solicitors and counsel?', and another said: 'fathers will be put off from coming to court and will lose contact with their children'.

These reflections led respondents onto issues of democracy and the rule of law. A barrister argued that 'the attack on public funding on Legal Aid generally—not just in family, but also housing, immigration, and crime—is making access to justice unavailable for the ordinary man in the street and it's becoming a society of two halves', and the Circuit Judge worried about how this undermined the legitimacy of the system: 'there is the wider impact on the justice system generally—all the cutbacks are I think giving people a perception that the law doesn't protect the vulnerable and the disadvantaged'. Another stated that 'increasingly justice is not a right.... It's becoming more of a privilege, or a benefit, as opposed to something that everyone should be entitled to'. In her subsequent comments, this barrister elaborated on the erosion of democratic accountability:

> now we've lost judicial review since LASPO ... we can't do anything via judicial review [funded by legal aid]. So now, if local authorities are doing anything wrong as far as a family is concerned, we're not in a position to challenge it. That is an erosion of people's rights. Particularly when you bear in mind that a lot of the cases that have had significant impact on people's rights have been conducted with the benefit of legal aid. So if you haven't got legal aid then one of the means by which the Government can be effectively challenged becomes less available.

Moreover, the reforms are, according to the Circuit Judge, having a 'chilling effect, making people less likely to be bold in terms of the way they use their powers' so that judges were 'deterred from trying to obtain representation for litigants under the exceptional rules'.

CONCLUDING REMARKS

The data discussed above suggest various ways in which we can think about the Coalition government's family law policy. We might focus on its contribution to the general process of state withdrawal from responsibility for unprofitable social relationships, the consequence in turn of the neoliberal commodification of all social and bodily necessities (such as the protection of and access to one's children). The resulting harms to vulnerable people and especially women are then legitimated through a discourse which reconstructs our moral horizons by depicting, first, welfare as a primary cause of those harms, and, secondly, its recipients as moral weaklings who are thus 'false citizens'.[69] State intervention would merely impede the development of an 'ethics of the self' which could re-habilitate such citizens. Further, the state in fact has a positive duty to protect the taxpayer against the depredations of such welfare recipients as single mothers.

Or we might, following David Luban, argue that the complexity of modern societies has made legal systems fundamental to protecting primary human rights and that the right to a lawyer is thus a 'derivative human right', and, further, that a state's failure to provide the mechanisms to enable people to know and understand their legal obligations and opportunities and to negotiate the legal system, and to provide them with support to do so if necessary, represents a move away from rule of law values.[70] Building on this argument, we might also reflect on the fact that the family law reforms and government policy in relation to the justice system generally are not only affecting the poor and vulnerable. The recent report by Trinder et al indicates that even those with high levels of education or professional experience struggle with aspects of the legal process. And this reduction in access to justice for private citizens generally is of course accentuated by ongoing court closures and rises in fees. This is a resiling by the state from one of its core functions which was indispensable to binding the polity together, and, which, through its provision of a public space where people could engage in dialogue and dispute, re-created the social order.[71] Evidently the reduction

[69] In the case of women, we can apply Skeggs's insight into the classed nature of femininity—in other words, these women are not 'true' women in the sense of deserving any particular protection: Skeggs, B, *Formations of Class and Gender* (London, Sage Publications, 1997).

[70] Luban, D, 'Is there a Human Right to a Lawyer?' (2014) 17(3) *Legal Ethics* 1.

[71] For instance, writing about the development of private law, Du Bois argues that its existence secures civil society as a realm of social interaction that is distinct from the state, and in this manner makes a vital contribution to the legitimacy of a society's political institutions: Du Bois, F, *Tort Law Recovered? From Alan Brudner's Revised Case for Tort Law to the Ethical Underpinnings of Liberal Democracy* University of Leicester School of Law Research Paper No 14–18, 15 June 2014. His argument resembles Habermas's conceptualisation of

of people to consumers renders this citizen right to engage in rights' struggles unnecessary. In fact, the reconfiguration of the state as a mechanism for global capital eviscerates these rights and makes the maintenance of such public spaces not only superfluous but positively undesirable. The blatant transgression by a government of its own norms demonstrated by its recent 'reform' of judicial review[72] suggests that legalism/the rule of law is now merely an inconvenience, supporting the argument of scholars such as Brown and Wacquant[73] that neoliberalism is antithetical to democracy.[74]

However, the production of a new moral compass takes time. Some commentators suggest therefore that while democratic politics have been profoundly damaged by the neoliberal, neo-conservative project, this is not irreversible and that public spaces remain where values can be expressed and contested.[75] This may be why the government feels the need to persist in its claims that 'we're all in this together',[76] and its deployment of medical metaphors which depict the crisis as a serious illness which, unavoidably, required a radical 'cure'. However in order to engage in the politics of resistance advocated by Crouch, it is important to speculate about how the government will respond to the disintegration of the machinery of justice described in this chapter, and the widespread opposition it is provoking. Several respondents expressed the hope that it would come to recognise the chaos and misery which the reforms are producing and that 'when the crisis is over' would re-invest in the family law system. As the above discussion should make clear, and the evidence that the savings which the reforms will bring will be negligible,[77] I consider such optimism a misreading of the neoliberal project. On the contrary, the disintegration of the private law justice system should be viewed as the ultimate goal; in other words the aim is to further the crisis to a point where it becomes common sense that, first, as a matter of practical economics, the system is too far gone and too expensive to save, and, secondly, that in any event, the state and justice system has no business in intervening in people's lives.

law as acting as an institutional expression of the lifeworld's moral and ethical development: Habermas, J, *Between Facts and Norms. Contributions to a Discourse Theory of Law and Democracy* (Cambridge, Polity Press, 1996).

[72] Sedley, S, 'Not in the Public Interest' (2014) 36(5) *London Review of Books*, 6 March, 29–30.

[73] Brown (n 6); Wacquant (n 9).

[74] See eg Crouch (n 2); Giroux, H, *The Terror of Neo-liberalism: Authoritarianism and the Eclipse of Democracy* (Boulder, Paradigm Publishers, 2004); Hall, 'The Neo-liberal Revolution' (n 3) 705–28; Ranciere, J, *Hatred of Democracy* (London, Verso, 2014).

[75] Crouch (n 2).

[76] Cameron, D, Transcript of a speech by the Prime Minister on the Big Society, 19 July 2010 at: www.gov.uk/government/speeches/big-society-speech.

[77] Cookson, *Unintended Consequences* (n 40); Law Society, *Transforming Legal Aid Consultation. The Law Society's Response to the Non PCT Proposals* (London, Law Society, 2013).

15

Casualties of Friendly Fire: Counter Productive Campaigning on Public Funded Legal Services

PETER G HARRIS

INTRODUCTION

IN AN 'AGE of austerity' when governments across Europe and beyond are under pressure to contain or reduce expenditure on public services and to limit the size of the state, those who wish to preserve or expand publicly funded legal services arguably need to be increasingly aware of the need to be

— careful not to undermine the position of those ministers and civil servants[1] within the government machine who are charged with ministerial and departmental responsibility for securing funding for such services; and
— alive to the need to be prudent in taking opportunities to help those within the government machine who share their wish to protect and promote such services

By way of cautionary tales, the history of legal aid in England and Wales over recent decades contains examples of behaviour which arguably ignored or continues to ignore those needs.

Within the government machine, responsibility for publicly funded legal services in England and Wales rests with the Lord Chancellor, who is also the Secretary of State for Justice, and his civil servants in the Ministry of Justice whose other responsibilities also include running the courts, civil procedural and substantive law, the regulation of legal services and prisons, but not the criminal law or the police, for example. Over the last three decades the Lord Chancellor and his civil servants have become increas-

[1] In the United Kingdom, career professional civil servants who remain in post even when governments change continue to be involved in advising ministers at the very highest level on public policy issues including those relating to both private and publicly funded legal services.

ingly vulnerable to pressure from the Treasury (the finance ministry in the UK) and from elsewhere in the executive branch of government to contain or reduce the expenditure on such services. As Woodhouse explains,[2] that pressure is nothing new and has been faced by successive Lord Chancellors and their civil servants over the last 30 years and under both Labour and Conservative administrations in the past as well as under the current Conservative/Liberal Democrat Coalition government.

Legal aid's vulnerability to expenditure cuts is arguably and in large part explained by the fact that, in the author's experience,[3] politicians of all political persuasions assume that no votes will be lost or gained by expanding or reducing the provision of publicly funded legal services. While legal aid was introduced by the Legal Aid Act 1949 as part of the post-World War Two programme of social welfare reforms, it has never attracted the same level of public and political attention and support as other reforms such as the introduction of social security, the foundation of the modern system of education and the creation of the National Health Service. It is a matter of speculation why legal aid has been treated as the 'poor relation' in the social welfare family. It may be the simple fact that many fewer citizens ever have reason or the right to benefit from legal aid while health and education services are regularly used by most if not all citizens. Or again it may be that legal aid has been tainted by a popular suspicion of the law and lawyers. That suspicion arguably has deep cultural roots. Readers may recall Dick's incitement in Shakespeare's Henry VI, 'The first thing we do, let's kill all the lawyers'[4] as well as the contemporary belief that there is a 'compensation culture' in the UK in which lawyers and their clients pursue frivolous claims for damages.[5] Whatever the cause, legal aid continues to have a low priority when compared with, say health or education, as demonstrated by the fact that while education and health budgets were 'ring-fenced' and protected from cuts under the austerity programme introduced by the UK Coalition government in 2010, access to justice and legal aid enjoyed no such protection. Further, cynics might also suggest that with the development of judicial review and tort law as a means of challenging or holding government to account, some parts of the executive have a positive, if perverse, incentive to seek restrictions on the availability of legal aid.

[2] Woodhouse, D, *The Office of the Lord Chancellor* (Oxford, Hart Publishing, 2001) ch 4.

[3] Peter Graham Harris was for 28 years a senior civil servant during which time he advised three Lord Chancellors on legal aid policy.

[4] Dick the Butcher is one of the rebels under Jack Kade who unsuccessfully challenged the rule of King Henry V1 of England in William Shakespeare's play, *Henry VI, Part 2*. In particular see Scene 2, 71.

[5] See *The Cost of the Compensation Culture*, Working Party Report, Institute and Faculty of Actuaries (October 2002); The Regulation Task Force, *Better Routes to Redress* (London, Cabinet Office Publications, 2004) and Publicity Team and Hand, J, 'The Compensation Culture: Cliché or Cause for Concern' (2010) 37(4) *Journal of the Law Society* 569.

To add to its vulnerability, legal aid over those decades has come increasingly under the control of the executive. Originally administered by the Law Society (which acts as the solicitors' trade association) and the courts and a demand-led service, its administration has been brought ever closer 'in-house', first by transferring the Law Society's responsibilities to statutory authorities run by government appointees (the Legal Aid Board and later the Legal Services Commission) and more recently by bringing the operation entirely 'in-house' as an executive agency of the Ministry of Justice and subject to close ministerial control.[6] In addition, the executive has increased its ability to determine which providers may supply legal services[7] and at what price and what categories and types of individual cases are to be funded. Thus, for example, the Legal Aid and Punishment and Sentencing of Offenders Act 2012 (LASPO) has excluded a raft of family proceedings from the categories of case which fall automatically within the scope of legal aid.[8] While clearly justified in terms of increasing value for money and targeting resources on priority cases, those controls have also made the Lord Chancellor ever more vulnerable to pressure from his colleagues to contain expenditure simply because he now has the power to do so. Readers might note, however, that without those controls, legal aid might well have declined as a means of providing access to justice simply as a result of a failure to address waste, inefficiency and 'provider capture' by the lawyers.[9]

'Executive capture' by the government of legal aid, if such it is, has arguably been reinforced by the implementation of the Constitutional Reform Act 2005. Before that Act came into force, the Lord Chancellor held a unique constitutional position as Head of the Judiciary, a Cabinet Minister and the Speaker of the House of Lords (the upper chamber of the British Parliament). By tradition, the post was always filled by a senior barrister and, in addition, was a 'final appointment' in the sense that Lord Chancellors were either, like Lord Mackay of Clashfern, not career politicians or were politicians at the end of their careers, such as Lord Hailsham. Those two facts meant that Lord Chancellors traditionally were members of the judiciary and the Bar. Hence, they had close relations and connections with both groups and shared the priority which those groups gave to access to justice including the provision of legal aid. Thus, for example, Nigel Lawson, when reflecting on his career in the Treasury as the Chancellor of the Exchequer, noted that Lord Chancellor Hailsham was not generally minded to pursue reforms which would be opposed by the legal profession and the judiciary.[10]

[6] The Legal Aid Agency, which is required by law to be headed by a civil servant responsible to and subject to directions given by the Lord Chancellor. See LASPO, s 4.

[7] ibid, s 27.

[8] ibid, s 9 and sch 1, pt I.

[9] Provider capture happens when the providers of a service organise and run that service primarily for their own benefit rather than for the benefit of their customers or clients.

[10] Lawson, N, *The View from No.11—Memoirs of a Tory Radical* (London, Corgi, 1993) 602.

Further, in the absence of career prospects within the ministerial hierarchy, Lord Chancellors were arguably less susceptible to pressure from the rest of the executive branch than a career politician would be. However, since the 2005 Act came into force, the Lord Chancellor has ceased to be Head of the Judiciary. Further, the tradition that he should be a senior barrister at the zenith of his career has also been abandoned and the current holder of the office is not a lawyer but rather is a middle ranking minister and a career politician. Hence, as recent attempts substantially to reduce legal aid funding arguably demonstrate (see below), Lord Chancellors may now be more susceptible to pressure from their fellow and more senior ministerial colleagues to contain or reduce the legal aid budget either to contribute to overall cuts in public expenditure or to release public funds for other areas of the public services which are seen to have a higher political priority.

The general vulnerability and low priority accorded to legal aid means that Lord Chancellors and their officials need all the help they can get in defending that part of their budget. Accordingly, those seeking to maintain or increase legal aid expenditure (be they the Lord Chancellor and his ministerial team within the Ministry of Justice, their officials or outside interest groups concerned with access to justice) arguably need to be aware of how the government machinery operates and to be careful not to undermine further the already weak position of Lord Chancellors in respect of legal aid. Those outside the Ministry and the government also need to be alert to opportunities to help the friendly elements within government. Possible examples of where they arguably failed to do so in the past include the following 'cautionary tales'.

CAUTIONARY TALES

The risk of pyrrhic victories is ever present in the competition for public funding. One such followed the Bar's success in the mid-1980s in securing increases in criminal legal aid fees. Under pressure from the Bar, Lord Chancellor Hailsham commissioned consultants to review criminal legal aid rates to establish whether and how far they had fallen short of 'fair remuneration for work actually and reasonably done' as contemplated by the Legal Aid Act 1974.[11] In the event, the consultants reported in 1985 that an increase of between 30 and 40 per cent was required to bring remuneration for criminal law work back into line. When the Lord Chancellor failed to persuade his ministerial colleagues that a substantial increase was justified, he offered the Bar a routine uprating of about 5 per cent. The Bar promptly instituted judicial review proceedings and eventually forced the Lord Chancellor and the government to settle the matter out-of-court, to pay their costs and to concede part of their claim.

[11] See Woodhouse, *The Office of the Lord Chancellor* (n 2) 189.

At an immediate and superficial level, that outcome might have been seen as a triumph for those who wanted a properly resourced criminal legal aid scheme that paid sufficiently competitive rates to attract competent advocates. However, it embarrassed the Lord Chancellor, who faced public criticism,[12] and outraged the Treasury, who struck back almost immediately by making it explicit in subsequent legislation that rather than being 'fair', legal aid rates in the future would have regard to public expenditure and be subject to Treasury approval.[13] In the longer term, some of those inside the Department believed that the Bar's 'success' in undermining the standing of the Lord Chancellor with the public, the Treasury and his ministerial colleagues marked the beginning of what then became a sustained and successful effort within government to contain legal aid spending, converting it from a widely available and demand-led system to the much narrowed and cash limited service that has now emerged from LASPO.[14]

It is not suggested that had the Bar acted with greater foresight or prudence on that occasion it would have stopped the long-term decline in the availability of legal aid. However, by undermining the most powerful 'sponsor' they had within the government, arguably the Bar contributed to the speed and the tone and direction of the policy which in later years manifested itself in Lord Chancellor Irving publicly labelling senior barristers who undertook legal aided cases as 'fat cats';[15] legal aid strikes by the Criminal Bar when fees were cut[16] and a serious fraud trial being halted because no senior barristers could be found who were willing to act for the legal aid fees on offer.[17]

The author recollects another narrowly avoided 'own goal' when in discussions with the Bar in the 1980s the profession argued that legal aid expenditure could be contained without cuts if 'weak and frivolous cases' were more effectively excluded from the scheme. The difficulty with that argument, as the author explained to the Bar Council representatives, lay in the fact that legal aid was generally granted only if there was a legal opinion from a practising barrister to the effect that the case had merit and a committee of practising barristers and solicitors confirmed that opinion and concluded that it was reasonable in all the circumstances that legal aid should be granted. Hence, the Bar's argument that too many weak and frivolous cases were being funded by the Legal Aid Fund amounted to an admission that its members and other lawyers along with their clients were 'ripping off' the legal aid scheme. Hence, had their 'weak and frivolous'

12 *The Times* 27 March 1986.

13 Legal Aid Act 1988, s 34.

14 See LAPSO, s 9 and sch 1, pt 2 and pt 3, which, for example, exclude most social welfare law from the legal aid.

15 *The Lawyer*, 22 July 1997.

16 *The Independent* 13 July 2014.

17 *The Guardian* 1 May 2014.

argument been pursued by the Lord Chancellor with his ministerial colleagues in trying to fend off Treasury pressure it could, in effect, have only fuelled demands for more, not less constraint on the provision of publicly funded legal services.

Another example of the 'unhelpful friends' of legal aid were the tidy-minded and fastidious individuals (including the author) who argued for the consolidation of civil and criminal legal aid funding within the budget of the Lord Chancellor's Department (now the Ministry of Justice). Before the Legal Aid Act 1988, while the costs of legal aid in civil matters and in magistrates' courts were met out of the Lord Chancellor's departmental budget, the cost of criminal legal aid in the Crown Court and on appeals therefrom were met out of the Home Office budget.[18] However, under the Legal Aid Act 1988, those two budgets were consolidated within the Lord Chancellor's vote.[19] At first sight that looked like a matter of simply clearing up the messy and fragmented arrangement in the 1974 Act and avoiding the constitutional infelicity of the Home Office, which was and is responsible for the detection and prosecution of criminals, having control of the funding of criminal defence services. However, fragmentation and the separation of the two budgets had the unrecognised advantages that while they remained fragmented each budget was considered and bid for separately by each department. Thus each budget provided a smaller and thus less enticing target than would a consolidated budget within one department's spend. In addition, the risk that criminal legal aid expenditure, which is the more difficult to constrain, would erode expenditure on civil and family legal aid was in practice avoided. With the consolidation of those heads of expenditure into one budget on one department's 'books', legal aid lost those protections and from relative obscurity became the target of increased Treasury interest and, as time progressed, and as might have been expected, criminal legal aid proved to be the 'cuckoo in the nest' putting ever greater strains on the budget to the detriment of civil and family legal aid until the point where, for example, most family cases and social welfare law have now been generally excluded from the legal aid scheme.

Once again, even if policy-makers had not been persuaded by tidy-mindedness and constitutional niceties and had the budgets remained separated, it would likely not have halted the long-term downward track of publicly funded legal services. However, arguably that bit of tidiness contributed to progress down that track.

A more recent example of 'unhelpful friends' can be found amongst those who opposed the funding cuts provided for under LASPO. In particular, some of those campaigning against the cuts appeared to be ignorant of the

[18] See the Legal Aid Act 1974, ss 17(6) and 37(5) respectively. The Home Office is the United Kingdom's ministry of the interior.

[19] See the Legal Aid Act 1988, ss 6 and 42.

counterproductive potential of arguing that the predicted savings would not be realised and of complaining that the Lord Chancellor had agreed to budget cuts too quickly and too easily.

So far as the alleged shortfall in the predicted saving was concerned, as part of the campaign opposing the cuts to legal aid, the *Law Society Gazette* publicised the carefully analysed and impressive report, *Unintended Consequences: the Costs of the Government's Legal Aid Reforms*, prepared by Dr Graham Cookson of King's College London as he then was,[20] saying that the report demonstrated that

> the legal aid cuts will have significant knock-on costs and are [quoting Dr Cookson] 'unlikely to make a significant contribution to reducing the fiscal deficit'.

The *Gazette* went on to explain that

> Cookson's economic analysis examined the likely impact of the cuts in three areas—private family law, social welfare law and clinical negligence, which the government claims will save £239m a year. He found that these elements of the proposals could cause unintended extra costs of at least £139m, realising a net saving to the public purse of £100m, less than half (42%) of the government's predicted figure.

And it again quoted Dr Cookson's findings that

> Numerous costs could not be estimated, and this figure is therefore likely to be a substantial underestimate of the true costs.... At approximately 42% of the predicted savings, this level of saving would make an insignificant contribution to the total spending cuts of £81bn per year that the government seeks to implement by 2014/15. The report concludes: 'This undermines the government's economic justification for the changes, especially given the numerous costs that could not be estimated'.

The *Gazette* article went on to itemise the knock-on expenses which the Cookson report argued had been ignored by the government as follows

> It finds that removing legal aid for clinical negligence will cost the NHS £28.5m a year, almost three times more than the predicted £10.5m saving.
>
> Knock-on expenses include the cost of the telephone triage service, the after-the-event premium for expert fees and reports, and the 10% damages premium paid in all successful cases, which will largely be borne by the NHS through the NHS Litigation Authority.

[20] Graham Cookson is now Professor of Economic and Public Policy at the University of Surrey.

> The report estimates knock-on costs of £100m per year for removing legal aid for private family law cases, set against a proposed budget saving of £170m, resulting in a saving of roughly 40% of the government's forecast. Mediation will be the single largest area of expenditure, with a knock-on cost of £42m per year. Other costs include £2m towards the telephone gateway, £22m for the increased use of alternative advice services, £8m for exceptional funding of cases and £3m due to problems caused by stress for those who give up trying to solve legal problems.
>
> The report suggests that the increase in the number of litigants in person will generate a knock-on cost of £273.50 per person, which will cost over £7m in private family law matters. Cuts to social welfare law, which the government expects to save £58m a year, will have knock-on costs amounting to £35.2m, generating a saving of 39 per cent of those predicted by the government.
>
> The Ministry of Justice's own impact assessment identified a number of potential knock-on costs, including reduced social cohesion, increased criminality, reduced business and economic efficiency, and increased costs to other departments. But, as the King's College report notes, the Ministry has identified neither their magnitude nor likelihood.

In welcoming the report, Desmond Hudson, CEO of the Law Society, which had commissioned it, said that:

> The Ministry of Justice has defended swingeing cuts to Legal Aid in civil cases, which will deny justice to thousands, on its need to contribute savings to the Government's deficit reduction programme. The Law Society accepts the need to achieve savings, but this report confirms that much of the Ministry of Justice's claimed savings are being achieved at the expense of other parts of government. This is kamikaze accounting and will do little to tackle the deficit while sacrificing access to justice.

The Cookson report represented a careful and impressive analysis of the costs and savings that might result from the government's proposals and as such was seen as highly persuasive. Hence, on its face it appeared to the Law Society and others as a powerful contribution to their case for opposing the cuts. However, had the report been accepted and acted on by the government it would likely have resulted in even greater cuts to the Lord Chancellor's budget and to legal aid funding than those which the Law Society and those others were seeking to resist.

The appeal to what might be called 'the Exchequer costs' of any proposal (that is the total costs of that proposal or policy across the whole government machine) is dealt with within the government machine by requiring the department whose policies generate costs in other departments to meet those cost either by persuading the Treasury to provide the resources needed by the other departments or, if necessary, by transferring part of its own budget to those other departments. Hence, had the government acted on Doctor Cookson's report it might have insisted that the Ministry of

Justice transfer £139 million to the other departments adversely affected by the changes to legal aid. Meanwhile, it would likely still have expected the Ministry to find the full level of savings agreed, namely £207 million. The result might then have been to generate even deeper cuts in legal aid and other expenditure for which the Ministry is responsible. To borrow a phrase from the CEO of the Law Society, that might truly be regarded by some as having indulged in 'kamikaze accounting'.

As to the accusation that the Lord Chancellor settled too early, it ignored the fact that settling early is a means of defending a low priority budget such as that for legal aid. The risk otherwise is that the low priority budget ends up, and loses out, in a competition with high priority budgets such as health or education. Indeed, when commenting on charges of being 'a lackey or dupe of the Chief Secretary of the Treasury', Lord Hailsham pointed out that the pressure to contain expenditure on legal aid also came from ministers of other departments who were in competition for the taxpayers' money.[21] And there is another advantage to early settlement in that it often allows the minister concerned to join the 'Star Chamber' of selected ministerial colleagues who gather as a committee towards the end of each annual spending round to decide between the competing claims from those departments which have not reached an agreement with the Treasury.[22] A seat in that 'Chamber' provides the ministers involved with the best opportunity to defend their own budgets, a consideration of particular importance when the budget being defended is, like the legal aid budget, of low priority. Arguably, an early and orderly retreat to a defensible line by securing an early settlement with the Treasury of the legal aid budget is to be preferred to a Custer's Last Stand, however disappointing that may be for the spectators.[23] To summarise the position, had the pressure groups' complaints been acted on and the negotiations with the Treasury re-opened on the basis that the savings claimed were false economies, the legal aid budget would likely have been cut even more severely as the kamikaze attack obliterated Custer's Last Stand.

[21] Lord Hailsham, 'The Office of the Lord Chancellor and the Separation of Powers' (1989) 8 *Civil Justice Quarterly* 308, 314.

[22] The Star Chamber was set up in the late-fifteenth century to supplement the work of the ordinary courts, its particular purpose being to bring over-mighty subjects of the king to justice. To that end, members of the King's Council as well as judges sat in judgment. The proceedings were secret and over time it became a feared political weapon. Hence, the informal adoption of its name for the ministerial committee which decides between competing claims for money from Departments in the United Kingdom who fail to reach an agreement with the Treasury.

[23] The occasion known traditionally as Custer's Last Stand occurred in 1876 in the course of the Great Sioux War when, in attacking a village of native Americans consisting of members of the Lakota, Northern Cheyenne and Arapaho tribes, the elements of the 7th Cavalry Regiment of the United States Army under the direct command of Lieutenant Colonel George Custer were annihilated, including Custer himself and several male relatives, in what became known as the Battle of the Little Big Horn.

PRUDENT OPPORTUNISM

The examples given above seek to demonstrate the need on the part of interest groups to be careful not to hinder or undermine those within the government machine who, in the face of heavy pressure, may nonetheless be doing the best they can to protect and promote publicly funded legal services. However, beyond applying the maxim of 'first, do no harm', there may on occasion appear to be opportunities for those outside government to aid those friendly elements within in maintaining or expanding legal aid. However, in doing so, those seeking to help those elements within government still need to keep at the forefront of their minds the harsh realities of public expenditure and the low priority accorded to legal aid (outlined earlier in this chapter) and hence to be prudent. To that end, outsiders arguably also need to be alert to the fact that official policy even on a single topic is often a compromise between competing and even contradictory policy objectives within the government.

A current example of the need for prudence and an awareness of contradictory policy objectives arguably exists in the provisions of LASPO. While Schedule 1 of that Act generally excludes most family, social welfare and some other proceedings from the scope of the legal aid scheme, section 10 makes those general exclusions subject to a power conferred on the newly created Director of Legal Aid Casework to grant legal aid in cases which are generally excluded by the Schedule where, in the absence of legal aid, there would be a risk of a breach of the applicant's rights under the European Convention on Human Rights (the Convention).

In the immediate aftermath of the enactment of LASPO, the pressure groups and commentators concentrated on complaining about the general exclusions of most family, social welfare and other proceedings. The general approach was well summed up in Mr Justice Cobb's contribution to the Family Justice Council's inter-disciplinary conference on the theme of family justice redefined, held in London on 7 February 2014 when he said:

> The Lord Chancellor's Guidance published for caseworkers assessing claims imposes a high threshold for eligibility for this [section 10] funding 'Will withholding of legal aid make the assertion of the claim practically impossible or lead to an obvious unfairness in the proceedings?' Comments made earlier in this conference today support the recalibration of this test. I further wonder whether the bar set for caseworkers to consider 'whether the applicant would be incapable of presenting their case without the assistance of a lawyer' could also be lowered slightly to permit for a more manageable target.

The judge went on to note that

> of the 572 applications for exceptional funding in family cases since April 2013, only six grants have been made. The Parliamentary Human Rights Joint Committee

> published its report in December 2013, expressing the worrying conclusion that the Government cannot rely upon the exceptional funding scheme as it currently operates in order to avoid breaches of access to justice rights. The Law Commission, which reported last month, reached similar conclusions.

The judge concluded by making a plea for 'the Government to look again at the fitness for purpose of s 10'.

However, during that aftermath, the author suggested a bolder approach. He pointed out that in effect there was already an established right to legal aid under the Convention where, in its absence, a party would not have 'practical and effective' access to the courts. Hence, section 10 represented an opportunity for the pressure groups and the courts to ensure that legal representation was available in otherwise excluded cases where nonetheless legal representation was necessary to secure a party's such access.[24] The author went on in that article to urge pressure groups to concentrate on using judicial review proceedings to challenge the Director of Legal Aid Case Work's refusals to grant of legal aid under section 10 and in that way to re-establish many if not all of the rights to legal aid that had existed before the implementation of LASPO.

In the event, the bolder approach advocated in that article has, at the time of writing, been adopted by the courts. In *Gudanaviciene and Others v Director of Legal Aid Case Work*,[25] Collins J concluded that the government guidance on the operation of section 10 was too restrictive and that there would be a risk of a breach of Convention rights under Article 6 if in the absence of legal representation a party would be unable to have an 'effective and fair opportunity to establish his claim'.[26]

Bringing that case before Collins J might therefore be seen as taking an opportunity to support friendly elements within the government machine, being on this occasion, those ministers and civil servants who had ensured the inclusion of section 10 in the Act and who believed that as a matter of principle or perhaps legal necessity citizens should receive publicly funded legal services where in their absence they would be denied 'practical and effective' access to the courts. But as ever in the world of politics, matters may not be that simple and interest groups may need to think and act strategically and with prudence before simply exploiting section 10 to its maximum degree.

It is clear that there is an underlying tension between the wish to comply with the Convention by providing effective access to the courts and the

[24] See Harris, PG, 'Legal Aid Cuts? What Legal Aid Cuts?' (2012) 42 *Family Law* 1267 and *Airey v Ireland* (1979) 2 EHRR 305, which had already established that the right to a fair trial under art 6 of the Convention would be breached where, in the absence of legal representation, a party would not have 'practical and effective' access to the court.

[25] [2014] EWHC 1840 (Admin).

[26] ibid at [50].

government's announced objective (outlined earlier in this chapter) of making substantial savings in the funding of legal aid. And, given the vulnerability of the legal aid budget to government cuts (which was also explained earlier), if section 10 were used to reinstate or even increase legal aid expenditure beyond its levels prior to the implementation of LASPO, it would likely provoke ever more drastic action by the government. For example, the government might repeal section 10 and thus simply exclude the types of case in Schedule 1 from the scope of legal aid altogether.[27] Further, an all-out exploitation of section 10 would also likely provoke a clash between the government, which rightly regards itself as having a democratic mandate to control public expenditure,[28] and the judges who rightly regard themselves as the guardians of the rule of law, of which access to justice is a vital element.

In the case of section 10, part of the answer may, for example, lie in the pressure groups, the legal professions and, so far as they may, the judges promoting means of resolving disputes by procedures which enable a litigant to enjoy 'practical and effective' access to the court or tribunal without legal representation or by diverting disputes to forms of Alternative Dispute Resolution such as mediation[29] or arbitration where legal representation is either unnecessary or not allowed. That more balanced approach towards maintaining access to justice would aid those friendly elements within the government machine to persuade colleagues against more drastic action even while section 10 is used to provide legal representation in cases which LASPO would otherwise exclude from the legal aid scheme.

CONCLUSION

It arguably is a common mistake for pressure groups who are faced with attempts by the government to restrict expenditure in their area of interest

[27] See Laws J's decision in *R v Lord Chancellor, ex p Witham* [1998] QB 575 where in respect of defamation proceedings he endorsed the view that as regards legal expenses 'it was for the Lord Chancellor's discretion to decide what litigation should be supported by the taxpayer's money and what should not', a view endorsed by Collins J, who distinguished between simply excluding categories of cases from the legal aid scheme altogether and requiring that certain conditions be satisfied if a type of case is to be supported by legal aid, such as meeting the requirements under s 10.

[28] The current budget deficit faced by the government is £8.5 billion (see Office for National Statistics, *Statistical Bulletin: Public Sector Finances*, September 2014). With all the political parties in the UK committed to protecting public spending on the health and education services for the foreseeable future, further and substantial cuts in other public services are likely to be unavoidable and long term. Therefore, if the judges are perceived, however unfairly, to be using the European Convention on Human Rights significantly to undermine attempts to cut public expenditure it would have the potential to fuel both the already existing antagonism towards the Convention amongst many politicians and attempts to rein in its operation in the United Kingdom.

[29] It should be noted that the UK Legal Aid Agency already has power under LASPO to fund mediation in family proceedings which are excluded by sch 1 of LASPO reflecting the government's policy of attempting to divert cases away from lawyers and courts.

to assume that the government is monolithic in the sense that the policy reflects unanimity within the government machine. Hence they tend to assume that taking any opportunity to attack or discredit any ministers or civil servants involved is not only justified but always in the service of their opposition to the government's proposals. There may also be a temptation to exploit ambiguities in policy in order to protect or promote spending in a particular area. The cautionary tales above describe a more complex world in which pressure groups might be well advised to recognise that their aims and values are often shared by some within the government machine and to avoid undermining the position of those friendly elements while at the same time being alive to the dangers of overstepping the mark when exploiting ambiguities in government policies in ways that may be immediately beneficial but in the long run seriously counterproductive.

Part IV

Innovation in Delivering Family Justice

16

Controlling Time?

Speeding Up Divorce Proceedings in France and Belgium

BENOIT BASTARD, DAVID DELVAUX, CHRISTIAN MOUHANNA AND FRÉDÉRIC SCHOENAERS

INTRODUCTION

THIS CHAPTER CONSIDERS the issue of judicial time spent dealing with family matters.[1] When considering the amount of time spent on conflicts that emerge during the breakdown of relationships, we seek to highlight the radical change in the perception of time that has affected civil justice. This analysis sits within the sociology of law and of justice, with an eye to issues of organisation and the logic of work applicable to members of the judicial system and, consequently, how the issue of time sets the rhythm of their activity. This study of the forms of judicial activity envisaged in their time dimension offers an illustration of the acceleration of social time,[2] which can be seen at the very heart of the institutions, both the justice system and the family. The transformation of judicial time is in fact doubly affected, because at the same time there have been significant upheavals in the nature of conjugality and parenthood. This 'revolution' has a time dimension: the increase in the number of breakdowns, the chain of successive unions and the resulting conflicts are the origin of the applications brought before the family courts. The judges find themselves in a position where they must provide answers to critical situations that are marked by urgency and by people who are suffering.

[1] An earlier version of this text has been published in French: 'Maîtriser le temps. L'accélération du traitement judiciaire du divorce en France et en Belgique' (2004) 19 *Temporalités*. This research has been supported by the GIP Mission de Recherche, Droit et Justice.

[2] Rosa, H, *Beschleunigung. Die Veränderung der Zeitstukturen in der Moderne* (Frankfurt-am-Main, Suhrkamp, 2005); Rosa, H, *Accélération. Une critique sociale du temps* (Paris, La Découverte, 2010).

To study the way in which these answers were framed and to analyse their meaning and the effect they had on the timing of proceedings, we compared the situations in France and Belgium. We found situations that were fully comparable with regard to judicial structures and prevalent views on regulating family dysfunction, but at the same time, we found certain significant differences that highlighted the crucial dimensions of the analysis. Examining the responses of the judicial institution to the pressure of time led to raising two main parameters: first, the strategy to deliver justice more quickly and efficiently and, secondly, the privatisation of the family and its consequence, viz the attempt to ensure that decisions related to the breakdown of relationships are taken by the parties themselves.

THE EMERGENCE OF A NEW TIME FRAME OF REFERENCE FOR JUSTICE

Judicial time has always been the subject of debate and criticism. However, the issues raised by this theme of time in justice and the length of an action have now changed course. Traditionally, the problem of judicial timing was its slowness. The slow pace of justice was proverbial, criticised, but considered insurmountable. It was denounced as often by litigants as by the professionals who interacted with judicial institutions and by the media who saw an intolerable discrepancy between it and the faster pace they themselves had contributed to creating.[3] For the judges and the professionals in judicial institutions, these delays were justified by professional elements, 'the ethos of the profession',[4] and by structural and organisational constraints. Praise for slowing processes down[5] highlighted the independence, the declared serenity and the 'standing back' of the judge in relation to the event, while in reality, it reflected the absence of material and human resources that would have allowed files to be handled in less time.

In the second half of the twentieth century, dissatisfaction with delays continued to rise. From the 1980s, this had a direct impact on how the system worked. It then developed into taking a more tangible and proactive approach to responsibility for the issue of time,[6] similar to that which was already being done in other sectors of society.[7] The new relationship with

[3] Commaille, J and Garapon A, '"Justices et médias", sous la direction de' (1994) 26 *Droit et Société* 9.

[4] Vigour, C, 'Ethos et légitimité professionnels à l'épreuve d'une approche managériale: le cas de la justice belge' (2008) 50 *Sociologie du travail* 71.

[5] Commaille, J, *Une sociologie politique de la carte judiciaire* (Paris, PUF, 2000).

[6] Schoenaers, F and Kuty, O, 'Analyse socio-organisationnelle des facteurs constitutifs de l'arriéré judiciaire. Le cas des juridictions belges et françaises du travail' in G de Leval and J Hubin (eds), *Espace judiciaire et social Européen* (Brussels, Editions Larcier, 2003) 97–122.

[7] Giddens, A, *Modernity and Self-Identity: Self and Society in the Late Modern Age* (Cambridge, Polity, 1991).

time is in fact at the origin of the demand for faster responses, and shorter processing times. This requirement follows both from the profound changes in the relationships between the institutions and their constituents[8] and from the complete renewal of the ideas related to managing the institutions. Indeed, there was decreasing tolerance for the distance between the state institutions and their public. In most cases, concern emerged for making them more transparent and affordable, according to the principle of accountability.[9] As regards justice, this movement was reflected in a whole series of innovations during the 1980s and 1990s in both France and Belgium. For example, greater consideration for the victims in criminal proceedings and for applicants in civil proceedings led to an improvement in communicating with and informing the public, with an emphasis on transforming the image of the institution. Similarly, the desire to provide a better response to social demands led to speeding up the proceedings. The desire to deliver justice more quickly has been endorsed by the highest legal authorities as evidenced under Article 6(1) of the European Convention on Human Rights: 'Everyone is entitled to a fair and public hearing within a reasonable time'.

At the same time, and after years of reluctance on the part of judges, judicial institutions became subject to managerial requirements via the principles of new public management, in particular the notions of planning, effectiveness and efficiency.[10] First the LOLF then the RGPP[11] in France, and the Copernic reform in Belgium, instruments for the modernisation of all public services, contributed to transforming significantly government and court activities. Organisational, management and legislative reforms were taken up with the explicit aim of speeding up judicial timing at every stage of the process—adjudication, hearing, drafting and execution. At first perceived as contrary to the fundamental principles of law and the administration of justice, these managerial imperatives are now part of the way courts operate, and have become central elements, again raising questions about customary practices in the justice system and their symbolism.

These developments found a variety of expressions in the day-to-day operations of the courts, with tensions sometimes exacerbated with regard to time. In fact, in an ad hoc manner, slowness continues to be celebrated. The search for serenity and truth and the time needed to understand situations are still used to justify significant delays.[12] This is especially the case

[8] Dubet, F, *Le déclin de l'institution* (Paris, Éd du Seuil, 2002).

[9] Pollitt, C, *The New Managerialism and the Public Services: the Anglo American Experience* (Oxford, Basil Blackwell, 1990).

[10] Schoenaers, F, 'Le Nouveau Management Judiciaire, tentative de définition et enjeux' in F Schoenaers and C Dubois (eds), *Regards croisés sur le Nouveau Management Judiciaire* (Liège, Editions de l'Université de Liège, 2008).

[11] *Loi organique relative aux lois de finances* and *Régie générale des politiques publiques.*

[12] Latour, B, *La fabrique du droit. Une ethnographie du conseil d'Etat* (Paris, La découverte, 2002).

regarding the criminal courts and assize courts or, in civil cases, appellate proceedings. However, more generally, expediting proceedings has become a central value and an objective for many decision-makers within the court systems, which leads them to dispose of cases as quickly as possible, even if it means not looking deeply into the substantive issues. Criteria for assessing and comparing courts have been developed. Everything is in place to promote 'productivity' and time-saving.[13]

Speeding up proceedings by managerialising justice is well documented in the field of criminal law, a field favoured by reformers of justice. Different analyses have demonstrated how time is perceived, lived, managed and 'orchestrated' here by the various groups of actors who contribute to handling cases, whether handling these in 'real time'[14] or in 'summary trials'—*comparutions immédiates*.[15] These analyses suggest that, in this area, acceleration goes hand-in-hand with strengthening the control of the state which seeks to deal with any form of social deviance without delay. This observation of a link between judicial acceleration and punishment moreover leads to questioning the direction of the developments in progress. Is their main effect not to reduce time spent in legal debate, and hence to change the conditions for dispensing justice?

This raises the question, therefore, of whether the same conditions are found in the field of civil justice, where the procedural principles differ greatly. We would argue here that this sector has also been affected by the movement to speed up justice, but according to specific requirements, particularly with regard to family justice.

SEGMENTING MARITAL TIME AND TRANSFORMING METHODS OF BREAKDOWN MANAGEMENT

The particular feature affecting judicial time in civil matters is the fact that the process is not the result of public action, as is the case in criminal law, but is based on the actions of the parties themselves. We therefore face a configuration in which speeding up judicial processing is not exclusively the product of the will and ideology of state organs, but rather the result of developments in the field of family law over the last few decades. If managerialising and researching organisational effectiveness falls within the services for family matters, it is because the search for a swift response appears

[13] Vauchez, A and Willemez, L, *La justice face à ses réformateurs* (Paris, PUF, 2007).

[14] Bastard, B and Mouhanna, C, *Une justice dans l'urgence. Le traitement en temps réel des affaires pénales* (Paris, PUF, 2007).

[15] Léonard, T, *De la politique publique à la pratique des comparutions immédiates. Une sociologie de l'action publique au prisme des configurations locales et nationales* (Lille, Université de Lille 2, 2014).

to be in response to the parties. According to one French judge: 'We are asked to do everything immediately. It's very difficult to manage. The parties are always pressed for time and want a decision now'. We thus return to the issue of the growing number of failing relationships and to the increasing expectations that affect regulating the situations that ensue, with their complexity and their share of conflicts and individual suffering.

For four decades, civil justice has been facing an ever-increasing number of matrimonial breakdowns. This phenomenon is one of the most striking signs of the change in the regime that has affected all family practices, marked by de-institutionalisation: 'Today, the form of private life that each person chooses has little need for external legitimacy, social conformity to an institution or morality'.[16] The movement to 'privatise' the family is boosted by the transformations that mark relationship breakdowns and by the 'privatisation of divorce'.[17] Unions have become precarious; divorces, or more generally, relationship breakdowns, are more frequent and more commonplace. Separation is now an everyday fact in the contemporary conjugal model. This development has had considerable repercussions on the activity of civil courts. In France, over half the civil cases are family law cases. There are more than 130,000 divorces a year, an even greater number of cases deal with the situation of children of unmarried parents and 55,000 cases deal with post-divorce proceedings. In Belgium, approximately 25,000 divorces are granted every year. These figures make resolving family litigation a 'mass dispute'. This growing trend is moreover accompanied by a very profound transformation in how these cases are handled. Over the last 30 years, the judicial handling of divorce has been transformed by the overall change in the character of couples and the transformation of means of dispute resolution.[18] Because the family has become empowered and privatised, the law, which stopped prescribing how a couple should be organised during the marriage, now acknowledges the freedom of the spouses to organise themselves as they see fit at the time they separate, provided they agree. It is in this way that the preference for a liberal-minded, negotiated model to deal with private disputes has been gradually affirmed, in contrast to the past excesses of legal and state interference in family functioning. It is now expected, even demanded, of the parties that they reach agreement on both the principle of the divorce and the practical details. The law has taken note of this preoccupation and fosters, as much as possible, arriving at a consensus.

[16] Singly, F, de, *Le soi, le couple et la famille* (Paris, Nathan, 2002).

[17] Cardia-Vonèche, L and Bastard, B, 'Les silences du juge ou la privatisation du divorce. Une analyse empirique des décisions judiciaires de première instance' (1986) 4 *Droit et Société* 497.

[18] Théry, I, *Le Démariage* (Paris, Odile Jacob, 1993).

JUDICIAL TIME AND FAMILY TIME: IRRECONCILABLE DIFFERENCES?

We set out to show here that the quicker pace that can be observed in the family courts becomes reality through a convergence of the two movements: the managerial revolution and the privatisation of family relationships. On the courts' part, the emergency is 'decreed': it is a matter of responding to the mass of files by considering this indispensable speed both for the viability of the service and for the sake of the litigants, who would like speedy justice. At the same time, this speed is only possible because it operates in coordination with another requirement, that of resolving family disputes by agreement. The pressure in favour of arrangements originating from the parties themselves, desirable for substantive reasons (ie preferring family democracy, preventing interference and seeking the best interests of the children), is the main factor that allows courts to remain afloat by allowing less time to deal with each individual case. It was this astonishing link between the desire for a quick answer and the need to deal with the reality of the family that we wanted to illustrate and to challenge here. How do we arrive at a situation whereby the conflicting spouses and their counsel conform to the requirements of efficiency expressed in each stage of the judicial process? What are the consequences of this speed in proceedings? Ever since the work of Pierre Noreau, it has been known that attention must be paid to the distinction between the time of the proceedings and the time as experienced by the couple, particularly in the case of family law where practical and emotional reorganisation require time.[19] The legal shaping of private conflicts prevents the feelings and realities experienced by divorcing couples from being expressed.[20] When law and court practice seek only to reduce the judicial timescale for divorce, is there not a risk of increasing, at least in part for the parties, the disconnection of times, with the risk that the differences between legal and judicial responses and the expectations of the persons concerned are all but irreconcilable? The interest in speeding up the legal process under all circumstances is not inconsistent with the singular rhythm of marital situations, often chaotic, comprising both progress and waiting time resulting from moments of agreement and disagreement, from the desire to break up or to pursue the relationship, and so on.

[19] Noreau, P, 'La superposition des conflits: limites de l'institution judiciaire comme espace de résolution' (1998) 40 *Droit et société* 585.

[20] Renchon, J-L, 'Droit et pauvreté affective' (1983) 10 *Revue interdisciplinaire d'études juridiques* 17.

A STUDY OF FIVE COURTS IN FRANCE AND BELGIUM

This chapter is based on the results of recent research carried out in five courts in France and Belgium,[21] which examines the wave of acceleration affecting courts, and the limitations and the obstacles encountered. France and Belgium display at once strong similarities and marked differences in the field of divorce law as to how the justice system is organised. The comparison has the heuristic virtue of bringing to light, through significant differences, the main features of the structure of judicial time for which a description is sought. The research approach used is empirical and inductive. It is based on detailed knowledge of situations encountered by the judicial branch: in the courts surveyed, we interviewed over 150 sitting judges, court clerks and lawyers and we also attended hearings.

The choice of courts studied is based on the idea that the size of the organisation affects the activity of the judges and starts from the way of thinking about and of managing time. Two pairs of courts of similar size in France and in Belgium were studied as well as a fifth, larger court, located in the Ile de France region. As far as the Belgian courts are concerned, one is located in Flanders and the other in Wallonia, the Flemish courts having the reputation of being 'ground-breaking' in terms of management.

We will first discuss the recent developments in divorce law in France and Belgium to demonstrate how the legislator has sought to speed up divorce proceedings. We will then consider the survey data to illustrate the different methods of speeding up judicial treatment of divorce cases. From these descriptive elements, we will reflect more generally on the conditions for achieving the acceleration of family justice and on its effects.[22]

Reforms that Promote Quick Divorces

The most obvious temporal dimension that judicial time offers, in particular in the eyes of legal professionals, is that of legal deadlines. Civil law and procedure organise the presentation of disputes submitted to courts and state that precise time benchmarks must be respected, without which proceedings would become null and void. Thus there have been many significant reforms in the two countries being considered to the law that applies to

[21] Bastard, B, Delvaux, D, Mouhanna, C and Schoenaers, F, *L'esprit du temps. L'accélération dans l'institution judiciaire en France et en Belgique*, research undertaken with the support of the Mission de recherche 'Droit et Justice', 2012.

[22] In this chapter, we will consider in particular the issue of divorce itself and we will also contemplate more broadly the decisions related to the effects of divorce, which are handled separately in Belgium, and separation of unmarried couples as well as post-divorce decisions, which, in France, are part of the jurisdiction of the Family Court judge.

marital separation. The objective of these reforms is to make divorce accessible so as to respond to the demands of spouses and to take account of the diversity of family situations, to promote as far as possible non-conflicted access to courts and, at the same time, to speed up the procedures.

In France, the objective of encouraging mutual agreements can be found in all legal provisions. Since the joint petition for divorce was introduced in 1975, the legislator has constantly reaffirmed it up to the 2000s.[23] The reform that came into effect on 1 January 2005, while maintaining the diverse character of divorce law, introduced more demanding conditions for seeking a divorce on the ground of fault, simplified those for divorce based on mutual consent and reorganised the other non-adversarial methods of resolution.[24] The current model of divorce, consensual, privatised as much as possible, possibly reviewable (since the judge may easily be seised of it to review the terms sought by the parties), is, from the perspective of those who promote it, by no means incompatible with speedy and efficient treatment of proceedings. This desire to speed up the process was expressed in a number of ways in the 2005 reform. Where joint applications for divorce are concerned, a single hearing would be necessary for the divorce to be pronounced whereas, previously, the parties had to appear before the judge twice, to confirm their agreement after a period of six months. Where the application for divorce is based on the breakdown of the marriage, the duration of separation necessary for the divorce to be admissible was shortened from six years to two years, a means to revive a procedure that had been little used precisely because of the length of this period under the old legislation. This reform had the expected effects: an increase in the number of divorces by agreement and a marked decrease in the average time required to deal with divorces because of speeding up joint applications for divorce.

> The proceedings for a divorce by mutual consent are now three times faster than they were for the earlier cohorts before the reform. While for the generations from 1996 to 2004, a divorce decree based on a joint application for a divorce by mutual consent would take approximately eight to nine months, in 2005, a divorce by mutual consent took three months from the application.[25]

In Belgium, a reform even greater in magnitude came into force on 1 September 2007. From the principle that the proceedings should not contribute to increasing the difficulties inherent in all marital separations, the legislator sought to

[23] Théry, I, *Couple, filiation et parenté aujourd'hui. Le droit face aux mutations de la famille et de la vie privée* (Paris, Odile Jacob—La Documentation française, 1998); Dekeuwer-Désfossez, F, *Rénover le droit de la famille. Propositions pour un droit adapté aux réalités et aux aspirations de notre temps* (Paris, La Documentation française, 1999).

[24] Law no 2004-439 of 26 May 2004 on divorce.

[25] Chaussebourg, L, Carasco, V and Lermenier, A., *Le divorce* (Paris, Ministère de la Justice, 2009) 47.

accelerate and 'humanise' divorce.[26] Three objectives were pursued: removing legal arguments over fault, simplifying and accelerating the procedure and establishing a true 'right to divorce'.[27] The draft law 'aims to abolish all causes for divorce and to replace these with a single cause, that is, irretrievable breakdown of the marriage'.[28] Arguments over fault thus appeared to be inadequate 'because the faults of one of the spouses, which could occasionally be outlined legally, frequently do not reflect the root causes of matrimonial disunity' and inappropriate 'because such arguments can only a priori inflame the tensions within the separated family, while the more fundamental objective should be to allow the spouses who are separating to do so respectfully'.[29] Furthermore, also included in the preparatory work is the need to simplify the proceedings by removing from these all legal obstacles likely to lengthen them unnecessarily. 'The authors of the draft law sought to simplify divorce proceedings, to speed up the course of these proceedings and to give them a practical efficiency that responds to the current needs of citizens'.[30] It is a question of breaking with a 'Napoleonic' vision of marriage[31] that sees a social interest in maintaining and preserving it and of substituting for it a more 'humanist'[32] approach, which corresponds to the new rhythm of reorganising the unions.

Once this reform was adopted, there was only one cause for divorce, that of 'irretrievable breakdown'.[33] In practice, this comprises five cases. If the application is unilateral, there are three ways to obtain a divorce based on an irretrievable breakdown: either the applicant proves that 'the matrimonial behaviour makes it reasonably impossible to pursue a common life and the resumption thereof', or the couple has been separated for a year, or finally the applicant may present the application before the judge twice, the applications being separated by a one-year interval. If the application is joint, there are two solutions open to the divorcing couple: the couple will be divorced if the spouses have been separated for six months or if the application for divorce is presented to the judge twice the applications being separated by a three-month interval.

[26] Draft law reforming divorce, Belgian Chamber of Representatives, 15 March 2006 (DOC 51-2341/001).

[27] Renchon J-L, 'La nouvelle réforme (précipitée) du droit belge du divorce: le «droit au divorce»' (2007) 4 *Revue Trimestrielle de Droit Familial* 1028.

[28] Draft law reforming divorce law and establishing no-fault divorce, Belgian Chamber of Representatives, 30 May 2000 (DOC 50-0684/001).

[29] Renchon, 'La nouvelle réforme (précipitée) du droit belge du divorce' (n 27).

[30] Draft law modifying divorce legislation with a view to establishing no-fault divorce, Belgian Chamber of Representatives, 9 November 2001 (DOC 50-1497/001).

[31] Bruley, Y, 'Mariage et famille sous Napoléon: le droit entre religion et laïcité' (2012) 14 *Napoleonica. La Revue* 111.

[32] Draft law reforming divorce, Belgian Chamber of Representatives, 15 March 2006 (DOC 51-2341/001).

[33] Pire, D, 'Le divorce pour désunion irrémédiable: un an d'application' *Actualités de droit familial. Le point en 2008*, Commission Université Palais—Université de Liège (coll), vol 103 (Liège, Anthémis, 2008) 7–64.

Though the legislator's ambition was to simplify divorce itself, the organisation of the courts and their jurisdictions remain extremely complex. No fewer than four judges may be involved. The justice of the peace in the domicile of the spouses is competent to record and organise the separation in all its aspects. In particular, the justice makes decisions on maintenance obligations. The judge of the court of first instance grants the divorce and also intervenes on the issues of maintenance, but only after the divorce. The juvenile court judge is competent regarding applications related to children born outside the marriage. Finally, applications may also be made to the interim relief judge (*juge des référés*), these applications relating to provisional and urgent matters. If we add to this the intervention of lawyers and notaries, the parties will find the system difficult to comprehend.

Two Ways to Speed up Divorces

The description of the applicable law and the competent courts does not exhaust the analysis of judicial time in civil matters. In addition to legal time limits, there are other categories of time: functional time, which legal professionals allow themselves for dealing with the cases, 'dead time', during which nothing happens, and 'strategic' time, which the parties use both to speed up the proceedings or to slow them down depending on their objectives and their interests. All these types of time are also affected by the pursuit of speed within the courts. To show this requires characterising the methods by which the court services and the judges are organised and work in practice. This analysis highlights the differences between the countries as regards to the methods. In France, one magistrate, the Family Court judge, hears the applications and organises his unit to respond to them; in Belgium, a court finalises the divorce itself while decisions related to its effects fall to other bodies. Different issues result as regards the issue of judicial time: in France, the issue is one of how to speed up the activity of a unit responsible for all family disputes, while in Belgium the issue is more complex, it is the distribution of time amongst different courts.

The Family Court Judge, Someone to Do Everything to Speed up the Divorce Proceedings

The work of the courts studied shows a dual movement of privatisation and acceleration, the two trends being interdependent. First, the courts start, correctly or not, with the principle that the parties would like to proceed quickly and maintain control of their separation; they encourage the divorcing parties in this direction by constantly appealing to self-regulation. Secondly, they are organised to resolve as quickly as possible the mass disputes that represent family cases with, in the background, the fear of finding themselves 'submerged' should the efficiency of the legal action weaken. In fact, unlike what happens in the criminal sector, the flow of family cases cannot be subject to any regulation at the jurisdictional level: no 'dropped cases', no 'third way' institutionalised proceedings that could give the impression of a legal answer, whether or not it is satisfactory, while relieving the functioning of the service.

The civil court itself can only hear the applications put before it. 'I must, particularly in the Family Court judge's functions, deal with large numbers of files', a young judge says. 'It's something felt very acutely. It's a shock at the beginning of your career'. Subject to high demand and with limited resources for which there is no guarantee that they will be maintained, Family Court judges in the three French courts studied are organising themselves to deal with it. 'We put this pressure on ourselves', one magistrate states. They all show the same determination in seeking efficiency and in the fight against delays, developing the same practices to frame the proceedings and 'control' the parties so as to maintain a satisfactory pace. This mobilisation is carried out, it should be emphasised, under the watchful eyes and under the control of the judicial hierarchy. Its effectiveness and the 'success' of these operations nonetheless remain dependent on the goodwill of the parties and their capacity to adhere to the model based on mutual consent being proposed.

The goal of the Family Court judges (*Juges aux affaires familiales*, often called JAF) is to fight dead time and reduce the time for dealing with cases. Their primary resources are their capacity to work and the registry's services so that the cases are examined and the rulings are rendered quickly. In their own words, they must 'motivate themselves'. But the pressure also comes from users. 'The parties are grumbling, the lawyers are grumbling', one court clerk said. 'I've got everyone on my back'. The Family Court judges indicate all the tension they feel: '*We* are permanently under pressure of quantity. If I devote a day to a file, I'll be under terrible pressure in the following days for the others. There are many reasons for this pressure, in particular chronic understaffing'. Family Court judges calculate the time they need to draft judgments according to the number and the complexity of the cases for which they are responsible. A 'management' rule set by the Chancellery provides that the decisions should be rendered within two months, failing which a 'red dot' appears on the court's statistical grid. If this deadline is passed, the judge must explain the lateness. It is noteworthy that the preoccupation with statistical efficiency which underpins all activities of the Family Court services generates, as elsewhere, other circumvention strategies. To avoid being penalised statistically for managing its stock of cases, the Family Court judges can, for example, strike off a file that has been dragging on because they have been waiting for an expert's report, or even open a new file when this report is submitted—with a new number, a new date, etc. In any event, the Family Court judges are, amongst the civil law magistrates, those who render the largest number of decisions: more than 80 judgments per month, well above the 45 that is the norm set by the Chancellery.[34]

One of the most obvious markers of accelerating the treatment of family law cases is found in the routinisation of the hearings. Judges themselves will often use metaphors to describe them: assembly line work, 'the slaughter' or 'the divorce factory'. The work is in some way 'mechanised'. 'The days are getting longer', one court clerk said. 'The other day, we finished at 6.45 pm having started that morning at 9.30 am'. Under these conditions, we can speak of a certain disengagement from the merits of the case, which the judges accept with difficulty while implicitly acknowledging it. The speed and the distance observed by the magistrate relate both to his position in the civil proceedings and to the preference given to self-regulation. Family Court judges, in general, emphasise that the limitation they impose on expressing emotions or relating the stories and situations of the couples—as dramatic as they may be in some cases—upholds the legal dimension of their action. They allow room for feelings, but only marginally. They refocus the hearing on relevant points, in the light of the law and the applications that have been submitted. Above all they seek to obtain solutions that the parties accept, while keeping the time spent handling the cases as brief as possible and avoiding getting 'caught up' in the emotions of the spouses.

Analysis of the functioning of the hearing reveals the pressure for self-regulation that pervades the entire system for handling matrimonial breakdowns. The best way for Family Court judges to save time is to influence the time of the parties involved: the divorcing spouses themselves or their lawyers. However, typically, wanting to influence the parties means 'make them do something', that is, getting something from actors deemed to be independent in the court. From this perspective, the family magistrates remain at a disadvantage as long as the parties 'don't play along' and instead continue their dispute. When in control of the agenda, the spouses may choose whether to be part of the judicial institution's desired perspective—a peaceful divorce in which the assistance sought from the court is kept to a minimum, so reducing the time devoted to it. When they choose to be a part of this perspective and appear before the court ready to agree with it, having settled issues related to the separation, children and division of the property, they are praised and encouraged.[35] In this case, the hearing lasts

[34] This figure clearly results from an aggregation of heterogeneous data. In some cases, it is a matter of complex decisions that require a longer report. In other situations, the decision may be drafted by the court clerk immediately at the hearing. This is the case where, exceptionally, the parties to the divorce give up their action. The justice strikes their case from the list, a decision quickly rendered and quickly notified, which eases both the hearing and the judge's work and improves productivity statistics.

[35] Bastard B, *Les démarieurs. Nouvelles pratiques du divorce* (Paris, La Découverte, 2002).

no more than a few minutes and the proceedings are particularly short.[36] There remain numerous situations in which the parties do not waive either their action or their conflict and seek the court's assistance to find answers to their disputes.[37] The question for the Family Court judges then is finding a way to mobilise the parties and guide them towards working out their disagreement and to return to the anticipated model of a peaceful divorce. In such situations—that is, in drawn-out disputes with a more or less elevated level of conflict—the judges use different strategies that are directly related to the question of time. For example, they propose as soon as possible to use the bridges that allow for returning to divorce by agreement, in particular, by signing, during the hearing itself, an 'acceptance report' by which the divorcing parties abandon their conflict on the principle of the divorce.

In the case of unresolved disagreements, judges see the parties as 'consumers of justice'.[38] They see time that extends as 'harmful', suggests one lawyer. They continue to give the parties signs of their reluctance to choose between opposing positions. However, the procedure contains all sorts of resources that can be used to extend the trial process:

> When one of the two parties wants to drag things out and the other wants speed things up, there's a lot of room for the parallel war in daily life—we cut the oxygen, we manipulate the children. The party without the means to fight this war suffers from the stalling tactics' (one lawyer).

In all these situations, the judges make efforts to reduce the areas of conflict and to seek to 'frame' the parties and their lawyers.

Controlling the time length of the trial process entails not only, for the courts, promoting the search for arrangements between the divorcing spouses, but also controlling the lawyer. Where divorce is concerned, the lawyers were traditionally held responsible not only for the conflicts in the case but also for the slowness of justice. Today the Family Court judges acknowledge the role lawyers have played in changing and contributing effectively to handling the cases, in particular through the work they do beforehand, on all divorces and especially on divorces by mutual consent. They nevertheless still hold on to some of their prejudices against lawyers. The confrontation that exists between the courts and the Bar is as persistent

[36] The recent study carried out by Le Collectif Onze provides a systematic analysis of the lengths of hearings—which shows that the time devoted to each case is between three minutes to one hour and 30 minutes, with an average of 18 minutes: Le Collectif Onze, *Au tribunal des couples: enquêtes sur des affaires familiales* (Paris, Odile Jacob, 2013) 15.

[37] There is also an intermediate situation: the parties may defer when to really commence a legal action. From the order *pendent lite*, they effectively have 30 months for this in the case of a contested divorce. This kind of situation creates, within the courts, a list of outstanding cases, which, if they do not create work, produce an uncertainty since judges and clerks don't know if or when they will lead to proceedings.

[38] Le Collectif Onze, *Au tribunal des couples* (n 36).

as one between two professional worlds that are at once similar and different in their working methods which are quasi-incompatible in relation to time. While the judges concede that lawyers are now participating in negotiating and finalising the agreements that the courts expect, they are, nevertheless, still a little mistrustful. 'It is said that divorce is something that goes on between the parties', one judge says.

> But this is not entirely true. Even if the parties agree on the pace of the proceedings, they will be confronted with certain cumbersome procedures, including those of the lawyers. Family law lawyers belong to artisanal organisations, subject to the problems of judicial organisation, which makes it impossible for them to manage their time seriously. The parties find themselves blocked by the deficiencies of their lawyers, by their failure to react.

Judges seek to control the lawyers during the hearing itself and, more generally, in the way the proceedings are conducted. In the hearing, the fact that lawyers are asked to keep a low profile is particularly sensitive in all consensual proceedings. The success of this type of procedure dictates that no point be disputed so that the lawyers, who could have played significant roles beforehand, often regret not having performed better before the court. They can sometimes be heard telling their client: 'I told you that this would not take very long'. But the time allocated to the lawyers to express their client's point of view has also been shortened in the context of litigation. The Family Court judges ask them to limit their submissions and above all to refocus on the points they mention in their written pleadings, and only those on which the judge must rule. This warning is sometimes brutal—particularly in the largest of the three courts observed. 'I reduce as much as possible the oral submissions part', says one Family Court judge. 'I am very familiar with the files. I give each fifteen minutes to check everything, which isn't bad. I still have another fifteen cases afterwards'.

More generally, Family Court judges seek to resist allocated 'dead time', which does not necessarily result from negligence on the part of the lawyers, but mostly from the multi-dimensional and multi-site nature of their activity. One of the most sensitive points relates to the resistance against applications for 'referrals' (*renvois*)—in which the lawyers agree, at the request of one of them to say they would like to postpone examining the case to a later date. 'Judges are obsessed with referrals. It's like they're having a tooth pulled. They are under statistical pressure' (a lawyer). For about three decades, since they were themselves mobilised to reduce time to handle cases, judges have continued to find ways to put mechanisms in place that are capable of spurring members of the Bar to respect the jointly-defined procedural deadlines. The question then becomes, in the context of 'pre-trial' civil procedures (*la mise en état*), one of defining the work of the lawyers in 'procedure contracts' or 'calendars' that, implemented and constantly discussed in the hearings dedicated to this, aim to set strict benchmarks and deadlines. These mechanisms have trouble achieving their objective:

> The pre-trial judge has some control. He asks each of the parties to conclude, to submit its arguments, evidence, documents, etc. He sets deadlines each time. We try to limit the deadlines, but we can't tell the lawyers: everything must be dealt with by such and such a date. That isn't possible. The people, the lawyers, everyone needs this judicial time. (a judge).

The elements raised, present in all courts, are combined specifically in each of them, according to the size, the story, the workforce they have, the institutional environment or the methods of its governance. Without purporting to identify the 'ideal/typical' methods from three cases, it is nonetheless possible to show how these different elements are focused to describe the forms of judicial time that prevail in the family law unit in each of the courts studied.

In the first court, maintaining speedy handling is at the origin of a 'virtuous circle' that preserves the efficiency of the service rendered and the comfort of the judges. The family law service has enough resources and has implemented ways of operating that allow it to receive applications from the parties within short time limits and to produce quick decisions. Furthermore, for litigation, the pre-trial is also quick. The judges show strong determination as regards lawyers and their work. The latter appear to accept the operating conditions by avoiding, in particular, fruitless debates. They participate in this way to regulate the whole.

A second configuration can be seen in the largest of the three tribunals: a kind of 'industrialisation' of handling divorce. Indeed, seeking speed does not appear here, as in the previous situation, as a means but more as an end in itself. Judges do everything they can to speed up and waste the least amount of time possible. The organisation of the work is marked by the desire to streamline divorce cases, which clearly originates in the large number of files to manage—over 600 new cases every month. Practical mechanisms have been implemented for reducing as much wasted time as possible in the various procedures. It is in this way that Family Court judges are vehemently opposed to applications to refer and systematically resist delays, in particular as regards the experts' role in conflicted divorces. Generally, hearings are conducted by the judge who sets the rules like a true 'master of time', regularly criticising lawyers for failing to handle their case properly. At the same time as being the day-to-day work of judge, maintaining the service 'above water' is also the work of the 'manager', the vice-president who is in charge of it, in particular through the constant administrative control that he performs in collaboration with the chief court clerk.

In the last court, there is a vicious circle, a cascading increase in delays in handling cases that has been developing gradually in the family law service and against which a collective action is being built. In fact, in the space of two years, the delays for a first notice have gone from two months to five or six months. The issue: chronic understaffing. The current delays appear to judges to be extremely long and harmful. Applications for referral have become increasingly frequent because of the same slow response from the service. At the hearing, lawyers are frequently heard explaining that they have not seen their client since the client consulted them and they thus do not have up to date information to allow them to represent their clients. Another consequence of seeking to obtain a quicker decision, and taking into account the structural delay of the court, is that parties make interim applications that both add a large volume of cases to the already overburdened existing litigation and that slow the activity all the more. In short, not only is the time lost troublesome, but it increases the workload which accumulates and prevents any return to normal. Judges suffer from this situation:

> Currently, when someone files a petition, it is examined five months later. It's huge, in family matters, when it's people who are separated and cannot agree on where the child will live. It's dramatic to wait five months before the situation has stabilised.

In this situation, a reorganisation of the courts was initiated to try to get the court back afloat: in particular, applications for referral, when they are not strongly justified, carry a new term of several months resulting in very adverse effects, so the hearing dates for the new cases can be kept to within a short period. The less cooperative are thus in some sense 'punished' by an extension of the deadlines for dealing with their cases.

Regardless of the local differences, it can only be noted that controlling time, in the judicial phase of matrimonial breakdowns, is a shared issue, which a judge analyses as follows: 'We intervene to give a rhythm and the lawyers and the parties can delay it or speed it up. It is not up to the judge to control time nor is it completely up to the parties. It is shared by both'.

THE PURSUIT OF ACCELERATION IN BELGIAN TRIBUNALS AND ITS UNEXPECTED EFFECTS

In the two Belgian tribunals studied, the same observations could be made as regards the 'mechanisation' of judicial activity. However, the issue of time is different when, as described above, the decision regarding divorce itself is distinguished from other aspects of the reorganisation of the family at the time of the breakdown. With regard to the principle of the divorce decree, the proceedings are carried out in two types of hearings organised by the court of first instance as regards granting the divorce. The first is the introductory hearing. It is the marker for all divorce applications, regardless of the legal basis. The second is the hearing on the pleadings. That is for 'contentious' divorces only, whose irretrievable breakdown has not been proven by the required separation time but rather by any other element provided.

The divorce reform has had a significant impact on managing hearings in the court of first instance. In fact, when it was implemented, the new procedure resulted in a significant inflow of applications, necessitating the creation of additional hearings. It seems to have had the effect of making divorce more 'attractive', in particular because of the reduced waiting times. At the same time, given that the trial judge is content to grant the divorce without considering the bases,[39] the number of files before the interim relief judge (competent, in particular, in maintenance issues when divorce proceedings have been submitted) has also increased. This overlapping in legal process is frequently observed: divorce gives rise to an application for interim relief then, a few weeks or even months later, to proceedings on the merits before the competent judge. To deal with this influx of files without significantly extending the time before they can be heard, hearings before the interim relief judge in one of the two courts studied have tripled.

Under the old divorce procedure, most of the proceedings, and thus the hearing time, were devoted to fault. Since this issue has disappeared from the stage of granting the divorce, the trial judge will henceforth have a limited role during the introductory hearing. His role comprises essentially noting that the legal deadlines are respected. One Walloon judge said: 'In fact, I am a recorder who checks the legal provisions'. This verification relates to divorce applications based on an irretrievable breakdown resulting from de facto separation, which make up a significant portion of the hearing files. Most of these are otherwise 'closed' at the time of the introductory hearing. In a single session lasting three to four hours the court can deal with 40 to 60 files. The rate of handling them is very high, about three to four minutes per case. The 'mechanisation' here is very real. One of the two courts has implemented a 'ticket' system to manage the queues like that used for queues at public services. Given the very short handling times for files, it would be futile and tiresome to set an order of appearance. The rule is thus that of 'first come, first served', with the exception that the parties who are represented by a lawyer are given priority. In reality, therefore, there are two queues with different tickets: those for files with lawyers and those for files without lawyers. The time for the introductory hearing is thus voluntarily 'routinised' or automated.

The reform seems here to have left the actors, applicants, lawyers and judges, little room to manoeuvre, appearing passive in the face of the well-oiled

[39] The judge of the court of first instance can deal with maintenance issues, but only after the divorce has been granted. Previously, it was the justice of the peace or the interim relief judge (*Juge des référés*) who was competent.

machinery of the procedure. This is particularly evident at a time when one or another of these actors behaves unusually. Such is the case of the judge who, faced with a couple whose desire to divorce seemed feverish to him and although the time for the de facto separation had been met, suggested they 'give it another try'. Another such example is of a man who, faced with his wife's desire to divorce him and drowning in grief, is unable to speak an intelligible phrase. The judge listened to him and tried within his means to help. As remarkable as they may be, these few suspensions in the frenetic pace of the introductory hearing have little effect on the course.

The efficiency of the divorce reform implemented in Belgium is clear. Divorces are quicker and easier than ever before. In that sense, divorce law is effective. If questions arise on the reasons for this success and on the factors that have allowed this speeding up of the procedure, there is no doubt that the obliteration of the role that the judge could play through the debate on the fault and in the context of granting the divorce is an essential element of this 'success'. Because the decision is based on the observation of a time period running or on a fact, the irretrievable breakdown, and no longer on the search for 'responsibility', with serious consequences for the future of the ex spouses, the judicial time to grant a divorce may be significantly reduced.

If the reform has sped up granting divorces, it has nonetheless introduced a distinction between granting the divorce and the timing of additional reorganisation needed. Thus, frequently, a granted divorce is not an organised divorce. If most couples agree on the act of divorcing, they do not necessarily agree on custody of the children, maintenance payments and property division. Granting the divorce was 'peaceful', but the arguments on the matrimonial breakdown and the animosity that it may generate have shifted, through an interconnected system, to decisions on the practical details of divorce. With the new procedures, a spouse may be quickly 'unmarried', but the notion of fault has not entirely disappeared. We are seeing a shift in the tensions and the conflicts, from granting the divorce to the methods for its settlement and the issues related to maintenance, custody of the children, division of property or occupation of the family home.

> To divorce quickly and efficiently, the spouse who wants it most will often accept the conditions set by the other without thinking too much about them. People go to the notary or the justice of the peace and they make an arrangement regarding occupation of the family home and custody of the children. They sign the paper and this arrangement is endorsed a few days or weeks later by the judge. They are happy at the time. Then a few weeks later, they realise that they've maybe not done the best deal. They want to review the terms of the separation contract. The judicial machinery starts up again. We are seeing an explosion in the number of applications before the juvenile court judge or before the interim judge to reconsider the terms of custody of the children, for example. (President of the Court of First Instance)

Indeed, the three juvenile court judges of one of the courts had to increase the number of civil hearings while also increasing the time for setting the hearings—up to three months at the most critical time instead of a maximum of three weeks and eight weeks at the time of our survey. Thus the reform could very well have had as a consequence the shifting of some tensions initially observed before the court of first instance to the interim judges, the justices of the peace or the juvenile court judge.

In addition to the incompleteness of the divorce at the time it is granted, the new legislation seems to have had another unexpected effect that will have significant repercussions on the life of the courts. It concerns the unstable nature of the decisions taken in the framework of a hastily granted divorce. As has been seen, from the moment when a spouse files the application to the moment when the divorce is granted, very little time has elapsed (two months), significantly less than under the old legislation. The law thus allows for a divorce marked by its immediacy, but this brief time generates a precipitous process that requires adjustments and subsequent recourse to the courts. Previously, a file that took longer to be handled could allow for a divorce to be organised more coherently, without prejudice to the impact of the suffering generated by the length of the judicial dispute. When the divorce was granted, its rules for application, both practical and in relation to the assets, were also more 'mature' and more stable.

If divorce reform seems to have achieved its objectives, it has nevertheless generated unexpected effects. And if its ambition was to 'humanise' divorce and make the procedure more peaceful, it is striking to observe that these objectives are only being achieved when we reduce or withdraw the 'human' aspect of the procedure, viz the active role of the judge, in particular, or the human dimension, viz the understanding of the individual process of separation. In other words, humanising divorce, as intended by the legislator, operates by 'dehumanising' the process.

Finally, we also note that a divorce granted in all its forms is not a finished divorce. Speeding up the process which precipitated in some way the possibility of getting 'unmarried' is not free of the impact in terms of organisation and the time needed for justice. As we noted, the parties appear enthusiastic for immediacy when they want to divorce. The new procedure allows this to be satisfied. The judges play the game of speed. Their 'mechanical' approach of granting the divorce in most cases attests to their desire to respect what appears to be the desire of the parties. The actors are thus left to 'tinker' with integrating the new situation and organising their separation. In any event, adding up the various procedures necessary to get a 'full' and 'stabilised' divorce, including all its matrimonial and patrimonial aspects, the question may be raised as to whether the result is not one part of a process that is just as long as it was under the framework of the previous legislation. In other words, and without certainty in this respect because elements are missing from this deduction, everything unfolds as though there were a kind of irreducibility of judicial time.

Some Revealing Differences

If the acceleration in handling family law cases is an imperative in the two countries, this wave is taking different paths: the greatest speed is observed in Belgium with the spectacle of hearings in which divorces are truly granted 'on an assembly line' from the moment the case is introduced; while in France, it offers the image of hearings in which, even when accelerated, divorce is the subject of more detailed handling. The observation of this difference in the concrete signs of acceleration can be referred to the more general structuring of the judicial professions in the two countries and to the construction of the state.

In France, the requirement for speed in divorce cases results from the judicial institution holding on to the control it has on every aspect of divorce, while accepting the privatisation of divorce. For the magistrates, the issue is to show that they 'see' all the situations and that they can intervene, where necessary, if the interests of the parties, and above all those of the children, have not been respected. We can see in this claim the extension, in the judicial framework, of the centralising role of the state and the expression of its interest in family cases. Family Court judges are moreover allied with the lawyers in each of the endeavours that are made to make divorce a purely administrative process. In fact, this control appears largely illusory not only because of the speed of the hearing but also because referring the decisions to the parties means that the magistrate practically never intervenes in the decisions submitted to him. Because the applications are joint, the role of the magistrate is symbolic, limited to the solemnity at the time of making the decision, which, it is worth noting, is meaningful for marking the change in the marital situation of the applicants and respondents but does not impart to him the role of 'decision-maker'.

In this regard, Belgium is following a very different path and we are witnessing a more marked 'liberalisation', in the sense of privatisation, of the divorce process. Everything is happening as though we are witnessing a more marked withdrawal of law, as of justice, as regards, at least, the issue of the couple. The abandonment of arguments about cause and the near-automatic granting of the divorce reflect this withdrawal so we can again refer to a more general socio-political analysis by highlighting the relative weakness of the Belgian state and the influence of liberal ideology in that country. Even so, different kinds of control remain, but they relate to the ancillary aspects of divorce which are referred to specialised courts.

ACCELERATION AND PRIVATISATION

Beyond these local differences, divorce and, more generally, separation, form mass disputes, which the legislator and the judges want to deal with rapidly in both countries, without substantial investment from the judicial institutions. Speeding up the handling of this litigation corresponds, in law as in practice, to the idea that there is a demand for quick answers from the applicants and the respondents—a demand that is moreover constructed by the actors. Magistrates and court clerks are constantly required to satisfy the demand and to respond to the applications that are submitted to them while preventing the services from becoming completely swamped.

The fact remains that, unlike in the criminal sector, the capacity to respond quickly to this type of case is contingent on the will of the divorcing couple. The possibility of closing the files depends on the existence of an agreement between the parties and their determination to divorce. When this does exist, the divorce is granted very quickly. In France, the magistrate formalises a decision to which he did not contribute and which he cannot possibly think he controlled, while in Belgium, the presence of the parties is no longer even required. When there is no agreement, we move into another temporal dimension where different parameters are at work. In France, it is the noticeable desire on the part of the magistrates to give the parties time or the capacity of the lawyers to impose their rhythm on the court by slowing it down where necessary; in Belgium, it is the segmentation of the courts and its fragmenting effect of the cases in the courts.

More generally, the acceleration in this kind of case refers to the notion of privatisation that makes it possible and justifies it. Handling divorces quickly is essential when the state has relinquished involvement, except in exceptional situations of public interest (in particular, where children are involved or where there has been domestic violence), in handling situations that are part of the private sphere. Beyond the local differences, acceleration goes hand-in-hand with the withdrawal of the judiciary who avoid, as far as possible in principle, adjudicating on the merits of cases, and in particular on the causes of divorce. The legislator and judges are refusing to decide in the place of couples. Recent data confirm this. For France,[40] divorcing couples 'get what they want' to a large extent (more than 90 per cent)—the agreements which they reach in this way moreover doing nothing more than reproduce the existing inequalities and gender stereotypes.[41] If this is the case, it is because a single model is necessary, that of the peaceful and, as much as possible, self-regulated divorce. There are thus two aspects to acceleration: that of 'humanisation', viewed restrictively, which consists in thinking that the people concerned are waiting for a quick answer to the application, and that of managerial efficiency.

[40] Guillonneau, M and Moreau, C, *La résidence des enfants de parents séparés. De la demande des parents à la décision du juge. Exploitation des décisions définitives reçues par les juges aux affaires familiales au cours de la période comprise entre le 4 juin et le 15 juin 2012* (Paris, Ministère de la Justice, 2013).

[41] Le Collectif Onze (n 36).

However, acceleration does come at a price. In Belgium in particular, the speed with which the divorce is granted translates into a shift in the time that is sometimes essential for decisions required for reorganising the family. The time of the divorce is therefore segmented, because of the recourse to different courts, each of which falls under unique legal and procedural rules. More generally, in France, as in Belgium, the withdrawal of the judiciary and the speed imposed on handling a greater number of cases leads, in some circumstances, to postponing the judicial reaction, even refraining from giving answers to the parties in the area into which they would like to draw the judges. The judges are not interested in engaging in fault or responsibility. The result is an astonishing paradox: under the pretext of 'humanising' divorce, that is, of stripping it of its dramatic and divisive appearance while moving in the direction of a desire for speed imputed on the parties, we end up handling them like items on an 'assembly line', and reducing any uniqueness in handling the situation of each couple: in short 'dehumanising' them.

This observation may be placed in a broader perspective on judicial time, which differs from the time as seen by the parties while coordinating with it.

Marital separation is an event that, sometimes appearing brutal, happens over a long period and is made up of misunderstandings, disputes and one-off conflicts. Separation is the result of a long-standing process, sometimes beginning when the couple formed, and it does not necessarily have a legal translation, at least not immediately. Divorce, a judicial moment, is thus nothing more than an episode limited by a conjugal trajectory that will continue beyond it. The time of justice is a short period in which this private conflict is found in a form, 'translated' by the intention of the institutions assumed to have given an answer—a collected time, which has its own specific features, defined by rules of procedure and depending on the functioning of the professions in the legal field.[42] The two types of time, private and judicial, do not correspond, even if there is movement back and forth between them, in particular with regard to subsequent appearances before the courts aimed either at formalising new provisions regarding, for example, the children of the couple, or at adjudicating on new conflicts.

This study suggests that the acceleration of judicial time in divorce cases makes the disjunction between these two types of time much clearer, as reflected in the regrets expressed by legal professionals who think that they are not giving enough time in these family dispute situations. Certain French judges deplore social pressure to consent, which has been made even stronger with the reform of 2005. The old divorce regime gave a little more time to the parties with, in particular, the period that ran between the two appearances before the Family Court judge in joint applications. With the reform, the same criticisms that were levelled at mutual consent when it was first introduced are thus reappearing and relate to the 'decoupling' of the

[42] Noreau, 'La superposition des conflits' (n 19).

time of the judiciary and that of the parties. The spouses go before the judge once, leave, and are divorced. The dispute is badly perceived in justice and its existence is being denied there, while it still has validity in the private sphere, but lacks a place for expression.

Speeding up the handling of cases exacerbates the hiatus between the parties' time and judicial time, the consequence of which is to increase the precariousness of the decisions taken. In both France and Belgium, magistrates highlight that, in the field of family law, they will have to deal more often with measures of a transitional nature, following the organisation of the relations between the partners. This sentiment refers to the fact that family structures are now less institutionalised after separation than during the marriage, and more generally to the idea that the organisation of family relationships has become more malleable, capable of being remodelled over time. In line with this now well-established observation, the relationship between the parties to a divorce and justice no longer takes the form of a single passage that aims to sanction the end of the marriage and formalise a new status of the people, but rather in an increasing number of situations, of reiterated remedies and of the anticipation of formalising successive statuses in family relationships. In addition, the commitment of the Family Court judges to management of these precarious situations risks weakening the force of the judicial decision.

In conclusion, it will be noted that acceleration in the handling of civil cases responds to 'reasons' identical to those that apply in criminal law but that they are also based on a different logic.[43] In both circumstances, as we have described, the changes introduced correspond to the general quest for efficiency of the public service of justice, a quest that is focused almost exclusively on use of time. Nevertheless, new standards for public management generate opposing effects. The acceleration of the handling of criminal cases relates, in the two countries, to maintaining *public policy* and the efficiency of the legal process on the social fabric. In civil law matters, the same acceleration has been made possible and is mainly due to the *privatisation* of family issues. In other words, while in criminal cases, the idea of speed is closely associated to strengthening the legal process in society, and necessary to punishment, this is not the case in civil law matters, at least as regards divorce and parent/child relationships. Acceleration corresponds de facto to a certain disengagement from the judicial apparatus and the state, where the affairs of the couple are concerned. Acceleration is everywhere, but its meaning indeed requires further examination.

[43] Bastard et al, *L'esprit du temps* (n 21).

17

When is a Family Lawyer a Lawyer?

LISA WEBLEY

INTRODUCTION

FAMILY PROBLEMS ARE amongst the most common disputes liable to give rise to the need for legal help: in her *Paths to Justice* study, Hazel Genn discovered that respondents undergoing a divorce reported problems in 59 per cent of instances and problems relating to children and money each in a further 19 per cent of cases.[1] And private family law matters cover a broader range of issues than divorce, including dissolution of civil partnerships, breakdown of cohabitation arrangements, ongoing disputes between family members about money, property and children, as well as domestic violence, child abuse and forced marriage concerns too—the full extent of family legal need is difficult to overestimate. Family disputes are distinguished from many others in that they often encapsulate multiple and interconnected problems, which may warp and shift as time elapses. They often involve third parties, principally minor children. At a difficult time in their lives when family support systems may be at breaking point, individuals are faced with a bewildering array of choices about the professionals and services they should use to help them to navigate complex procedural rules in a rapidly changing family law landscape. And to make matters even more challenging, the accessibility and affordability of legal advice and representation have been greatly reduced by decades of legal aid reform in England and Wales culminating in the recent Legal Aid, Sentencing and Punishment of Offenders Act 2012 (LASPO) that has removed most private family law matters (absent domestic violence and a small number of exceptional factors) from the scope of the scheme, further reducing access to legal professional advice and assistance for

[1] Genn, H, *Paths to Justice: What Do People Think About Going To Law?* (Oxford, Hart Publishing, 1999) 200.

an estimated 210,000 people.[2] It is thus unsurprising that legal professional bodies and others argue that we are facing a crisis in family justice.

It may be no coincidence that legal aid reforms occurred hard on the heels of legal services reform, which opened up the market in legal services with the aim of increasing consumer choice and access to services at a price consumers can afford. With this in mind, this chapter will first delineate the private law family justice context in England and Wales; it will then consider when a family 'lawyer' is acting as a legal professional providing legal services that fall within professional regulatory frameworks. It will also examine an emerging trend of family legal services offered in less traditional environments by people who may not always be admitted lawyers subject to regulatory oversight. I conclude that while there are serious concerns about the market's ability to protect consumers and ensure the maintenance of the rule of law, the developing legal services market may hold some potential to increase the public's access to family legal help if the emerging services and service providers are regulated to reduce the risk of exploitation and harm.

'PRIVATE' FAMILY DISPUTES

The family justice landscape has changed markedly since the early-1980s. Parliamentarians and policy-makers have largely moved from an ideology of family justice, delivered by legal professionals in the shadow of or in the full glare of the court, to an ideology of individual private ordering such that recourse to the courts is an exception rather than an expectation.[3] This is demonstrated by the development of thinking about divorce, from that set out in the 1966 Law Commission discussion paper *Field of Choice*,[4] to the more recent report in 1988 *Facing the Future*.[5] The privatisation of divorce from court-adjudicated outcomes to negotiated settlements was an early indication of this ideological shift, which has been followed by changes to the divorce process itself (the introduction of the Special Procedure and the development of the divorce process as a largely administrative one),

[2] See Cookson, GD, *Unintended Consequences: the Cost of the Government's Legal Aid Reforms* (King's College, London, 2011) 50.

[3] There were 28,542 petitions filed for divorce and 29,197 decrees absolute made in January to March 2014 but only 10,259 financial remedy (formerly 'ancillary relief' cases) started and 8098 cases with a disposal in January to March 2014 demonstrating that nearly 2/3 of all divorces involve a negotiated property and financial agreement rather than an adjudicated outcome: Ministry of Justice, *Court Statistics Quarterly Report January to March 2014 Ministry of Justice Statistical Bulletin* (19 June 2014) www.gov.uk/government/uploads/system/uploads/attachment_data/file/321352/court-statistics-jan-mar-2014.pdf.

[4] Law Com No 6, 1966.

[5] Law Com No 170, 1998. See O'Donovan, K, *Family Law Matters* (London, Pluto Press, 1993) for a discussion of divorce law and its assumptions at 110–14 in which she discusses the development of law from guardian of justice to guardian of procedural fairness.

to the ousting of much of the court's child support jurisdiction (the Child Support Act 1991) and latterly the withdrawal of the state's role in assisting with new child support problems unless the parties pay a fee to the Child Maintenance Service. This mirrors political dynamics discussed in the section below on family justice and the legal aid scheme—universalism was replaced with neoliberalism[6] that has at its heart individualism, personal choice and responsibility. There has been a marked reduction in the role of the state and the influence of the old professions in favour of a greater role for market-based models of service provision.[7]

That is not to say that the state has withdrawn entirely from supporting access to professional help in the context of private family law disputes. Other professionals have been invited into the publicly funded arena; indeed, this was one of the driving forces behind the Family Law Act 1996.[8] Family mediators' publicly funded role continues even in the face of savage legal aid cuts—such is its importance that separating couples must demonstrate that they have attended a mediation information and assessment meeting (MIAM) to consider using mediation, or have exemption from that requirement, before a family case is listed for a hearing.[9] The professional role of family mediators embodies the ideal of personal responsibility for one's own decisions and actions. Further, the profession operates within a minimalist regulatory framework that is largely market driven, and requires pragmatic, skills-based professional training that is no greater than is necessary to ensure competence.[10] Family mediators are the new market-fit professionals; they are also the gatekeepers to the court process, where once this was the role of an admitted lawyer.

The debate about whose norms should be used in the context of private ordering is also a live one, given that markets confer consumer choice and UK family mediators do not need to be admitted lawyers or even legally

[6] For a discussion of the very varied meanings given to the term neoliberalism, see Jessop, R, 'From Thatcherism to New Labour: Neo-Liberalism, Workfarism, and Labour Market Regulation' in Overbeek, H (ed) *The Political Economy of European Employment*: *European Integration and the Transnationalization of the (Un)Employment Question* (London, Routledge, 2003) 137–53.

[7] Webley, L, 'Legal Professional De(re)regulation, Equality and Inclusion and the Contested Space of Professionalism in England and Wales' (2015) 83(5) *Fordham Law Review* 101.

[8] Douglas, G and Murch, M, 'Taking Account of Children's Needs in Divorce: A Study of Family Solicitors' Responses to New Policy and Practice Initiatives' (2002) 14(1) *Child and Family Law Quarterly* 57, which may also suggest that there is a role for other professionals in this area.

[9] This change came into force on 22 April 2014 following the introduction of the Children and Families Act 2014, s 10 and follows a similar requirement with respect to access to adjudication on divorce. There is some early anecdotal evidence to suggest that some courts are not enforcing this requirement, particularly where the parties are unrepresented.

[10] Webley, L, 'Gate-keeper, Supervisor or Mentor? The Role of Professional Bodies in the Regulation and Professional Development of Solicitors and Family Mediators Undertaking Divorce Matters in England and Wales' (2010) 32(2) *Journal of Social Welfare and Family Law* 119.

qualified. Some commentators have sought to distinguish between mode of dispute settlement and the role of the law in reaching the outcome, citing confusion in the policy debates between the two.[11] They contend that legally compliant agreements are essential regardless of the mode of dispute resolution used to reach them; agreements made outside a legal framework can breed long-term inequality, particularly for women.[12] Given the relatively low starting base of public legal understanding, the ever-changing family law canon, and the relatively new public legal education movement in England and Wales, this gives rise to concerns about informed consent in the context of mediation agreements where a party is not legally represented to an adequate extent (or at all). A negotiated settlement may not be fair even if it is accepted, and a poor settlement for the primary child carer may have long-term impacts on children and on society more generally. These individual inequalities and their collective societal impacts were, interestingly, some of the thinking behind the introduction of civil legal aid in the later-1940s. The solution was to introduce a means by which everyone could enforce their legal rights, rather than to rely on the ability of a privatised market applying individually negotiated norms to deliver fair solutions.

ACCESS TO FAMILY JUSTICE: LEGAL AID

There is undoubtedly a strong nexus between welfare ideology and social policy with respect to family legal aid provision in England and Wales. The civil legal aid system was established as a state/market partnership through the Legal Aid and Advice Act 1949 by the Attlee Labour government as part of the welfare consensus that emerged after the Second World War.[13] The system was administered by the legal profession on behalf of the state, the day-to-day provision was provided by private practice lawyers, but payment for that work was made from general taxation in conformity with the Middle Way ideology of collective provision of social services, provided by and to serve the practical needs of a liberal market.[14] Civil legal aid

[11] See Lewis's study examining assumptions made about lawyers in the policy literature: Lewis, P, *Assumptions about Lawyers in Policy Statements: A Survey of Relevant Research* no 1/2000 (London, The Lord Chancellor's Department, 2000).

[12] Fiss, O, 'Against Settlement' (1984) 93 *Yale Law Journal* 1073. See further Webley, L, *Adversarialism and Consensus? The Professions' Construction of Solicitor and Family Mediator Identity and Role* (New Orleans, Quid Pro Books LLC, 2010). For a discussion of current policy on civil justice and ADR, see Genn, H, 'What is Civil Justice For? Reform, ADR, and Access to Justice' (2012) 24 *Yale Journal of Law and the Humanities* 397.

[13] Alcock, P, *Social Policy in Britain*, 3rd edn (Basingstoke, Palgrave and New York, MacMillan, 2008) 186–88.

[14] ibid 186–87. See further Sommerlad, H, 'Some Reflections on the Relationship between Citizenship, Access to Justice and the Reform of Legal Aid' (2004) 31(3) *Journal of Law and Society* 345.

was established as a means through which people could enforce and defend their legal rights in-keeping with a democratic citizenship model that provided equal access to justice guarantees (for the poor *and* those of moderate means). Essentially it facilitated a redistribution of risk rather than a redistribution of wealth.[15] Its introduction was driven by the need to provide access to divorce assistance post war[16] although a new focus on citizenship required a broader remit. Given that the twin doctrines of the rule of law and the separation of powers demanded that a claimant's legal dispute against the state be administered and conducted by a lawyer independent of the state, a private practice model of legal aid was established.[17]

Neoliberal Reforms: The Free Market Model

At its height, an estimated 80 per cent of the population were eligible for civil including family legal advice and assistance (including court representation). By the early-1990s, after the Conservative reforms, the eligible population had dropped below 40 per cent.[18] Eligibility for matters still within the scope of the scheme has plummeted yet further.[19] Why were the reforms considered necessary? The burgeoning legal aid bill appeared to be incompatible with the government's aim of public spending retrenchment to counteract the economic difficulties of the early-1980s. The Thatcherite era was firmly grounded in a free market model that sought to address social issues with reference to market principles, to limit a 'dependency culture' and to incentivise creative private solutions that encouraged consumer sovereignty.[20] There was real concern in government that the legal

[15] 'An outstanding characteristic of expenditure on legal matters is that people may, through no fault of their own, be involved in litigation, the costs of which bear no relation to their financial circumstances and against which they could not reasonably be expected to make provision in advance': National Assistance Board, Public Record Office, *AST 20/40 Draft Memorandum on Legal Aid*. See MacGregor, S, 'Welfare, Neo-Liberalism and New Paternalism: Three Ways for Social Policy in Late Capitalist Societies' (1999) 23 *Capital and Class* 91, 100; Spencer, M, 'Public Subsidies without Strings—Labour and the Lawyers at the Birth of Legal Aid' (2002) 9(3) *International Journal of the Legal Profession* 251, 270; Moorhead, R, 'Legal Aid in the Eye of a Storm: Rationing, Contracting and New Institutionalism' (1998) 25(3) *Journal of Law and Society* 365, 367.

[16] Morgan, R, 'The Introduction of Civil Legal Aid in England and Wales, 1914–1949' (1994) 5(1) *Twentieth Century British History* 38, 45.

[17] Spencer, 'Public Subsidies without Strings' (n 15) 259; Morgan, ibid 68.

[18] Thomas, P, 'Thatcher's Will' (1992) 19 *Journal of Law and Society* 1, 9; Sommerlad, H, 'Managerialism and the Legal Profession: a New Professional Paradigm' (1995) 2 *International Journal of the Legal Profession* 159, 165.

[19] The legal aid calculator may be of use to those who wish to gain an impression of income and capital levels that allow people to be eligible: http://legal-aid-checker.justice.gov.uk/family/. For a discussion of the implications of the drop in legal aid eligibility in family matters, see Cookson, *Unintended Consequences: the Cost of the Government's Legal Aid Reforms* (n 2) ch 6.

[20] Alcock, *Social Policy in Britain* (n 13) 184–86.

aid system was leading to perverse incentives in-keeping with Murray's neoliberal thesis:[21] artificial supplier (lawyer) induced demand.[22] It was claimed that individuals were fuelling a litigation culture as there were few disincentives to initiating legal proceedings when the state was paying for much of the bill and a protective costs shield insulated the legally aided party from being required to pay the legal costs of the successful opponent. Neoliberalism required that the state liberalise and privatise the market, which it attempted to do through a greater use of client means-testing, a reduction in client eligibility, a real terms cut in legal aid payment rates and for the first time a hard cap on civil legal aid expenditure.[23] The administration of the scheme was also transferred from the profession to a new statutory body, the Legal Aid Board (LAB), who were to regulate the legal aid system on best value principles. The government introduced a market-based solution to access to justice, a fee regime known as conditional fee arrangements, which was a forerunner of the 'no win no fee' agreements often employed today.[24] These arrangements were intended to shift financial risk from the state to the profession, for all but the poorest in society.

Current Legal Aid Provision in Family Law Matters

As of 1 April 2013, since the introduction of the provisions in LASPO an individual will usually only be eligible for legal aid in private family proceedings (including divorce, dissolution of civil partnership, property, finance and children matters) where there is evidence that they are subject to domestic violence and they meet the stringent financial eligibility criteria.[25] There are exceptions, largely to protect children and young people (to prevent children from being removed from or to be returned to the jurisdiction, to allow children to make an application to the court in family proceedings, to protect

[21] Murray, C, *Losing Ground: American Social Policy 1950-1980* (London, Basic Books, 1984); see also Deacon, A, *Perspectives on Welfare: Ideas, Ideologies and Policy Debates* (Milton Keynes, Open University Press, 2002).

[22] See Smith, R, 'Legal Aid on an Ebbing Tide' (1996) 23(4) *Journal of Law and Society* 570, 571–72; Moorhead, 'Legal Aid in the Eye of a Storm' (n 15) 376; Moorhead, R and Pleasence, P, 'Access to Justice After Universalism: Introduction' (2003) 30(1) *Journal of Law and Society* 1.

[23] See Goriely, T, 'Rushcliffe Fifty Year On: The Changing Role of Civil Legal Aid within the Welfare State' (1994) 21(4) *Journal of Law and Society* 545; Thomas, 'Thatcher's Will' (n 18) 9; Smith, 'Legal Aid on an Ebbing Tide' (n 22) 571; Spencer (n 15) 265.

[24] These were developed further through the Access to Justice Act 1999. See Spencer, M, 'The Common Law Legacy and Access to Justice: Contingency Fees and the Birth of Civil Legal Aid' (2000) 9(2) *Nottingham Law Journal* 32.

[25] For the official information provided to the public in this regard, see 'Legal Aid for Family Matters', available at www.justice.gov.uk/legal-aid-for-private-family-matters, and for the information members of the public are likely to access about legal aid eligibility, see www.adviceguide.org.uk/wales/law_w/law_legal_system_e/law_taking_legal_action_e/help_with_legal_costs_legal_aid.htm.

those who may be about to be or have been forced into marriage, to comply with some European provisions) and also to encourage use of family mediation. Domestic violence is broadly drawn[26] to cover psychological, physical, sexual, financial or emotional abuse but the evidential burden is high so as to meet the threshold of victim and is currently the subject of a judicial review challenge.[27] Family legal aid is retained for people deemed to be vulnerable by virtue of their perceived victim status or their age, but all others are largely required to find solutions to their family problems without recourse to public funds for legal help, court fees or experts' reports. 15,000 fewer people in the last quarter received family legal aid for court representation, and a further 40,000 fewer received family legal advice, legal help.[28] The Ministry of Justice's own statistics[29] indicate that the number of people receiving legally aided family legal representation fell from 33,847 in the first quarter of 2013 just prior to the introduction of LASPO to only 18,762 in April–June 2014. And these reductions do not appear to be as a result of diversion from court to family mediation—the number of publicly funded family mediations appear to have fallen 40 per cent as between the year leading up to the introduction of LASPO (30,662 in 2012–13) to the first year of the LASPO reforms (13,354), although the success rate of mediation, if success is measured as agreement, is up from 66 per cent to 79 per cent.[30] More people are attending MIAMs since they became compulsory, although there is some disagreement about whether this is leading to an increase in referrals to mediation proper.[31]

[26] *The Home Office Information for Local Areas on the Change to the Definition of Domestic Violence and Abuse* March 2013, available at: www.gov.uk/government/uploads/system/uploads/attachment_data/file/142701/guide-on-definition-of-dv.pdf.

[27] Public Law Project, 'High Court to Hear Rights of Women's Legal Challenge to Restore Access to Legal Aid for Victims of Domestic Violence' Press release (18 September 2014) www.publiclawproject.org.uk/news/43/press-release-high-court-to-hear-rights-of-womeneys-legal-challenge-to-restore-access-to-legal-aid-f.

[28] General Council of the Bar, 'Thousands of Families Shut Out from Justice Since Government Cuts' (3 October 2014) www.barcouncil.org.uk/media-centre/news-and-press-releases/2014/october/thousands-of-families-shut-out-from-justice-since-government-cuts/; and further, General Council of the Bar, 'New Legal Aid Figures Show the Depth of Legal Aid Cuts' (2 October 2014) www.barcouncil.org.uk/media/305997/141002_new_legal_aid_figures_show_the_depth_of_legal_aid_cuts__attachment_.pdf.

[29] Ministry of Justice, *Legal Aid Statistics in England and Wales Legal Aid Agency Apr to Jun 2014* Ministry of Justice Statistics Bulletin (25 September 2014) www.gov.uk/government/uploads/system/uploads/attachment_data/file/358092/legal-aid-statistics-apr-jun-2014.pdf.

[30] Otterburn Legal Consulting, *Transforming Legal Aid: Next Steps. A Report for The Law Society of England and Wales and the Ministry of Justice* (February 2014) https://consult.justice.gov.uk/digital-communications/transforming-legal-aid-next-steps/results/otterburn-legal-consulting-a-report-for-the-law-society-and-moj.pdf.

[31] See eg National Family Mediation (NFM) Chief Executive Jane Robey's comments in 'News and Comment: Legal aid work in family cases drops 27% compared to the same quarter last year' *Family Law* 25 September 2014, available at: www.jordanpublishing.co.uk/practice-areas/family/news_and_comment/legal-aid-funding-in-family-cases-drops-27-compared-to-the-same-quarter-last-year#.VFj8xTSsUuc and contrast those with comment on the figures M Lopatin obtained as a result of a Freedom of Information request: Baksi, C, 'Civil Legal Aid: Access Denied' *Law Society Gazette* 7 April 2014, available at: www.lawgazette.co.uk/law/civil-legal-aid-access-denied/5040722.fullarticle.

Instead more people appear to be attempting to navigate the court process alone rather than negotiating agreements in private.

The effects of the reforms have given rise to a range of (potentially) unintended consequences. At this early stage it appears that the reforms are not leading to greater levels of private ordering. Instead they are leading to greater numbers of self-representing litigants.[32] Statistics published by the Children and Family Court Advisory and Support Service (Cafcass) indicate that in the year immediately preceding the reforms only 18 per cent of family law cases commenced with both parties self-representing, 60 per cent with one self-representing and 22 per cent where both parties was legally represented. In the eight months immediately following the reforms both parties were self-representing in 42 per cent of family law cases, one was self-representing in a further 54 per cent of cases and in only 4 per cent of cases did both parties begin the case with legal representation.[33] Some argue that the wide publicity associated with the legal aid reforms means that fewer people are attempting to secure legal aid (the exceptional funding figures—for those who do not meet the standard legal aid criteria—would give some credence to these claims, as would the drop in the number of calls to the Civil Legal Aid Advice Line, the compulsory gateway into the legal aid system). Whatever the reasons for the sharp rise in self-representing litigants in family law cases, the figures and the results are undeniable. The Cafcass figures are bolstered by those from a study undertaken by the Bureau of Investigative Journalism in conjunction with the Magistrates' Association, and magistrates overwhelmingly believe that the rising number of self-representing litigants has a negative impact on the court's work (97 per cent of n461), including concerns about equality of arms, time delays and the undermining of the principle of justice.[34] The time judges need to spend on each case is greater when one or both parties are self-representing, costs saved on legally aided representation may be being transferred to the court service instead, with additional unexpected costs to the public purse

[32] Self-representing litigants are sometimes referred to as unrepresented litigants, litigants in person or those appearing in person. I have chosen to use self-representing litigants given that this may be a marginally more familiar term for those from non-common law jurisdictions. For research on the difficulties they face, see Moorhead, R and Sefton, M, *Litigants in Person: Unrepresented Litigants in First Instance Proceedings DCA Research Series 2/05* (London, Department for Constitutional Affairs, 2005) www.law.cf.ac.uk/research/pubs/repository/1221.pdf; and Williams, K *Litigants in Person a Literature Review Research Summary 2/11* (London, Ministry of Justice 2011) www.gov.uk/government/uploads/system/uploads/attachment_data/file/217374/litigants-in-person-literature-review.pdf.

[33] NAPO, 'Money Saved on Legal Aid is Being Spent on More Court Time' in *The Impact of Legal Aid Cuts on Family Justice A Report by the Family Court Unions Parliamentary Group* at 4–5, available at: www.napo.org.uk/sites/default/files/The%20Impact%20of%20Legal%20Aid%20Cuts%20on%20Family%20Justice.pdf.

[34] Ling, V, 'Legal Aid Cuts Impact Statement' (Legal Action Group, July 2014) www.lag.org.uk/magazine/2014/07/legal-aid-cuts-impact-statement.aspx. See more at: www.lag.org.uk/magazine/2014/07/legal-aid-cuts-impact-statement.aspx#sthash.SGEpATKu.dpuf.

also estimated to be high including the cost of those who give up and gain no settlement or redress.[35]

It is not just legal professionals and their respective representative bodies—the Law Society and Bar Council—that are expressing concerns about the depth and breadth of the family legal aid cuts. Judges often reluctant to engage in public policy discussions given the deference of the judiciary to parliamentary enactments within a constitutional framework founded on parliamentary supremacy, have also expressed concerns both in private to the Secretary of State for Justice and in public in individual family law cases.[36] The judiciary has set up a working group to consider ways in which judicial training should respond to the high numbers of self-representing litigants.[37] Parliamentarians have also publicly expressed their grave concern;[38] retired senior family law judges have also entered the debate.[39] The chorus of criticism about the withdrawal of private family legal aid has reached unprecedented levels. The courts currently have to pick up the deficits in affordable legal service provision and litigants' lack of legal process and knowledge. But could the new legal services market provide ways to deliver cost effective quality assured legal advice, assistance and if necessary legal representation too?

THE REGULATORY CONTEXT OF FAMILY LAW PRACTICE

As indicated earlier, civil legal aid reform followed sweeping changes to legal professional services introduced by the Legal Services Act (LSA) 2007, which may have contributed to the ease with which a government faced with serious budgetary constraints felt emboldened to remove most private law family matters from the scope of public funding. But the position is more nuanced than that. Contrary to many other jurisdictions, most legal activities are not reserved to admitted (authorised) legal professionals in England and Wales; there are only six reserved activities that must be undertaken by qualified and admitted lawyers.[40] The reserved areas are the exclusive preserve of those authorised to undertake them, and are: the exercise of rights of audience (ie appearing as an advocate before a court); the conduct

[35] Cookson (n 2) and further, Pleasence, R and Balmer, N, *How People Resolve 'Legal Problems' A Report to the Legal Services Board* (PPSR, Cambridge, 2014).

[36] See eg Amelia Hill, 'Parents' legal aid wait to fight enforced adoption of son inhumane, says judge' *The Guardian* 7 January 2015 www.theguardian.com/law/2015/jan/07/parents-legal-aid-wait-adoption-son-inhumane.

[37] Baksi, 'Civil Legal Aid: Access Denied' (n 31).

[38] See *The Impact of Legal Aid Cuts on Family Justice A Report by the Family Court Unions Parliamentary Group* (n 33).

[39] Baroness Butler-Sloss, 'Legal Systems: Rule of Law Motion to Take Note' HL Deb 10 July 2014, vol 755 col 348.

[40] In most instances it is a crime to undertake reserved activity work if you are not an authorised legal professional: LSA 2007, ss 14–17.

of litigation (ie issuing proceedings before a court and commencing, prosecuting or defending those proceedings); reserved instrument activities (ie dealing with the transfer of land or property under specific legal provisions including registration of land); probate activities (ie handling probate/estate matters for clients); notarial activities (ie work governed by the Public Notaries Act 1801); and the administration of oaths (eg swearing affidavits, taking oaths).[41] No single branch of the legal profession (Barrister, Solicitor, and Fellow of the Chartered Institute of Legal Executives) is authorised to conduct all six reserved activities although it is possible for professionals within each branch to undertake further accreditation to gain additional authorisation to undertake more areas of reserved work. Family mediation and arbitration are not reserved activities, nor are negotiations in family law matters, and nor is advising a client on family law or assisting a client to draft a consent order which they ask a court to ratify as a full court order, even for payment of a fee. And the generic term 'lawyer' is not legally defined in England and Wales and is open to anyone to use without caveat. Consequently 'when is a family lawyer a lawyer?' is a more contestable question than it may appear to be at first glance.

All non-reserved forms of legal work are open to anyone, legally qualified or otherwise and so much family law work is not 'law' at all for the purposes of regulatory or disciplinary oversight. There are no minimum entry standards for these types of work (even though there are minimum standards for entry into the three main branches of the legal profession), nor currently ethical or regulatory mechanisms for those who are not members of any of the legal professional bodies. It may be possible for a client to sue a service provider for breach of contract or tort for inadequate professional services subject to limitation clauses contained within the lawyer-client contract. This is not new, but the introduction of the LSA 2007, which allows for Alternative Business Structures (non-lawyer ownership of firms, multidisciplinary organisations and the delivery of reserved activities by companies and other business entities) has shed light on our very narrow unauthorised legal practice rules and the potential opportunities for the legal services market. It has shone a light on a market ripe for expansion and has allowed for capital investment by non-legal professionals to aid its development.

The Legal Services Act 2007: Access to Justice via the Ultimate Free Market in Legal Services?

The Conservative governments' approach not only changed the civil legal aid system, it has also encouraged the legal profession to adopt a business-led

[41] ibid, schs 2 and 12.

market model in all areas of work; the dominance of a monolithic conception of old-style professionalism was challenged and different branches of the legal profession began to compete against each other for market share.[42] Even the terminology used by government and by sections of the legal profession reflected this switch: the 'practice of law' became the 'provision of legal services', 'legal professionals' became 'legal service providers'.[43] Although some sections of the profession resolutely resisted these changes, most notably the English Bar, others embraced them wholeheartedly.[44] The access to justice discussion had shifted from universalism to individualism,[45] mediated by market principles.

The LSA 2007, so avowedly pro free market, was enacted at the height of the economic boom by the New Labour government as a champion for rather than a detractor from the market model.[46] The LSA 2007 uncoupled much of the machinery of professional complaint (if not professional censure) from the original professional bodies. The admission and disciplinary parts of the historical professional bodies were hived off to independent bodies with majority lay representation; the membership service and the campaigning arms remain within their control. Consequently, the admission, regulation and discipline arms of the solicitors' profession now rest with the Solicitors Regulation Authority (SRA), for barristers they rest with the Bar Standards Board (BSB) and for chartered legal executives with Ilex Professional Standards (IPS), while the Law Society of England and Wales, the General Council of the Bar and the Chartered Institute of Legal Executives respectively continue to act as professional associations for their members. Consumer complaints are made to the Legal Ombudsman which has exclusive jurisdiction for complaints' redress in the first instance although discipline rests with the SRA, BSB and IPS. Professional autonomy has been supplanted. The LSA 2007 also established an independent oversight regulator, the Legal Services Board (LSB), which has statutory powers and duties to ensure that the regulatory objectives of the LSA 2007 are realised by the front-line regulators the SRA, BSB and IPS via intervention if

[42] See MacGregor, 'Welfare, Neo-Liberalism and New Paternalism' (n 15) 92; Thomas (n 18) 2–3; see also Abel, R, *English Lawyers between Market and State: The Politics of Professionalism* (Oxford, Oxford University Press, 2004). Thomas (n 18) 8–9, argues that professional deregulation and developments in favour of an enterprise culture were not wholly government led, as some of these policies reflected what was already happening in some sectors of the legal profession.

[43] Thomas (n 18) 5.

[44] The Chairman of the Bar Council indicated: 'justice cannot be measured in terms of competition and consumerism; justice is not a consumer durable; it is the hallmark of a civilised and democratic society' *The Times* 3 July 1989 as cited by Thomas (n 18) 5.

[45] MacGregor (n 15) 110. See also Moorhead and Pleasence, 'Access to Justice After Universalism' (n 22).

[46] See Jessop, 'From Thatcherism to New Labour' (n 6).

necessary. The regulatory objectives of the LSA 2007 are set out in section 1 of the Act as follows:

> (1) In this Act a reference to 'the regulatory objectives' is a reference to the objectives of—
> (a) protecting and promoting the public interest;
> (b) supporting the constitutional principle of the rule of law;
> (c) improving access to justice;
> (d) protecting and promoting the interests of consumers;
> (e) promoting competition in the provision of services within subsection (2);
> (f) encouraging an independent, strong, diverse and effective legal profession;
> (g) increasing public understanding of the citizen's legal rights and duties;
> (h) promoting and maintaining adherence to the professional principles.

The regulatory objectives pose a number of interesting paradoxes: how does the LSB seek to improve access to justice when the family justice system is being configured apparently to reduce it and Alternative Dispute Resolution (ADR) as such falls outside its scope? How does diversion to ADR support the constitutional principle of the rule of law if a disputant is not able to afford legal help to determine whether the issues he or she faces are ones of fact, discretion or of public interest? How can consumer protection be assured when so few areas of family practice are reserved to admitted regulated lawyers? And how can the Legal Ombudsman transform the experience of disgruntled or exploited clients when it only has jurisdiction over admitted legal professionals? Perhaps outside investment in Alternative Business Structures that deviate from a traditional model will provide opportunities for innovation, competition and price reduction, but some legal work, such as advocacy services, is less likely to be susceptible to the workings of a liberalised, deregulated market given that these are reserved activities that take place in a highly regulated courtroom environment. And innovation with limited regulation may pose real challenges to the public's perceptions of the rule of law and on a practical level to the LSB's ability to succeed at consumer protection.

NEW MODELS OF FAMILY LAW PRACTICE?

There has been much rhetoric about, yet limited evidence of, a revolution in legal service delivery for family matters;[47] most changes have been reinventions of the standard models with some cost savings brought about by technological

[47] For insight into the potential future direction of legal services, see Susskind, R, *Tomorrow's Lawyers: An Introduction to Your Future* (Oxford, Oxford University Press, 2013).

advancements or the use of paralegals to undertake the more routine aspects of family legal practice. But the LSA 2007 has emboldened businesses that have not traditionally offered legal services to enter the market in ways similar to those through which they provide other professional services, to offer clearly advertised fixed fee packages. The Co-operative Legal Services basic self-managed petitioner divorce service costs £119, they have a range of more extensive and lawyer-managed services that cost up to £570 (petitioner) £900 (respondent).[48] The service delivery is not that innovative (other than its accessibility online), the legal work is undertaken by admitted lawyers or those working under their supervision. But unbundled legal services have often been the preserve of commercial practice rather than 'High Street' provision, and clients may be more inclined to seek out services that offer a transparent fee structure and a clear indication of the work that they can expect to do and to be done for them.

For those even less able to pay, law school student law clinics are now beginning to take on family law cases (Huddersfield, Liverpool John Moores and Westminster universities, for example) when once family matters were viewed as staple legal aid work and not the subject of clinic casework. But, pro bono provision is spread thinly and there is patchy coverage in rural areas (universities tend to be based in towns and cities) plus demand far outstrips supply. These services, while welcome, remain at the more traditional end of the spectrum given that they are staffed by would-be lawyers (law students) working under the supervision of law academics, many of whom are former or currently practising solicitors or barristers. They are often highly supervised and regulated and they offer services to relatively few clients when compared to a business model of practice as they are often subsidised as part of an educational mission.

An increasing number of other organisations are offering family legal help over the internet, some with legal helplines, some through internet video meeting facilities, others via chat messenger applications. Some are not-for-profit public legal education initiatives,[49] others provide legal self-help guides as a means to draw traffic to their sites where they provide other services (such as lawyer comparison sites to allow members of the public to find admitted lawyers at the right price and quality).[50] But there is a growing number of seemingly very competitively priced businesses advertising family legal services where it is not always easy to determine whether the purported and signposted 'lawyers' are admitted professionals in good standing, are formerly admitted and now retired, suspended from practice, struck off, never admitted but legally qualified, or never legally qualified. The companies are very easy to find via Google, their credentials rather less obvious

48 See www.co-operativelegalservices.co.uk/family-law-solicitors/.
49 See Divorce Aid: www.divorceaid.co.uk/ as an example.
50 eg AccessSolicitor.com: www.accesssolicitor.com/.

without a phone call and some targeted questions.[51] As indicated above, anyone is able to refer to themselves as a 'family lawyer' regardless of their educational or professional background—yet often even law academics and legal professionals in the UK when told this are amazed—I hazard that most of the public would believe that someone referring to themselves as a lawyer would be a legally educated, admitted and a regulated member of the legal profession. Further, non-admitted 'lawyers' are not subject to the same insurance requirements nor are they overseen by the Legal Ombudsman.[52] Clients seeking redress may struggle to obtain satisfaction, if things go wrong, other than via recourse to the courts—the very thing that the LSA 2007 sought to limit with the establishment of the Legal Ombudsman—, yet this is the logical extension of a fully privatised market in legal services. The difficulty with this market is the knowledge asymmetry between potential client and the service provider, given that the service provider may use terminology suggestive of professional standing—'lawyer'—and is under no obligation to indicate the potential shortcomings of routes to redress in respect of their services.

But it is not just the market in family law advice and assistance that has developed over the past few years; the market in family legal help in court has also moved on a pace. There is a developing trend of paid McKenzie Friends who historically have been pro bono assisters to self-representing litigants. The McKenzie Friend tradition developed as a pro bono aid for people who found themselves in court without a means to pay for a barrister to represent them. Advocacy services are matters reserved to certain types of admitted lawyer (principally barristers, but solicitors and some Fellows of CILEX also have advocacy rights). However, as McKenzie Friends do not technically act as advocates (they may sit next to the self-representing litigant and advise them quietly on law, procedure and tactics) they do not have to be admitted. In recent years some McKenzie Friends have offered their services for a fee in a new guise as a Litigation Friend. Some have even been permitted to address the court as a quasi-advocate (this is within the judge's discretion although a Practice Direction indicates that judges should check the individual's CV before they extend this courtesy to a McKenzie Friend). The LSB Consumer Panel's study on paid McKenzie Friends suggested they offer some potential access to justice benefits but also raise some

[51] This is the subject of research that I have recently started, to determine the extent to which new legal service providers that advertise on the internet are staffed by admitted professionals who are delivering services via a new business model, qualified professionals who while not admitted are legally qualified, or those with limited or no formal legal qualifications.

[52] The jurisdiction of the Legal Ombudsman is to be widened to cover regulated claims management professionals, although there do not appear to be plans at this stage to bring the unregulated legal sector within scope: www.legalombudsman.org.uk/.

real concerns.[53] My own anecdotal evidence from a small unrepresentative sample of barristers who have appeared against Litigation Friends suggests cause for alarm: some Litigation Friends have no training beyond attending a brief course to prepare them to appear and they may be motivated to take on the role after a bitter experience as a litigant in their own family proceedings. They may not be aware that they must not mislead the court, that their first duty is to the court, and that they must leave aside all personal views about the law nor pass judgement on their client or the other party. Perhaps it is time for direct access barristers to advertise fixed fee prices for their services given that the fees charged by some McKenzie Friends are not far below a brief fee. The LSB has also noted anxiety that members of the public may believe these types of service provider are legitimated, regulated legal professionals (some of course will be, but it is clear some are not). But given the statistics above on the rising number of self-representing litigants in family cases, many people will be faced with the daunting prospect of representing themselves or relying on the services of a McKenzie Friend who may be expert, professional and learned or who may be seeking to walk around the reserved advocacy rules to provide representation with no knowledge of the law, court procedure or legal ethics with a personal axe to grind.

CONCLUSIONS

Many will continue to campaign for the reintroduction of legal aid for private family law matters, but in the meantime we are left with the difficulty of finding ways in which the market can provide affordable, quality-assured services that meet the needs of a very wide range of family law clients. Granularity of service provision is needed, including many of the non-legal forms of social style support that family lawyers have traditionally provided for no additional payment.[54] The new market in legal services may provide

[53] LSB Consumer Panel, *Fee Charging McKenzie Friends* (April 2014) www.legalservicesconsumerpanel.org.uk/publications/research_and_reports/documents/2014%2004%2017%20MKF_Final.pdf and the LSB's response of September 2014 is available at: www.legalservicesboard.org.uk/what_we_do/responses_to_consultations/pdf/20140902_LSB_Response_To_LSCP_McKenzie_Friends_Report.pdf, noting at 2: 'However, some of the observations in the report mean that we are cautious about formally accepting fee-charging McKenzie Friends as a legitimate feature of the evolving legal services market. In particular, we are concerned that they may be misleadingly perceived to be offering a service underpinned by the same standards and consumer protections that are provided by a regulated professional'.

[54] See Moorhead and Pleasence (n 22) for a summary of the arguments about the appeal of a one-size fits model but the need for this to be resisted; and further Abel, L, 'Evidence-based Access to Justice' (2009–10) 13(3) *University of Pennsylvania Journal of Law and Social Change* 295; for evidence of the broad range of non-legal services provided by family lawyers, see Eekelaar, J, Maclean, M and Beinart, S, *Family Lawyers* (Oxford, Hart, 2000).

a means to drive down costs, as companies like Co-op Legal Services are able to cut overheads through economies of scale, investment in technology and reduction in client-facing office space and provide client-lawyer partnerships that allow those who can to do some of the administrative work themselves.[55] These services may provide affordable access to justice for those of more modest means, and their delivery may lend itself to a less distanced, impersonal and anxiety-inducing interaction between client and lawyer. They may also provide access to legal employment for the very large numbers of law graduates who are unable to secure a training contract or a pupillage so as to gain full admission to the legal profession (and may bolster the status of legal executives who may train and gain full qualification in a broader range of legal environments than can solicitors and barristers).[56] But consumer protection concerns will persist unless it becomes mandatory for all services clearly to signpost the current legal professional standing of all their advisers and in-court representatives plus their insurance cover.

The legal professional bodies could do more to assist the public: there is no easy means by which a potential client may vet the professional standing of any lawyer (there is no single roll against which a member of the public could check standing, even were they to think to do so and have the means by which to achieve this). Further, the Legal Ombudsman's jurisdiction needs to be extended beyond the work of admitted legal professionals to all legal service providers. This will not be easy—when is a service a legal service so as to be within the Ombudsman's jurisdiction? But given that other countries reserve all legal activities to admitted professionals and have devised means by which to identify when a service is a legal one, this cannot be insurmountable for us. Nor would we be unable to develop a nuanced approach to redress so as to distinguish between pro bono and for profit providers.

Even then while complaints may be addressed, matters of ethics and professionalism will be left to the market rather than professional censure as for other forms of service provision. Some will argue that this is in-keeping with most professional service markets. Yet no other service delivers the rule of law commitment that undergirds our society (and our markets). The blurring of the boundaries between reserved and unreserved activities, between legal professionals, lawyers and others, coupled with the fiendish complexity of the legal system and the different professional denominations,

[55] For some of the more technologically innovative approaches to legal service delivery see the ReinventLaw channel: http://reinventlaw.com/main.html. For research on their potential to improve access to justice and also their limitations, see Smith, R and Paterson, A, *Face to Face Legal Services and Their Alternatives: Global Lessons from the Digital Revolution* (Glasgow, Strathclyde University, 2013) www.strath.ac.uk/media/faculties/hass/law/cpls/Face_to_Face.pdf.

[56] See Webley, 'Legal Professional De(re)regulation, Equality and Inclusion and the Contested Space of Professionalism in England and Wales' (n 7).

reservations, disciplinary and regulatory contexts all lead to a terrifyingly difficult situation for the public to navigate. We are at risk of undermining the public perception of family justice, particularly in our family courts wherein the administration of justice is made corporeal. The market may be able to provide a range of educative, self-help, partnership-model services to allow some family disputants to make reasonably informed decisions, fill in the necessary forms[57] and to mediate resolutions to their disputes. But unless we simplify our court processes and procedures to make lay participation not just a choice but the goal, we must allow the vulnerable and those of limited means to obtain publicly funded legal representation to obtain access to family justice. Advocacy is a reserved activity for very good reason. The courts have to embody justice. If we lose that we lose the foundation of our society. Yes, the market may be able to deliver greater access to family legal help, but only if the market is regulated in a way to promote fair competition between all professionals. It appears that everyone is a family lawyer now, but not all are regulated equally.

[57] See the Dutch Legal Aid Board's *Rechtwijzer* site www.hiil.org/news/rechtwijzer-game-changer, which is a truly ground-breaking way to provide access to family justice, for those who are internet literate. For a discussion of the relative strengths and weaknesses and a greater range of examples including telephone hotlines and websites, see Smith and Paterson, *Face to Face Legal Services and Their Alternatives* (n 15). For Australian responses, see Dewar, J, Smith, B and Banks, C, *Litigants in Person in the Family Court of Australia A Report to the Family Court of Australia Research Report no 20* (Family Court of Australia, 2000). For a key recent study in England and Wales, see Trinder, L et al, *Litigants in Person in Private Family Law Cases* (Ministry of Justice, 2014).

18

New Ways to Seek Legal Information and Advice on Family Matters in England and Wales: From Professional Legal Services to Google and Private Ordering

MAVIS MACLEAN

INTRODUCTION

THIS VOLUME REPRESENTS a response from scholars in a variety of jurisdictions, common and civil law, with and without various forms of public support for access to family justice, to widespread change in access to law and the legal professions in managing family matters. The preceding chapter from Lisa Webley describes the impact on the legal professions of the deregulation and marketisation of legal services in England and Wales, compounded by the reduction in availability of both private resources and public funding due to the economic recession. We may expect to see a move away from traditional professional client care, including legal information, advice and support, towards the separation out of these elements which will then reach the user through new and separate channels. This chapter starts from an acknowledgement that this change is occurring, as in other jurisdictions, in a neoliberal policy context, and looks at new developments in accessing legal information and advice services. With a tradition of generous legal aid in family matters, pro bono work has not in the past been focused in this area, though this too may be changing. But two new developments are beginning to emerge following the restriction of legal aid for family matters under the Legal Aid and Sentencing and Punishment of Offenders Act 2012 (LASPO) and the financial obstacles for all except those with considerable resources to seeking full legal services from the legal professions. We are seeing increased interest in low-cost internet access to as yet largely unregulated information services, while those dependent on public funding for legal advice are now directed for conflict resolution towards mediation. Mediation has remained in scope for funding after LASPO, and may offer general legal information, but not advice. The boundaries between information and advice are, however, a little indistinct in practice if not in theory. These two new developments, it is suggested, do not so much fill the gap left by the impact of reduced public and private spending on legal advice but circle around it, like a bagel with a hole in the middle. Nevertheless we need a clearer picture of how legal information and advice are being provided and whether current developments are likely to be able to sustain universal access to a family justice system. This chapter can do no more than begin to describe the development and scope of some of the new forms of web-based advice, and raise questions about the provision of information and advice within Alternative Dispute Resolution, drawing on data from a research project in progress at the Oxford Centre for Family Law and Policy (OXFLAP) on the Delivery of Family Justice in England and Wales in Post Modern Society.

The provision of web-based services and their links to the legal profession will be addressed first. This route to justice will then contrasted with the provision of information and advice by lawyer mediators and non-lawyer mediators in the mediation setting. The role of lawyers, though changing, is not disappearing.

WEB-BASED SERVICES: A CONTINUUM FROM INFORMATION TO ADVICE

The recent development of divorce-related services offered over the internet is perhaps the most innovative but least understood part of the changing landscape for legal information and advice in family matters.

Richard Susskind[1] has described what he called the decomposition of professional work into its component parts. He suggested that we will soon no longer see traditional lawyers offering what is sometimes called 'the full legal', taking care of the client in every aspect of a case, often with a strong personal relationship, but instead we may see people who are not necessarily accredited members of the legal profession working in the legal sector, offering legal services and legal help in new ways. We may expect less individual client care, and more digital availability of legal information, legal documents and maybe some advice. Alan Paterson and Roger Smith have looked at the issue in depth for the Nuffield Foundation,[2] stimulated by the

[1] 'Beyond the Professions' *The Guardian* 19 June 2014.

[2] Paterson, A and Smith, R, *Face to Face Legal Services and Their Alternatives: Global Lessons from the Digital Revolution* (London, Nuffield Foundation, 2014).

response of the Coalition government's programme of unprecedented cuts to public expenditure following the financial crisis, which included a cut of £350 million from the £2 billion annual budget for legal aid. They were encouraged by the success of digital services in other jurisdictions, particularly the *De Rechtwijzer: eerste hulp bij conflicten*, developed by the Legal Aid Board in the Netherlands as part of a drive to reduce public spending on legal assistance by moving away from traditional representation in law centres towards self-help at law counters, together with a new free interactive advice service for family disputes, which includes the calculation of child maintenance amounts.[3] Current research to evaluate *De Rechtwijzer* is optimistic about levels of success. There are, however, concerns about the limitations. If, for example, a mother and father do not agree on the amount of income stated by either parent, a child maintenance assessment cannot take place. Limitations to the scope of these services were also documented recently for England and Wales in experimental empirical research reported by Catrina Denvir in her doctoral thesis 2014[4] on how young people use websites to address legal problems. She found that they could find relevant factual information, but were not able to envisage the next step without talking to someone they trusted. Parents were mentioned. The websites could provide information, but not advice and support, both of which may be particularly important if action is needed in family matters.

How far has this digital legal revolution progressed in England and Wales? The most recent large-scale data come from a report from YouGov-SixthSense, a well-regarded market research company, entitled *Family Law–Divorce*, published in August 2013,[5] which suggested that, following the restrictions to legal aid for divorce-related issues in the aftermath of LASPO, there was likely to be an increase in 'DIY' or do-it-yourself divorce because of increasing inability to pay privately for legal help. 24 per cent of their sample of 866 UK adults aged over 25 who had been involved in divorce proceedings in the last five years had met the financial criteria and used publicly funded legal help. Such a group in future would need to look for free or low-cost help. They also found that a quarter of their total sample had not used any kind of legal help, and that among the younger group aged 25 to 35, a third had opted for trying to arrange their own divorce. In the five years up to 2013, only 6 per cent of the YouGov sample had used web-based services, mainly to download the necessary forms. This is only a tenth of the

[3] These developments are being carefully monitored: see eg Dijksterhuis, B, *Users' Opinion about Online Self Help Tools on Alimony Payment*, Paper to the RCSL Legal Professions Group, Frauenchiemsee, (Free University of Amsterdam, July 2014).

[4] Denvir, C, *What is the Net Worth? Young People, Civil Justice, and the Internet* PhD Thesis (University College, London, 2014).

[5] The full reports can be accessed at: http://sixthsense.yougov.com/general-market-reports/family-law-divorce-/family-law-divorce-.aspx. A summary is available in (2013) 43 *Family Law* 1086–89.

60 per cent who had used a solicitor. But the prediction of increased use of web-based services may nevertheless be well founded. YouGov also looked at legal costs for divorce, which, while considerable, were not as high as sometimes suggested. Of their sample who had divorced before the legal aid cuts arising from LASPO came into effect, nearly half of the divorces had cost under £2000, a further quarter over £5000 and only 6 per cent over £20,000. By comparison, total legal fees for those arranging their own divorce were less than £200 for a third of the group, and less than £500 for two-thirds. When higher figures are quoted for legal costs, they quite often refer to final contested hearings, which occur only rarely. For example, the National Family Mediation (NFM) website quotes Novitas Investments as saying that the average cost for solicitors' fees is £40,000 per party in London and £13,000 each outside London. The cost of a contested final hearing in a big money matter can be well over a million pounds. But a case observed for our study recently which included financial issues and which resulted in an order of the court by consent without a contested hearing but with the help of a solicitor cost £750.

It seems that we are far from universal use of digital legal help, though this may change as the technology develops and the financial incentives remain or increase. But in an unregulated setting without effective quality control, there are questions about what kind of function these services perform and at what cost to the user, both direct, in the form of charges, and indirect, in terms of the possible impact of less than optimal service. We need to know more about what exactly is on offer. Is it general information or information specific to the individual? Earlier attempts to provide general information following the Family Law Act 1996 proved unpopular, as people wanted advice as to their personal circumstances, not general information. We also need to know where costs are arising. Who is providing this information and advice: is it a 'lawyer' in the sense of a practitioner accredited to the profession of solicitor or barrister with lengthy training and professional accountability, or a paralegal with a similar regulatory structure but more limited expertise, or an individual with an interest in the subject (perhaps with access to professional legal advice), or just wanting a job to do? What is the relationship between these digital services and the work of accredited legal professionals? What kind of matters can be dealt with online and where is the point at which face-to-face help is required?

To examine these questions, as part of an exploratory study of changing legal services in family justice,[6] OXFLAP carried out a small survey from Oxford of online divorce services in 2013, updated in 2014, to try to discover what is being provided by internet services. Is it information or advice? Who is providing these services (solicitors, barristers, paralegals or

[6] 'Delivering Family Justice in Post Modern Society' Research in progress (Oxford, OXFLAP, Department of Social Policy and Intervention).

others), at what cost, what kinds of clients find them helpful, and how do these services fit into the larger picture of support for men and women going through the process of separation?

We used the following search terms on Google in summer 2013 and autumn 2014: DIY Divorce, Divorce Advice, Divorce Petition Forms, Divorce Papers, Online Divorce. Using the first page of Google entries, we found 41 entries in 2013, with little change in 2014, many of the names coming up more than once.[7] The majority of entries were from law firms advertising their services, including the Co-op Legal Services (n=10). Two counsellors and one mediator also presented their services. There were also four independent advice services (Citizens' Advice Bureaux, Mumsnet and Netmums, the Independent Money Advice Service), two government websites offering forms and three commercial services offering legal documents and notes of guidance or help with financial problems. But there was also a group of six services which we have termed the New Specialist Providers offering a new kind of online divorce service which we will address in more detail below.

If we approach these new ways of accessing information and advice from the consumer perspective, various difficulties emerge. The names of a number of services are confusing; quite often a firm of solicitors used a name which gave the impression of something less traditional, for example 'Alternative Family Law' or 'Divorce Rights'. At the same time, some of the non-law firms used titles which gave the impression of being a more traditional law firm, such as 'Divorce Aid: Solicitors', which on further investigation turned out not to be a firm of solicitors but an agency which helped potential clients identify an appropriate firm of solicitors for their needs. If the consumer chooses a service, what might they be offered? We found a wide range of products, ranging from simple document handling to some document checking (analogous to the service provided when a passport application is checked by the Post Office for a small fee), to packages offering to support the working out of a financial agreement, sometimes described as supported divorce, managed divorce, and even solicitor-supported or solicitor-managed divorce. There was little evidence of willingness to become involved in child-related matters. The distinctions between these descriptions may be difficult for a potential user to understand, especially as such a client is likely to be under considerable stress, and to be a first-time user without experience of this kind of service or problem. Those providing the service may be accredited professionals regulated by the Solicitors Regulation Authority who have professional indemnity insurance, or they may have some kind of business relationship with accredited professionals, or they may not. Costs range from free access to legal information, though there are usually costs

[7] We rely on the earlier data updated where necessary.

for any form of advice, to several hundred pounds for solicitor-managed divorce including a financial agreement. The divorce or separation issues dealt with range from non-conflicted divorce without ancillary issues to the negotiation of quite complex financial arrangements. Some of the information provided was of high quality, and was similar to the kind of information available on a number of law firm websites without charge, particularly those formerly offering legal aid for family work.

The first name to come up in response to our google search has remained the same over the last two years, Quickie Divorce. This claims to deal with (or perhaps have their website visited by) over 15,000 people a year, which could mean almost 20 per cent of the total divorcing population in England and Wales. The website offers to initiate a divorce petition immediately for £37, the price remaining the same since last year. Court fees are not mentioned. In addition, for the higher price of £67, 'you can have all the divorce forms you'll need to send to the court completed for you'. When we called the advertised phone number the reply was quick and friendly, but the speaker was insistent that they could only deal with cases where there was no dispute. When asked about a consent order, we were told that this is included in a more expensive package costing £135. When asked if Quickie Divorce staff were solicitors, the answer was a clear no, but accompanied by the explanation that financial consent orders would be sent out to an external solicitor to be checked. In sum, Quickie Divorce was offering a low-cost document handling service for cases without issues to be resolved. It could provide a useful, cheap and accessible service for those divorcing without issues, but was unlikely to be able to help in those cases where difficulties emerge during the course of proceedings, and could be problematic where there was power imbalance between the parties where financial information might be concealed. Although there was no claim to be offering legal advice, other than as to process and choice of service, nevertheless this kind of procedural advice can have grave consequences, for example when choosing in which jurisdiction to bring proceedings, with far-reaching legal implications. The distinction between information and advice is not easy to draw, and those providing information without professional indemnity insurance would be unable to offer redress for misinformation or what was in effect poor advice. But the impact of limited or misinformation can be wide-reaching and any error or misjudgement could be costly.

Divorce Online offers a range of services starting from £45 for all the forms needed and a guide to filling them in, and sample letters to send to the court. In autumn 2014 they were still charging £189 for managed divorce with £229 for a clean break and £385 for a solicitor-managed divorce. When asked over the phone whether they were a firm of solicitors, the answer was 'No, we are paralegals, qualified to take two people who are willing through the divorce process. We deal with amicable divorce'. Again this is a useful service for those seeking an amicable divorce, and offers good value for money, with input from solicitors present but clearly defined and visible.

Forms and process and even consent orders can be effectively supported with web-based good quality information, and support with form filling, so long as there is no dispute over fact or potential outcome. Information can be specific on the finely tuned and interactive websites. But when specific information shades into general and even specific advice and support, individualised professional input will be needed. Not surprisingly, mechanisms have been developing to bridge these gaps, through web service use of legal advisers, and links to enable users to move from information through to professional advice and support in increasingly complex packages. Wikivorce is an interesting example of formal cooperation between a web-based enterprise and an established firm of solicitors. Individual solicitors have also set up their own websites. And the Co-op Legal Services have set up a consumer-oriented structure which enables the client to move from purchasing basic forms, securing assistance with completing them to limited legal help and full legal service as necessary, to be charged for as needed. These will be discussed in more detail below.

Perhaps the most impressive online service was and remains Wikivorce, a not-for-profit service set up by Ian Rispin to provide high quality legal information, advice and more. Wikivorce offers a price comparison table, comparing costs for fixed price deals in a number of other firms, including Nelsons, which is said to have the cheapest fees, and Woolley & Co as the most expensive by a factor of eight. Wikivorce offers a free Divorce Calculator for use by parties. This asks for information on the husband's and wife's income, and a description of, first, their household income needs, divided into essential expenditure and childcare costs and, finally, a schedule of assets and liabilities. The Calculator also gives a precise account of how a court would approach any such calculation, with the first portion of income allocated on prioritised needs, and any surplus allocated under the heading of lifestyle, taking into account contributions made and compensation for detriment. The Calculator and accompanying text are clear, well-informed and detailed but would require good language skills and a clear head from any potential user. Following the reference to solicitor-managed divorce, a follow-up phone call asked whether there were solicitors working for Wikivorce. The answer was no, but that Wikivorce worked with a firm of solicitors called Brethertons. On following up with the firm, it was learnt that this was indeed the case and that there was an arrangement whereby the legal firm kept the website information up to date and accurate with respect to the law, and in return received access to potential private clients. When a client used a Wikivorce package, the firm provided the solicitor element, and was available to be called on for further assistance if the matter became too complex or conflicted for the simple Wikivorce package. The lawyers would decide when such a point had been reached, and offer to take the case on, having agreed a fee. The firm has an excellent reputation for good quality, reasonably priced work. Wikivorce benefits from having a high quality website, the firm benefits by having access to a stream of clients, and the clients get a good quality service at a reasonable price, and successful symbiosis is achieved.

This kind of connection between a website and a law firm can work well in a variety of ways. In the case of Wikivorce, the web is the starting point and base. But the balance may be different. For example, a family solicitor of many years' experience working as a consultant with a central London law firm has set up a website for the firm offering low-cost web-based work, but is able to do more for users by way of filling in forms as an accredited solicitor than a non-lawyer would be able to do, and to offer more complex advice, support and representation in his professional capacity, charging accordingly. This way of working clearly fits Susskind's[8] description of 'decomposition', with each element of work being done by the most cost-effective person, and goes further than the more common term 'unbundling' which simply describes the solicitor as defining which elements of a case will be included in his work for a particular price.

The final example of integrated digital- and lawyer-based information and advice linkage is Co-op Legal Services (CLS), where originally only young and enthusiastic solicitors were recruited to provide a good value, high quality service with a range of options which could be accessed in a flexible way. A client might begin by using the free initial conversation and website information, buying the basic divorce pack, with guidance on how to fill in the forms, and have them checked, and then if necessary move to a lawyer-supported package which, if needed, could become the 'full legal' service with face-to-face meetings as well as representation in court. This venture was launched with great enthusiasm in 2012 and received a positive response from the public, though difficulties arose later due to problems in other parts of the Coop business. Nevertheless, CLS has gained a reputation for high quality innovative work, including help with evidencing domestic violence to achieve exemption from the exclusion of private family work if applications for legal aid are a possibility, and a contract with NFM for mediation, though this has not been widely used. The service remains however still on the way to productivity and profit.

To attempt to summarise, the new specialist web-based providers range from the CLS, which was initially fully staffed by accredited solicitors, offering a flexible set of legal services accompanied by web-based document handling, to Wikivorce, which began at the opposite end of the spectrum. From being a specialist web-based information service, this has developed effective links with a law firm, and legal advice at various levels of complexity can be purchased. The non-lawyer digital DIY low-cost services for non-contested

[8] See Susskind, 'Beyond the Professions' (n 1).

divorces work well for those without issues. At the far end of the spectrum in terms of quality of service there remain poor quality services which offer free advice, which on examination is usually not advice but only information, and is rarely free beyond the first approach. For example, Just Answer asks how important your question is to you, and charges are set in accordance with your answer. The quicker the response required the higher the fee. Overall, however, wherever problems were complex and the service was of high quality, we found that lawyers were involved.

LEGAL INFORMATION AND ADVICE IN MEDIATION (ADR AND PRIVATE ORDERING)

How do these findings relate to the other potential source of expanding access to legal information and advice in the private ordering world of Alternative Dispute Resolution, in particular family mediation? In England and Wales the mediation of family disputes has been encouraged since the 1970s, developing from the conciliation movement which had tried to reconcile parties whose relationship was breaking down. Mediation tries to help the parties find their way to an amicable individual settlement on how to arrange their finances and childcare after separation. Governments have been supportive, as they have long been suspicious of the legal profession's role in divorce, appearing to believe (despite the evidence)[9] that lawyers working at arm's length in an adversarial system are likely to increase hostilities in order to maintain their professional status and associated rewards. Instead of going to lawyers and courts to settle disputes in a public arena, it was thought that private conversation and negotiation facilitated by a mediator would lead to increased ability to manage the separation, and to outcomes which the parties would 'own' and therefore accept. Others, including the author, remained concerned that divorce was being characterised as a dispute or series of disputes, rather than a difficult transition during which it is important, particularly for the more vulnerable party, to be well informed about the legal framework and practical aspects of the change, and to be supported in case dispute does arise in order to reach fair and informed settlement. The role of the legal framework is to provide a clear statement of social norms and access to the means of working within them, with some guarantee of compliance for a negotiated settlement. There are many ways of working through the divorce transition, and more than one source of information, advice and support may be needed at different stages. A couple approaching separation may have no dispute, but may not know what they will or should do, or be expected to do, to fit within the

[9] Lewis, PSC, *Assumptions about Lawyers in Policy Statements* (Lord Chancellor's Department Research Series February 2000 no 1/00).

legal framework. Legal information and perhaps advice at that stage may prevent a dispute, and thus the need even for mediation, arising. If a dispute emerges, mediation appears to be a useful additional service, but is not a substitute for legal information and advice given that divorce includes a change in legal civil status, often sale and purchase of houses, division of other assets, and long-term financial planning as well as provision for the welfare of children, and that there is a possibility of imbalance between the parties in knowledge and bargaining capacity. This need for legal help is recognised by government in LASPO through the provision of limited funding for help from a lawyer and mediators. In financial matters mediators are advised to encourage clients to check their position with their own lawyers. Mediation takes place outside the legal system, does not require practitioners to have full legal training or accreditation, and cannot lead to binding or enforceable agreement without further support from the justice system.

Governments in England and Wales, as elsewhere, turned to mediation as an attractive and cost-effective solution to the problem of increasing public spending on family legal disputes as the divorce rate increased. Mediation received strong government support in England and Wales throughout the 1980s, leading up to the attempt to introduce information meetings as part of the Family Law Act 1996 which were designed to encourage people to mediate.[10] But this part of the Act was not brought into effect, and government instead began to require anyone seeking legal aid to first see a mediator who would encourage the use of mediation. When the government set up the Family Justice Review in 2010 the terms of reference included the statement that 'mediation and similar support should be used as far as possible to support individuals themselves to reach agreement about arrangements, rather than having an arrangement imposed by the courts'. The statement yet again ignores the fact, now documented by Hitchings et al, that most arrangements are currently reached through solicitor-led negotiation and though they can be made into consent orders of the court for enforceability they are rarely court imposed.[11] The Children and Families Act 2014 has taken the process a stage further and anyone making an application to the court in a private law matter is now required to attend a meeting (MIAM, Mediation Information and Assessment Meeting) to learn about mediation and be assessed for their suitability. In the virtual absence of publicly funded legal information or advice after LASPO, apart from pro bono work,[12] the mediator now appears to be a potential source of such help, though not, of course, of legal representation or support. Might mediation be contributing

[10] Lord Chancellor's Department, *Looking to the Future: Mediation and the Ground for Divorce* (Cm 2799, 1995).

[11] Hitchings, E, Miles, J and Woodward, H, 'Assembling the Jigsaw Puzzle: Understanding Financial Settlement on Divorce' (2014) 44 *Family Law* 309.

[12] *In the matter of D (a child)* [2014] EWFC 39.

to meeting the now unmet need for legal information, advice and support which has followed LASPO? Or should we question the existence of such a need, and are family matters being successfully 'delegalised' and privatised, to be dealt with in other ways? In the Child Support Act 1991 government some time ago began the process of removing what had been legal matters from the legal arena by making child support the subject of administrative decision-making, and recently went further towards emphasising the advantages of private decision making within the family and introducing charges for using the state system. Are courts and lawyers now to be no longer the service of last resort, but to disappear altogether from family matters?

It is hoped not, as family law fulfils a number of essential functions, particularly in a diverse society, by providing a framework which encapsulates the protection of human rights within the family where power imbalances are inevitable and emotions run high. If this is so and there is unmet need, what kind of contribution might mediation make? According to the Family Mediation Council Code of Practice (para 2.1), mediation is intended 'to assist participants to reach the decision they consider appropriate to their own particular circumstances'. Given this guidance, what can mediators contribute to this unmet need? What kind of legal training do mediators have, and what kind of legal information, general or specific, can they provide? Could such information in practice amount to advice? Drawing on data from both observation and interviews in the Delivery of Family Justice project, the legal training and qualifications which mediators might draw on is set out, and the Codes of Practice for mediators considered, together with what was observed in practice after sitting with non-legally trained mediators and lawyers who have trained as and work as mediators.

Training

Given the different routes to practising as a mediator, with five organisations, including Resolution (the association of family lawyers) originally providing NFM accredited courses, it is not surprising that the legal content of training is hard to define.[13] A nine-day NFM foundation course comprises three days on intake and assessment of suitability for mediation, three days on children matters and three days on finance and property. These training days are made up of short periods of information-giving by trainers, including video presentations, periods for role play and discussion in small groups, with the whole group of about 20 participants coming together for reflection and discussion. Each of the subject areas touches on both

[13] This section is informed by Webley, L, *Adversarialism and Consensus?* (New Orleans, Quid Pro Quo, 2010) 71.

family law and other sources of information, and the inevitable overlapping makes it difficult to be precise, but it is estimated that the nine days includes approximately three hours of family law training, with written materials provided. The aim of the training is to enable the mediator to give general legal information when appropriate, and to be able, if both parties agree, to indicate when a proposal being made falls outside the legal framework and would not be acceptable to a court if the matter were to proceed to a hearing. There may be difficulties if only one party wishes to hear this information. Further qualification by accreditation to be able to undertake publicly funded work requires preparation of a Portfolio, but legal knowledge was not one of the items specifically identified for assessment. But the legal trainer said in interview:

> we teach, if you don't know, get legal advice either yourself from colleagues or from our legal consultation service, or advise the client sees a lawyer … most NFM mediators go into services and have colleagues, but sole practitioners vary in legal knowledge. They should have an update each year when they reapply for membership of NFM, but it's not always on finance.

At the second day of a Resolution foundation mediation training course dealing with children issues, the emphasis observed was not primarily on legal training as those being trained were practising lawyers. Webley points out however that a solicitor's training may include no family law training at all. The law degree or the legal conversion course known as the Graduate Diploma in Law, including the subsequent Legal Practice Course, plus the two-year training contract, which must include the Professional Skills Course, are designed to provide generic legal skills considered to be transferable across subject areas, but do not necessarily include a family law element, though for accreditation as a specialist family lawyer further experience is required.

Codes of Practice

What do the codes of practice for mediators say about offering legal information or advice? Note the mediators may also be qualified as solicitors, and may practise in one field or both, with lawyer mediators offering mediation as one of many services available from their law practice, or offering sessions for another law firm. Non-lawyer mediators also offer sessions within a law firm, or work within a mediation service, or as sole practitioners. Charges by lawyer mediators are usually at the same rate as for legal advice, but of course there are two clients not one, and the meeting is usually 90 minutes, rather longer than many lawyer-client sessions, and there is little preparation time and no contact outside sessions.

Having set out the purpose of mediation as being to assist participants to reach the decision they consider appropriate to their own particular circumstance (para 2.1) the Family Mediation Council (FMC) Code states:

> 5.3 Mediators must remain neutral on the outcome of a mediation at all times. Mediators must not seek to impose their preferred outcome on the participants or to influence them to adopt it, whether by attempting to predict the outcome of court proceedings or otherwise. However, if the participants consent, they may inform them that they consider that the resolution they are considering might fall outside the parameters which a court might approve or order. They may inform participants of possible courses of action, their legal or other implications, and assist them to explore these, but must make it clear that they are not giving advice.
>
> 5.7.1 Mediators must have special regard to the welfare of any children of the family. They should encourage parties to focus on the needs and interests of the child as well as on their own and
>
> 5.7.2 (mediators) must encourage participants to consider the children's wishes and feelings.
>
> 6.15 The mediator must inform participants of the advantages of seeking independent legal advice when desirable in the course of the mediation … before any final agreement, and inform them of the risks and disadvantages if they do not do so

As of October 2014 discussion is in progress about moving towards a unified code of practice. There is still some difference between the code used by solicitors working as mediators and non-lawyers working as mediators with respect to the role of law. Full agreement has not yet been reached, and some differences between lawyer mediators and non-lawyer mediators remain with respect to how far the mediator may suggest proposals, how they should respond to proposals which sit outside the legal frame, and how far they refer to the law in sessions. The Solicitors Regulatory Handbook 2011 quoted on the Law Society website gives general rules and principles for solicitors' practice, including mediation. The principle of not giving advice is described as permeating this code. But, similarly to the FMC Code, para 5.6 states 'the mediator may suggest possible solutions and help to explore them', 5.7 that they 'should assist to identify information and documents and how to obtain them' and 5.9 that 'parties should be helped to reach resolutions which feel appropriate to them in their particular cases, these may not be the same as those arrived at in the event of an adjudication by the court'. At 5.9 it is stated that the mediator should inform the parties if they consider the decision falls outside what a court would accept (whereas the FMC Code merely states that a mediator 'may' do this) and should terminate if the solution proposed is unconscionable or fundamentally inappropriate.

If we are to consider mediation as a source of legal information and advice, what can we assume is on offer? A number of questions arise:

What is the state of knowledge? Non-lawyer mediators have little formal legal training but are encouraged to seek legal advice for themselves, and to send clients to seek legal information and advice. Under legal aid regulations, any mediation which receives public funding must be about a justiciable matter in dispute, and not purely a therapeutic or supportive intervention. Lawyer mediators may not have had a specific family law component in their training but they will have practised family law and are expected by the Law Society to have detailed knowledge of core areas of family law and of legal process.[14]

What does the code of practice require? The basic framework for mediation is that the parties are negotiating, the mediator is facilitating. General legal information is expected, but legal advice may not be given. In practice however the distinction between information and advice is not always clear. What constitutes legal advice? A sign saying 'Private Property' is legal information. But a sign saying 'Unauthorised vehicles will be clamped' appears to go beyond merely providing information. It certainly seeks to influence decisions. If this is characterised as information and not advice, then most 'traditional' legal advice provided by lawyers to their clients is not advice either, since it will usually take the form of pointing out legal consequences of actions, which a client is not obliged to follow.

And when is a proposal outside the legal frame? The Children Act 1989 requires the interests of the child to be given paramount consideration. The NFM Code of Practice only asks for parents to be advised to think about their children's needs as well as their own. If a parent thinks about the child and then puts the needs of, say, a new partner first, while not being in any way an abusive or neglectful parent, is this outside the legal framework? A mediator affiliated to the FMC mediator may, if the parties agree, 'inform' when a proposal is outside the legal frame. The Law Society mediator may make suggestions for proposals and must 'inform' if the proposal is outside the legal frame. Mediators are required to 'assist' in exploring options, but in doing so it may be difficult to avoid indicating a preference for one option over another, and if only one option is presented any assistance will in effect amount to advice. The giving of legal information may in practice have the same effect as providing advice. This has profound consequences because, as has been explained, public funding has been withdrawn for most family legal advice, yet it remains for family mediation. Leaving aside these issues, what in practice can the mediator offer by way of legal information and advice? The non-lawyer mediators may have limited legal information, in which case we must hope for caution in providing advice. The

[14] ibid, 102.

lawyer mediators have all the relevant information but may see themselves as forbidden to share it, and certainly not able to give advice which is other than neutral. They are, however, able to make suggestions, within the legal framework, and are required to question proposals which are outside what a court would accept.

As part of our study we have now observed over 20 mediation sessions, and present two examples concerning the provision of legal information or advice.

The first is taken from a financial session conducted by Rex, a non-lawyer mediator. During the third and (hopefully) final session with a couple in their forties with two children aged 10 and 12, the question of child support was being discussed. The father had used the Child Support Calculator, and accepted the total figure. But he proposed withholding a certain amount regularly for larger expenses such as school trips. The mother was horrified by this suggestion as she believed that the even the full amount would leave her under financial strain in caring for the children, who were to live with her, with frequent and staying access with the father. Rex did not express support for the proposal, but gave no reasons for this when asked why by father. The couple became angry with each other, and the father was frustrated by Rex's lack of support without apparent reasons. The session ended acrimoniously. After the session Rex commented to the observer that he was pleased that he had not been drawn into giving the couple the information he had about how the child support amounts are set to meet basic day-to-day requirements and not the kind of extra costs the father had in mind. But that could be seen as general information, in the sense of being an explanation of the structure of the child support system. It could become specific information if related to this father's proposal and this mother's refusal, and even advice if Rex had gone further and explained that he had not supported the idea because it lay outside the intention of the scheme or what a court would accept. But withholding the information/advice did nothing to promote agreement; giving it might have promoted informed and fair settlement.

The second example comes from a session conducted by a solicitor also working as a qualified mediator. Carol was meeting with a couple of similar age, who were moving on to talk about finance but wanted to report on the agreement they had reached following a previous session about how their daughter, aged 12, should be looked after. The mother had wanted a settled routine, weekdays with her and overnights with dad only at weekends. The father wanted more flexibility over mid-week overnight stays. Agreement had clearly been reached between the couple. But Carol asked whether they had discussed the plan with their daughter and what she thought about it. The couple had not done so, wanting to present their daughter with something secure and 'sorted'. But Carol, as a lawyer, drew on the Children Act 1989 requirement to place the interests of the child first and foremost and to take into account her wishes and feelings. Carol re-opened an agreed element of their separation arrangements and suggested (advised) that they consider sending their daughter to have a private session with the specialist child-qualified mediator. She used her legal knowledge to press for welfare paramountcy, seeking the best possible outcome for the child even though an agreement had been made.

These are two extreme examples of the accessibility of legal information and advice in mediation and its possible implications. Given that, as noted above, the legal framework in family matters puts children first and looks for flexibility in finance, it is important to see how it may be accessed through the current maze of training requirements and codes of practice which lack clarity about how far a mediator may go in this direction.

CONCLUSION

If we accept that the legal framework is of value in protecting the vulnerable and promoting fair agreements in family matters in times of stress, it follows that parties need to know what the law requires and how they can agree enforceable decisions in the shadow of the law. Among the lawyer mediators there is a wealth of relevant information and potential advice. It is hard to see why this should not be used to best effect by the lawyer mediator, seeing the parties together using their mediation training, but without restricting their potential use of legal information and advice. For a solicitor, the interests of the client can already include the interests of the family. The Law Society's protocol on family law can be considered to extend the solicitor's duty to act in the best interests of the client to include the best interests of other adult family members[15] as it does already under the Children Act 1989 with respect to the children. The Solicitors Regulation Authority Handbook, 2011, para 3.6 goes as far as to permit a solicitor to act for both parties

> where there is a client conflict and the clients have a substantially common interest in relation to a matter or a particular aspect of it, … if: (a) you have explained the relevant issues and risks to the clients and you have a reasonable belief that they understand those issues and risks; (b) all the clients have given informed consent in writing to you acting; (c) you are satisfied that it is reasonable for you to act for all the clients and that it is in their best interests; and (d) you are satisfied that the benefits to the clients of you doing so outweigh the risks.

[15] Webley, ibid 164, observes that solicitors need to consider both parties when redressing power imbalances.

The door may be ajar for recognising the validity of the provision of legal advice to both parties within a mediation session.

However hard government tries to restrict the role of lawyers in family matters, and despite the economic costs associated with the provision of legal services, when we look at the new ways of accessing legal information and advice we find the lawyers playing an important part, not only through new attention to pro bono work, and new ways of marketing traditional services, but also underpinning both IT developments and the mediation process.

19

Can there be Family Justice Without Law?

JOHN EEKELAAR

THE DOWNGRADING OF FAMILY LAW

SOME MONTHS AFTER the sharp reduction in legal aid availability for private law family matters came into effect in England and Wales on 1 April 2013,[1] a specialist legal aid family lawyer told Mavis Maclean and me of a visit from a client, a lone mother living on benefits, who had said that the estranged father of her two-year-old child had appeared and 'taken' the child with him. As she did not qualify under the few remaining categories where private law legal aid was available, the solicitor had to say there was nothing she could do for her. The solicitor was leaving practice in disillusion and disgust. In November 2014, it was reported that private law court applications in family matters in the Bristol area were running at 36 per cent lower since the legal aid changes, and nationally that in nearly three-quarters of such cases that did go to court, either one or both parties were not legally represented.[2]

This cannot be said to be an unforeseen, or even unintended, consequence of government action. There has been a widespread and apparently growing belief that, at least in the areas covered by 'private family law', the law should have little or even no place. I noted this first after the UK Coalition government first announced its plans in 2010 to cut back drastically on legal aid in such cases.[3] It expressed the view that 'issues' that arise from a person's 'own personal choices' were not likely to be considered 'of the highest importance' for legal aid, and that not everyone involved in such disputes is entitled to 'a particular outcome in litigation'.[4] The resultant legislation

[1] Legal Aid, Sentencing and Punishment of Offenders Act 2012.

[2] Wildblood, S, Goldingham, C and Evans, J, '"The Way we Are": Accessing the Courts after LASPO' (2014) *Family Law* November Issue.

[3] Eekelaar, J, '"Not of the Highest Importance": Family Justice under Threat' (2011) 33 *Journal of Social Welfare and Family Law* 311.

[4] Ministry of Justice, *Proposals for the Reform of Legal Aid in England and Wales*, Consultation Paper CP 12/10 (2010) para 4.19.

(Legal Aid, Sentencing and Punishment of Offenders Act 2012 (LASPO)) has retained its availability in private family law cases only in specific circumstances where a party is deemed to be 'vulnerable' (largely as a result of violence, for which there must be objective evidence), and certain international cases.[5] It is not accepted that being at risk of injustice in a family dispute can in itself be seen as creating such vulnerability. As Moses LJ said:

> Analysis of Part 1 of Schedule 1 shows that the statute seeks to confine civil legal services which the Lord Chancellor must secure to cases which are judged to be of the greatest need. Those cases are identified by reference not only to the circumstances which an individual might face but also by reference to personal characteristics or attributes, for example, children or those suffering from mental ill health.[6]

In that case the High Court held that the attempt of the Lord Chancellor to impose further restrictions on legal aid that would exclude funding even of those 'needy' cases if the claimant did not satisfy residence requirements was illegal as falling outside the purpose of the 2012 Act. But the attempt to exclude those cases shows that the government does not see the state's role as seeking to secure justice as an end in itself, but only as providing limited assistance to people who resort to the legal system to secure special provision (such as special education) or protection (for example, against violence). Like welfare benefits, therefore, it was thought legal aid should not be available to foreigners. The idea that everyone should be treated justly under the law appears to be abandoned. Therefore the government has not produced resources to assist people who may now appear in court without representation as a result of these changes. It must be concluded that in its view it would be better if such people did not use the courts at all: they should simply get on with their lives.

This approach is manifested in the interpretation given by the Lord Chancellor (who is also the Secretary of State for Justice) to the provision in the 2012 Act allowing legal aid to be granted 'in exceptional circumstances' to cases falling outside the permitted categories of 'need'. One of these is where 'it is necessary to make the services available to the individual under this Part because failure to do so would be a breach of (i) the individual's Convention rights (within the meaning of the Human Rights Act 1998)'.[7] The courts have viewed this as referring primarily to the ability of individuals to

[5] LASPO, ss 8–10 and sch 1, pt 1. An exception is made in 'exceptional circumstances' where failure to provide legal aid would breach someone's rights under the European Convention on Human Rights. This is extremely difficult to operate in practice, and was enacted simply to make the legislation appear to be compatible with the UK's obligations under the Convention.

[6] *R (on the Application of the Public Law Project) v Secretary of State for Justice* [2014] EWHC 2365 (Admin) at [37].

[7] LASPO 2012, s 10(3).

access the procedures necessary to protect their Convention rights (such as the Article 8 right to respect for private and family life). As Collins J stated:

> since the procedural requirements exist in order to make effective the protection provided by the relevant Article, the ultimate question must be whether denial of legal aid would either cause or produce a risk of causing a breach of a requirement needed to avoid a breach of the substantive right conferred by the relevant Article.[8]

Whether such a breach could occur must, in the words of the European Court of Human Rights,

> be determined on the basis of the particular facts and circumstances of each case and will depend, inter alia, upon the importance of what is at stake for the applicant in the proceedings, the complexity of the relevant law and procedure and the applicant's capacity to represent him or herself effectively.[9]

However, the guidance given by the Lord Chancellor stresses how rarely legal aid should be granted where Article 8 rights are in issue, asserting that the threshold is whether 'withholding of legal aid make(s) assertion of the claim practically impossible or lead(s) to an obvious unfairness in the proceedings'.[10]

Judges have stated that this threshold is too high.[11] In *Q v Q; Re B (A Child) Re C (A Child)*[12] the President of the Family Division, Sir James Munby, suggested that if the legal aid authorities did not make provision in a case where a party would thereby be denied protection of Convention rights because they were applying too high a threshold, they might need to be supported from

[8] *Gudanaviciene and others v Director of Legal Aid Casework and another* [2014] EWHC 1840 (Admin) at [40].

[9] *Steel & Morris v UK* (2005) 41 EHRR 22 at [61].

[10] *Lord Chancellor's Exceptional Funding Guidance (Non-Inquests)* (Feb 2013) para 10. Available at: http://legalaidhandbook.com/2013/02/26/lord-chancellors-guidance-published/. The Guidance states (para 43) that in applying this test: 'The following matters may be particularly relevant: Are the proceedings likely to be unusually emotive for the applicant? All private law proceedings are likely to be emotive for the applicant to some degree but this factor alone will very rarely be sufficient to demonstrate that legal aid is required to avoid a breach of art 6. In relation to the complexity of the proceedings: how complex are they in comparison to the complexity of the proceedings in *Airey v Ireland*? Caseworkers should take into account that large numbers of litigants in England and Wales represent themselves in family proceedings every year and that, although the family justice system may not always be easy to navigate, it is rarely likely to exhibit the degree of complexity seen in the *Airey* case. In relation to legal and factual complexity: for example, does the case involve unusually complex questions of trust law? What support (other than legal representation) is the applicant likely to receive? Caseworkers should take into account that judges are used to dealing with unrepresented parties in family proceedings and the court may be supported by, for example, CAFCASS in reaching a decision'.

[11] See n 8 and n 12.

[12] [2014] EWFC 31.

court funds. Running throughout the President's judgment is an emphasis on the needs of justice and fairness (including the entitlement to a 'fair' hearing under Article 6 of the European Convention on Human Rights), especially in regard to the conduct of proceedings and use of experts. This indicates that the general policy of restricting legal aid to cases of vulnerability and need is itself flawed, since the requirements of justice and fairness extend beyond such categories.[13] The President expressed himself even more strongly in *In the matter of D (a child)*.[14] The local authority had obtained a care order regarding the child but allowed him to remain with the parents (who had learning difficulties). For those proceedings the parents were entitled to non-means-tested legal aid. The authority now wished to place the child for adoption. For these further proceedings legal aid was now subject to a means test and the husband's monthly earnings were very slightly above the (very low) eligibility limit of £733. He was therefore unable to afford legal representation in a matter that could result in the permanent removal of his child. The President described this as 'shocking'. In fact, a law firm provided its services free, leading to the caustic comment by the President:

> Thus far the State has simply washed its hands of the problem, leaving the solution to the problem which the State itself has created—for the State has brought the proceedings but declined all responsibility for ensuring that the parents are able to participate effectively in the proceedings it has brought—to the goodwill, the charity, of the legal profession. This is, it might be thought, both unprincipled and unconscionable. Why should the State leave it to private individuals to ensure that the State is not in breach of the State's—the United Kingdom's—obligations under the Convention?[15]

DISCOURAGEMENT OF THE USE OF LAW

A conspicuous example of the policy imperative that people should sort out their problems themselves occurs in the government website giving guidance and information regarding 'child maintenance' between separated couples, 'Child Maintenance Options'. The government writes that: 'There are no laws that say how parents should arrange child maintenance'[16] and that 'the most important thing about family-based arrangements though, is that you

[13] See *Airey v Ireland* (1979) 2 EHRR 305 where the ECtHR held that Ireland was in breach of Mrs Airey's art 6 rights because it was not realistic in the court's opinion to suppose that she could effectively conduct her own case, despite the assistance which the judge would afford to parties acting in person, in the family litigation in which she was engaged.

[14] [2014] EWFC 39.

[15] ibid at [31(vi)].

[16] www.cmoptions.org/en/other-arrangements/statutory-service.asp. The 'Child Maintenance Options' does not make it clear that it is a government site.

and the other parent can decide between yourselves what, when and how you will both support your child'.[17]

To underline this, a government poster was issued on 29 November 2013 promoting mediation which announces:

> Family mediation can help you agree on arrangements for your children, or what happens to your home and finances, if you are divorcing or separating. You can do this without going through court or involving big legal fees. The majority of people who start mediation reach an agreement. Family mediation is:
>
> — **Quicker and cheaper** than long court battles
> — **Less stressful** than court—with less conflict between you and your partner
> — **Easier on your children** when parents cooperate with each other.
>
> Plus:
>
> — It gives you **more control** over decisions than if you go to court—and you can both agree to change arrangements if circumstances change
> — It can improve communication and **make things easier for the future**
> — If you can't afford mediation you may be able to get **Legal Aid to help pay for it**—visit www.gov.uk/check-legal-aid.

It is notable that the only references to law as an alternative to mediation are in extremely disparaging terms: 'long court battles' and incurring 'big legal fees'. Yet study after study has shown that use of the law seldom involves going to court, and, if it does, 'long court battles' are very rare. Lawyers settle most matters by negotiation and agreement, probably well over three-quarters of cases they deal with.[18] The poster makes no reference to the possible importance, or even relevance, of legal advice. Legal aid is mentioned only in the context of paying for mediation. The poster does not even mention that where someone is eligible for legal 'help' to pay for mediation, a small amount of 'help' will also be available for legal advice during the mediation and after it concludes. Early information suggests that those who use mediation make little use of it. They may well be unaware of it.

The government-constructed web app, Sorting out Separation, which offers guidance to parties contemplating divorce or separation, has a similar reticence, though at some points (and sometimes via links provided) users

[17] www.cmoptions.org/en/family/index.asp.

[18] The research is summarised in Eekelaar J and Maclean, M, *Family Justice: the Work of Family Judges in Uncertain Times* (Oxford, Hart Publishing, 2013) 7 and ch 3. Recent research in the UK found that only 5% of the sample of 399 financial orders had been made after adjudication. The authors write: 'The role that solicitors apparently play in negotiating (and advising on) a large proportion of out-of-court settlements is at odds with the popular view that lawyer involvement necessarily means litigation': Hitchings, E, Miles, J and Woodward, H, *Assembling the Jigsaw Puzzle: Understanding Financial Settlement on Divorce* (London, The Nuffield Foundation, 2014).

will become aware of the importance of legal help. For example, the tab 'Money and Finances' has general advice on how couples should discuss these issues together: only through going to some of the links provided will reference to legal advice be found. A similar approach is taken regarding housing, though the window on mortgage and rent issues does refer to the value of professional legal advice, as indeed where the parties cannot agree on who should stay in the family home. There is a tab entitled 'Legal' which gives a brief summary of the law on certain issues, and helpful links, but even here the window for 'negotiation' contemplates negotiation between the parties alone. However, there is a tab entitled 'when do I need a solicitor?' which, after saying it is not always necessary to involve a solicitor, continues:

> Solicitors can help you understand your own legal position and help you and your ex-partner to reach an agreement without going to court. They can help you come up with a legal document if there are things that you want to rely on for the future—like what to do with the house or pension. A solicitor can write letters for you and negotiate an agreement with your ex or their solicitor if they have one.

There is no language of commendation or encouragement to follow that route. And of course, legal aid will generally not be available for this service.

In arguing for recognition of law's importance, I do not mean to suggest that other services are not important. The Ontario Law Commission has rightly emphasised that

> It is crucial that family problems be viewed in a holistic manner, both to help identify whether the problems really need resolution in the family legal system or whether the resolution of other matters (financial or mental health issues, for example) will either mean that a couple finds that they do not need to break up, after all, or if they still want to dissolve their relationship, it is easier to address the legal aspects.[19]

But law and lawyers are an essential element within this. The Ontario Commission considers a variety of ways in which these may be delivered, including the development of multidisciplinary, multifunction centres, 'unbundled' legal services, enhanced use of 'trusted intermediaries', law students and possibly paralegals.[20] It is also perhaps significant that, although lawyers were originally absent from the Family Relationship Centres set up

[19] Law Commission of Ontario, *Increasing Access to Family Justice through Comprehensive Entry Points and Inclusivity, Final Report* (February 2013) 3: this perspective runs throughout the report.

[20] ibid 59–72.

in Australia, the Australian government later changed this policy to enable legal services to be included in the model. An evaluation of the first five years of the centres concluded that

> Having begun life mainly as a default alternative to legal interventions and court processes, it is likely that FRCs' real strength will lie in their emerging capacity to work constructively, not only with other relationship services and networks, but with family lawyers and the courts.[21]

There must be concern, in England and Wales, that the continued blindness to the importance of legal services (albeit as part of a wider package of services) in private law family disputes, will have damaged supply of such services to the less well-off in society so severely that it is becoming increasingly difficult to see how they can easily recover.

A Revealing Exception

There has, however, been a concurrent counter-theme to the hostility to law in family matters seen mostly in the context of the debate over post-separation parenting in which government has seemed anxious to use the law as a means of promoting the idea (in various permutations) of 'shared parenting'. Here the law is seen as being useful in sending 'messages'. For example, in justifying proposals to promote 'cooperative' parenting in legislation, the UK Coalition government stated in 2012: 'The aim of the legislative amendment is also to reinforce the expectation at societal level that both parents are jointly responsible for their children's upbringing'.[22] How successfully this could be done through legislative statements is debatable. According to Australian research, a similar legislative measure may not have in itself resulted in an increase in the number of 'shared care' arrangements agreed between the parties (as opposed to judicially imposed shared care, which did increase). However, it seems to have led to more such arrangements in contexts where a parent had concerns about the child's safety. So it is possible that the presence of the legislation created a perception that the law required that such concerns be subordinated to the goal of shared parenting.[23] There is also a danger that public perceptions (usually influenced by a press that

[21] Moloney, L, Qu, L, Weston, R and Hand, K, 'Evaluating the Work of Australia's Family Relationship Centres: Evidence from the First 5 Years' (2013) 51 *Family Court Review* 234.

[22] Consultation Paper, *Co-operative Parenting following Family Separation: Proposed Legislation on the Involvement of both Parents in a Child's Life* (London, Department for Education, 2012) para 3.2.

[23] Kaspiew, R, Gray, M, Weston, R, Moloney, L, Hand, K, Qu, L and the Family Law Evaluation Team, *Evaluation of the 2006 Family Law Reforms* (Melbourne, Australian Institute of Family Studies, 2009).

is not given to appreciating, or conveying, subtle nuances) will misconstrue the content of the legislation. For example, section 11(2) of the UK Children and Families Act 2014 requires courts in England and Wales 'to presume, unless the contrary is shown, that involvement of that parent in the life of the child concerned will further the child's welfare', but goes on to state that '"involvement" means involvement of some kind, either direct or indirect, but not any particular division of a child's time'. One wonders how far people, especially if not legally advised, will be aware of this qualification, or, if so, how it will be understood.

There does seem to be an inconsistency here. But there is also a more worrying feature. It is arguable that the areas where the role of the law in private family disputes is being downplayed, and people left to their own devices, are those where it mostly operates in support of women and children, who are less able to protect their interests in a law-free environment. But government sustains its belief in the importance of law in the matter of shared parenting, where it could be seen as working mainly to protect the interests of men, despite its expression in the language of children's welfare.

LAW AND LEGAL PROCESSES

Perhaps, though, I am putting the position too strongly. The government view may not be that the *law* itself is unimportant, but that *legal processes (including consulting lawyers and negotiating through them)* should ideally play no part in resolving 'ordinary' family disputes. Some of the wording cited earlier might suggest this. After all, there is no suggestion that people should be constrained from using lawyers, or courts, for that matter, *if they are prepared and able to pay for it*, and initiatives have been taken both in the private and public sectors to enhance access to legal *information*, for example, on websites and helplines. Also, as remarked earlier, under the new legal aid provisions for private law family cases, public funding for mediation includes a small additional amount for legal advice (although this is not mentioned in the government poster).

However, I do not think that the distinction carries much weight in this context. For even if the provisions of the law can be clearly understood by people without needing to obtain professional advice, which is a large assumption, it is of little use to them if they have no or little access to legal resolution or enforcement mechanisms. This seems to be well understood with regard to interactions between citizens and state agencies. It is not thought enough simply to place statements of citizen's rights in relation to police powers, or other exercises of state authority, on websites, or in leaflets handed out in police interview rooms. Information must be understood, and the individual must have capacity to use the knowledge. Why is it different with regard to relations between individuals? The Ontario Law Reform Commission stated this well:

> For the law to be effective for those who are subject to it, access to knowledge about the law *and capacity to negotiate the law, with or without assistance*, is as important as 'the law' itself. A 'good' statute has limited value if it is difficult to understand and *accessing the rights* it provides formidable.[24]

This does not, of course, mean that individuals should be encouraged to use legal processes to resolve all personal disputes in accordance with legal norms: that they must always seek to 'vindicate their rights'. Often, perhaps even usually, acting responsibly requires one to refrain from exercising one's legal rights.[25] So perhaps there could be another defence of the apparent hostility to law. It may be that all that is being promoted is that non-legal mechanisms for resolving disputes should be tried *first* and only when these fail should legal processes be used.

It often seems that this is indeed the case. In many jurisdictions parties must undertake mediation before being permitted to proceed to court hearings. In England and Wales, this was required in the days when legal aid was still available for private law family disputes. Apart from special cases, this would not be granted unless the applicant had first seen a mediator to be encouraged to use mediation.[26] Now, in all cases, before making an application in family proceedings the applicant will have to attend a mediation information and assessment meeting (MIAM).[27]

Since, as I have said, departing from one's legal entitlement may be the right and responsible course of action, there cannot be any objection in principle to such efforts. Indeed, as remarked earlier, it is, or has been, common to do this through negotiation conducted with the assistance of lawyers. Even judges encourage settlement, sometimes at an actual hearing, and usually if there has been a Financial Dispute Resolution (FDR) hearing. Everything, however, turns on practical details, and, often, the nature of the issues. This is because such compromises are only right and responsible if they are voluntary, and this requires knowledge about, and the realistic possibility of, alternatives; in this case, those provided by the law. For those who have to rely on legal aid, there is no alternative to mediation: if that fails, legal aid does not suddenly become available for recourse to the law.

[24] Law Commission of Ontario, *Increasing Access to Family Justice through Comprehensive Entry Points and Inclusivity, Final Report* (n 19) 5–6 (italics provided).

[25] See Eekelaar, J, *Family Law and Personal Life* (Oxford, Oxford University Press, 2007) 127–28.

[26] Family Law Act 1996, s 29.

[27] Children and Families Act 2014, s 10.

The perplexing thing, at least in England and Wales, is that government promotes the use of mediation *in place of* the use of lawyers. At present it seems that the take-up of mediation is very low. There is therefore a danger that less well-off people whose relationships break up will increasingly be left without assistance either from lawyers or mediators. The consequences of this are hard to predict.

Private Ordering and the Role of the Law

Another defence of this approach is the belief that the parties themselves are better able to judge the fairness of an outcome than a third party. This view received a significant boost from the Supreme Court's decision in *Radmacher v Granatino*, which concerned the enforceability of an ante-nuptial agreement, where the majority stated:

> The reason why the court should give weight to a nuptial agreement is that there should be respect for individual autonomy. The court should accord respect to the decision of a married couple as to the manner in which their financial affairs should be regulated. It would be paternalistic and patronising to override their agreement simply on the basis that the court knows best. This is particularly true where the parties' agreement addresses existing circumstances and not merely the contingencies of an uncertain future.[28]

This has been enthusiastically followed up by Munby J in *S v S*, where the parties were asking the court to make a consent order based on an award made by an arbitrator. Munby J endorsed that statement, and added that

> There is no conceptual difference between the parties making an agreement and agreeing to give an arbitrator the power to make the decision for them. Indeed, an arbitral award is surely of its nature even stronger than a simple agreement between the parties.[29]

But whether or not outcomes agreed between the parties are more likely to be 'fair' than one reached, or approved, by a third party, it should not be thought that this approach supports the view that the law and legal processes should have little part to play in private law family disputes. Under private ordering, parties are to be *held* to agreements apparently freely entered into. The majority in *Radmacher v Granatino* were insistent that both ante- and post-nuptial agreements were *contracts*.[30] The Law Commission has now

[28] *Radmacher v Granatino* [2010] UKSC 427 at [78].
[29] *S v S* [2014] EWHC 7 (Fam) at [19].
[30] [2010] UKSC 427 at [63]: see Lady Hale's dissent at [138].

reinforced this by recommending that statute should expressly confirm that 'qualifying nuptial agreements' should be regarded as binding by courts when parties separate, except insofar as the court may consider it necessary to depart from it in order to meet the 'financial needs' of the parties or as required in the interests of the children.[31] So far from banishing the law, this imports a whole legal discipline into the private domain: the law of contract. Contracts need to be properly established; they need to be interpreted; they may be re-negotiated; they need to be enforced. The Law Commission's proposals add a variety of additional requirements for nuptial agreements, including that both parties act on separate legal advice.

While *Radmacher* and the Law Commission were concerned only with financial and property matters, there are some who would extend this to all aspects of intimate relationships. Lenore Weitzman was an early advocate of this[32] and Martha Fineman is a contemporary one.[33] In the world advocated by these writers, all aspects of living together would be subject to bargaining. The result would be to extensively legalise intimate life. The home would become like the workplace, family law a domestic version of employment law. Fineman envisions that provisions 'such as those found in equity (such as unjust enrichment or constructive trust), partnership, and labor law could provide rules for decisions in disputes involving sexual affiliates'.[34] One consequence is that contract law would apply to all kinds of sexual activities because 'there is no obvious reason that sex should be excluded from some contractual schemes (private bargaining) while it has been an explicit part of another contractual scheme (the services requirement in the marriage contract)'.[35] A tort of intentional infliction of emotional harm might be developed.[36] Of course this remains largely in the realm of speculation. But it shows that it may be difficult to break free from the need for legal regulation.

[31] The Law Commission, *Matrimonial Property, Needs and Agreements* (Law Com No 343, 2014). The qualification regarding children is not mentioned in the list of recommendations, but is clear in the draft bill set out in app A of the report.

[32] Weitzman, L, *The Marriage Contract: Spouses, Lovers and the Law* (London, Macmillan, 1981).

[33] Fineman, MA 'The Meaning of Marriage' in A Bernstein (ed), *Marriage Proposals: Questioning a Legal Status* (New York and London, New York University Press, 2006) ch 1: see review by Eekelaar, J (2012) 8 *International Journal of Law in Context* 320.

[34] ibid 58.

[35] ibid 61.

[36] A similar situation might, it seems, potentially arise in Islamic marriages according to the analysis by Pascale Fournier of the treatment of *mahr* (dowry payment by a husband to the bride). Fournier writes that, 'between (two possibilities created by high *mahr* or "a ton of jasmine") lies a continuum of bargaining possibilities ... (which) range from agreeing to better or more sex during marriage to entering or not entering the labour market ... A woman can thus use her *mahr* to bargain for the custody of her children or for a sort of alimony, even if these would have been denied to her under a regular divorce': see Fournier, P, *Muslim Marriage in Western Courts: Lost in Transplantation* (London, Ashgate, 2010) 28.

JUSTICE AND THE ROLE OF THE LAW

Thus far I have not said anything about justice. I have simply referred to an apparent downgrading of the role of the law in private law family matters. What, then, has this to do with the question: can there by family justice without law? After all, one could say that, historically, in all societies, legal, or at least social, norms have played a central role in governing family relations, and that the results might not strike the modern observer as always being exactly fair, especially between men and women. That, however, is to miss the point of the question: it is not whether law is a sufficient condition for family justice, but whether it is a necessary one. Mavis Maclean and I looked briefly at this at the beginning of *Family Justice*.[37] We distinguished between behaviour-focused and outcome-focused disposals of family problems. In the first, the objective was primarily to bring an end to the dispute—to achieve a degree of workability to a relationship that had become unworkable. The actual effect on any matters that might have been in dispute (whether it be financial dispositions or living arrangements) was not relevant. As long as the parties were prepared to work with whatever the outcome was, that was sufficient. In the second, the focus was on the outcome itself: a disposition or arrangement would be identified, and it was the responsibility of the parties to try to work with it. We argued that, for such an outcome to be 'fair', both the outcome and the way it was reached (the 'comprehensive outcome') would need to be perceived as such by an 'impartial spectator' (the phrase comes from Adam Smith, via Amartya Sen).

In our context, the 'impartial spectator' was the family justice system. This was seen comprehensively as including, inevitably, the relevant legal norms, but also courts, lawyers (when advising and representing parties) and mediators when resolving disputes. We observed that whether or not legal norms themselves are considered just went beyond the scope of our discussion as they were 'political questions which raise issues of justice at another level'.[38] However, the fact that the family justice system operated within a legal framework was of 'first importance' because it provided criteria according to which the 'impartial spectator' could assess the fairness of outcomes.

This does not imply that all family disputes must be resolved by, or overseen by, such an entity. It is very important that there should be scope for behaviour within relationships that is not legally regulated. Otherwise where would be the opportunities for kindness between partners, and manifestations of parental affection to children? But this takes place within a framework of norms (rights and duties) which should be reasonably accessible if disputes arise. This must imply the availability of legally informed assistance where information in itself may not be sufficient.

[37] Eekelaar and Maclean, *Family Justice* (n 18) 15–17.
[38] ibid 17.

But there is a final, and slightly different, reason why the law is important in family contexts. It concerns the question whether there are certain obligations which should not be subject to bargaining. I don't think we would be happy with a pre-nuptial contract that removed *all* obligations by one party to provide any care or support for the other during the marriage (leaving aside any obligation after the marriage) or any right whatsoever and in any circumstances to seek dissolution of the marriage. Would we accept a contract that stated that neither party would seek to resolve issues that arose at the dissolution of their relationship in a just manner? Even more so, surely we would not permit parents to agree that one of them should have no obligations to their children. The law simply states that parents have these obligations by virtue of being parents. So when the UK website, Child Maintenance Options, proclaims: 'There are no laws that say how parents should arrange child maintenance'[39] and that 'the most important thing about family-based arrangements though, is that you and the other parent can decide between yourselves what, when and how you will both support your child', is this suggesting that the parents are completely free to bargain over whether one of them needs to perform that obligation? Can one them make that performance dependent on what benefits he or she gets out of the arrangement? Family justice is concerned with more than simply bargaining, fairly or otherwise. It is concerned with upholding and underwriting some elemental features of personal relationships. It cannot do this without the law, and effective means of upholding it.

[39] www.cmoptions.org/en/other-arrangements/statutory-service.asp. The 'Child Maintenance Options' does not make it clear that it is a government site.

Index

www.ingramcontent.com/pod-product-compliance
Ingram Content Group UK Ltd.
Pitfield, Milton Keynes, MK11 3LW, UK
UKHW020132290926
15471UKWH00003B/444